THE BIG BOOK OF

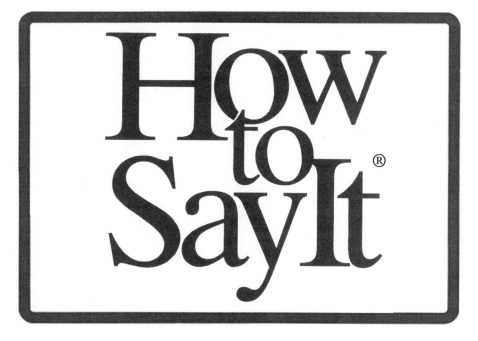

BEST

includes the complete texts of

How to Say It® Best by Jack Griffin

&

How to Say It® When You Don't Know What to Say

by Robbie Miller Kaplan

A member of Penguin Putnam Inc.
375 Hudson Street
New York, New York 10014

www.penguinputnam.com

Previously published as *How to Say It® Best*, copyright © 1994 by Jack Griffin
and *How to Say It® When You Don't Know What to Say*, copyright © 2004 by Robbie Miller Kaplan.

Prentice Hall® is a registered trademark of Pearson Education, Inc.

Library of Congress Cataloging-in-Publication Data available upon request
Special Markets ISBN: 0-7352-0424-1
Printed in the United States of America
10 9 8 7 6 5 4 3 2 1

Contents
How To Say It® Best

Introduction   xi

PART ONE
THE MAJOR SUBJECTS   1

Accepting an Appointment   3

After Dinner Speeches   8

Anniversaries   14

Awards and Tributes—Accepting   19

Awards and Tributes—Presenting   24

Birthdays   30

Business Meetings   35

Charity Events   44

Commencements   50

Community Meetings   59

Congratulations   67

Dedications   73

Eulogies   79

Farewells   87

Fraternal Organizations and Commercial Clubs   94

Inaugurals   102

Introductions   111

Invocations   117

Keynote Speeches   123

Master of Ceremonies   134

Occasions of Triumph   142

Occasions of Crisis   150

Officers' Annual Reports 158

Patriotic Occasions 164

PTA and Other Parents' Groups 173

Retirements 180

Reunions 189

Sales Meetings and Presentations 196

Thanks 209

Weddings 215

Welcomes 221

PART TWO
SPECIAL SUBJECTS 229
Featured Speaker 231

Children's Group 237

The Impromptu Speech 241

Panel Discussions 246

Press Conferences 250

Radio 256

Television 258

Toasts 260

PART THREE
THE NUTS AND BOLTS 275
Architecture 277

Audience Give and Take 284

Body Language 285

Clothes 289

Comfort 290

Diction, Pronunciation, and Grammar 292

Getting Personal 294

Hecklers 295

Humor 296

Lighting 297

Nerves 298

Off-Color Language, Remarks, and Stories 300

Publicizing and Publishing 301

Reading, Memorizing, Rehearsing, and Winging It 302

The Right Word 304

Slang 305

Surviving Mistakes 306

Typing the Speech 308

Using Facts and Figures 309

Using Quotations 310

Visuals 312

Volume, Tone, and Pace 315

APPENDIX 319

Sources of Anecdotes 321

Sources of Facts, Figures, and Statistics 323

Sources of Quotations 325

Toast Collections 328

Speech Collections 328

How To's 329

INDEX 333

Contents

How To Say It® When You
Don't Know What to Say

Introduction   347

PART ONE
COPING WITH LOSS   351
What is Grief? Understanding the Process of
Mourning and How You Can Help   353

PART TWO
BASIC COMMUNICATIONS   361
What Can I Say? Communications That Comfort   363
What Can I Do? How to Listen   374

PART THREE
COMMUNICATION IN TIMES
OF ILLNESS AND DEATH   381
Illness   383
Death of an Adult   397
Death of a Child   419
Birth of a Stillborn or Death of a Newborn Baby   430
Suicide   440
Miscarriage   451
Pet Loss   460
Mental Illness   468

PART FOUR
COMMUNICATING IN THE FACE OF CRIME AND VIOLENCE
475

Nonviolent Crime   477

Violent Crime   483

Sexual Assault or Rape   490

Domestic Violence   499

Natural Disaster   505

Terrorism   511

Legal or Criminal Problems   519

PART FIVE
COMMUNICATING ABOUT PERSONAL AND FAMILY ISSUES
525

Infertility   527

Adoption   534

Baby or Child with Special Needs   543

Physical Disability   551

Separation   561

Divorce   568

Job Loss   578

Financial Troubles   589

Caregiver Responsibilities   595

Personal Disappointment   605

ABOUT THE AUTHOR   611

INDEX   613

How to Say It BEST

CHOICE WORDS, PHRASES, & MODEL SPEECHES FOR EVERY OCCASION

JACK GRIFFIN

PRENTICE HALL

Introduction

It's all a bad dream. A sea of faces, staring eyes above folded arms, all focused on the brightly lit lectern. You cross the stage to that lectern, assume your position behind it, grip its sides, gaze up and out at the faces, at the eyes, the folded arms. You open your mouth to speak . . .

Almost everyone is afraid to speak in public, and many people are downright terrified by it. What can happen? The audience will walk out. They'll think you're stupid. They'll hate you. They'll ask you things you don't know. You'll be heckled. You'll make a terrible mistake. You'll forget what you have to say. You'll forget how to read. You'll forget how to talk. Your voice will crack. You'll throw up. You'll pass out. You'll forget to zip your fly or button your blouse.

Now relax.

The truth is, even the best and most experienced speakers are scared. So are great athletes, musicians, dancers, race-car drivers, actors. Like them, the great speakers have simply learned not merely to control their fear, but to savor it, to harness it, to use it. How? By knowing their craft. Know how to take the hurdles, hit C above high C, dance *Swan Lake,* find the groove at Indianapolis, penetrate to the heart of Hamlet, and your fear becomes the fuel that drives your performance. There is a thin line between being scared and feeling the exhilaration, the high, of being out front, the focus of attention, a winner.

Why does making a speech seem so daunting and frightening a task? Because a speech can be magic. Think about it. A speech is an opportunity to change the world with words. Using words, Abraham Lincoln transformed a costly, narrow Union victory at Gettysburg, Pennsylvania, into the moral turning point of a heartbreaking war. With a speech, telling his nation the only thing it had to fear was fear itself, Franklin Delano Roosevelt headed off revolution and despair in the depths of the Great Depression. Through speech after speech, Winston Churchill held England together as it stood alone against the Nazi hordes that had engulfed Europe. John F. Kennedy challenged America to greatness with his inaugural address. And Martin Luther King, Jr., used language rather than force of arms to move the world beyond the corrupt and corrupting hatreds with which it had been encrusted (it seemed back then) forever.

Now, if you're the President of the United States, prime minister of England, or a great Civil Rights leader, your words really can change the world. But the world consists of an infinite number of smaller worlds—communities, corporations, individuals. Even if you are only a PTA parent speaking to other parents and teachers, your words can change *your* world, or an important part of it: your child's school. If you are a sales manager speaking at a meeting of your sales force, your words can change your world, your company's world, and the individual worlds of your sales people. Your words can put more money into your company, your own pocket, and the pockets of those who work with and for you. Your words can mean the difference between prosperity and mere survival—or between survival and failure.

Abracadabra. Never doubt that words can work magic.

That's what this book is about—not how to fill time with a few words because you have to, but how to fill your listeners' minds and imaginations with the *right* words, the words that will persuade, motivate action, evoke good feelings, whatever the occasion calls for, whether it's convincing the town council to appropriate funds for a life-saving traffic signal at a hazardous intersection, motivating a sales force to reach this year's projection, or telling your district manager, at her retirement dinner, all that she's meant to the company for the past thirty years.

You do have one problem, however. Athletes, musicians, dancers, race-car drivers, and actors spend years, even a lifetime, learning, practicing, and perfecting their craft. You're not a professional speaker, and—perhaps—you're no Lincoln, Roosevelt, Churchill, Kennedy, or King, either. You don't have years, let alone a lifetime, to get ready for a speech that has to be delivered a week and a half from today. Maybe you don't even have a week and a half. Maybe your boss just stuck his head in the doorway and asked you to "say a few words" at the sales dinner tonight.

That's also what this book is about: How to prepare a speech for most any occasion. How to create a speech when the ideas and the words just aren't flowing. How to write a speech on a week's notice, a day's notice, a few hours' notice. Or no notice at all —how to make yourself ready for the dreaded "impromptu" speech.

Actually, "how to" is not the most accurate phrase in this case. You will find in this book plenty of advice on "how to" write and deliver speeches, from topics such as body language, to finding sources of illuminating quotations, to the mechanics of typing a speech on readable pages. Each of the thirty-nine alphabetically arranged chapters in "Part One: The Major Subjects" and "Part Two: Special Subjects" is devoted to a specific speaking situation or occasion—Birthdays, Business Meetings, Commencements, Eulogies, and so on—and begins with a brief introduction, a checklist of what to include in a speech for the occasion in question and a checklist of what not to include. In addition to the "how to" information within each chapter, "Part Three: Nuts and Bolts" provides more extensive discussions of such important general topics as wearing the right clothes; coping with nerves; when and how to use humor; when and if to use off-color words, phrases, and stories; whether to read, memorize, or wing it; and so on. An "Appendix" provides a valuable listing of essential resources for the speaker and speech writer, including where to find just the right facts and figures, the most colorful anecdotes, and the pithiest quotations.

But it is the subtitle of this book that gets to the heart of the matter. Most of *How to Say It Best* consists of choice words, phrases, sentences, and paragraphs for every speaking occasion. Advice, tips, and rules are important, of course, but perhaps the most valuable rule of speech writing (so valuable that it is more than mere advice or a simple tip) is to *show* rather than *tell*. This does not mean you must use "visual aids" (though sometimes a speech does call for them), but that, whenever possible, you should appeal to the five senses of your audience through image and example. Lincoln did not say it was bad practice to shift allegiances in the middle of a campaign, but that you shouldn't change horses in midstream—a vivid image that was even more vivid to a nineteenth-century audience of backwoodsmen who crossed streams on horseback every day. Lincoln *showed* more than he *told*, and that is what this book does, too. Instead of telling you what kinds of words and phrases to use in writing an after-dinner speech, the chapter on after-dinner speeches includes an alphabetical list of words and phrases especially appropriate to such speech-making occasions—together with a short list of words to *avoid*. Instead of talking about sentence structure, it supplies sample sentences, including openers, point makers, and closers. You will also find examples of fully developed paragraphs and, for each chapter, at least one complete speech.

The words, phrases, sentences, paragraphs, and speeches are intended to save you precious time. Use them to get your own ideas flowing. You may find that a few choice words or phrases will be sufficient seed from which to sprout your own speech. You may find it more useful to borrow entire sentences or to appropriate some of the sample paragraphs, modifying them with your own words or words from the chapter's list. You may even be able to adapt to your own needs a complete sample speech. Whatever procedure works for you is the right one.

Now relax, write your speech, face your audience, and let the magic begin.

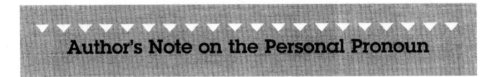

Author's Note on the Personal Pronoun

The English language makes it difficult to avoid sexism without taking refuge in such awkward pronoun combinations as he/she, his or hers, and the like. Therefore, I have tried to use the masculine and feminine pronouns evenly but arbitrarily throughout this book.

▼

▼

▼

The
Major
Subjects

▼▼▼▼▼▼▼▼▼▼▼▼▼▼▼▼▼▼▼ Accepting an Appointment

Given an award or honored with an appointment to some post of responsibility, most people respond with humble protests of surprise and even unworthiness. The speech accepting an appointment is, however, no time for modesty—feigned or genuine. The last thing you want to convey to your listeners is that they have elected, chosen, or appointed someone inadequate to the task and undeserving of the position. Of course, your stance should not go to the other extreme of empty boastfulness, but it should embody and broadcast self-assurance. Your remarks should reassure your listeners that they have chosen wisely. In fact, it may be helpful to think of this kind of acceptance speech as a form of the speech of congratulation. You are not congratulating yourself, but your listeners for having placed their confidence in you.

If self-assurance and congratulations is the dominant tone of the successful acceptance speech, gratitude and openness come next. Make sure that your listeners appreciate how grateful you are to them. Demonstrate your openness by appealing to them for their cooperation and assistance in the tasks that lie ahead.

WHAT TO SAY

Express your pleasure and gratitude in accepting the position.

Acknowledge your own hard work and experience; you feel rewarded because your efforts have come to fruition.

If appropriate, acknowledge your opponent (in an election) and/or your predecessor.

Acknowledge and address the traditions of the position you are accepting; make your audience aware that you fully appreciate the nature of the responsibilities you are undertaking.

Enumerate problems to be resolved and goals to be achieved; to whatever degree is possible, keep the tone of this positive.

Convey your responsiveness to those who appointed or elected you to the position; invite their input and ask for their cooperation and assistance.

What Not to Say

In contrast to what is appropriate when you accept an award, do *not* express surprise or shock.

Do not patronize or cast blame on your predecessor(s).

While it is acceptable, even desirable, to challenge those who appointed or elected you, do not attempt to "shake them up," scold them, or announce that you're going to do a lot of things they won't like. In general, avoid the tough-guy image.

Do not offer protests of unworthiness and demonstrations of modesty, whether feigned or genuine.

Words to Use

accept	difficult	maintain
acknowledge	dream	opportunity
aid	duty	pleased
aspire	excel	pleasure
assistance	faith	positive
attain	faithful	realistic
aware	firm	resolve
blessed	goal	responsibility
challenge	grateful	reward
challenging	guidance	solemn
collaboration	help	strength
commitment	highest	strong
cooperation	honored	stronger
culmination	hope	support
delighted	improve	will
deserved	loyal	wonderful

WORDS TO AVOID

blame	mistakes	undeserved
errors	status quo	unworthy
incompetence		

PHRASES TO USE

address the needs

august company

aware of the extraordinary responsibilities

cannot do this alone

dedicate ourselves to

delighted to serve

distinguished company

distinguished tradition

give you all I've got

give you my best at all times

go the extra mile

honored to serve

hundred percent

meet the challenges

need your support

not let you down

profound respect

proud to have been selected

sacred trust

solve the problems

thrilled to serve

will never forget

work together

SENTENCES TO USE

As the old saying goes, my door will always be open.

I promise to make you pleased—and even proud—that you have chosen me.

I pledge to you my loyalty, skill, fortitude, and concentration.

I am eager to get to work—and to work with you.

I am fully aware of the responsibilities I am accepting along with this position.

I am deeply honored by the confidence you have placed in me.

I intend to be the best [title of position] ever to serve you.

I'm awfully good at what I do, but I cannot do this job alone.

Let us begin to work together.

Please join me in acknowledging my predecessor, [Name].

This is one of the great moments of my life.

Words cannot express the pride I feel right now.

SAMPLE PARAGRAPHS

1   Except for the birth of my son, this is the greatest moment of my life. Also—except for the birth of my son—this is the scariest moment of my life. Thrilled and honored as I am by the confidence you have shown in me, I am also profoundly aware of the great responsibility you are entrusting to me. Well, through the years I've managed not only to avoid doing bodily harm to my son, I believe I raised (with no little help from my husband) a pretty great kid. I am similarly confident that I will not only manage to avoid wrecking our company, but, with your help, I will raise it to new heights.

2   I have to admit to you that what I feel most at this moment is—selfishness. Oh, I am very much aware that you have thrust upon me great responsibility that will demand long hours and self-sacrifice and sleepless nights. But what I most feel is that now—right now—you have given me the culminating moment of my career. And I hope you'll indulge me for, say, fifteen seconds, while I pause to bask in it.

3   Thank you for this honor and this responsibility. We have a lot of work to do together, and before I take the pleasure of running down a long list of individuals I wish to thank and acknowledge, I want to run down a somewhat shorter list of the challenges that face us and the goals I would like to achieve.

4   *Opportunity*: I've been thinking a lot about that word as I am about to begin my new job. It is not just an opportunity for me, but an opportunity for all of us to reshape this company, to make it more competitive and more responsive to the vision that—together—we must develop over the months and years to come. It sounds strange, I

know, and awfully self-centered, but the opportunity you have given me is an opportunity you have given to yourselves, to all of us.

SAMPLE SPEECH

I began here at Transwestern Industries a quarter-century ago. Don't be alarmed. I'm not going to recount my entire career. This is, after all, supposed to be an enjoyable occasion! But what I want to say is that it is easy for me to think of this appointment as the culmination—the summation—of my career with you. This is what it all adds up to. (And it's about time, I should think!)

But the problem with this kind of thinking is that it makes the great honor you have given me and the confidence you have placed in me seem like nothing more than preludes to retirement. So I don't want to accept the position of president of Transwestern as a summation, but as a beginning.

I'm not saying that I intend to throw out everything that came before me. We have been led by a succession of great presidents, paramount among them Sarah Walton, who now begins a most richly deserved retirement. Leaders like her have made it unnecessary to "reinvent" this firm.

But they have given us plenty to build on, plenty of opportunities to strike out in new directions. Let me outline what I see as the most important of these:

[list]

Of course, these new directions will present their own sets of challenges. We will, in the months and years to come, have to address—aggressively and successfully—such problem areas as:

I look forward to the opportunities no less than I do to the challenges. I can say this because I know what a great organization I have to work with. *I* look forward to the challenges, because *we* will be facing them together. I am confident that—together—we are facing an exciting and most profitable period. I am deeply grateful to all of you for giving me the opportunity to embark with you on this adventure.

▼ ▼ ▼ ▼ ▼ ▼ ▼ ▼ ▼ ▼ ▼ ▼ ▼ ▼ ▼ ▼ ▼ ▼ ▼ ▼

After-Dinner Speeches

There are no set rules or magic formulas for after-dinner speeches, and, obviously, such speeches may cover almost any subject, depending on the context of the occasion. But there are some guidelines to bear in mind. If you have been given a subject, proceed accordingly. If, however, the choice is yours, you should consider the following:

Who is my audience? What interests them?

What is the nature of the occasion? What's on the agenda?

What are my strongest areas? What interests me most? (Note: These two things may not be the same. If they are not, think about going with your greatest interest rather than your highest level of expertise. Your speech will probably be fresher and more enthusiastic for it.)

Are there areas of current controversy that beg to be addressed?

If there are to be other speakers on the program, find out who they are and what topics they intend to address. It is also a good idea to determine where you are in the batting order. If you are the last one up to the plate, better keep it brief. Finally, ask yourself this key question: What do I know that nobody else in the audience knows? That alone is often a good place to start thinking about your speech.

In the early 1790s, the great Austrian composer Franz Josef Haydn wrote one of the most popular of his more than one hundred symphonies. He called it the "Surprise" because, two-thirds of the way through the quiet second movement of the piece, there is a sudden, sharp, and very loud chord. Haydn knew that his audience would hear his symphony after a big Viennese dinner washed down with copious amounts of wine. Commonly, the satisfied burghers would drift off into sleep, lulled by the slow and stately music of the period. Haydn knew his audience, and he knew the conditions under which they would listen to his music. He wanted, in a good-natured way, to shake them up a bit, and he succeeded.

Similarly, the after-dinner speaker needs to be aware that, at the after-dinner hour and following a formal meal often accompanied by alcohol, his audience will be fat and happy enough, but not necessarily acutely alert. Ideally, all good speeches are stimulating. If the physician's primary directive, as given in the Hippocratic Oath, is "First, do no harm," then the speaker's prime dictum is, "First, don't put them to sleep." This is particularly critical in the after-dinner speech. You can avoid inducing somnolence by carefully observing the preceding guidelines, which really boil down to a blindingly obvious point: Speak on a subject of great interest to your audience. Add to this a special emphasis on another element that should be basic to any good speech: Use real language, laced with nouns and verbs rather than abstract adjectives, filled with real objects and scenes rather than abstract ideas and concepts. Along with this, use your own experience to *tell* a story. An after-dinner tale goes down much more easily than an after-dinner speech. Finally, the after-dinner speech particularly benefits from all the good humor you can inject. You are, after all, expected to be something of a dessert—not a meat-and-potatoes main course.

What to Say

Since after-dinner speeches vary so widely in range of subjects and context, I will offer only general guidelines.

> Begin with a surprise, a particularly stimulating or provocative statement. This is an after-dinner speech, but, reflecting the dinner itself, begin with a verbal appetizer.

> Depending on the hour and the nature of the occasion, you may win many friends in the audience by assuring them that you will be brief. (If you do this, make sure that you are, indeed, brief. Promising a short speech and delivering a long one—even if it's good—will make your audience uncomfortable and resentful.)

> Choose either a light, humorous subject and tone or a subject of surefire urgency, of certain concern to your audience. Face the fact that your audience may think of the after-dinner speech as the "price" they must pay for the meal. Managers often motivate employees with the carrot-and-stick strategy. Unfortunately, the timing of the after-dinner speech means that the carrot is on the wrong end of the stick.

> Stress positive subjects.

> If at all possible, tell a story; that is, frame as much of what you have to say as a narrative.

If at all appropriate, use humor liberally.

To the degree possible, relate directly to the listeners in the room. The after-dinner speech is one speaking occasion in which it is usually quite appropriate and even highly desirable to get personal. Think of the success, for example, of the Friars' Roasts and similar occasions.

WHAT NOT TO SAY

Avoid lecturing, which means steer clear of abstraction and complex reasoning. Provoke thought, but do not demand it.

Avoid negativity and bad news. The after-dinner speech is usually not the appropriate occasion for discussing crises, problems, and failures.

Avoid blame.

Avoid long speeches.

WORDS TO USE

amusing	fulfilled	satisfied
brief	funny	short
cash	interesting	stimulating
celebrate	irresistible	story
congratulate	money	success
delightful	penetrating	surprising
entertaining	pleased	tale
exciting	prosperous	urgent
fabulous	provocative	wealth
fantastic	remarkable	
fruition	rousing	

WORDS TO AVOID

argument	disaster	dreary
confusing	discussion	dull
crisis	dispute	hopeless

lecture	loss	technical
lengthy	patience	trouble
long	problem	

PHRASES TO USE

a brief tale

a true story

affects every one of us

best time

bizarre story for you

can't afford to miss

can't live without

chalk talk

don't reach for the Pepto Bismol yet

exciting developments

exciting news

exciting times

fascinating story for you

funny thing happened

great success

happened to us all

important points

in this together

listen carefully

most crucial

most important

most interesting

most promising

most significant

most unforgettable

peak moment

real life

stimulating possibilities

strange but true

test your imagination

test your skill

things that matter

toward the future

uncommon man/woman

urgent interest to you

we all know

we depend on it

you can't help loving

you can't make up stuff like this

you have to hear this

you won't believe this

SENTENCES TO USE

Here are three extraordinary facts to digest with your meal.

Okay, we've just eaten and drunk ourselves into a pleasant stupor, and morning's several hours away, but I'm about to give you your wake-up call early.

Let me be direct: You can't live another minute without hearing what I'm about to say.

How about a little entertainment?

I am a merciful man, and this will be brief.

We are about to make history.

Think a moment: Who is the stupidest person you know?

I would rather hang myself than give an after-dinner speech.

I have some late-edition news that will affect every man and woman in this room.

Do you want more money?

This was a great meal, but have you had enough and are you completely satisfied?

I have a confession to make.

Can you keep a secret?

This is strictly between you and me.

The only thing harder than speaking to a roomful of lawyers is speaking to a roomful of lawyers who have just eaten.

SAMPLE PARAGRAPHS

1   I wish that everybody in this community could have a meal as good as the one we have just enjoyed. The bad news, of course, is that there are many among us who can only dream about a banquet like this. The good news is that, together and united, all of us in this room can do something to help, to give hope, and to make a genuine impact right now. Let me talk to you—briefly—about what we can do.

2   I have a confession to make. I stand before you a fraud. When Jack Smith, your delightful and all-too-persuasive chairman, asked me to

speak to you tonight about successfully marketing your dental practice, I said, sure. After all, I'm a dentist, and I live in a big house, drive two expensive cars, own my own set of golf clubs—so I'm obviously also a successful dentist. Therefore, whatever I've done to market my practice, I must have done well. So I accepted Jack's offer. Then I went out and did some research—there *are* books on marketing your practice—and I discovered that I had been doing it *all* wrong. I'm no expert, and I'm here to tell you why.

3 Uncle Charlie, in Arthur Miller's great play *Death of a Salesman*, has a very memorable line: "No man," he says, "no man ever has enough salary." The first point I want to make in talking with you tonight about employee compensation is never, *ever* let the people who work for you read *Death of a Salesman*. The second point is that there *are* ways to keep your personnel from feeling like Uncle Charlie.

SAMPLE SPEECH

Ladies and gentlemen, take a good, long sip of your after-dinner coffee, because: *This is a test.*

You are on an airplane flying from Detroit to Denver. Fate has seated you next to the chief engineer of your closest competitor. He's got that little tray table down, and he's spread out drawings for a new valve—just the kind of valve you are currently bidding on. Your firm needs that contract, really needs it. You yourself could use a raise or a bonus, what with two kids in college and another soon to be. Furthermore, you notice that this fellow's company was obviously thinking along the lines you have been—except that they're already into the finished drawings.

You're not stealing anything. You're not whipping out your Minox to snap the drawings. You're just looking. And doesn't this guy have it coming to him, what with being so careless about displaying the drawings in a public place? He's asking for it.

Here's the test: Do you look at the drawings and learn what you can from them? Or do you turn away from them?

Remember, your company needs the contract. Remember, you need the money.

I'm not really going to ask you to wrestle with this one, not after so fine and full a meal and at this hour of the evening. I also have to tell you that *I* cannot answer the test question for you. In all honesty, I'm not sure I can answer it for myself.

What the "test" does tell us all is that our industry—and business in general—desperately needs guidelines for ethics. We need a common understanding of just where the boundaries lie.

I do not propose to pontificate to you on what should constitute these boundaries. It's not so easy that it can be settled by the speech of an evening. Instead, let me tell you a few stories about real-life ethical situations we have encountered at Lebhaft Enterprises. Like all good stories, they each have a beginning, middle, and end. What they lack is a moral. I'll let *you* supply that element.

Then I propose to leave you alone, step down, let us all finish our coffee, drive home, and get ready for another business day in which we will be confronted by a multitude of ethical questions in a very real world.

[Narrate anecdotes.]

Anniversaries

Anniversaries are almost certainly productive of more speeches than any other event. Unfortunately, it is also true that anniversaries spawn more dull and half-hearted speeches than any other event. But, with a little preparation, this does not have to be the case. Indeed, anniversaries are natural occasions for very engaging talks.

Why?

Everyone loves to reminisce, to pore over old family albums, to listen to old rock 'n' roll, to watch the black-and-white relics of television's Golden Age. Few things, in fact, are more delightful than memory.

There are, then, only two secrets to delivering a successful anniversary speech: First, make the occasion a collective reminiscence. But, second, don't stop there. Evoke the past, relive it—*then* look to the future.

Anniversary speeches are among the simplest talks to structure. At their most basic, they have only two parts: the past and the future. Why, then, do so many of these talks go so wrong? Speakers fail to make the memories real. They feel obliged to make a few "profound" observations, which usually translate into abstract clichés bolstered by hollow adjectives. Replace these with the flesh and blood, the sights and sounds of real memories, real things described with verbs and nouns and lots of proper names and brand names. Evoke the fabric of real life. Let your listeners *see* what you are talking about.

WHAT TO SAY

Travel back through time. When XYZ, Inc., was founded in a Muncie, Indiana, garage, what were the hit songs, the popular TV shows, the most talked-about books, the hottest movies, the price of gasoline, the price of Coca-Cola®, a loaf of Wonder Bread®, a DuMont® television set?

Celebrate the founder, owner, the early guiding light. Give a capsule biography of her or, better yet, zero in on a few revealing anecdotes.

Dramatize the changes that have occurred in the industry, the school, the organization. Highlight changes that the company, college, club—whatever—played a role in.

To this panorama of change, counterpoint the qualities that have remained constant: commitment to excellence, concern for people, regard for the community, and so forth.

Remind your listeners that they partake in a tradition and a heritage.

Urge your listeners to maintain what is good and enduring about the past, even while they move forward to face the challenges of the future.

Suggest that, as good as things were in the "good old days," there are even better, more challenging, more rewarding, more exciting days to come.

WHAT NOT TO SAY

While it is very effective to use statistics sparingly, do not overdo it by reciting long lists of facts and figures gleaned from old annual reports.

Do not lament the passing of the Good Old Days.

Do not patronize or belittle the accomplishments of the past.

Do not fail to look forward to the future.

Avoid high-flown rhetoric. "Four score and seven years ago" worked well—once. But that was it.

Avoid being so personal, dwelling exclusively on insider anecdotes, for example, that you alienate the majority of your audience.

WORDS TO USE

adaptability	flexibility	memories
astounding	forward	memory
challenge	founded	milestones
confidence	founder	past
create	future	progress
creative	goals	recall
dedication	grand	remarkable
determination	great	rich
determined	hallowed	stubborn
development	honored	tradition
emotion	hope	vision
emotional	innovation	wonderful
establish	inventive	
extraordinary	landmarks	

WORDS TO AVOID

errors	limitations	odd
funny	mistakes	outmoded
good old days	narrow	silly
guys	never again	

PHRASES TO USE

always cared for

always eager

always sensitive to

always the best

anticipate another fifty years

astounding development

best of the past

blessed stubbornness

celebrate the heritage

celebrate the past

commitment to the community

commitment to the future

did not shrink from

enduring qualities

enduring values

face the challenges

firm foundation

forward-looking

honor the past

in the best tradition

in the finest tradition

look forward to the future

major effort

never quit

open to change

partake of the heritage

recall the past

remarkable qualities

steady progress

story of remarkable growth

sustained effort

tradition of excellence

tradition of greatness

tradition of innovation

tradition of service

value of the past

willingness to change

SENTENCES TO USE

It has been fifty years since Ebenezer Hardwick turned his Thirteenth Street garage into Hardwick Rejuvenator, Inc.

When it all began, milk was 35 cents a gallon, you could buy three apples for a nickel, most houses were priced in the four-figure range, and a Ford Model T cost $300.

We have come through the adventure of our first decade.

Congratulations on your first hundred years.

It is a pleasure to stand between the past and the future and to contemplate the history we have made and have yet to make.

We are here to recall the past and look ahead to the future.

Even the most optimistic of people back in 1955 would not have dared to predict the phenomenal growth we have achieved.

SAMPLE PARAGRAPHS

1   I knew Ebenezer Hardwick back when he started this company in 1945. The war was over, money was tight, and I said to him, "Eb, you're out of your mind. It will never work, and it certainly will never last." Fifty years have been quite sufficient to persuade me that I was wrong. It gives me great pleasure today to fess up to that and to congratulate Hardwick Rejuvenator on its first half century.

2   When blustery old General Braddock was beaten at the Battle of the Wilderness during the French and Indian War, all he could say was, "Who would have thought it?" Now that *we* have emerged, victorious and very profitable after a decade of ups, downs, and in-betweens, and I find myself in the position of making a tenth anniversary speech, about all I can say is, "Who would have thought it?"

3   Okay, let's admit it. In 1948, the big event for most people was not the founding of our venerable club. It was, of course, the premiere broadcast of the "Milton Berle Show." The few fortunate families who owned that nine-inch DuMont® or Admiral® or RCA® gathered about the set to watch a middle-aged former vaudevillian cavort across the screen in a dress and a wig. How could we hope to compete with that?

SAMPLE SPEECH

Here we are, twenty years later. I'd like to tell you that my most vivid image of 1975 is of George Burnside—our faithful and fearless leader—braving a late March blizzard to cut the ribbon across the door of the first MegaMore Store. I'd like to tell you that I remember how proud we all were that the *Sun* sent a reporter and photographer to cover the grand opening. I would enjoy recalling with you the difficulty George had making those oversize prop scissors slice through the ribbon, and how he finally just tore the thing with his teeth. It would be fun to recall the opening-day crowds, and how relieved we were that the customers did, after all, show up.

But what I *really* remember about 1975 is that I wore a brown polyester leisure suit with a five-inch-wide tie depicting, I think, the fall of the House of Usher, and that my white shoes were made out of a kind of plastic that the EPA has since banned.

Not all of us looked that bad in 1975. Actually, now that I look at the old-timers here, it occurs to me that, yes, all of us *did* look that bad. Well, we had a lot to learn.

And learn we did. We learned, more often than not the hard way, what almost everyone else already knew about retail marketing. But we learned fast, and we learned enough to survive. Then people like George, and Esther Fisk and Edward Laszlo and Howard Lemmick (no longer with us, I'm sorry to say) learned a lot more. They learned how to sell hardware better than anyone else had ever sold it before. In 1978, we opened a second store. A third and fourth followed the next year. Then they started coming by the half-dozen—each year, right up to this twentieth anniversary.

Let's take a breath, then. We've earned it. Let's take pleasure in recalling so wonderful a past. But I trust that you will join me in taking even greater pleasure contemplating—dreaming about—a future that promises even more.

Awards and Tributes—Accepting

If you have a hard time taking a compliment or accepting an award, you're not alone. It's a problem for most of us. From an early age we are admonished in no uncertain terms to be "modest," because nobody likes a bragger. Mother or father wags a finger at us to point out that people who are too full of themselves look foolish and, sooner or later, fall on their faces. The truth is that such injunctions against feeling good about our accomplishments never breed true modesty, but instead make us seem graceless and ungrateful when we are complimented or given some form of positive recognition. A good acceptance speech can overcome the ingrained taboos of childhood and not only let us claim our just deserts with poise and grace, but with generosity to ourselves and to those who present the award. The speech is an opportunity to savor the pleasure of recognition as well as to give others the pleasure of having bestowed that recognition. It gives to those who present the award the satisfying feeling that they have acted right and have made a wise choice.

What to Say

Express your pleasure in accepting the award.

Express surprise, even shock, if the award really is unexpected.

Express your affection and respect for the organization giving the award.

Convey a sense of modesty—but don't overdo it. Leave your audience convinced that the award has, after all, gone to the right person.

Share the award with others who deserve it, naming names and always associating a role with the name. ("I couldn't have written word one without the love and support of my husband, Bill Blake, and no one would have published the words I did write had they not passed under Bill's editorial blue pencil.")

Acknowledge your competitors generously, praising their ability, hard work, and, where appropriate, their sportsmanship.

Recognize your colleagues and co-workers.

Use humor—it's the most effective way of conveying a sense of genuine modesty without resorting to cloying self-effacement—but use it carefully. Make it clear that you take the award seriously.

Be brief, especially if you are one in a list of honorees.

WHAT NOT TO SAY

Don't "confess" your unworthiness. It is ungenerous to yourself and even less generous to the givers of the award.

Neither patronize nor run down your competitors.

Resist the temptation to acknowledge every last person with whom you have ever come in contact. A tedious recital of names is meaningless to your audience and, worse, suggests to them that the names are, if the truth were known, equally meaningless to you.

WORDS TO USE

accept	goodwill	proud
acknowledge	grateful	recognition
amazed	gratified	reward
awed	happiest	source
blessed	help	strength
culmination	high	support
delighted	highest	thank
deserved	kind	thankful
dream	love	thrilled
faith	overjoyed	ultimate
firm	overwhelmed	uncomplaining
flabbergasted	pleased	unexpected
generosity	pleasure	unstinting
generous	positive	untiring
gift	pride	wonderful

WORDS TO AVOID

embarrassed	mistake	undeserved
luck	silly	unworthy

PHRASES TO USE

approval from those I so
  deeply respect

august company

bowled over

culmination of my career

deeply moved

delighted to pay a debt of gratitude to

feel so good

give full credit to

great thrill/honor/pleasure

greatest admiration

happiest day of my life

highest regard

honored to accept

no one could be more happily
  surprised

on behalf of my colleagues/
  friends

peak experience

pleasure to receive

praise from good friends

praise from honored colleagues

profound respect

proud to have been selected

recognition of my colleagues/
  friends/associates

share this award with

ultimate high

what a wonderful shock

you have been so
  generous/kind

SENTENCES TO USE

I am thrilled to accept this award.

I must be dreaming, but please don't wake me up.

I never thought it possible to feel so good standing in front of so
many people.

I share this award with my wife/husband, [name], and children,
[Names], who have given me the support, love, and time that
enabled me to complete this project.

I have not been this excited since the day my son/daughter was born.

I am delighted to be here tonight.

In accepting this honor, I am delighted to acknowledge the indispensable contribution of [Names], who provided support and advice at every stage of the project.

It is a joy to be recognized so generously.

My friends, I thank you.

Now I really do feel as if I've accomplished something!

Talk about the light at the end of the tunnel!

What a pleasure to bask in the approval of honored colleagues!

You are kind beyond words.

You have made me a very happy man [woman].

SAMPLE PARAGRAPHS

1 Two weeks ago, our chairperson, Mary Wheeler, phoned me at home. At least, she *said* she was Mary. I thought she was an imposter and it was a crank call, because she was telling me that the committee had decided to present me with the Golden Spear. But, before the call was over, Mary had convinced me that she was, indeed, Mary, and this was no joke. What a thrill!

2 I am deeply honored and moved to receive this award, which I accept on behalf of the small army of fund raisers who have worked so tirelessly. I could not have asked for a more inventive, imaginative, and cooperative group, though I don't kid myself by assuming that they did all that they have done for *me*. They—we—worked for the children whose lives this great fund will benefit.

3 I have always regarded you as the arbiters of all that is good in our profession. Now that you honor me with this award—well, what can I say? I was right!

4 I have a confession to make. I've always coveted this award, and I have dreamed over and over of standing here, just as I'm doing now. What I never imagined is how good it would actually feel! You've given me an incredible gift: a moment in real life that's better than a dream. Wow!

5   This award will go into my office, but it also belongs to Benjamin West, in research and development, Shirley Church, in marketing, and Frank Fader, in design. I invite them now to drop by at any time to visit *their award*.

Sample Speech

In the fifteen years I've worked for Global Enterprises, I've known nothing but kindness, support, and encouragement from my colleagues and supervisors. Discussions were always lively and criticism direct and honest—yet always aimed, I felt, at helping me create a better product, a product that pleased the customer and in which I personally could take pride. Every exchange with my friends here has made me a better designer and, therefore, more and more delighted with myself. If this goes on much longer, in fact, none of you will be able to stand me!

So now, in addition to all you have given me year by year, you present me with the Silver T-Square, which, I am all too aware, puts me in company with such extraordinary designers as James Darrell, José Pizarro, and Penny Lane. I hope they're happy with my presence. As for me, I'm dazzled, and as I endeavor to be worthy of their company, I take comfort in the knowledge that I will continue to enjoy the same abundance of critical support that has taken me to this podium this evening.

My good friends, colleagues, and mentors, I thank you for this honor.

Awards and Tributes—Presenting

Few speaking occasions offer more opportunity for pleasure than presenting an award. Cynical folks believe that human beings delight in cutting each other down to size, in criticizing and finding fault. The fact is that most of us feel good when we have occasion to deliver praise. It gives us pleasure to make another person feel appreciated. If that person is our employee or appointee, the award becomes a kind of self-congratulation as well. If the recipient of the award is a colleague or co-worker, we find that we are happy to be on a winning team with her. And if we have simply been chosen to present the award, that in itself is an honor.

The effective presentation speech embodies, first and foremost, the speaker's pleasure and delight in presenting the award. Keep that positive emotion uppermost in your mind, and it is difficult *not* to deliver a good speech.

WHAT TO SAY

Express your pleasure in presenting the award and/or having been chosen to present the award.

Unless your audience is well aware of it, define the purpose and significance of the award. Even if the award is a familiar one, you may cite particular aspects of it that apply to the recipient. ("The Bingo Award is given for meritorious service. If anyone has consistently given 'meritorious service,' it is tonight's honoree . . .")

Establish your connection (if there is one) with the honoree. Talk about her as a person, a colleague, a friend.

Paint a picture of the character of the honoree.

Cite the tradition of this award, the caliber of those who have received it in the past.

Explore the nature and significance of the honoree's accomplishment(s). How does the honoree's accomplishment(s) affect your listeners? ("Joe's work means a 15 percent increase in our market share this year, and that, of course, contributes to the security and prosperity of each and every one of us.")

Cite and celebrate sacrifice and dedication.

Keep it brief, especially if the honoree is one of several.

WHAT NOT TO SAY

Do not dispute the choice of the honoree in any way.

Do not denigrate the award in any way.

Explore the nature and significance of the honoree's accomplishment(s), but do not embark on an exhaustive and monotonous laundry list.

Exercise extreme care in the use of humor. Unless you are very skillful, humor at the honoree's expense may sound like denigration.

WORDS TO USE

accomplishment	high/highest	restless
admiration	honor	sacrifice
awe	hope	self-sacrifice
brilliance	humor	service
caring	innovative	steadfast
character	judgment	steadfastness
commitment	legend	stewardship
courageous	legendary	thrilled
dedication	love	tradition
delight	meaning	ultimate
dependable	meaningful	uncomplaining
fearless	old-fashioned	unshakable
generous	passionate	urgent
genius	personality	vision
gift	pleasure	vital
helpful	praise	wise
heritage	progress	
hero	rescue	

WORDS TO AVOID

doubtful	pro forma	supposedly
dubious	routine	usual
finally	safe	
obligatory	silly	

Phrases to Use

an inspiration to us all

celebrate a great woman/man

created an industry

didn't have to twist my arm

do not present this lightly

followed some very tough acts

gathered here to honor our friend

generosity and self-sacrifice

gives me great pleasure

highest regard

I am honored

in the best tradition

long overdue

my dear friend and colleague

my good friend

my mentor and friend

my respected colleague

no thought for himself/herself

one of my all-time heroes

paved the way

proud to have been selected to present

raised the state of the art

rare privilege

someone to whom we owe much more than a gold-plated figurine

story of dedication

thrilled to have been chosen

thrilled to present

unsung until now

Sentences to Use

I am honored—thrilled—to present this award to Helen Overton.

I always told you that, someday, you'd get what's coming to you.

In a world too often filled with injustice and fraud, it is wonderful to see someone get the recognition he so justly deserves for so genuine a record of accomplishment.

I have never been so delighted to give something away.

This award, for "exceptional accomplishment," goes to a most exceptional person.

I am honored to induct Frances Borth into a most distinguished group.

Bill Waterman is more accustomed to giving than receiving.

I confess that I feel it is almost as great an honor to have been asked to give this award as it is to receive it.

It is impossible not to admire, to like, and to respect Paul Drake.

If Samantha Johnson feels half as good about getting this award as I do about presenting it to her, she's walking on air.

If we had a few days to spare, I'd review with you Ben's record of achievement.

I have the enviable job of presenting a most coveted award to a very deserving person.

SAMPLE PARAGRAPHS

1   I must let you all in on a little secret. There is one person here tonight who doubts that Bev Tressor deserves the Romney Award. That person is—Bev Tressor. Like many extraordinarily talented, capable, self-sacrificing, and thoroughly committed people, she is the only one around who is not fully aware of just how terrific she is. I hope this award convinces her.

2   Our Annual Achievement Award was established in 1967 to "recognize and celebrate innovation in the development, design, and marketing of widgets." Reflect just a moment on the number of design innovations for which Les Moore has been personally responsible— no fewer than twelve, including three patents—and you can appreciate what an easy time the Awards Committee had in choosing this year's honoree.

3   Phyllis Payne and I go back—and back and back—more years than we care to count. Suffice it to say that we were very young, and so was this company, when we first began to work together. We collaborated on many projects, including the development of the wash-

board transistor, but even when we weren't formally working together, I sought her out to discuss my problems and my ideas. They weren't always of a technical nature, either. I'd come to Phyllis as quickly with a question concerning my son's school homework or what to buy my wife for an anniversary gift as I would about interpreting the figures from the latest batch of performance tests. She is a person you just naturally rely on for help, encouragement, and great ideas.

SAMPLE SPEECH

John, you once said that award ceremonies reminded you of funerals and that receiving public recognition must be the last step before embalming.

John, I am about to give you an award. Please forgive me.

But this is one more thing you have to do for all of your friends and colleagues here at General Sales: Sit there calmly and patiently and accept our praise, our thanks, and our gratitude. We promise to stop just short of embalming.

It would take hours to reel off your accomplishments since you joined General Sales in 1979. It would take too long even just to hit all the highlights. You'd sit there, squirming with modesty, and it would all be too painful for us to watch. I'll spare you and the audience by simply observing that, thanks in no small part to the innovations you have introduced over the years, General Sales has grown from a $15 million company to a $35 million giant. I am being conservative when I say that 65 percent of us owe our jobs in large part to the work of John Doan.

John, whether you like it or not, we present our Outstanding Contribution Award to you for having played a significant role in shaping this company and this industry and for having contributed to our collective success and mutual prosperity. You have made—and I know you will continue to make—a big difference in our lives. This award is our way of saying thanks.

▼ ▼ ▼ ▼ ▼ ▼ ▼ ▼ ▼ ▼ ▼ ▼ ▼ ▼ ▼ ▼ ▼ ▼
Birthdays

Birthday speeches range from a few words spoken before an informal gathering to a more elaborate address given at a full-scale banquet. Usually, the speaker is either a close acquaintance of the person whose birthday is being celebrated or is himself the object of the celebration.

If you are called upon to speak at a friend's birthday, make sure first that you know who will be among your listeners. Are they close friends of the honoree? Or do they know him less well than you, perhaps only in a business or professional capacity? Your task is to be as personal and anecdotal as possible without, however, alienating your listeners by demanding of them an insider's and intimate's knowledge, which they may not possess. Humor and warmth are the keynotes in this situation.

If you are called upon to speak at your own birthday celebration, you can't go wrong focusing on the milestone you have passed and poking a little fun at yourself. You should also graciously thank all of those who are celebrating with you.

THINGS TO SAY

At a party for another:

> Quotations are frequently overused in speeches, but the birthday speech is a good occasion for trotting them out. Peruse a good book of quotations (see the Appendix for a list of some of the best) and find something appropriate to the age and/or profession of the honoree.

> Compare the honoree to other, more famous folk who accomplished something at this particular milestone. ("Well, George, now you're forty. That's the age at which Joseph Conrad published his first novel. You already have a dozen books to your credit. . . .")

> Go back in time to the year of the honoree's birth. What happened back then?

> Express the group's collective affection and respect for the honoree.

At your own party:

Poke gentle fun at yourself.

Offer good-humored mock words of wisdom "at your age."

Express satisfaction with your life, your career, your family, and your colleagues.

Point out the "advantages" of growing older.

Graciously thank those who are celebrating with you.

What Not to Say

Avoid such ungrateful cliches as "you shouldn't have done this."

Avoid false attempts at profundity.

Avoid bitterness and recitations of woe; this is a celebration.

Avoid remarks so personal that they exclude your audience.

Words to Use

beautiful	goodwill	pleased
beginning	graceful	pleasure
brilliant	grand	renew
buddy	gratitude	revel
celebrate	health	sincere
confidante	heartfelt	spirit
delighted	helpful	spirited
diminish	honor	toast
esteem	humor	tribute
experience	joy	undiminished
feast	joyous	wisdom
friend	kind	wise
fun	kindness	wit
future	loyal	years
generosity	pal	

Words to Avoid

aged	feeble	infirm
decrepit	final	last
end	frail	old

Phrases to Use

best birthday anyone could ask for

best of health

blessed with so much

celebrate a new beginning

celebrate a great occasion

each year is a new beginning

embrace experience

friend to everyone

gather together

grateful to you all

legacy of service

passed a milestone

pleasure to recall

proud to know him/her

rich in friends and colleagues

sense of humor

share his/her experience

share wisdom

thankful for my friends

what a great day

you have been so generous

you have been so kind

young at heart

youthful imagination

zest for life

Sentences to Use

At a party for another:

What can you say about sixty years of Mr. Martin Rolls?

Bill, you're way past middle age. When are you going to grow up?

Let's congratulate Sarah Cone on eighty years of a very full and very productive life, and let's congratulate one another on having had our first eighty years of Sarah Cone.

The last thing Pete Williams wants to hear at his birthday party is a list of his *past* accomplishments.

I am proud to call Frank Farmer my friend.

All of us in this room share one great distinction: We have had the privilege of knowing and working with Mary Watson.

Sophie Tucker said "Life begins at 40." That would make Mike ten years old today.

At your own party:

I'm not getting older, I'm getting better—and I have a very long way to go.

I am overwhelmed by all that you have done for me.

This is one terrific party.

Don't feel bad for me. In dog years, I'm only twelve.

I suppose you are all waiting for me to say something wise.

This is the first surprise party anybody's ever given for me. I only wish I had been prepared for it.

I have been blessed with a wonderful family and extraordinary colleagues.

You've already given me the best gift I ever got: your friendship.

Sample Paragraphs

At the party of another:

1   You think that I'm here to celebrate Moe Greenburg's fiftieth birthday? Actually, I'm here to celebrate the twenty-five years that Moe has been a part of my life—a friend, a mentor, a colleague.

2   Congratulations, Sally, on having gotten another year older —among friends who love you. Eastern religions teach us that everything you do comes back to you in time. Well, look at all of your friends. You've racked up an enviable stock of great karma.

3   On the day you were born, October 27, 1962, Premier Nikita Krushchev offered to remove the missiles he had planted in Cuba. In other words, your birthday coincides with the avoidance of World War III—and you've been working miracles ever since. You graduated number one in your law class at Harvard. You became a brilliant attorney and joined this firm. You've won more cases than you lost— with a little help from some of the rest of us, of course. And you always manage to get at least 250 extra pages out of a photocopier toner cartridge that everyone else has given up for dead.

At your own party:

1   I am very touched and very grateful that you have remembered me in this way. I feel supremely blessed in that I can close my eyes and look back from each birthday to savor memories of all the great people I have known and worked with; then I can open my eyes and see wonderful people like you here and now, people with whom I can look forward to many years of work and friendship.

2   You people will find any excuse to celebrate. When I was a young man, we waited for really big occasions—like when the hunting party brought down a mastodon.

3   I want to join in the congratulations that have been hurled at me. I congratulate myself on having found a job I love, having been able to stick with it for so long, and having been able to work at the job I love with the people I love. If there's one thing I've learned, deep into my middle age, it is that the most valuable asset anyone ever has is friends and family—and friends who are just about the same as family.

SAMPLE SPEECHES

At a party for another:

This birthday party has been a raw deal for you, Ed. We all chipped in and bought you a very nice gift—more expensive than any of us could afford individually. Or, at least, it cost more than any of us individually would have been *willing* to spend. But, extravagant as it is, it's just one gift given on one day in the year. You, on the other hand, give every one of us a gift 365 days of the year. You give yourself: your expertise, your wisdom, your understanding, your compassion. I'm afraid I'll have to stop short of "your good looks," but you get the point.

Ed, all of us here at Acme Retreads thank you for your great generosity, thank you for being you. We are proud, pleased, and honored to celebrate your birthday, and we look forward to spending many more of them with you.

At your own party:

This would be very embarrassing for you if I were one of those old fossils who hates birthdays, who looks upon them as milestones along the road to oblivion, who looks back at the same time each year and thinks about all that he has lost. Well, that's not me.

I have lived a long time, and I haven't lost anything—only gained. Sure, money has come and gone. Some dear friends and family are no longer living. But, on balance, I have gained. I have gained experience, friends, opportunities to love and to be loved. It's amazing. Each year I seem to gather more—dear friends like all of you.

So, that's why I love to celebrate my birthday—even more now than when I was a kid. And because I love it so, I thank you for this warm and wonderful celebration.

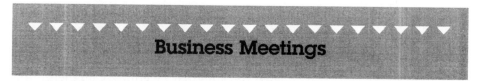

Business Meetings

The kinds of public speaking that business meetings call for include a number of the speech-making subjects covered elsewhere in this book. You may want to consult, in particular, Congratulations, Introductions, Luncheon Meetings, Occasions of Crisis, Officers' Annual Reports, and Sales Meetings and Presentations. In this chapter, we will consider some general guidelines for speaking at business meetings. These include some very important nonverbal steps you can take to help make any business meeting a success.

Foreign business people and those who are not involved in the corporate world are amazed by the Great American Business Meeting as an anthropologist might marvel at having discovered a ritual of mass masochism practiced among a remote tribe. There seem to be two virtually unshakable principles that govern our business meetings:

1. The Universal Corporate Motto—"At X Industries, meetings are our most important product." Thoughtlessly obligatory meetings are the norm in American business.

2. While everyone acknowledges the absolute need for meetings, no one expects them to be useful and productive.

The result of this bizarre combination of governing principles is what psychologists call cognitive dissonance. American corporate workers set up meetings, discuss meetings, and flock to meetings nevertheless convinced that the meetings not only will be, but have to be a waste of time and resources.

An anthropologist must look objectively upon the cultural practices she studies, no matter how strange they may seem. But there is nothing wrong with a business person taking a long, hard look at the way most of us conduct business meetings and simply saying, This is crazy, and it has to stop.

WHAT TO SAY AND WHAT NOT TO SAY

Here, then, are some modest guidelines for planning meetings that work (for a change):

1. Is this meeting really necessary? If it is within your power to do so, review your company's schedule of regular meetings. Can their number be productively reduced and/or their duration shortened? By the same token, before you call your next special meeting, think about it. Is the subject of the meeting something that could better be handled, say, with a memo that asks others to submit ideas?

2. Think about schedules. When is the best day in the week and time of day for your regularly scheduled meetings? Monday morning is generally neither a good time to handle crises nor to entertain new products, projects, and ideas. People tend to be overwhelmed at the opening of the week. Friday afternoons, especially during the spring and

summer, are also a bad idea. You may think that businesslike behavior dictates running roughshod over human behavior, but just as businesses are finding that their workers are most productive when the furniture and tools they use are designed ergonomically—to fit them—so you will find that productivity is enhanced when schedules mesh with social, emotional, and physiological imperatives.

3. Think about schedules for special meetings. This can be difficult, since it involves coordinating the plans of however many people will be involved in the meeting. Begin by taking into account holidays, including religious holidays you may not celebrate but that are very important to others, and other periods you know will call for the absence of certain employees. Once all these dates are anticipated, circulate a memo announcing the meeting as far in advance as possible. You may also find it helpful to take advantage of the latest technology. If your office has personal computers linked in a network, investigate the latest in "workgroup scheduling" software that is now available. Such programs take a lot of the guesswork, drudgery, and need for last-minute alterations out of scheduling meetings.

4. Think about the meeting site. For regularly scheduled meetings, you may or may not have much of a choice. Perhaps you have one conference room where all meetings must take place. In this case, see to it that everyone is seated comfortably and that nobody feels crowded. Set the thermostat to a comfortable temperature—a little too cool is far better than too warm. Think about moving a special meeting out of the office, perhaps to a restaurant or hotel or perhaps to someone's home. This makes a routine convocation a special occasion and telegraphs the message that the business transacted on this day is especially significant. For larger meetings and conferences, devote serious thought to the site. Cost will be an important factor, of course, but always take the time to visit the room. Find out what other meetings will be taking place simultaneously with yours. You don't need the Fraternal Order of Gophers holding their Annual Orgy next door.

5. Arrange the room so that everyone can see and hear the speaker.

6. Make sure in advance of the meeting that all audio-visual equipment is working properly. I remember reading in a hilarious book about good manners that, if you must blow your nose, do not then take the handkerchief away from your nose to look at what you've done. Of

course, everyone does just that. Similarly, a book of meeting manners—if one existed—would tell you never to tap the microphone, blow into it, say "Testing 1, 2, 3," or ask "Is this thing on?" But, of course, everyone does it. It is a strange tic that most of us can't get rid of, but the fact is that testing the mike in front of your audience certifies the meeting that follows as a Strictly Amateur Production.

7. Make sure the hotel knows where and when your meeting is. Of course, they *should* know. Of course, it is their *business* to know. But you'd better notify the switchboard anyway, or you are sure to have key participants wandering aimlessly in the lobby and halls.

8. Start on time. It is supremely irritating to be summoned to a particular place at a particular time only to find that you have to wait for the event to begin. With every minute that passes, you lose a little more of your audience's commitment.

9. Prepare an agenda and distribute it in advance. Do not, however, distribute copies of speeches in advance. You don't want people rustling papers and following along as you speak or others deliver their talks. If appropriate, distribute copies of the speeches at the conclusion of the meeting.

As to your speech on the occasion of a business meeting, it will be helpful to observe these guidelines:

1. Arrange for someone to introduce you. An introduction is like a frame for a picture. It heightens—sets off—the importance of what it contains. Don't omit this or leave to chance.

2. Avoid the masochistic trap of the Great American Business Meeting, the conviction that the meeting is part of everyone's job, no one is getting paid to have a good time on the job, and, therefore, there is no need to make what you have to say interesting. Yes, people are accustomed to boring business speeches. This is all the more reason to make yours interesting.

3. The great enemy of interest is disorder. How many speeches have you heard that begin something like this: "I have a few random thoughts to share with you" or "Here are a few observations," or "Let me review some notes," or even, "Bear with me while I go over a number of items?" Organize your material rigorously. Bumbling and ram-

bling may have been endearing in Charles Dickens's Mr. Macawber, but it will not work for you.

4. Avoid spontaneity. Does this commandment shock you? It is true, nobody likes to converse with a rigid person who sounds as if he is speaking from a script. It is also true that our culture puts a high premium on spontaneity. We treasure the off-the-cuff repartee of a Noel Coward or the improvisatory hilarity of, say, Robin Williams. Okay. If you have the wit of the former or the wild imagination of the latter, disregard this guideline. But, if you are like most of us, it is better not to depend on spontaneity. Think about what you have to say, organize it, and write it down. But also read point number 5 next.

5. The most annoying—that is, aggravating as well as boring—type of speaker subjects her audiences to a "spontaneous" ramble. The second most annoying type of speaker reads from his script in a droning, stumbling manner. Just because you've written the speech out does not mean that you are absolved from practicing it. Strive to put some life into what you say. The basics of this are covered in Part III, but for now, remember to slow down, give value to each word, be aware of the meaning of what you are saying, and don't be afraid to open your mouth. (Literally: Don't speak with your teeth clenched or your chin in your chest. Sing out.) You will also find in Part III some guidelines for typing the speech. Yes, that's important. Handwriting (even your own), single-spaced type, faded type, a script with a lot of corrections and interlineations are all very difficult to read well out loud. It is also important to know what kind of lighting will be available. If you're showing slides, will you be able to see your script? It is a real gamble to depend on the presence of a podium light, to rely on its working, and to count on its illuminating the entire page adequately. While we're at it, don't forget your glasses or contacts.

6. Keep it concrete. Define issues sharply. Back up generalizations. Don't be afraid to use statistics. Contrary to popular belief, statistics do not bore people. This said, be aware that the indiscriminate and excessive use of statistics reeled off laundry list fashion will not only bore but will utterly bewilder your listeners. Use statistics—sparingly but fearlessly—to make your point.

7. Keep it concrete, part 2. Statistics—numbers—are not the only way to make your speech real. Use nouns and verbs in preference to adjec-

tives. Use objects and events in preference to abstract concepts. Vivid speech does not require flowery or ornate description. It thrives on sharp, simple nouns and verbs, words your audience can appreciate with their senses of sight, hearing, smell, taste, and touch.

8. Beware of slides. For at least the past two or three generations, Western humankind has been overloaded with "multimedia input": words, pictures, music all together and in an endless stream. Slide shows in and of themselves do not make much of an impact. Quite the contrary, a slide-show speech presented, say, after lunch in a darkened room may well be the miracle cure to which even the most hopeless case of insomnia will yield. By all means, use visual aids that are required to illustrate the points you need to make. But do not use slides in the mistaken belief that they will dress up your speech or in the *tragically* mistaken belief that they will keep your audience awake.

9. Make your speech the start of something. You may feel obligated to come up with all the questions and the answers in your speech. In our culture, people are obsessed with "getting the last word." Better to make your speech the first word rather than the last. What you say should stimulate thought, consideration, debate, and discussion—not discourage it. Invite ideas rather than try to head them off. That means, at the very least, don't put down the ideas and suggestions of others.

10. You will find in Part II a chapter devoted to question-and-answer sessions, but a few words concerning questions and answers are useful here as well. Don't be afraid of questions. Invite them and answer them as best you can. If you don't know an answer, say so—and invite audience members to do their best with an answer. Do not dismiss or ignore any questions. At the same time, do your best to keep any one person from monopolizing the question-and-answer exchange. Your audience is likely to become resentful if they are obliged to act the part of silent witness to a prolonged conversation between you and one other person. Try lines like, "Is there anyone here who can respond to that?" Or even, "Can anyone else elaborate on that question?"

11. Keep your speech as short as your subject will permit. Don't short-change your audience or your topic, but do practice economy.

WORDS TO USE

Obviously, much of your vocabulary will depend on the subject of the speech, but here are some words generally useful in any business meeting:

address	criticize	innovate
agenda	develop	innovative
ahead	discuss	inventive
appreciate	effort	invite
begin	encourage	nurture
brainstorm	establish	open
build	exciting	prioritize
collaborate	forward	priority
consider	foster	productivity
consult	fresh	renew
creative	grateful	team
creativity	hear	understand

WORDS TO AVOID

absolute	patience	routine
boring	perfect	rules
drill	random	unchangeable
lengthy	recite	unprepared
long	rigid	
no	rough	

PHRASES TO USE

a matter of survival and prosperity

address the issues

affects each and every one of us

all the bases covered

areas calling for improvement

clear up any problems

consider our choices

discuss strategy

encourage innovation

encourage questions

entertain all suggestions

establish our ground rules

evaluate our options

explore the issues

feel free

get in and out

get to the heart of

invite comments

invite your participation

keep this as brief as possible

lay out [number] points

make the connections

of vital concern

open to discussion

open up the possibilities

plenty of time for discussion

raise all issues

significant progress

thoughtfully consider

throw it open

to the point

vital questions

will be brief

work group

SENTENCES TO USE

Here are the issues, as I understand them.

I am going to begin by stating three problems, which I want us to solve before we leave here today.

I don't intend to leave you with any answers, just questions.

I want to establish some definitions and directions, then throw the meeting open to discussion.

I am always thrilled to meet with all of you.

I intend to share with you my understanding of our most desirable goals and our most pressing problems.

I'm not sure what you are expecting, but I promise you an exciting meeting.

It is always exciting to get together like this.

Please help me to add to this list.

The subject for today is motivation.

This meeting is about you, your future, and how much money and happiness you expect to derive from this corporation.

You asked for this meeting, and I'm glad that you did.

SAMPLE PARAGRAPHS

1   It is my pleasure to welcome you to a concentrated session of what we do best at Lacksall Industries: innovate. I want briefly to review the highlights of our performance this past year and outline what I think are the challenges and opportunities we face. Once I've laid these out, I invite your comments and remarks on strategy.

2   What we accomplish today, no less than what we fail to accomplish today, will affect the immediate welfare and future prosperity of each and every one of us. It is a pleasure to meet with you in order to determine our collective destiny. Let's not blow this meeting, ladies and gentlemen. Let's get right to work.

3   We are gathered here to save our lives. Each day we do business, the task at hand is first to save our lives, then to improve them, to build on what we have, and to create anew. We should have fun doing this—and I am confident that you will enjoy today's meeting—but we can never allow ourselves to become complacent. Let's begin by setting out some ground rules for this meeting, then continue by outlining its primary goals.

SAMPLE SPEECH

It is a pleasure to gather together with all of you in order to shape the future. Those of you who find five minutes to spare at the end of your workday might be familiar with the television commercial that tells us, "In the car business, you either lead, follow, or get out of the way." That, of course, is true of any business, and our task today is, first, to decide which of these three options we will take, and, second, to formulate strategies accordingly.

You realize, of course, that the opening of my speech is fixed, rigged, and entirely phony. I know you all very well, and, knowing you, I already know that, for us, there is no choice other than to lead.

So we have our work cut out for us: What steps do we take in the coming year to maintain our leadership position in those segments of the market where we presently lead? And what steps do we take to achieve leadership in those areas in which we presently follow?

You have all studied the annual report, and you understand that we have the largest market share in the following areas: [list]. Of these, however, [number] have shown significant erosion of market share.

We recognize [number] product areas in which we are a player. We cannot, this year, expect to achieve market leadership in all of these areas. However, I propose as a reasonable goal for the next 365 days, that we do pull ahead in the following: [list].

My job up here at this podium is almost finished. I have the questions. I have the problems. I set the goals and propose the tasks. You are in a much more powerful position than I am. You have the answers, the means, the strategies, the methods. Let's begin by reviewing, in detail, this year's performance in our leadership areas and then in our "followship" areas.

Joe Madison, vice president for marketing, will review these figures for you and make some analytical comments.

Then we will hear from Flora Darien, Pat Nearing, Frances Borth, and, once again, Joe Madison, all of whom have strategies to propose to you. I stress the word *propose*. Nothing is carved into stone. Everything is open to discussion and subject to the kind of creative evolution I have grown to expect from meetings like this.

Let's get started.

Charity Events

Speeches at charitable events fall into two categories, which are often related. You may be called upon to speak to a charitable group, or you may be asked to speak on behalf of one. In the first instance, your task is usually to reaffirm the importance of the work of the organization, congratulate your listeners on what they have achieved, and outline goals to be met in the immediate future and the long term. If you are appealing to others for aid, for support of an organization or cause, your task is one of salesmanship—salesmanship in an exalted and glorified form, perhaps, but salesmanship nonetheless. An effective plan is to begin by establishing the need for the work of the organization, then to discuss how the organization has addressed, plans to continue to address, and (with your listeners' help) could better address the need you have described.

The word *charity* is derived from the Latin word for love, *caritas*. As it is a stale and dull activity to speak of love in the abstract, so it is flat and unprofitable to discuss charity in such a way. Whether you are speaking to the charitable group—as it were, preaching to the choir—or making an appeal on behalf of the group, your focus should be on people: the people who are hurting and being helped and the people who are doing the helping. Statistics are fine, in their place, but they need to be juxtaposed with vivid pictures of individuals.

WHAT TO SAY

Congratulate your audience on their fine work, but do not foster complacence.

Clearly establish the need for the work of the organization.

Vividly illustrate how the organization addresses the need you have established.

As clearly and fully as possible, outline specific goals and requirements.

Speak in terms of cause and effect, action (or inaction) and consequences.

Invite your audience to consider what would happen if your organization did not exist.

Keep it human. Talk about individuals. Use vivid examples and anecdotes.

WHAT NOT TO SAY

Avoid complacent self-congratulation.

Avoid abstraction.

Never shame your listeners into contributing. Keep the act of contributing in a totally positive light. Never suggest that it is anything other than voluntary.

Words to Use

abandon	hand	ongoing
aid	happiness	open-hearted
better	heart	plight
bless	help	progress
blessed	hope	protect
children	human	receive
clothing	humanity	research
comfort	humankind	revitalize
community	hunger	shelter
continual	improvement	strength
despair	inspiration	strong
desperate	inspire	sustenance
donate	joy	urgent
donation	kindness	value
emergency	legacy	values
family	lend	vital
food	light	voluntary
gift	love	volunteer
giving	necessities	want
goodness	need	

Words to Avoid

compel	handout	rejected
dirty	helpless	shame
diseased	lame	sick
dole	must	useless
force	outcast	waste

PHRASES TO USE

all part of the community

better life for all

blessed gift

cannot do this without you

choice is always yours

consider the consequences

depend on all of us

depends on our generosity

desperate situation

family of humankind

feel good with good reason

generous donation

generous gift

gift of giving

good work

greatest gift you can give

have a right to be proud of yourselves

help them help themselves

human assets

invaluable service

irreplaceable service

more than the government can do

please give this careful thought

please use your imagination

pressing need

sustained giving

there but for the grace of God go I

time is running out

tremendous difference

urgent need

valuable contribution

very real need

whatever you are capable of

willingness to give

you can help

you can make all the difference

your brother's keeper

SENTENCES TO USE

If not you, who? If not now, when?

I have a gift for each and every one of you: the opportunity to give, to make a difference in our world.

My heart is filled with joy in contemplating the accomplishments of the past year.

I want to tell you about a family I know.

What would our community be like without music [without a library, without a recreation center, etc.]?

What if you got sick and couldn't pay for a doctor, for medicine, or even for a place to stay?

Let's imagine our neighborhood without the Meals Tonight Program.

SAMPLE PARAGRAPHS

1   Charity, the saying goes, begins at home. I believe this is true, but I also believe that many people define home too narrowly, limiting it to the space within the four walls they happen to inhabit. Our home is this community we love, and our family is all the people in it.

2   I love to remember what it was like when I was a kid. My folks loved me, and, although we certainly weren't rich, there was always plenty to eat. At Christmastime and on my birthday, there were toys. Our house was warm. These are simple things. Take just one of them away, and childhood can be a pretty scary time. Take more than one away, and it can be a terrifying disaster.

3   What I have to say to you tonight is very simple. This past year, your hard work has meant that Clarksville still has a fine symphony orchestra for all of us to enjoy and to derive inspiration from. With your continued hard work, our community will enjoy the orchestra for yet another year. But with even harder work—extra effort from every one of us—the orchestra can add two free concerts to the season, bringing the wonderful gift of great music to children, families, and senior citizens who otherwise simply could not afford to attend a concert.

SAMPLE SPEECH

Drugs. Gangs. Guns. Dropouts. Delinquents. Death. These are words, these are things that should have nothing to do with children and childhood. But I see by the looks you are giving me—by the nodding of heads—that all of you know only too well how crime, despair, and drugs threaten to reach out to what is most precious to us: our children, our legacy, our future.

It is a wicked world, many of you are thinking, a world gone crazy. You'd like to protect your children, but you feel helpless, unable to do anything except hope, hope that the bad things don't happen to you and your family.

When I agreed to work for the Neighborhood Association I did so in the belief that there was, in fact, very little I could do to help the world. I am not a rich man, nor a powerful one. I own no great business. I hold no elective office.

But I do live here, in this neighborhood, with the rest of you. And, I realized, if I change my neighborhood, well, I *have* changed the world. Crazy and strange as this wonderful community sometimes seems, it is, after all, part of the world.

Most of us think of the empty lot on Foster and Kimball as an eyesore. But a few of us here at the Neighborhood Association see it as an oasis, a paradise, a haven, a place of joy and salvation.

Following this meeting we will distribute to each of you a proposal for a supervised playground to be built on the lot at Foster and Kimball. The details are in the plan, which I invite you to read and discuss following my remarks. But I'll jump right now to the bottom line—actually, *two* bottom lines.

The first is that we need to raise $250,000 now, to build the playground, and $50,000 annually to support it.

The second is that this supervised playground will mean that the children of our community will have an alternative to those horrible words—those horrible things—I mentioned at the opening of my remarks.

Here is my analysis of this double bottom line: I have never seen a more spectacular bargain.

Commencements

Commencements come in all sizes and levels of intimidation. Perhaps your local middle school or junior high has asked you to speak. Perhaps the alumni association of your old high school has called on you. Or you may receive a request from your alma mater or some other institution of higher learning that has deemed you important enough to address its graduating class. In whatever variety it comes, the invitation to speak at a commencement is flattering and a little overwhelming. There are few audiences as demanding as junior high schoolers, and if you are speaking at a university function, your audience may be very large indeed and quite distinguished.

Your first task in preparing for the commencement is to accent the positive. The invitation to speak is not to be confused with a midterm exam, although some of the same teachers and professors who administered such exams to you may well be in the audience. Rather, it is one of the greatest votes of confidence you are ever likely to receive. No matter how big or small the commencement, you should regard the invitation as among the highlights of your speaking career (likewise no matter how big or small). Prepare accordingly.

Begin your preparations by finding out as much as you can about the commencement program:

▼ Will there be other speakers? If so, try to find out what their topics will be. If you cannot get specific information of their topics, at least find out who they are and what their areas of expertise are, so that you can steer clear of these areas and therefore stand a better chance of avoiding a redundant topic.

▼ If there are other speakers, request that you speak first or at least near the beginning of the program. Spirits generally run high at commencements, which means that audiences tend to be fidgety. If the event is taking place outdoors, the weather can be a problem for an audience wearing itchy caps and hot gowns while sitting on hard folding chairs.

▼ Find out who will introduce you. Send that person a full resume or, if you have one, a curriculum vitae. You should highlight whatever you would most like emphasized about yourself. Better yet, why not write your own introduction and send it to the introducer? She will not be offended at having words put into her mouth. Quite the contrary, she is likely to be grateful for having been spared yet one more task. A concise paragraph will do. See the chapter on "Introductions" later in this book.

▼ All commencements are special events, of course, but you should ask if there is anything exceptional about this one. Will any special degrees be given out? Any firsts? Lasts? Important additions to the academic program? Retirements of distinguished or popular professors? Significant accomplishments that will be recognized—or *should* be recognized? Awards? Is this the largest graduating class ever? Does it include the first graduates of a particular program? Does it include an exceptionally large number of graduates in a particular program?

▼ Finally, ask how long you are expected to speak. Then plan to use only about 50 to 60 percent of that time. If you are the featured speaker, a fifteen-minute speech is ample. Even if you were allotted a half hour, no one will feel cheated.

The next phase of preparation is discovering your material. Many presentations you are asked to make involve research. If, for example, you are asked to speak to a convention of marketing specialists, you will probably want to gather some case studies to use as examples of techniques, principles, future directions, and so on. In the case of a commencement, you must assume that you were chosen to speak because of something special in your background and your position in the community. Begin there. Assume that, since you have been chosen for your experience, the most valuable words you have to offer must come from your experience. What have you learned and put into practice that will be useful to the graduates? Think long and hard about this, and construct your speech around it.

WHAT TO SAY

A great commencement speech comes from the heart, from your personal experience, but most commencement speeches should also embody the following elements:

A traditional opening. Much like a formal letter, commencement speeches begin with a formal salutation. Address the president (or chancellor) of the university by name, the deans (by name, unless they are too numerous), faculty, graduates, and honored guests: "President Adams, distinguished deans and faculty, graduates, and honored guests, it is my privilege and pleasure . . ." If the commencement features an especially well-known or distinguished guest, include him or her in the salutation: "President Adams, Deans Perkins, Smith, and Reynolds, distinguished faculty, graduates, Cardinal Wolsey, and other honored guests . . ."

Set a high tone and stay there. This does not mean that you should use flowery and ornate language. Nor does it mean that you should studiously avoid humor. It does require that you deliver a speech in harmony with the atmosphere, spirit, and significance of the event, a speech that reflects high hopes, aspirations, goals, ideals, and achievements. Inspire your audience. Make them feel good. This is a proud and happy occasion, a culmination of one phase of many lives and the launching of a new and hopeful phase. A commencement is both a culmination and an inauguration.

Praise and congratulate the graduates.

Praise and congratulate the parents—who have provided the inspiration, support, and the cash necessary to the achievements that are being celebrated.

Praise the school. In this, be as specific as possible. If you are an alumnus, draw on your own experience. Or cite some specific programs or policies that distinguish the institution.

Glance back at the past, but emphasize the future. A commencement does not merely pass the torch, it asks the graduate to seize that torch and hold it higher and run farther and longer with it than those of the preceding generation.

Emphasize choice: The graduates have the intellectual equipment to make informed moral choices in order to create a better future for everyone.

Cite challenges and opportunities. What does the world have to offer? Compare the present threshold of opportunity and challenge with what you faced x years ago.

Invite a challenge to the status quo. Invite bold thought and the courage to make sweeping change.

Emphasize responsibility to the community, the nation, the world, and the planet itself. A commencement signifies passage into citizenship in the fullest sense.

Balance the big picture with the individual and intimate. Emphasize the importance of family relationships. An education should help you be a better lawyer, doctor, leader, and father, mother, wife, or husband.

Fall back on integrity—the ageless injunction of the Oracle at Delphi: "Know thyself."

WHAT NOT TO SAY

Say nothing to belittle the graduates' achievement.

Avoid invidious comparisons with other schools or past graduating classes.

Unless you have been invited to speak as an athlete, avoid emphasis on the institution's sports programs.

Avoid concentration on narrow definitions of success. "Proctor College has produced the highest-paid accountants in the entire Southeast." This is nothing to be ashamed of, but it is, frankly, too narrow an achievement to highlight in a commencement address.

Avoid gratuitous humor—humor for its own sake. This is a joyous but serious occasion.

Avoid protestations of modesty, inadequacy, and a sense of intimidation. You may *feel* all these things. That's perfectly normal. But why should you suggest to the graduates, parents, and faculty that those in charge have selected the wrong person to speak on this most important occasion?

Major commencements are newsworthy events, even if the coverage is strictly local. Say nothing to reporters that might embarrass the institution. Keep your remarks positive and celebratory, in harmony with the speech itself. It is best to avoid speaking to reporters or granting interviews before the speech. You owe your words and your full attention to the institution and the occasion. Ask reporters to speak to you after the ceremony.

WORDS TO USE

achievement	goals	rebirth
active	health	rebuild
actual	honor	reinvent
anew	hope	renaissance
aspiration	innovate	renewal
beauty	innovative	rescue
begin	integrity	restless
bold	inventive	revise
build	investment	scholars
challenge	judge	self-esteem
choice	judgment	self-knowledge
choose	knowledge	selfless
commence	labor	skill
commitment	lasting	solid
community	limitless	spirit
compassion	limits	spiritual
compete	model	stake
confidence	new	stewardship
congratulate	nurture	strive
courage	opportunity	stubborn
courageous	passion	sweat
create	passionate	technical
creative	pleasure	technology
creativity	potential	threshold
dedication	praise	thrilling
development	precious	tradition
education	predict	treasure
emulate	pride	truth
endure	privilege	understanding
enduring	proactive	valuable
exciting	profit	value
experience	progress	values
foster	prologue	wisdom
frightening	real	wonderful
future	realize	work

WORDS TO AVOID

authority	exclusive	over
clique	finished	retreat
club	hopeless	routine
desperate	impossible	security
discouraging	inadequate	silly
doomed	insiders	spent
elders	jobless	status quo
empty	money	success
end	outworn	ticket

PHRASES TO USE

accept nothing secondhand

accept the challenges

adjust your aspirations upward

aspire to excellence

challenge all accepted ideas

choose the right course

community of peoples and nations

community of scholars

compromise no ideal

create new challenges

do not shrink from

enlarge your scope

eye on the future

face the challenges

invent the future

make your own world

meet the challenges

move forward

never lose compassion

open mind and open heart

optimistic skepticism

pride of accomplishment

recognize your stewardship

reject all that is narrow

reject the status quo

remake your generation

respect the best of the past

serve the community

the global village

true to yourselves

worthwhile goals

Sentences to Use

Be prepared to invent what you do not have and to reinvent whatever you take from those who have gone before you.

Honor the achievements of the past, but do not be a slave to them.

I have learned, after twenty-five years as a physician, that narrow self-interest simply does not work, not for yourself, not for your neighbor, not for your world.

I congratulate you on what you have achieved, and I rejoice for the world that will be made better by your continued achievements.

My profession has taken me all over the world, and travel has taught me many lessons, this one above all: The horizon is not a limit, but an invitation.

The torch has been passed to you in the expectation that you will hold it higher and carry it farther than we have been capable of.

We are so very proud of you, and we expect so very much of you.

You are our hope and our glory.

You have been given—you have earned—the gift of knowledge, and you must now bestow in return the gifts of service and hope.

Sample Paragraphs

1   I am not going to deny that one purpose of a college education is to allow you all to earn more money. Certainly, I have profited financially from my four years at Hughes University. You'll leave here, go on to graduate school or directly into the corporate world. This institution has carved out a fine reputation in that world, and you'll get a good job. But the real profit comes later—for some, just a little later. For others, quite a bit later. But, if you're alive to yourself and to all that you have learned here, it *will* come, sooner or later. It is the knowledge that all that you gain for yourself is of very limited value. It is the knowledge that in service to others lies your real treasure, a treasure beyond all imagining, a treasure multiplied by the number of lives you touch.

2　Let's begin with congratulations. First, to the parents, who have raised these young people to value the education offered to them, and who have supported their children through four financially and emotionally demanding years. Second, to this institution, which has dedicated itself to preserving what is best of the past and to inventing the future boldly and fearlessly. At last count, its graduates have been responsible for no fewer than 23,000 United States patents. Finally, to you, the graduates of this class. I spoke of an "education offered" to you—as if what you have learned had been handed to you. Really, of course, it was nothing more or less than an *opportunity* that was offered—the opportunity to educate yourselves, to work toward knowledge. This day signifies the culmination of one phase of your hard work and it signifies that you have made a grand beginning to build all that you can upon the knowledge you have earned. Let me talk to you a little about what you might build.

3　You will take much with you when you leave this university. You will have partaken of a rich store of knowledge, wisdom, and the collective judgment of a great and learned faculty. Knowing as I do the traditions of this school, you will have also imbibed a spirit of openness and ruthless investigation tempered always with compassion. Yet there is so much that cannot be given to you: the courage to do right as you see it, the will never to compromise what you know to be true, the determination to know yourself and to live up to your *best* self. These things you must find within yourself. And you must nurture them, even when it is far easier to abandon such things, to sell even your best self to the highest bidder. Believe me, you will often be tempted to do just that.

Sample Speech

President Gooch, distinguished deans and faculty, graduates, and honored guests, it is always a pleasure to return to my alma mater, and it is a rare and extraordinary honor to be asked to address the graduating class of 199X.

Alma mater. Do you know, ladies and gentlemen, this is the first time I have used that phrase seriously, that phrase that seems so quaint, so archaic. But, ever since President Gooch asked me to speak, it is that very phrase that has been on my mind. *Soul mother*, the mother of one's soul. It seemed to me to express the affection I have never stopped feeling for this great school even through the passage now of twenty-five years since I sat where you fine young men and women now sit.

Corny? No. Not at all. Your parents, who have paid mightily for the privilege of sending you here, and yourselves, who have worked so hard to excel here, may find it hard to think that what you have received in the four years that have passed has been a gift. No, you say, you've paid for it all, you've worked so hard for it all. But it is a gift nevertheless, no matter what it cost in money and sweat and anguish and nerves and sleepless nights before open books.

For I know from experience that this great university—like any great institution of *higher* learning—nurtures not only your mind, but your spirit, your very soul. It cannot force you to be a good person, a compassionate person, a civilized person, no more than any mother can compel a son or daughter to be these things. But it provides models, examples, object lessons, and the nurturing soil in which these things can take root. The university is certainly part of this world. Your university has produced some of this nation's most influential politicians and jurists, some of its wealthiest industrialists, and its most aggressive managers of commerce. Yet it is also apart from this world, borrowing from it only what is best and offering it for your consideration.

I am going to say it outright. A great university trains your very soul.

It is up to each of you to make the best use of the training you have received here—to go on to be the best doctor, lawyer, social worker, accountant, manager, teacher, scientist, writer, musician, artist that you can possibly be. But that is hardly enough. It is up to each of you to develop your soul to be the best soul it can possibly become: caring, compassionate, truthful, far-seeing, selfless.

Knowledge without a great soul mastering it is barely human. It is, in fact, monstrous. And, looking out at your fine, hopeful faces, I know that you are not monsters. I know that, fresh from your Soul Mother, you are receptive to greater experience and determined to confront the many challenges and realize the even greater number of opportunities the world offers.

So, when I wish you every success, it is not simply to prosper in your law practice, business career, or medical endeavors. It is to succeed in cultivating your souls, which have been so tenderly nurtured, and to carry the fruit of that cultivation to others, who will surely benefit from it. I wish you success in making a kinder world and a brighter world, a place of more and more spectacular intellectual accomplishments, of more fantastic inventions, and of healthier, happier, freer, and more loving individuals. What I am wishing for you is that you do for the world—for those with whom, through deed and word, you come into contact—what your alma mater has done for you. Be true to yourselves and give of that truth to others. Impart knowledge, wisdom, and your best judgment. But, most of all, remember that the people whose lives you touch are more than minds. They are whole beings, and it is your responsibility to address, to respect, and even to love their wholeness.

I love this school, and because I do, I look forward to a world that will be, in ways great and small, transformed by each of you.

Thank you.

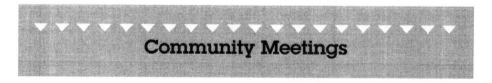

Community Meetings

At the root of public speaking is the community. It is no accident that the first great epoch of oratory was the product of classical Greece, the cradle of democracy. The Greek orators and, later, the great Roman rhetoricians regarded speaking as the primary means of creating, guiding, and perpetuating a community. When you get up to address members of your community, you are participating in a great tradition. This does not mean that you need the oratorical skills of a Demosthenes or a Cicero, but it does require that you keep uppermost in mind the same object they had: Persuasive public speech appeals to and fosters a sense of community.

This is not an idle, pie-in-the-sky ideal. The folks who are present at community meetings are rarely unified. Often, they are divided. An appeal to one faction or the other is not likely to prove ultimately useful or persuasive. It is unlikely that you will resolve all differences. The workable goal is to appeal to the common good, the common interest, the common concerns, the common cause. Regardless of your position, your message should be that, whatever our differences, we are all in this community together.

What to Say

Create and appeal to a sense of community.

Use imagery that suggests participation in a common cause and working toward a common goal. ("We may be very different people, but we are all in this lifeboat together.")

Demonstrate a willingness to listen, to hear all sides, to entertain all points of view.

Do not respond too quickly to questions. First, be certain the questioner has completed the question. Don't cut her off. Then take whatever time is necessary to consider your answer. You may even say, "Let me think about that one just a moment." It is better to be perceived as thoughtful than to be seen as someone who has a "quick answer to everything."

State, outline, and review the issues clearly. Do not push your point of view to the exclusion of others, but take all into account so that your audience will be persuaded by your arguments rather than feel bullied by mere verbiage.

Acknowledge the faults in what you have to offer—but make it clear that the benefits outweigh any faults.

Invite others to *explain* their points of view.

In reviewing alternatives, compare apples to apples and make sure that others do the same.

Construct the speech of persuasion as you might construct a good sales letter. Before you throw away that next batch of junk mail, take a look at one or two of the sales letters you have been sent. There are infinite variations in the details and language, but any good sales letter has five basic parts:

1. It gets the reader's attention.

2. It identifies a need the reader has.

3. It shows how the product or service in question can fill that need.

4. It persuades the reader to buy—often with some special offer.

5. It prompts action.

Consider building your community-oriented speech similarly:

1. Get your listeners' attention by asking a provocative question, making a bold statement, making a promise.

2. Identify a community need—one that, despite differences, is common to the audience.

3. Explain what you propose and show how it will fill that need.

4. Persuade your audience by comparing and contrasting your proposition to others.

5. Prompt action by telling your audience what their next step is. Don't leave them with a feeling that, yes, we *really should* do something about such and such. Give precise directions for action.

WHAT NOT TO SAY

Avoid appealing to factionalism.

Avoid attacking personalities. Address the issues, not the people behind them.

Avoid name calling.

Do not attempt to cut off or stifle opposing points of view. Allow all sides to be heard. Your arguments must stand on their merits and on the quality of your presentation. Unless you have a small army—or its equivalent—to back you up, bullying will not work, at least not for long.

Avoid emotional responses to emotional assaults. If an exchange becomes heated, it is best to withdraw from it for a time. Do not withdraw in anger or disgust, but appeal to the community. ("We are all upset by this issue. Let's take a few moments to collect ourselves and consider how we can act more effectively together.")

Do not back your audience into a corner. Most people resent being told they have no choice. It is better to make clear just what choices are available and why this choice is superior to that.

Words to Use

accepting	democracy	positive
account	demonstrate	progress
accountable	determine	proper
act	direction	proposal
action	discuss	protest
all	elect	receptive
answer	evaluate	report
benefit	everyone	respect
better	free	responsibility
calm	goal	responsible
challenge	hear	revise
change	imagine	right
choice	improve	scenario
choose	investigate	share
citizens	judge	solution
collaborate	justice	solve
commitment	learn	team
common	listen	teamwork
community	neighbors	together
consider	open	truth
convince	orderly	value
cooperate	outline	values
create	participate	vote
creative	persuade	weigh
decide	plan	
deliberate	popular	

WORDS TO AVOID

(all ethnic and other slurs)	force	ripoff
closed	ignorant	steal
compel	liar	stupid
criminal	lies	them/us
enemy	must	thief
fat cats	outsiders	wrong

PHRASES TO USE

a house divided

anticipate problems before they become unsolvable

assess the need

avoid emotion

avoid empty argument

benefit the community

common good

common cause

compromise is valuable

consider all points of view

coordinate our efforts

determine our common goals

discuss fully

formulate an effective response

greatest benefit

honorable compromise

in this together

invite alternatives

least harm and most good

love thy neighbor

make the choice

mutual benefit

not productive

open to discussion

open to suggestions

plan of action

plan together

pull together

respect one another

respect the minority

take the time to think this through

team effort

this is our community

through unity and teamwork

united we stand

we are a team

we are the community

we make and remake this community every day

weigh the options

weigh the choices

what's best for all of us

workable solution

work together

work toward a solution

Sentences to Use

I have an offer to make to each and every one of you.

Without so much as talking to a single person here, I know that six out of ten of you have been the victims of street crime.

Let's work together to find a solution.

I do not pretend to have *the* answers, but I have *some* answers, and I would like us to consider them.

Let us remember that we are neighbors.

We can pull in opposite directions, or we can determine, here and now, in what single direction we should move.

This much is clear: the choices are ours to make.

The burden is on me to demonstrate to you the effectiveness of what I propose.

I have a promise to make to you.

Let me outline the issues.

Let us look at the issues and the answers.

We have a choice: to shout at each other or to speak together in a way that will change conditions for the better.

I have been wrong before, and I am very willing to be shown that I am wrong again.

This community is challenged, and how we choose to respond to the challenges can make us a better or a much worse place in which to live.

If you own any vehicle that runs on wheels, I don't have to tell you that our streets are falling apart.

Are you prepared to see a child killed on the corner of Broad and Smith?

As surely as I am standing here and you are sitting there, the sewer main beneath Elm Street will rupture today, tomorrow, in a week, a month, a year—sooner or later.

We can ignore politicians, and we can even refuse to listen to one another, but we cannot turn a deaf ear to what the structural engineers have to say.

SAMPLE PARAGRAPHS

1   Please let me ask you a question: Do you want fifty-five new jobs in this neighborhood? That was an easy one. Now let me ask you to think about a tougher question. Are you willing to allow a major zoning variance to get those jobs? That's what you will have to allow if my company is to move in here and grow with this community. The advantages of the variance are obvious, for your community as well as for my company. Are there significant drawbacks? Let's outline what's involved, and then it will be up to each of you to decide.

2   I come to you with hopeful news from Heller Memorial Hospital. Our neighbor, twelve-year-old Johnny Sparks, is off the critical list. For that, of course, all of us here are thankful. Let us continue to send Johnny our best thoughts and prayers to help him in what will be a long and painful process of recovery. But, while concentrating on such thoughts and prayers, let's not lose the power of our collective outrage. Johnny would not be in that hospital if the town had installed the traffic signal we have petitioned for so long.

3   Don't be surprised if you soon see M-1 tanks rolling down the streets of our community. No, it won't be an invasion. Soon, it will be the only way anyone will be able to negotiate our crumbling streets. In the past three weeks, I've talked to four people who have suffered broken axles driving within a few blocks of their homes. *Broken axles!* Up until a month ago, I went my entire life without meeting anyone who had actually broken an axle. Now there are four in the space of three weeks and within a mile of this room.

Sample Speech

You can't fight city hall.

End of speech. Goodnight. Go home—while it is still worth living in.

Or instead of bowing mindlessly to a cliché, let's fight it with another: *Don't believe everything you hear.*

Can't fight city hall? What do you think city hall is for? Every day a small army of lawyers and lobbyists make their living fighting city hall. Let's get this much straight: We can do the same.

Now, we have a choice. We can fight loudly but uselessly, individually, separately, and piecemeal. Or we can begin this very evening to lay out the issues and develop a plan.

Each of us produces lots and lots of garbage. That much is a fact of life. Something has to be done with it. That is also an immutable fact of life. Our city wants to take not only our garbage, but garbage from ten other wards, and burn it here, in a plant to be constructed on a site bounded by Lord, Lovett, Lowe, and Lemming Streets. That is three blocks from our neighborhood's central business district and six blocks from one elementary school, one high school, and a day-care center.

We don't want it here.

Well, every community says that. To which our city responds, We've got garbage and we've got to get rid of it—if not in your neighborhood, then in someone else's.

That is, indeed, a problem. Or it *would* be a problem, if what the city is saying were true. If our city's statement of the situation were accurate, it would not, of course, change the fact that we don't want the incinerator here, but it would make our task at least morally more difficult: *We* don't want the problem. Let somebody else have it.

Much as we love our community, none of us is eager to pass the buck to someone else.

But the truth of the matter is that the city's statement of the situation is not only inaccurate, it is short-sighted, it is just plain incorrect, mistaken, and wrong. Our community board has filed a study with the city showing no fewer than three locations, zoned exclusively for manufacture, relatively remote from residential and retail areas, that offer ample acreage for the proposed incinerator.

We don't *have* to give this problem to someone else, because there does not *have* to be a problem.

Ladies and gentlemen—neighbors all—our choice is frighteningly simple. We can fail to fight city hall. We can let the administration build the incinerator precisely where it will do the most harm, where it will threaten our health and our children's health, and where it will burn up not only garbage, but the investment each and everyone of us has made in a home, a business, a life here.

Or we can begin here to map out a strategy for fighting city hall. They may not know it, in the bureaucracy, but the battle is not just for us, but for our entire city—your city, my city, and, yes, *their* city. After all, how many neighborhoods can this town afford to destroy?

I propose that we review the city's plan and work up a point-by-point response to it. Then we take the battle into the public hearings and, if necessary, into the courts. I further propose that we secure the best legal counsel we can obtain. I have a list of potential firms to read to you. The first step, however, the first action we must take is to organize a fund-raising effort to amass the war chest we are going to need.

No fight comes free. Let's consider the particulars. . . .

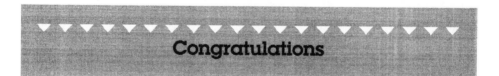

Congratulations

Highly paid motivation consultants tell us in detail what the old saying has long told us in a more general way: You catch more flies with honey than you do with vinegar. In any organization, it makes good sense to congratulate employees and associates on exceptional performance and notable accomplishments. It helps to ensure that such feats will be repeated. More than that, it makes everyone involved simply feel good.

Congratulations are generally quite brief, always contain an element of celebration, and often combine this with thanks for a job well done or for an accomplishment that benefits the organization as a whole. The congratulatory remarks can be quite simple, even rather formal, yet still strike the congratulatee and other listeners as sincere. However, the most effective congratulations reflect your relationship to the honoree. These are often frank expressions of admiration tinged with good-natured humor.

WHAT TO SAY

While it is a good idea to keep your remarks brief, make sure that your listeners understand what the honoree is being congratulated for, what his accomplishment means to himself, to the organization, and to everyone within earshot.

Wherever possible, inject a personal note.

Express admiration and pride.

Where appropriate—and, in one way or another, it almost always is—combine thanks with the congratulations.

Use good-natured humor. It is a sign of genuine regard and affection that everyone, honoree and audience alike, will appreciate.

Acknowledge the participation, collaboration, cooperation, and support of others.

WHAT NOT TO SAY

Beware of appropriating—or appearing to appropriate—credit due to the honoree.

Avoid references to luck, good fortune, coincidence, accident, or anything else that might tend to diminish the honoree's accomplishment.

Do not get carried away with your humor. This steals centerstage from the honoree and therefore seems graceless. Taken to excess, humor also tends to diminish or even denigrate the accomplishment being recognized.

Don't be afraid to inject a personal note, but beware of inadvertently delivering an autobiographical dissertation that steals the focus from the honoree.

Avoid lengthy speeches. Leave plenty of time for the honoree to say something.

Avoid invidious comparisons between the honoree and anyone else.

WORDS TO USE

admire	generous	performance
beloved	genius	praise
best	homage	progress
brilliance	honor	rare
brilliant	honored	resourcefulness
concentration	ingenious	respected
congratulate	innovative	revered
contribution	inspiration	sensational
cornerstone	inspirational	service
dedicated	invaluable	super
dedication	inventive	sweat
epoch-making	labor	unique
example	lofty	valuable
exceptional	marvel	willingness
extraordinary	model	wonder
finest	momentous	
foundation	perform	

WORDS TO AVOID

accident	dumb luck	luck
accidental	exploit	lucky
break	finally	obligatory
dumb	fortune	shocked

PHRASES TO USE

always delights and surprises us

a pleasure to congratulate

catalog of awards

congratulations and thanks

credit where credit is due

depend on him/her

embodies the values

great achievement

greatest respect

headed a fine team

hearty congratulations

here to praise

highly honored

hit the heights

in the finest tradition

join me in congratulating

makes this a better organization

never gave up

our applause

outstanding performance

owe him/her a debt of gratitude

pillar of this organization

power of invention

reflects credit on us all

rely on him/her

routinely extraordinary

service to us all

significant contribution

spectacular achievement

splendid achievement

splendid record

take for granted

through sweat and smarts

too modest to admit

wonderful person

SENTENCES TO USE

Come up here and get a hug.

I for one never thought you'd get this far.

I couldn't have done better myself—and I really do mean that!

I want to say that achievements like this are not a daily occurrence, but you have made them *seem* almost routine.

I know I speak for everyone here when I extend our congratulations and thanks for a great job.

It is exciting to anticipate your next achievement.

Just when I thought it was safe to relax, you come up with something like this.

Please join me in congratulating the entire research team on a magnificent achievement.

This is a marvelous achievement of which we all can be proud.

We are proud of you.

You did one hell of a job.

You are a pleasure to work with.

Your record is so consistently magnificent that you are in danger of being taken for granted, like a force of nature.

Your presence has been an inspiration to all of us.

SAMPLE PARAGRAPHS

1   I've asked you to take a few minutes out of your busy day to join me in congratulating Jane Leary, who, as you've probably heard by now, has just received the Dolton Award for Excellence in Advertising. That she has achieved such excellence is no news to *us*, of course, but I thought congratulations were in order because now the world at large has also acknowledged her achievement.

2   For the first time in the history of the Kennel Klub, our Pomeranians have swept the County Competition, the State Show, and the Grand National. Of course, we can be proud of our dogs—and we'll do our best to congratulate them. But I don't want to overlook the hard

work, skill, and dedication of members Esther Warren, Sarah Fishkill, and Arthur Morris. They bred, groomed, and trained this year's roster of champions.

3　People tell me that, being Irish, I'm always looking for an excuse to celebrate. Maybe. It's true, we haven't won any particular award, and while we've been doing very nicely with this quarter's sales, thank you, it has not, on balance, been a banner year. But I suggest to you that we do have plenty to celebrate. We have come through a recession period in which we have still managed growth, albeit modest. Even more important, we have a development program that promises great new products in the months ahead. So, let's stop a moment to pat ourselves on the back.

SAMPLE SPEECH

Today we have the pleasure of recognizing the achievements of three of our most successful salespeople, William Wall, Betty Hagan, and Shirley Samson.

It is easy enough to express their achievement this quarter in numbers. All have broken the $250,000 mark. This, of course, is great for them and for our company. Through their efforts, we are all a little bit more secure and prosperous.

But I want to congratulate them all on something more than mere numbers. Through their integrity, knowledge, and enthusiasm, they have done far more than coax our customers into parting with cash. They have cultivated a loyal clientele. They have, in the very best traditions of this firm, served the market and served it admirably.

Skill, integrity, resourcefulness, loyalty—these things are less tangible than cash, but they speak louder and they last longer. I have always been less interested in closing this or that sale than in building one strong relationship after another.

Please join me in congratulating Bill, Betty, and Shirley on a record of which we can all be proud.

▼ ▼ ▼ ▼ ▼ ▼ ▼ ▼ ▼ ▼ ▼ ▼ ▼ ▼ ▼ ▼ ▼ ▼ ▼

Dedications

Dedications partake of tradition, superstition, and noble aspiration. They are meant to mark a beginning, to announce to all within hearing the intention, purpose, and hopes of a project, a program, or a building. They are also meant to confer good fortune on an enterprise, and, by perpetuating a tradition of dedications, also to acknowledge the enterprise as something of significance. Dedications are serious occasions, yet hopeful ones. A skillful speech can set the tone not only for the event, but for an entire project. This does not mean that the speech should be highflown and somber. Quite the contrary, the dedication should communicate the anticipated joy of labor in a good and worthwhile cause.

Prepare for the dedication speech by first determining what role you are to play in the ceremony. Will you be the only speaker? Will you be the principal speaker? If not, ask the program planners what they might like you to speak on. If you are the sole or principal speaker, learn all you can about the project, program, or building you are helping to dedicate. Ask the planners of the ceremony to give you a thumbnail history and summary of the project and to list high points. If you are already familiar with the project, you should begin by making a similar summary and list for yourself. Generally, as with any speech, the more you know about the subject, the better—with one caution. There is a danger that you are *too* close to the project, that you might take for granted important facts about it and therefore fail to make your audience fully aware of the significance of the undertaking. The more familiar you are with the project, the more carefully you should ask yourself: What does my audience need to know in order to appreciate the purpose, significance, and benefit of this undertaking?

WHAT TO SAY

Welcome those present, singling out any special guests for mention by name.

Acknowledge the honor of speaking on this occasion.

State the task at hand: "We are here to dedicate . . . ."

Concisely explain the nature of the project, program, or building.

Concisely summarize the significance of the project, program, or building.

Mention or introduce the principals who are or will be involved in the undertaking.

Acknowledge those instrumental in authorizing, planning, and funding the undertaking.

Express hopes for success, prosperity, benefit, and so forth. If appropriate, ask for God's blessing.

Express your belief that the undertaking will, indeed, succeed.

What Not to Say

Avoid gratuitous or trivializing humor.

Avoid invidious comparison with other, similar undertakings.

Do not cast doubt on the enterprise: "Many people will tell you that there are already too many shopping malls in this area and that another one doesn't stand a chance. Well . . . ."

Words to Use

adapt	change	enterprise
ages	children	evolve
anticipate	commitment	extraordinary
aspire	completion	faith
belief	consecrate	favorable
believe	decades	foretell
bold	dedicate	fortune
centuries	dedication	future
century	develop	generations
ceremony	emotional	grandchildren

heritage	potential	strive
hope	pray	striving
investment	prayer	success
labor	predict	successful
launch	preserve	survive
legacy	profit	thrill
marvel	progress	thrive
monument	prosper	tradition
noble	self-sacrifice	undertaking
plan	send-off	wonderful
pledge	sincere	years

Words to Avoid

attempt	falter	test
chance	gamble	try
dark	hedge	unpredictable
delay	maybe	weak
doubt	murky	uncertain
doubtful	regret	
dubious	risky	

Phrases to Use

all our good wishes

dedicate our efforts

dedicate this monument

express in glass and steel

express in concrete form

good of all

have no fear

improve our lives

informed optimism

insures success

investment in our children and grandchildren

investment in the future

launch this project

let us thank

make a better world

monument to service

monument to the hands, hearts, and minds

new horizons

our highest hopes embodied

our prayers go with

predict great things

public good

public service

remarkable progress

state of the art

technological masterpiece

the common benefit

the common good

this is our pledge

we believe in this enterprise

we cannot fail

we stake our fortunes and reputations

Sentences to Use

A project of this magnitude is the product of profound faith and unshakable resolve.

Allow me to present the woman most directly responsible for this program.

I am proud to dedicate this monument to brain, heart, and muscle.

I am proud to dedicate this monument to our company's vision.

I wish everyone who is and will be associated with this enterprise the best of great good fortune.

In dedicating this building, we dedicate ourselves to serve the needs for which it stands.

It is a great thrill to be—quite literally—in on the ground floor of an enterprise such as this.

Only when we realize the full scope of this undertaking can we appreciate the level of dedication this project represents.

The time for planning and debate has ended as we roll up our sleeves to begin the day-to-day work of what promises to be a great institution.

This structure represents our hopes for—and faith in—the future.

We ask God to help us use this new facility wisely, effectively, and justly.

We launch this product line in the belief that it will not only profit us, but benefit our customers as well.

SAMPLE PARAGRAPHS

1   I am proud to participate in the dedication of this fine facility. The product of vision and hard work, it will make the lives of many in this neighborhood richer, fuller, and more fulfilling. We have gone too many years without a supervised recreational center. Now we—and our children, and their children, and for generations afterward—will benefit from a beautiful center for enjoyment, education, and recreation.

2   Let us launch this program with a full awareness of just what it is that we are beginning here. For years, we denied that there are citizens in our community who can neither read nor write—people who are cut off from much that our civilization has to offer and who, on a daily basis, are endangered in a world of hazards that reveal their warnings only to those fortunate enough to be literate. This new center means that the days of denial are over. We are beginning a new era. We are, in fact, welcoming new citizens to this community.

3   I know most of you who are making this great project possible, and because I know you, I am certain that this enterprise will succeed—succeed even beyond our greatest hopes for it. Nevertheless, you will forgive me if I ask that we pray for the success and prosperity of this undertaking. Those of you who don't feel particularly comfortable with prayer, I ask that you cross your fingers and wish us the good fortune that even the best-favored enterprise can benefit from.

SAMPLE SPEECH

I am thrilled, proud, and flattered that Principal Hunter asked me to return to Allen High—my own high school—to dedicate the new network of personal computers.

Allen High combines tradition and innovation. Its most hallowed tradition is to do whatever is necessary to ensure that the students at this institution are given the best education possible, one that embodies the state of the art, that partakes of the highest level of prevailing thought and technology. Our world runs on networked computers, on the ability to create information and to share it with others in order to create fresh, new insights. We must use the gifts technology offers. We must not shy away from them. This new, state-of-the-art computer network will allow our students to use the gift of technology—not just to meet short-term vocational goals, but to become accustomed to living in a community built of knowledge, information, and cooperation. This computer network has no end of technological lessons to teach, but, even more important, it gives a new dimension to the way in which our young people can come to think of and define and shape a truly *open* society.

The computer network we are dedicating here is more than a collection of plastic, copper, and silicon. It is a lesson in democracy, a lesson in and a commitment to the democratic ideal of society in which everyone has a stake and in which all are invited to participate and take responsibility for fashioning their own fate.

Let us acknowledge the hard work of Principal Hunter, of Superintendent Perkins, of the computer science faculty, and of the parents and industry leaders who have had the vision to provide financial and technical support for this project.

To the students who will benefit from this installation, I ask that you treat it with care—but that you use it boldly, creatively, inventively. With the guidance of your fine teachers, use it to learn about your world and to create new worlds. In the best, most profound, and most human sense of the word: Have *fun* with it. Like any great tool of learning, it should give you all great joy.

And now, please join me in officially declaring this computer network open and operational.

Thank you.

Eulogies

Perhaps no speaking assignment is more urgent or more intimidating than the eulogy. The nature of the occasion usually means that the speaker is given very short notice. Depending on the speaker's relation to the deceased, he may be making the speech under considerable emotional stress. But even more than these anxiety-arousing factors, there is the pressure—mainly self-applied pressure—to say something adequate to the memory of the deceased, something that will be consoling, memorable, and inspirational for those who are left to mourn.

Depending on your personality, your relation to the deceased, and your relation to your audience, dealing with death can be very difficult. There is no getting away from that fact. But the eulogy itself, while a challenging assignment, is not an impossible task. Realize the following:

▼ No one expects your speech to make all the pain go away.

▼ No one expects your speech to be the absolute and final word on the deceased, the perfect expression of the sum total of the man or woman's worth.

▼ Your listeners recognize the difficult nature of your task and tend to be particularly sympathetic and receptive.

▼ Your listeners are already focused on the subject of your speech.

▼ Unless the deceased was a controversial figure about whom a wide variety of people had ambivalent feelings, you enjoy a bond of unity with your listeners. You are united in mourning, respect, and affection. And even if the deceased was not universally loved, your audience shares with you a sense of decency and decorum that makes them receptive to your message of remembrance. In short, difficult as it may be to deliver a eulogy, you can embark on the task secure in the knowledge that your audience is with you.

There are three general principles so universally applicable to eulogies that we might as well call them rules:

▼ Speak from the heart, from your best feelings about the deceased.

▼ Evoke and share memories of experiences that you believe reveal the deceased at his most characteristic and best.

▼ Speak no ill of the dead. The admonition contained in this ageless saying seems obvious enough. The point is that you are not Saint Peter presiding over the Pearly Gates. It is not your role to weigh the worth of the deceased, to pass judgment on him or her. Mention only the good, only the best. Evoke only affection and admiration. The word *eulogy* contains the key to your task: It is derived from the Latin *eulogium* and the Greek *eulogia*, both meaning praise.

Finally, while it is true that funeral and memorial service attendees make a very favorable "audience," do be aware of your listeners' relation to the deceased. Are they mostly family members? Are they employees paying tribute to their CEO? Are they members of a community mourning the loss of a respected and beloved fellow citizen? Are they co-workers of the deceased? Members of the same club or organization? Be aware of how your relation to the deceased reflects or differs from that of your audience.

WHAT TO SAY

If you are the first or only speaker, state the purpose of your speech: "We are gathered here to remember Robert D. Williams."

Emphasize the unity of feeling in the room, the bond you and your listeners share. In an important sense, your mission is to speak on behalf of the other mourners.

Admit feelings of grief and pain.

Stress the value of the deceased—not just to you and his family, but to the organization, the company, the community. What would your firm, your club, the world have been like *without* him?

Speak from personal experience—from your knowledge of and relation to the deceased. Find a few endearing and revelatory anecdotes that show him at his best.

Stress the very best qualities of the deceased. Give those qualities names: kindness, thoughtfulness, selflessness, wisdom, a sense of humor.

Do not hesitate to inject humor into the situation, if a sense of humor or some humorous and endearing quirk were part of the personality of the deceased. ("Pete would have refused to come to this funeral if he knew it meant he'd have to wear a tie.")

If you will miss the deceased, say so, yet emphasize your sense of good fortune for having known her.

Talk about the deceased as a wife, husband, mother, father, son, or daughter.

Make use of memorable quotations from the deceased.

Read or quote from relevant literature.

Do not be afraid to address the deceased, using the pronoun *you*.

While it is very effective to share with your audience common memories of the deceased, it is also emotionally moving to reminisce about the childhood and early years of the deceased and other aspects of his life of which your audience may be unaware.

WHAT NOT TO SAY

Avoid abstractions and clichés.

Avoid highflown rhetoric. Share memories, not mere words.

Cast no doubt on the reputation or achievements of the deceased. Do not judge him or her.

Do not dwell on tragedy, misery, or pain.

In the case of an accidental or premature death, do not stress the "senselessness" of the incident. The point of the eulogy is not that the deceased met with a meaningless death, but that he led a life rich in meaning.

WHEN WORDS FAIL

No matter how well prepared you are, it is possible that you or others will become overwhelmed with emotion. Do not try to talk your way through such an episode. If you need time to compose yourself, excuse yourself, step back, and take the time you need. If someone in the audience requires assistance, pause while that person is being attended to. If you are too overcome to continue, it is best to yield to your emotions. Apologize briefly, if you are able, and step down. Under the circumstances, no one will think less of you.

WORDS TO USE

affection	fulfilled	lucky
affectionate	fulfillment	memory
beautiful	full	open-hearted
beauty	generous	pain
beloved	gift	peace
bereaved	God	quiet
blessed	grief	recall
brief	heal	recollect
calm	healing	recover
calming	heart	rejoice
celebrate	heaven	remember
character	heritage	rich
comfort	honor	serene
comforting	humanity	share
community	humor	shock
compassion	joy	solace
consolation	kindness	sympathy
console	laugh	time
contribution	legacy	touched
delight	life	transformed
enjoy	live	typical
enthusiastic	living	wise
faith	loss	wishes
fortunate	love	

WORDS TO AVOID

absurd	dust	senseless
dark	emptiness	shameful
darkness	empty	inconsolable
despair	hopeless	useless
destroyed	inexplicable	vain
devastated	insignificant	vanity
doom	meaningless	waste

PHRASES TO USE

a person of great character

acts of kindness

always there for you

blessed with such memories

boundless energy

cannot be replaced

cannot be taken from our memories

definition of character

devoted father/ mother/son/daughter

difficult to express

eager to help

example shall live in our hearts

filled with love

go the extra mile

good fortune to have known

great memories

great shock

has not left our hearts

helping hand

legacy of good work

legacy of service

legacy of wisdom

life of contribution

life of service

light up a room

long-term commitment

loved by all

made a difference in so many lives

modest and unassuming

offer condolences

one of a kind

pay our last respects

remain a happy memory

reflect on this great life

remember his/her example

rich memories

seek solace

smiling face	we shall miss him/her
the first one you would call	words of kindness
time will ease	words of wisdom
time will heal	would not want us to grieve
unbounded generosity	years of guidance

SENTENCES TO USE

As much as we loved and respected Dave, his family has suffered an even greater loss.

Ben would not want us to waste time grieving for him, because wasting time was the only thing this most tolerant of men could not tolerate.

Bill, we will miss you.

Each of us has a favorite George story.

Fred, we all had so much fun. Why did you leave the game so early?

Instead of somber and empty words of comfort, let me offer you some memories of Jane.

It was impossible not to like Martha.

Let's give up this idea of mourning Sarah and concentrate instead on continuing the work she began.

Now that you are gone, to whom can we complain?

Phil did something wonderful and significant for each of us in this room.

She was so stubborn so much of the time that I simply cannot believe she let herself be taken from us.

The first words Martin ever spoke to me were, "What can I do to help?"

We are here to remember our dear friend and valued colleague, Ralph Nemerson.

We will learn to continue without Ruth's ever-valuable contribution, but I pray that God will give her family the strength to endure in the coming days and to thrive, as she would want them to, in the coming months and years.

We won't get over this loss, but we can hope, at least, to cope with it and manage it.

SAMPLE PARAGRAPHS

1   It is easy to feel sorry at a funeral: sorry for the departed one; sorry for the grieving family; sorry for oneself. I'll tell you whom I feel sorry for today. I feel sorry for all the many people who did not have the rare and wonderful opportunity of meeting, of knowing, of working with Pat Butler.

2   One of the greatest things about Cynthia Broadhurst was her refusal to pigeonhole people, to tie them up into neat little parcels with this noun or that adjective and file them away. She regarded each and every one she met as a unique, multifaceted, complex human being with whole worlds of heart and thought to share. Now I'm supposed to stand up here and do to Cynthia what she refused to do to anyone else. Try as I might, I can't put her away with this word or that: kind, generous, wise, beautiful, cheerful, helpful. These words are all true enough, but she was much more than what little they can convey.

3   Patty, you've really done it this time. Any excuse to gather your best friends into one room! But, this time, you've gone too far. Much too far. As the song says, we will miss your bright eyes and sweet smile. We will miss your kind words, great advice, and a level of energy that was highly contagious. We will miss all the great talk, the great conversation, the sharing of ideas. In fact, now that I think about it, *this* is the only one-sided conversation I've ever had with you.

4   Let's be selfish for just a moment. Let's realize something. We are shocked and saddened, but we will survive the passing of Barton K. Fletcher. Even more, we will continue to benefit from all that he has done to make this company an industry leader. We will benefit from his restless drive to innovate and to perfect. We will benefit from the

care he took to insure our security. We will benefit from his example as we continue to build the business he began. It is a terrible loss, but, following a life so rich, full, creative, and generous, we are left, strange as it may seem to us at this sad moment, with a gain, a prof-it.

Sample Speech

Edward Pelican was the only perfectionist I ever liked. He would not rest until the last detail of a project was completed to his satisfaction. To tell you the truth, I'm surprised he allowed the good Lord to take him from us. I would have expected him to argue God into making this or that modification first before he pronounced him finished. "Lord," he might have said, "You've almost got it. But let's work a little more on my double chin, shall we?"

Ed hated to see things slip. He saw chaos in compromise, and he insisted that everything our firm created had to be the best we collectively were capable of producing.

If you did not know Ed well, this might all sound pretty awful.

But it wasn't. In fact, working with him was something very like a miracle, a kind of daily miracle.

He made you work in ways you never thought of working before. He brought out your best. He brought out *more* than your best. Who among us would dare seriously to aspire to create a perfect design? Impossible, right? Crazy to try. Well, Ed dared—and, more important, he got each of us to dare as well. He made the pursuit of perfection "routine procedure" around here.

The result was not a bunch of neurotic engineers with ulcers. The result was—is—an R & D program that is the envy of the industry, staffed by engineers who learned to be better than what they thought of as their best. Neurotic? No. Happy, fulfilled, proud. And it was largely thanks to Ed.

I believe I speak for many of us here, if we are really honest with ourselves. I graduated from a very good engineering program at a fine university. I've got the diplomas to prove it. But, let me confess, it was Ed who finally and fully taught me how to be an engineer—in the fullest, most highly perfected traditions of the profession. If I owed him nothing else, I would owe him that much. But I—we, all of us here—owe him so much more. He was a great engineer, a great mentor, a great example, and a very, very great friend. We are better engineers and better human beings for having known and worked with him.

Farewells

Occasions of farewell come in two broad varieties: either you are leaving or someone else is. This chapter applies to such occasions as a move to another department, a different company, a change in career, and the like. Speech-making essentials appropriate to retirements are considered in their own section.

Why make a speech when you leave or someone else leaves a job, a department, or a firm? Think about it this way. How would you feel if a friend were visiting with you and, at the end of the evening, simply got up, donned his coat, and walked out the door without saying a word? An effective farewell is more than a polite gesture. It is an essential one. For a whole range of reasons—from simple human decency to keeping your options open at the firm you are leaving—it is vitally important to give those you are leaving behind or the person you are sending off the right feelings. These feelings include thanks, gratitude, a certain regret, satisfaction in a job well done, acknowledgment of great performance, and pleasure in fond memories.

If you are leaving, your object is to make a graceful exit that keeps a welcoming door open. If you are giving someone else a send-off, let him know that he will be missed and wish him well in whatever he is undertaking next.

WHAT TO SAY

If you are leaving:

If appropriate, briefly explain why you are leaving.

Express affection for the organization and people you are leaving.

Thank those you are leaving.

Recall exciting or successful projects.

Summarize any accomplishments you share with those you are leaving. ("We were a great team, who, together, created some very successful programs.")

Express regret or bittersweet feelings about leaving.

Tell your listeners how you will remember them. Mention some specifics, including anecdotes and personalities.

Tell your listeners how you would like them to remember you.

If possible and appropriate, promise to return, at least to visit.

If another is leaving:

Be sure your listeners know what the occasion is all about. Briefly explain why the person is leaving.

Express regret tempered with good wishes for luck and success.

Thank the person leaving and praise her. Mention some specific accomplishments.

If the person leaving was a longtime associate, flash back to the "old days."

Get personal. Recall an anecdote or two. You might prepare for the speech by asking some of the person's closest associates to supply you with a few recollections.

Evoke a feeling of unity or family.

WHAT NOT TO SAY

Whether you are leaving or sending someone else off, do not slam the door. Say nothing mean or ungenerous. Complain about nothing and no one. Avoid sarcasm. Don't gloat.

If you are leaving or sending another on his way under unfavorable circumstances, it is almost certainly best to avoid any formal, public speech, ceremony, or acknowledgment.

WORDS TO USE

admiration	example	privilege
admire	experience	profited
advice	faithful	progress
affection	fond	proud
benefit	fortunate	recall
bittersweet	generosity	regret
celebrate	generous	send-off
committed	grateful	share
compassion	gratitude	shared
congratulate	guidance	standards
created	humanity	thanks
creative	learned	thoughtful
decency	learning	touched
dedicated	love	treasure
enriching	loyal	understanding
enrichment	memories	valuable
enterprise	mutual	wisdom
ethical	pleasure	
ethics	pride	

WORDS TO AVOID

angry	bitter	escape
bail out	cheated	failed

failure	ousted	tired
fired	quit	unfair
glad to go	rescued	unjust
mediocre	robbed	weary
mistake	shabby	

PHRASES TO USE

all your new endeavors	hard work
always reliable	keep in touch
best of luck	learned a great deal from
best wishes	mixed emotions
bittersweet emotion	mixed feelings
confidence in you	mutual benefit
debt of gratitude	never forget
deeply committed	new venture
deeply touched	no fear for your future
difficult moment	on behalf of
eager to lend a hand	one of the molders of this firm
earned the admiration of	proud to have served
earned the affection of	pull myself away
earned the respect of	tear myself away
express my admiration	time has come to leave you
fortune smile upon you	treasure this experience
give back	treasure you in my heart
good fortune	we marveled at
good times and bad	win-win experience
great learning experience	won't be the same without you
hard to leave	your legacy to the firm

SENTENCES TO USE

For me, for my career, and for my family, the time has come for a change.

I owe this company a great debt of gratitude.

I am stepping into a new career.

I will treasure my memories of this place—and of each of you—as long as I live.

I guess this is what the word *bittersweet* is all about.

It has been my pleasure and privilege to work with all of you for the past ten years.

It is not an easy thing to leave so many good friends.

My tenure here has been among the most personally and professionally rewarding experiences of my life.

This is a very difficult moment for me.

You have all taught me a great deal.

On behalf of Kramer Industries, I wish you the best of luck in your new endeavor.

Our best wishes are with you as you launch a brand new career.

This organization is better for having had you as a member.

We will miss you.

We won't let you lose touch with us.

While I am sorry, very sorry to see you leave us, I congratulate you on your new endeavor, and I know that you will make a great success of it.

You have meant a lot to this firm and to the many people here who call you friend—myself among them.

You've made a difference here: in our policies and practices, in our bottom line, in the lives of each of us.

SAMPLE PARAGRAPHS

1   One of the great things about this company is that we are at all times encouraged to try new directions and undertake fresh enterprises. That is precisely what I have done here for the past twelve years. Now it is time to take yet another direction—out the door and into my own company. It is a step about which I am simultaneously excited, frightened, and touched with sorrow at having to leave my friends here, with whom I have so enjoyed working.

2   I still remember with vivid pleasure how proud and thrilled I felt six years ago when I walked through the doors of Appleby and Crumb for the first time. The pleasure I take in this job has never flagged, has never left me. But now it is time to take on a new challenge as I accept the call to public service. Please know that I leave you having learned much from you and having drawn strength and inspiration from your unfailing support.

3   I am deeply touched by this send-off. I really wish I didn't have to leave in order to get a party like this. To tell you the truth, excited as I am by the new horizons that lie ahead, I wish that I did not have to leave you in order to travel toward them. But if there is one thing above all else that this marvelous company has taught me, it is the necessity of evolution and change.

4   I'll be frank. There are employees you hate to see go, and there are others you don't much care about. I am so very proud of all that you have done here, and I am also proud that you are leaving us to take on a position of so much responsibility and potential. I know that you will do very grand things in your new job. I will point to you with pride and say, "She got her start with me." But I hate, I really do hate, to see you go.

5   I know I speak for everyone here when I thank you for the seven great years you have given us. Great? They were the years that saw the publication of some of our most distinguished books, including [list]. It would be greedy to wish for another seven years like that. So I'll contain myself and simply wish you the best of luck in your new endeavors.

6 I hate clichés, and I particularly hate the one that goes: All good things must come to an end. It always seemed to me so arbitrary and obnoxious—and, unfortunately, true. You are leaving us.

SAMPLE SPEECHES

1 Saying goodbye to so many dear friends is very hard. You've meant a great deal to me personally and professionally. Among you and from you, I learned this business of ours. I learned a vast technology, but I learned much more. I took my Ph.D. here in ethics and decency, in understanding and encouragement. I am leaving you, but I will take with me into a new phase of my career absolutely everything you have taught me.

And I'll be taking much more than a collection of lessons, however valuable they are. I'll take my memories of Ed, who can tell a joke better than anybody; of Michelle, who can't tell a joke to save her life, but who remembers the birthday of every employee here—*as well as* the birthdays of their spouses, sons, and daughters; and Peter, tireless in his decade-old quest to start a bowling league among us. Don't give it up, Pete.

I would be lying if I didn't admit that I am excited by the prospect of moving to a new place and starting something I've worked toward for a long time. But it is like leaving your family: something you have to do, but something that's not any easier for having to do it.

Thank you for this wonderful, generous send-off. I will keep in touch by phone and letter, and I will travel back to Anytown every time I get the chance. It has been wonderful.

2 When you devote eighteen years of your life and career to a company, I guess you can't be accused of using the place as a "stepping-stone" to a better job. So I won't try to make you feel guilty. You've given us eighteen great years, years that saw this company quadruple in volume of business, years that produced the product lines for which we are now best known, including [list].

Henry, you've given us a lot. I wish I *could* make you feel guilty, because these eighteen years make me want more than anything another eighteen just like them.

Not just because we'd probably quadruple revenues yet again. Not just because, together, who knows what exciting new products we'd come up with. But because we've grown accustomed to your brilliant conversation, your kind heart, your enthusiasm for new ideas, and your truly terrible jokes—lame as a one-legged spider, jokes you never give up on despite the fact that not one of them has ever produced an audible chuckle. I saw John smile at one of them once, but he later admitted it was indigestion.

I've done all my pleading with you in private, Henry. I know these people have no desire to see me cry. So, on behalf of Baker Research, let me thank you for eighteen years of genius and 100 percent commitment and let me extend to you all best wishes and bright fortune in the years ahead. You are a credit and an asset to any organization, and whatever particular company you may work for, you will always be what you have been here: a great and positive force in this industry.

Best of luck, Henry. We'll miss you.

Fraternal Organizations and Commercial Clubs

Speeches delivered to fraternal organizations and commercial clubs are usually devoted to reporting on the organization's programs and activities, planning future programs and activities, and proposing new members and nominating officers. Club meetings sometimes also include featured speakers, a topic discussed in a separate section in Part Two.

Clubs customarily emphasize two kinds of values: comraderie and service to the community. Regardless of its content and purpose, your speech should reflect these values—as well as any others peculiar to your organization.

WHAT TO SAY

1. Reporting on programs and activities:

Give a capsule overview of the nature and purpose of the project, program, or activity.

Enumerate the main features and principal goals.

Evaluate the success or progress of the program or activity. What goals have been achieved? Exceeded? Fallen short of?

Stress the benefits of the program.

Introduce entertaining or revealing anecdotes concerning the program or activity.

Thank those who have worked hard to make the project, program, or activity a success. In the case of failure, stress the positive contributions of those who struggled valiantly to make the program work.

2. Proposing future programs:

Establish a need, either within the organization or in the community at large.

Propose ways in which your organization might address the need.

Stress the benefits—but try to anticipate drawbacks and objections.

Invite proposals. Or present your plan and invite discussion and response.

Try to conclude by outlining action—the next step. This does not mean that a proposal speech is successful only if it prompts an immediate, headlong plunge into the program. The "next step" might consist of an agreement to discuss the proposal at the next meeting or to begin researching the feasibility of the project, costs, and so on.

3. Proposing new members (This is a special kind of introduction, which emphasizes the qualities you know your fellow members value):

Stress the candidate's position in the community, industry, or profession.

Emphasize your friendship or association with the candidate. How long have you known him/her, and in what context? What makes him/her a good friend?

List the candidate's best qualities, which should reflect the values of the organization.

Emphasize the candidate's enthusiasm and eagerness to become a member.

4. Nominating officers:

List the personal requirements for the office in question.

Nominate your candidate, asserting that she fills the bill perfectly.

Demonstrate just why your nominee is the best person for the job. Run down the list of desirable qualifications and provide evidence of the nominee's strengths in one area after another.

WHAT NOT TO SAY

In general, avoid remarks that do not contribute to a sense of community and an atmosphere of brotherhood and sisterhood. This does not mean that everyone must always be in agreement on every issue. There is nothing wrong with disagreement and debate. However, do not turn disagreement into division and dissension.

Avoid personal attacks. Address issues, not personalities.

Avoid placing blame.

Avoid invidious comparisons—either between one member and another or between your organization and another.

WORDS TO USE

action	agenda	ameliorate
advise	aid	assist

balance	friendly	positive
brotherhood	friends	practical
brotherly	future	principles
budget	generous	program
by-laws	goal	progress
cause	guide	project
celebrate	help	realistic
charitable	heritage	reasonable
commitment	hope	repay
community	humanitarian	sane
compassion	ideal	sanity
compassionate	idealistic	sisterhood
comradeship	ideals	sisterly
contribution	improve	steer
create	kindness	stretch
develop	lead	success
devoted	legacy	support
devotion	navigate	supported
effort	negotiate	traditions
establish	optimistic	unity
extra	organization	unwavering
faith	original	valuable
feasible	philanthropic	welcome
fellowship	philanthropy	worthwhile
founded	pioneer	
founders	plan	

WORDS TO AVOID

absolute	must	unchanging
against	obedience	unwelcome
defend	obey	versus
exclude	showdown	
exclusive	ultimatum	

Phrases to Use

address the question

all-out effort

allocate resources to

benefit to us all

best direct our resources

best for all of us

choose among the options

come to an agreement

common goal

community responsibility

cooperative spirit

desires of everyone

devote resources to

differences of opinion

energetic commitment

enhance comradeship

enhance our image

establish a plan

feasibility study

flexible agenda

future of the community

help our neighbors

human and financial resources

image of the organization

improve the community

in unity is strength

invest in the future

investment of time

lay out a plan

listen to our members

listen to the community

minority opinion

move forward

needs of all

needs of our members

promote understanding

protect the minority

reach a consensus

realize major benefits

regard for our neighbors

report on the progress

respect the minority

serve the community

service to the community

shape our community

spirit of brotherhood/sister-
hood

spirit of cooperation

use friendly persuasion

useful projects

vote on the question

win-win proposition

work together

worthwhile cause

SENTENCES TO USE

I am responding to our president's call for proposals of projects worth our investment of time, money, and talent.

I take pride in nominating for the office of president one our most distinguished members, Simon Standish.

If anyone ever deserved to be a Knight of the Golden Circle, Peter Hayes qualifies without question.

It is my privilege and pleasure to nominate for membership a very good friend and a sturdy pillar of this community.

Let us bear in mind our by-laws, which outline a mission of aid and assistance to our neighbors.

Let's begin by admitting that our project did not produce the results we had hoped for.

No one has worked harder or more effectively for this organization than Mary Reynolds.

Our progress in achieving the goals of this program gives us much to be excited about.

United, there is nothing we cannot accomplish.

We can do better than this.

What I propose partakes of the spirit of our founding goals even while it addresses the needs of today and tomorrow.

SAMPLE PARAGRAPHS

1   Our organization is about winning: winning for ourselves, and winning for others. I am pleased and proud to bring us just such a winning opportunity. I would like to propose my good friend and colleague, Sheila Moore, for membership in Phi Beta Beta. It is one of the best things I can imagine doing for a very good friend, and inducting Sheila into our membership is certainly one of the best things I can think of doing for this organization.

2 With unity and careful planning, we can continue to make a big difference in our community. We must not let the fact that there are so many worthwhile issues to address overwhelm us. I propose that each member draw up a list of at least five potential programs, and that we form a committee to review these lists and make preliminary recommendations concerning the allocation of next year's funds for projects that are most needed and that we have the resources to handle most effectively.

3 I am responding to what some have called a crisis among the membership. Certainly it is true that there is a great deal of disagreement over what activities should be funded in the coming year, and there is a good deal of questioning concerning our immediate and long-term goals. Do these things constitute a crisis? I prefer to see such doubts and questioning as healthy and invigorating antidotes to stagnant inactivity. Dissent does not equal crisis. However, let us conduct our discussions frankly, but in the spirit of brotherhood and sisterhood. United, we can accomplish a wide variety of goals.

SAMPLE SPEECH

Madame chairperson, officers, and members, I am very happy to come before you this evening to report on the progress of Operation Summer Camp. Right now, some of you who have been most closely involved with the project are thinking that I'm either a terrible liar or a perfect fool. Why should I be "happy" to report on a project that has fallen significantly short of its current goal?

Well, let me tell you why.

First, let's get what some might understandably call the "bad news" out of the way. We had set as our March goal the raising of $9,500. March has come and gone, and we have raised $4,897.

How can this be interpreted as anything other than disappointing?

Let's step back for a moment and recall what has happened between the time we originally set the goal fourteen months ago and these last three months, during which we collected almost $5,000. First, we were hit by a nationwide and local recession, which saw in this area alone the loss of some 1,400 jobs. Second, January and February gave us some of the worst winter weather we've had in these parts for the past fifty years. Even when our fund raisers could reach potential contributors, they were occupied with financial survival on the one hand and, I dare say, physical survival on the other. Many of the strongest and previously most generous contributors we have not even been able to call on yet.

Do these sound like excuses to you?

Then let me point out a few statistics. I spoke to Pete Hamilton, chairman of the Unified Way, who reports that contributions to his organization are down 45 percent. I spoke to Gordon Pelham, of the Green Cross, who reports a 61 percent drop. Finally, I had a discussion with Reverend Moore at First Methodist. Offerings are down 43 percent.

Given the adverse conditions stacked against us, and in the prevailing context of sharply declining rates of giving, we have a lot to be pleased with in assessing our progress toward making Project Summer Camp a reality.

It's spring again. The back of winter is finally broken, and the economy at least seems to be getting no worse. I can promise you that we will go out into the community again, with redoubled energy, to reach our final goal of $25,000 by July 1.

We will begin by approaching those we had scheduled for appeal during the first phase, but whom the weather prevented us from contacting. These, as I have said, include some of our best prospects. We will follow this up by approaching those scheduled for the spring appeal. Then we will end by returning to those who did not contribute or who contributed less than they might have. We will offer them a second opportunity to make a big difference in the lives of the children of our community.

I am happy, then, to report that we are making progress—reasonable and, under the circumstances, even hopeful progress. I am also happy to report that, while some of us may be disappointed, we are all thoroughly committed to seeing this fund-raising effort through to a successful conclusion by July 1.

Inaugurals

It is a statistical inevitability that very few readers of this book will ever be called upon to speak at the inauguration of the President of the United States either as a guest or as the main attraction. However, somewhat less public inaugurations take place every day in the worlds of business, non-profit organizations, and local politics. You may well be called upon to make a speech at your own inauguration or at the inauguration of another.

The main purposes of an inaugural speech are to mark an orderly transition from one leader to another and to set the tone of the administration that is about to commence. Depending on the particular circumstances of the appointment, you may want to make a speech either proposing or supporting radical change or pledging to continue a hallowed tradition. In either case, and regardless of whether you are the inauguree or a featured speaker, bear in mind that inaugurations are occasions of hope and new beginning—even if the "new beginning" is merely a changing of the guard. Inaugurations are not an occasion for disparaging one's predecessor, nor for forecasting doom and broadcasting despair. If your organization faces a crisis or hard times, by all means address such issues, but address them hopefully and positively.

Inaugurations are less about politics and issues than about leadership and feelings. A good inaugural speech should reassure your listeners that a capable leader and administrator is stepping into a post of trust. It should create a feeling of confidence and communicate the new office-holder's 100 percent commitment to his or her responsibilities. In accomplishing this task, tone and rhythm are almost as important as content. Speak firmly, confidently, and slowly enough to give each word weight and significance. Think about the balance and rhythm of your sentences. While you should avoid bombast, don't be afraid to take the high road, favoring carefully balanced sentences over terse statements of fact. Finally, and perhaps most important in our democratic society, the speech should communicate a sense of unity, of teamwork, of cooperation and pulling together. Inaugural speeches may separate one administration from another, but they should emphasize the continuity of beliefs, ideals, and goals that underlie orderly change.

WHAT TO SAY

If you are the inauguree:

Acknowledge a new beginning—even if it is only a new beginning to perpetuating what is best about a tradition.

Find an effective metaphor for a new start, hope, ambition, and potential. At his inauguration, President Bill Clinton observed that, while the season was in deep winter, the mood of the nation was at spring.

Acknowledge the work, dedication, and achievements of your predecessor. This is especially important if he was your opponent.

Outline the major challenges and opportunities your administration and your organization face. How—briefly and generally—do you propose to deal with them?

Assert your commitment to your organization's ideals.

Assert your commitment to your constituents' needs and desires.

Emphasize unity, the need for cooperation and consensus.

Ask for everyone's help, cooperation, and commitment.

If you are a featured speaker:

Acknowledge the honor of having been asked to speak.

Why did you accept the invitation? Talk about your respect for the inauguree, your confidence in her, what (in general terms) you hope and expect she will achieve.

Assure your listeners that they are in good hands, that they have chosen a fine leader and administrator.

At appropriate intervals, address the inauguree directly.

Urge support for the inauguree.

Emphasize unity, the need for cooperation and consensus.

Look toward the future.

WHAT NOT TO SAY

Neither disparage nor patronize your predecessor.

Do not threaten your listeners with imminent doom. Don't evade crisis and challenge, but emphasize the positive and affirm your intention and ability to meet difficulties.

Do not lecture or admonish your listeners. Do not criticize them for past behavior (for example, a habit of big spending).

Do not contribute to disunity. Avoid speaking in terms of "us" versus "them." Avoid creating a fortress or bunker mentality.

WORDS TO USE

account	cooperation	hope
accountability	courage	intelligence
accountable	create	legacy
adapt	creation	liberty
ahead	desirable	open
appeal	determine	ordain
appointed	discover	perpetuate
attain	elected	pledge
aware	establish	posterity
best	explore	potential
blessed	flowering	praise
blessings	foresight	progress
build	forward	promise
challenge	foundation	realize
challenges	freedom	reform
change	fullfil	resolution
children	fulfilled	resolve
choice	future	respect
choose	generations	responsive
collaboration	grandchildren	reveal
commitment	grateful	revise
confront	heritage	revitalize
consensus	honor	sacrifice

service	together	willing
strength	tradition	willingness
stewardship	unity	wisdom
thankful	will	

WORDS TO AVOID

dire	failed	regime
doom	failure	revolution
eliminate	final	revolutionize
end	hardship	rid
exclude	hopeless	status quo
exhausted	incompetant	sweep out
exploit	maintain	threat
fail	radical	trouble

PHRASES TO USE

achieve our objectives

act fairly

act from compassion

act deliberately

act generously

address everyone's needs

affirm our commitment

aim higher

always grow and develop

a people united can never be defeated

ask for your input

ask for your contribution

aspire to be the best we can be

attain our goals

build collective confidence in ourselves

collaborate on a brighter future

depend on one another

discuss all contemplated actions

do not reject the past

enjoy the benefits

establish our priorities

evaluate our priorities

evolve in an orderly fashion

exercise leadership

exercise my best judgment

exercise vision

face our problems

faith in the future

feel compassion

honor the service of

keep the faith

look ahead

look forward

make careful plans

meet the challenges

move ahead with confidence

move forward with hope

no challenge is too great

100 percent committment

perpetuate what is best from the past

pledge our mutual loyalty and cooperation

pledge to our children

pledge to you

promote progress

provide for our posterity

public service

pull together toward our common goals

realize our full potential

realize the common good

reap the rewards

reevaluate the past

regard for our posterity

rely on your advice

remain responsive

respect for all

secure for our children

service above all else

strengthen our resolve

think beyond ourselves

think beyond the short term

think clearly

unwavering loyalty

weigh means and ends

welcome the challenges and opportunities alike

whatever is necessary

will not mortgage the future

work together

SENTENCES TO USE

If you are the inauguree:

After careful thought, after listening to all sides, after weighing the means and the ends, let us move boldly forward together.

I am about to make some promises to you, and I expect you to hold me to them.

I am no less eager to face the coming challenges than I am to realize the approaching opportunities.

I cannot promise to solve all of the problems that confront us, but I do pledge to devote 100 percent of my mind, heart, and will to meeting all of the great challenges ahead.

I invite—I welcome—disagreement and debate, but always in a spirit of cooperation and in the pursuit of our common goals.

I look forward to a bright future with you.

In truth, this is a very intimidating office, but, with your help, support, and guidance, I embark on it with total confidence.

Let us put aside "me" and "you" in order to devote our energy to "us."

Together, we can create an increasingly vigorous and more profitable organization.

We are agreed on our priorities; now it is my job to see that we address each of them effectively.

Within the spirit and traditions of our founding principles, I intend to move forward boldly and without hesitation.

If you are a featured speaker:

I know that I speak for all of us when I express full confidence in our new president's ability to lead this organization to new heights.

It has been my pleasure to call Henry Mason a friend and a colleague for more than twenty-five years.

Join me in welcoming Mary Johnson to a great office vital to us all.

Let's not delude ourselves into thinking Jane Selkins is beginning an easy job, but, with our support, she will lead our organization to greater levels of excellence.

On behalf of the membership, I congratulate you on taking office and pledge to you our loyalty, support, and—you can be sure—our most creative criticism.

Over the years, we have come to expect great things from the man we have just elected as our new chairman.

We expect nothing less than a 100 percent commitment from you, and, in return, you will have our 100 percent cooperation.

When I speak of giving our new chairman our full support, I do not mean that we owe him blind obedience.

SAMPLE PARAGRAPHS

If you are the inauguree:

1   It is tempting at this moment to tell you that our road will be an easy one, that we have prospered for decades, and that we will prosper for decades more—without having to sacrifice, plan, or even think. It is true, we are a large organization blessed with substantial funds. Perhaps I could get away with easy assurances and thoughtless promises. But that is not why you elected me to this office. We have done well—yes, for decades—but the time has come to do even better.

2   In taking office, I embark on an exciting journey with you, filled with the potential of discovery and opportunity and—let us face reality— rife with hazards. The opportunities are too rich not to share and the hazards too menacing to face alone. Let us, then, remember at all times that we are traveling together in one and the same vessel. By all means, let us discuss the course, declare our ports of call, remain alert to the opportunities, and be wary of the rocks and reefs. Let us communicate. Let us not hesitate to disagree and debate. But let us not forget that we have each invested so much of ourselves in this one common enterprise. We must work together as a spirited crew to navigate successfully, reaching the fabulous shores we know of and others we have yet to discover, while avoiding all that threatens to break us apart.

If you are a featured speaker:

1   Like many of you, I have found frequent occasion to disagree with the man we have named as our new chairperson. I have also found that, invariably, such disagreements produce a dialogue, and from that dialogue new and creative solutions, possibilities, and plans emerge.

We are welcoming a chairperson who is not afraid to lead, but who is receptive and open to suggestions and criticism. I'm sure Ronald Gerdts uses the pronoun "I" as much as anyone else does, but I also know that he uses "we" more than most of us do. He rightly sees our greatest strength as the diversity within our vital unity.

2   Please join me in welcoming into office a woman who, I firmly believe, is destined to be one of our most successful, innovative, and creative presidents. The road ahead of her—indeed, ahead of us all— is difficult. We can expect many challenging twists and turns and, I'm sure, even some detours. Negotiating this highway will demand skill and vigilance, and Sarah Walton will need all of the support and cooperation we can give her. But the road ahead promises also to take us into new and exciting territory, vast markets as yet untapped. We will behold new vistas, undreamed of until this moment. Sarah Walton, whose creativity has been proven to us time and time again, will not fail to seize the new opportunities, which, together, we can shape into new sources of profit and progress.

SAMPLE SPEECHES

If you are the inauguree:

Ladies and gentlemen, you have honored me by electing me to this most challenging and demanding office. I will endeavor to do honor to that office and to serve you in accordance with the finest traditions of this organization. My predecessor, Hiram Bolders, certainly honored the office and this organization, compiling a record of innovation and service that is at once enviable and challenging. I know that he will understand when I announce my intention to build on what he has begun, but to build even higher and stronger than he might have imagined possible.

Hiram, you have set a lofty standard for this organization and for this office. I *promise* to live up to that standard. I *hope* to surpass it.

I do not come into this office, then, intending to reinvent everything. Thanks to the great work that has been accomplished before me, there is no need for this.

But neither do I come into this office as a mere caretaker. It is my intention to direct the efforts of this organization even more vigorously than before toward the following goals:

[list]

Let us build on our collective experience, which teaches that it is not sufficent merely to preserve and maintain the gains of the past, but constantly to develop and innovate.

I am aware that a policy of continuous experimentation—and I propose nothing less—makes many people uncomfortable. But, then, we are not in business to be comfortable. We are in business to excel, to serve, and to advance the industry.

I ask you all, then, to join me in the collective discomfort of a corporately formed spirit of restlessness and dissatisfaction with things as they are. What is more, I ask that you join me in this enterprise freely and gladly. The years ahead will be challenging. They will involve risk. But I promise that, if we commit ourselves mind, heart, and soul, they will be joyous years, years profitable in every sense.

Ladies and gentlemen, I look forward eagerly to working with you and working for you.

If you are a featured speaker:

We are here to welcome and usher into office our new chairperson, Edward Mulberry. He comes to this position at a time of great opportunity tempered by formidable challenge. Our community has enjoyed unprecedented growth during the past two years, which has opened up many new opportunities for business and industry. Unfortunately, the prevailing economic climate during this same period has worked great hardship on individuals and businesses alike. As chairperson of the Chamber of Commerce, Edward Mulberry faces the task of building on the opportunities while addressing the economic challenges. We are asking him, like the Colossus, to straddle two shores: opportunity and need.

Ed, you face a difficult assignment. But I'm not going to call it an unenviable one. Through opportunity no less than through challenge, the best among us grow stronger, realize their fullest potential, and, in leadership positions, guide us all to be better than we ever thought possible. Ed, you are among the best of us. I have known you long enough to be confident that you will not shrink from the demands of opportunity nor of need, of lack, of want. You are a vigorous administrator and an aggressive thinker, but I have, time and again, seen that aggression governed by compassion.

All of this being true, ladies and gentlemen, we can face the promising but always uncertain future sure, at least, of one thing. We can be sure of Edward Mulberry. We can be sure that, in him, we have a responsive leader, committed to the aggressive harvesting of opportunity, yet determined to aid those whose current condition temporarily bars them from claiming a share of that opportunity.

We are fortunate to have Ed as our new chairperson, and I ask that you join me now in officially welcoming him to his post.

Introductions

I could, fair and square, make this a very short chapter indeed. The single best piece of advice I can give concerning introductions is to sit down, pick up the phone, and dial the featured speaker. Ask him to send you a paragraph introducing himself. You could ask for a resume or a curriculum vitae and write the introduction using that. But why stop there? Ask the speaker to write an introduction specifically intended for the occasion.

Sometimes it will be just this easy. Of course, even if you get a prepared introduction from the speaker, you may find that it needs work. After all, these words will be coming out of your mouth, so you'd better be happy with what you're going to say. If the speaker's introduction is boring, brighten it up. If it's too detailed, cut it down. If—and this is often the case—it is too modest and self-effacing, add to it; if necessary, call the speaker back and ask for more: "Ms. Peckham, you're being far too modest in your introduction. Can you give me a few more details concerning your work in Brazil?"

Whatever you do, include in your introduction more than one repetition of the speaker's name, hit the highlights of her credentials, and mention the title of the speech. Beyond these basics, your job is to "warm up" the audience, to create the basis of an emotional and intellectual bond between them and the speaker. Keep the tone of your remarks warm and, to the degree possible, personal. Communicate your intense interest in what the speaker has in store for the audience. Above all, keep your remarks brief.

WHAT TO SAY

Mention the name of the speaker more than once. Make sure beforehand that you are pronouncing the speaker's name correctly. If necessary, write it out phonetically. If you have any doubts at all, confirm the pronunciation with the speaker herself.

What connections can you make between the speaker and the audience? What concerns do they share? For example, in introducing a corporate leader to an audience of environmentalists, you might say: "Some of us have gotten to know Robert Halle through his work as one of a small but influential corps of industrial leaders who are deeply committed to protecting the natural environment."

Conclude your introduction definitively. Do this by facing the audience, not the speaker, and finding a strong concluding statement: "No one is better qualified to speak to us on this subject than this evening's featured guest, Maureen Casey." With that, turn to the speaker with a confident smile. Initiate (or join in on) a round of welcoming applause. Shake hands with the speaker, and be seated.

If the speaker thanks you for your introduction or acknowledges you in some other way, respond with a nod and smile. Such gestures are more than parts of a polite ritual. Your body language in relation to the speaker communicates a wealth of information to the audience, providing them with the initial cues that will influence their response to the entire speech.

Be brief—but not terse. Your introduction should be generous without being excessively long.

What Not to Say

Don't stumble over the speaker's name. Audiences are usually much kinder than a nervous speaker gives them credit for, but, quite frankly, this kind of mistake will not be forgiven. Worse, it reflects less on you than on the poor speaker, the perception of whose importance is diminished by your error. If he were really worth listening to, your audience feels, you would have taken the trouble to get his name right.

Avoid clichés—hoary old standbys like, "This woman needs no introduction," or "Without further ado," and the like.

Don't upstage the speaker by trying to outshine him.

If you are unsure of the speaker's subject, don't guess: "I expect Mr. Rayburn will talk about the treasury crisis." But what if Mr. Rayburn has no intention of talking about it?

Don't preempt the speaker's material. Perhaps she has let you in on some startling revelation or has revealed her conclusion. Don't let any of *her* cats out of *your* bag.

Don't make impossible promises that can lead only to disappointment. "You are about to be treated to the most brilliant speech you are ever likely to hear." Why not drive a stake into the poor fellow's heart and be done with it?

Avoid poisoning the well with unfair comparisons. "We all remember what an entertaining speaker Joe Benteen was. Let's see how Ben Marker measures up." Nor are you being helpful when, in introducing the number two speaker of the evening, you offer such judgments as, "Peter Woerner's a tough act to follow—but that is just what our next speaker must do."

Avoid all negativity or sarcasm. "I know we're all fat and happy after that fine meal, but try to stay conscious long enough to hear what Wendell Barrett has to say."

Don't allow your introduction to degenerate into a laundry list of qualifications. That is, don't pull out the speaker's resume and read from it. Such documents were never meant to be read aloud.

Don't talk too long.

Words to Use

advanced	forthright	practical
anticipate	fortunate	practitioner
anticipated	frank	pragmatic
anticipation	futurist	privileged
applaud	gratitude	professional
applause	greet	prognosticate
arbiter	guru	progressive
authority	hard-hitting	provocative
bold	honest	research
brilliant	ideal	respected
celebrated	idealist	reveal
courageous	idealistic	revealed
crucial	inspirational	revelatory
daring	intellectual	revered
data	investigate	secret
dean	investigative	soothsayer
delighted	judge	sought-after
delightful	judgment	stimulating
discover	kindly	successful
discovery	Merlin	surprising
educator	motivational	thinker
excited	no-nonsense	thrilled
exclusive	noted	trendsetter
expert	physician	triumphant
faculty	pleased	valuable
famed	pleasure	vital
fascinating	polished	warmly
favorite	popular	well-known

Words to Avoid

ado	guess	quiet
amusing	Heeeeeeeeeeeere's (Johnny)!	relax
fantastic	lengthy	silence
good	listen	sit back
greatest	must	ultimate

PHRASES TO USE

among the best

among the most influential

experienced viewpoint

explore the topic of [topic]

expresses much that we believe

fortunate to have with us

gain insight

get an insider's look

gives us direction

good fortune to have

held in justifiably high esteem

highly entertaining

highly talented

information we cannot afford
be without

insider's point of view

join me in welcoming

look forward to

look forward to his/her stimulating remarks

most highly qualified

most highly respected

most sought-after

much in common with us

no one is better suited

no one is more qualified

pleased to present

predicts the trends

provide insight into

puts into words

rare treat in store

sets the trends

share his/her experience

shares our concerns

tells us of things to come

will report on

will speak on [subject]

words of vital importance

SENTENCES TO USE

It is my great pleasure to introduce Sam Streeter, professor of business administration at Brandex University, who will speak to us on a subject of vital interest, "Option Strategies for the Serious Investor."

Thoracic surgeons have been listening to Dr. Helen Gunderson for more than two decades, and now it is our turn.

Walter Monfort, long regarded as the dean of antique porcelain appraisers, makes precious few public presentations.

I'm not shy about telling you that Susan Dyer is my idol.

When the subject of the credit counseling profession comes up, so does the name of tonight's featured speaker, Paul Mooney.

People are always talking about Frederick Post, so we thought it high time that he had an opportunity to talk about us.

Please join me in warmly welcoming one of the most influential thinkers in our profession, Dr. Mary Rogers.

What a thrill to introduce a person I have worked with and admired for many years now.

SAMPLE PARAGRAPHS

Note that a paragraph-length speech is often ample for an effective introduction.

1   This evening's featured speaker, Ronald Peterson, has written widely on a topic of vital concern to each and every one of us gathered here: rent stabilization and control. A real-estate attorney and consultant to the Municipal Arbitration Board, he sees the issues from the point of view of the landlord as well as the tenant. It is a valuable and perhaps unique perspective, which is reflected in the title of Mr. Peterson's talk, "Rent Control: A Balanced View."

2   Like most of you, I have eagerly waited for and then devoured every book our featured speaker has written. It's been quite a feast, since Jenny Frontis has just published her twenty-first book on the subject of Maine Coon cats. To say that this makes her the world's foremost authority on the breed is, if anything, an understatement. Tonight, she asks—and answers—the question: "Can I Train My Maine Coon?" Please join me in welcoming Jenny Frontis.

3   It gives me great pleasure and pride to describe Walter Lipscott as my mentor. I partook of three years of the twenty-five he devoted to Newton University, where he was instrumental in establishing the Department of Business Statistics. I am confident in saying that he has

taught more of us how to make use of statistics in business than anyone else in the field. As much as I learned from him in class, I learn something more each time I talk to Professor Lipscott. I look forward, then, to what he will tell us all this evening about "Statistics for Retailers."

Sample Speech

"Everybody talks about the weather, but nobody does anything about it." Few clichés are more familiar than this one. Tonight's featured speaker seems to have taken this old chestnut as a personal challenge. John Wesley Powell Professor of Earth Science at Southeastern University, the author of the Cranford Prize-winning *Climate and Weather Modification*, and special consultant to the U.S. Secretary of the Interior, Jane Claypool devotes her professional life to "doing something about" the weather.

Dr. Claypool is rightly credited with having established the science of micro-climate modification—though perhaps "credited" is not always the appropriate term. Her work has shaken up a good many traditionalists in the field of climate study, an area not accustomed to controversy. So I am not going to invite you to sit back, relax, and enjoy her talk, which is entitled "Controlled Thermonuclear Manipulation of Hemispherical Climate," but, rather, to lean forward, get a good grip on the arms of your chairs, and prepare to be stimulated.

Please join me in welcoming Dr. Jane Claypool.

Invocations

Even in thoroughly secular settings, invocations are a common feature of formal and ceremonial occasions. Despite the separation of church and state that prevails by law at all levels of American government, most formal and ceremonial events are preceded by an ecumenical invocation (and often concluded by a similar benediction), and both the U.S. Senate and the House of Representatives have official chaplains. It is, then, quite possible that you, too, will from time to time find yourself participating in events that call for an invocation. While this hybrid cross between a prayer and a brief speech is usually the province of an ordained priest, minister, or rabbi, you may be asked to deliver the invocation if clergy is for some reason unavailable or in situations where a layperson is specifically desired. For example, faculty meetings at church-affiliated institutions of higher learning often begin with an invocation delivered by a lay faculty member.

What do you do if you are called upon to deliver an invocation? To begin with, accept the assignment only if you are intellectually, morally, and emotionally comfortable with it. It is best to avoid the assignment if you would feel hypocritical in carrying it out. Second, know your audience and the occasion. Is the event primarily religious or secular? Can you be certain the audience is made up entirely of people of a particular faith, or will you be addressing a mixture of Jews, Protestants, Hindus, Muslims, Catholics, and others? If possible, ask someone familiar with the event what is required of you. Does the audience expect a more-or-less conventional prayer? (And, if so, can you deliver it?) Or is something more generally inspirational acceptable and appropriate? The works of spiritually minded philosophers and writers are good sources of inspiration and content for such "secular" prayers. Ralph Waldo Emerson, Henry David Thoreau, Martin Buber, Plato, W. B. Yeats, and the like are good sources of secular spirituality. Any substantial dictionary of quotations will save time in locating an appropriate thought.

WHAT TO SAY

Determine what is expected of you: A more-or-less conventional prayer? An inspirational "secular prayer"?

If you like, make use of inspirational quotations.

Offer thanks for blessings received—prosperity, a successful year, security, the opportunity to serve the community, the opportunity to advance knowledge, the opportunity to advance the state of the art of your industry, and so on.

Celebrate the human spirit—generosity, compassion, the quest for truth and knowledge.

Pray for peace and prosperity.

Pray for the community.

Pray for those "less fortunate."

Pray for the wisdom and strength to allow your organization to achieve its goals, or to continue to prosper, or to confront and resolve problems, crises, and challenges.

Pray for understanding and tolerance.

Remember, this is in essence a prayer and should, therefore, be brief. Thirty to sixty seconds is quite adequate.

Except in special situations (for example, a meeting of the Knights of Columbus or of the community service committee of your synagogue), make the invocation as ecumenical as possible.

WHAT NOT TO SAY

Unless you are absolutely certain of the religious convictions of the audience, avoid appeals to saints, to Jesus, Allah, Buddha, and the like. In a secular or ecumenical setting, the invocation should be more broadly spiritual than narrowly religious.

Humor, in some form or another, is appropriate to most speaking occasions. But not here! Certainly, an invocation should not be lugubrious, but its intent is earnest and, therefore, its tone should be solemn.

Except in very special circumstances, do not run beyond sixty seconds. What constitutes special circumstances? Perhaps an important member of the organization has recently died, and you wish to honor him by including a remembrance as part of an invocation for an event from which he is absent. Perhaps your organization has just come through a major crisis, which you want to acknowledge in the invocation.

WORDS TO USE

aid	forgive	peace
ask	fortunate	please
assist	gentle	pledge
aware	God	power
awe	grace	pray
bless	guidance	prayer
blessing	guide	promise
celebrate	hallowed	rejoice
challenge	heart	remember
challenges	help	remembrance
commit	holy	renew
commitment	hurdles	request
compassion	impress	sensitivity
courage	infinite	steward
covenant	inspire	stewardship
crisis	invoke	strength
dear	joy	tender
direct	joyous	tenderness
disappointments	kind	thankful
divine	lead	thanks
earnest	might	unwearied
earnestly	mindful	weary
energy	obstacles	will
enthusiasm	offer	wisdom

WORDS TO AVOID

For most secular occasions, avoid all narrowly sectarian references (to Jesus, Allah, Blessed Virgin, and so on).

defeat	revenge	strike
destroy	sin	vengeance
hell	sinful	devil
joke	smite	

PHRASES TO USE

bless our endeavor

bless our enterprise

direct our hands and hearts in this work

give us the courage to face our problems

give us the wisdom to act justly and creatively

grant us the patience and vigilance our mission demands

guide our steps

guide us in all we do

guide us in the decisions we must make

guide us to be the best we can be

guide us to peace and prosperity

guide us today and tomorrow

hear our prayer

help us always to remember our responsibilities

help us to act morally and ethically

help us to advance our industry and serve humankind

help us to be true to ourselves that we may be true to others

help us to help our neighbors

help us to maintain our faith

help us to realize our fullest potential

help us to serve our community

help us to treat one another with kindness and compassion

light our way

we are thankful for your bounty and many blessings

SENTENCES TO USE

Bless this meeting convened in good will for the benefit of those we serve.

Give us the strength to overcome the obstacles we shall surely meet, and the wisdom to make good use of the opportunities we shall surely find.

Give us the strength to sustain us in the arduous and challenging work that lies ahead.

Give us the wit to respond with agility, to meet all crises, and to use all opportunities to benefit our community and build our future.

God, we ask that you bless our enterprise and guide our hearts and hands toward its successful completion.

Help us to serve our community, our industry, and our customers with integrity, ingenuity, and responsibility.

Help us to see clearly on this hopeful journey, always to steer aright, and never to swerve from our goals.

Help us to conduct our business in a moral, ethical, and kind-spirited way.

Help us to act such that our children will regard us with pride today and remember us with love tomorrow.

We ask that you bless this convocation and give us the wisdom to make the many difficult decisions that are necessary.

SAMPLE PARAGRAPHS

Note that a single paragraph is often ample for an effective invocation.

1   We ask you, God, to bless this gathering, which is a meeting of people who earnestly desire to do their work in the best possible way, to benefit their community, to advance the art and science of their profession, and to leave to their children a better world. Please give us the wisdom and vision to plan adequately and act correctly to achieve these ends. Amen.

2   God, we thank you for blessing this most successful—most prosperous and productive—year, and we ask that you give us the will and the wisdom to use wisely that which we have gained. We ask that you guide us in making just, moral, and sensitive decisions. We ask that you help us never to neglect our community. We ask that you give us joy in our work. And we ask that our work help others to realize better health and greater happiness. Amen.

3   The poet e. e. cummings wrote a delightful line that seems to me wonderfully appropriate for tonight's gathering: "We thank you, God, for

most this amazing day." As we settle down to the business of this evening, let us ask the Lord never to allow us to forget that each of the days granted us is, indeed, amazing—filled with wonder and the wonder of opportunity. Let us approach our work tonight in the freshness of that spirit.

SAMPLE SPEECH

This morning, God, we begin a meeting for the purpose of planning the curriculum we will offer our freshman students. God, we are well aware of the importance of what we are about to do, and, being well aware of it, we ask for your help in giving us the clarity of vision and the sharpness of imagination to create a curriculum that will be of greatest benefit to our students.

God, we ask that you guide us in this work, so that we do not falter in carrying out the task entrusted to us. We know that nothing is more important than educating our children. We ask, therefore, that you create in us a spirit of collaboration and cooperation that sees beyond this or that academic discipline or department. We ask that you help us always to focus on what is best for our students.

And God, we ask even more. We ask that you infuse in us a spirit of joy and continual freshness as we go about this difficult and demanding work. We ask that you give us the skill needed to impart this spirit to our young charges, to instill in them a joy in knowledge and intellectual achievement.

Humbly and in goodwill, God, we ask of you all this. Amen.

Keynote Speeches

In music, the keynote is the first note of the diatonic scale. It is the tone that establishes the key of a musical composition, and, as any musician will tell you, it is the key that creates the mood, the feeling of a piece. In its strictest sense, a keynote speech outlines the subjects to be addressed by other speakers at an event. At political conventions, for example, the keynote speaker is expected to state the major issues facing the party's candidates and the nation at large. Keynote speeches, however, do not always set out a rigorous outline. What all successful keynote speeches do have in common is the function of establishing the tone of a meeting or program.

A keynote speech, of course, can be about any number of subjects, from strategies for marketing sports shoes to launching a national political convention. But, whatever the subject, occasion, and context, to be asked to deliver the keynote speech is a great honor and a great responsibility. What you say will go a long way toward establishing the emotional tone of the event—upbeat or down, hopeful or grim, positive or negative. You also have the opportunity of preparing the audience intellectually for the subject matter to be addressed in the course of the event. In this way, the keynote speech functions as a combination introduction and table of contents, helping the listener to absorb what is to come.

Perhaps more than any other speaking assignment, the keynote speech requires careful preparation. Depending on your position and role within the organization, you may be expected to take a strong hand in establishing the content of the program your speech will launch. In this case, your first step is to outline that content, then incorporate it into your speech. In most cases, however, you are neither expected nor required to act so autonomously. More realistically, then, your first step may be to poll key members of your organization—managers, officers, advisers—in order to assess just what issues the program will address. This may well involve weeks of meetings, discussions, and brainstorming sessions. Once these issues, themes, and priorities have been decided upon, they become the skeleton of the speech. You may also be asked to make the keynote speech for a program that is already established. In this case, you must contact the speakers and obtain in advance their speeches or outlines for them. At the very least, you must ascertain what they intend to talk about. If you are unfamiliar with any of the speakers, you should also request their resumes.

Whether your role is relatively autonomous or the result of meetings, advice, and consultation, you will want, at some point before the event, to coordinate your speech with what others intend to say. This can be a delicate task, especially if your position or role in the organization is not clearly defined. Are you expected to assign subjects to the speakers? If not, you will have to be careful to avoid seeming to dictate to them. You need to decide how closely you and the other speakers need to agree. Is there a "party line" to which you all must adhere? If so, you will have to take steps to ensure that nothing you establish in the keynote is contradicted by one or more of the other speeches in the program. If there is room for more variety of opinion, your keynote speech will need to establish this. In these cases, it is best that the keynote speaker restrict herself to defining broad areas of concern and major themes to be addressed rather than lay down immutable principles and anticipate absolute conclusions. It may even be advisable to be very explicit about the variety of opinions to which your audience will be exposed. The keynote speech may celebrate such diversity rather than seek to limit it.

As there is no one subject for a keynote speech, there is no one tone. Of course, all other things being equal, the keynote should create an upbeat, energetic, optimistic feeling. But blithe optimism will seem ludicrously out of place at the beginning of a program intended to deal with a pressing crisis. The best general guideline is to create a tone that is most constructive. This usually means creating a tone that is as upbeat and optimistic as circumstances allow. In a difficult situation, do your best to find the most positive, constructive elements and fully develop them.

WHAT TO SAY

Plan well in advance.

Make sure you fully understand your role in the program. Do you have primary responsibility for establishing content? If not, how will it be established? Coordinate your speech with those of the other speakers.

Devote care to structuring your speech logically. To a greater or lesser degree, the keynote speech is an outline of what is to come in the program. There is no single "right" way to structure the speech, but the following should be helpful:

1. Welcome your audience and program participants.

2. Set the tone. (See the discussion at the end of this list.)

3. Give the program relevance and urgency by establishing its context: "We are gathered together at a moment of crisis as well as opportunity."

4. (Optionally) State or affirm the principles of the organization.

5. (Optionally) Enumerate the problems and opportunities the organization confronts.

6. (Optionally) What must the organization do to address the problems and opportunities it faces?

7. Outline the goals of the program, meeting, or conference.

8. (Optionally) Say something about how each speaker will address these goals.

9. (Optionally) Highlight the diversity of opinion to which the audience will be exposed.

10. End with an affirmation of the constructive, creative nature of the program.

Devote care to setting the proper tone. Usually, this will be a feeling of optimism, energy, hope—the emotions of a constuctive approach to life itself. Be careful, however, to avoid hollow optimism at inappropriate occasions. Nevertheless, always attempt to establish the most constructive tone in any situation. If you are delivering the keynote at a meeting of a corporate giant undergoing forced downsizing, it would be foolish to begin by telling your audience that things look peachy. But it would be just as foolish to give them the feeling that the future is indeed grim. Your keynote, in this case, might establish downsizing as positive evidence of the proactive adaptability of your company. Yes, times are very hard. Yes, people will lose their jobs. Yet the organization will not only survive, but it is demonstrating its essential health by an ability to adapt to adverse conditions. Adaptibility, you might point out, is the hallmark of any healthy organism.

What Not to Say

Leave nothing to chance. The keynote speech is no place to wing it. Orderliness and direction are important in any speech, but they are especially important here.

Avoid depressing or browbeating your audience.

Avoid hollow, inappropriate optimism.

Avoid making promises you cannot keep. ("The speakers in this program have the answers to all of your questions.")

Beware of poisoning the well. Don't make remarks that will sabotage or be directly contradicted by the speeches that follow. Know what the speakers are going to say—or do not try to anticipate them to any degree. If you are giving the keynote for an inherently controversial meeting, prepare your audience for controversy so that they do not expect absolute harmony. Controversy is legitimately a part of most programs. However, if your audience expects adherence to a "party line," controversy will seem like *destructive* dissent or simply evidence of poor planning (a failure to "get one's act together").

Don't steal the other speakers' thunder. While it is useful to anticipate and even outline the content of the program in your speech, don't step on anyone's conclusions or preempt such items as astounding statistics, surprising revelations, and the like.

Don't tell your audience how to feel about, react to, or judge the program. Statements like "You cannot fail to agree with" beg—demand—to be contradicted. Better to say, "I believe most of you will agree with our speakers' analysis of the situation, but, whatever you conclude about this evening's program, I am confident that you will find the experience stimulating."

WORDS TO USE

accomplishment	analysis	choices
achievement	angle	clients
adapt	answers	climax
adaptibility	approaches	commence
address	assurance	confident
advance	bold	confront
adventure	celebrate	courage
age	celebration	courageous
aggressive	challenges	crisis
alternatives	change	culminating

culmination
data
decide
decision
delighted
determine
direct
direction
discoveries
embark
epoch
era
establish
ethics
evaluate
evolve
evolution
exciting
experiment
findings
flexible
future
goals
guide
guidelines
honor
hope
hopeful
illuminate
imagination

imaginative
important
information
informative
innovative
interpretation
issues
journey
market
marketplace
merchandise
new
offer
opinions
opportunity
options
optimistic
organize
outline
perspectives
plan
positive
predict
predictions
pride
priorities
problems
procedures
production
products

profit
progress
prosperity
protocols
proud
questions
reevaluate
relevant
remember
renew
report
revise
rules
scenario
statistics
stimulating
stride
strides
strive
tackle
themes
time
transform
universe
unwavering
value
values
variety
vital
world

Words to Avoid

adhere
boxed in
cornered
dead

dire
done
doomed
dreary

exhausted
finished
gloom
hopeless

must	retreat	surrender
obey	retrench	tired
quit	strict	

PHRASES TO USE

abide by our principles

act with prudence

affirm our convictions

agenda for the future

array of perspectives

balance prudence with decision

capitalize on our strengths

cautious optimism

climate conducive to profit

create our future here and now

creative approaches to problems

determine our goals

developed our agenda

diversity of points of view

emphasize creativity

establish our priorities

every reason to be optimistic

examine our motives

explore new directions

explore the issues from all sides

face this crisis as we have others in the past

go forward boldly

hear reports by

hear from all sides

help us to think through the difficulties

lay out a strategy

live up to our principles

make a difference

make this a part of our agenda

order our priorities

outline the issues

plan for the future

predict the trends

predict trends to come

present an analysis of

prevailing atmosphere

prevailing emotions

proceed surely but with caution

range of viewpoints

reach some positive conclusions

realize our full potential

renew our resolve

responsive to changing conditions

set forth the issues

set our goals

take a fresh look

take necessary steps

teach us to play to our
  strengths

welcome to your future

SENTENCES TO USE

It is vital to the health and direction of an organization to restate—
and reevaluate—guiding principles from time to time.

I welcome you to our annual convention, in which it is our task to
reevaluate and, where necessary, reinvent this industry.

Our speakers this evening will address five areas of particular concern: [list].

You will hear many points of view in the course of this program, but
all of us here are united by a single purpose: to serve this community
in the best way possible.

We are united by one goal: to get a fresh and unbiased view of our
operations here and abroad.

As we review the year and look forward to the next, we have every
reason to be proud and to be hopeful, but we must not allow ourselves the deadly luxury of complacency and self-satisfaction.

It is my hope that what you will hear tonight will not be "enjoyable"
or, heaven forbid, "relaxing," but, rather, invigorating, tantalizing,
exciting, and energizing.

I hope that you will leave this program, not reassured, but restless,
eager to do battle with our competitors and to cultivate an ever-rich-
er harvest of clients and customers.

We face many challenges, but behind each challenge is an opportunity.

SAMPLE PARAGRAPHS

1   Will Rogers was famous for saying, "All I know is what I read in the papers." Will Rogers was a fine man. But I hope that none of you are following his example. Pick up almost any newspaper these days, and you'll read about how our industry is "in crisis." Ladies and gentlemen, sometimes it's enough to make you want to jump ship. But what the newspaper stories don't talk about is all the opportunity that is the flip side of this so-called "crisis." *This* theme—opportunity—not the newspapers' theme—crisis—will be the focus of our series of meetings this weekend.

2   It is a great honor to be asked to make the keynote speech this evening. It is a great honor and a tremendous responsibility. I realized, when I began planning this talk, that what I said would set the tone for what follows. And I also realized that, essentially, only two sets of themes were available to me: debt and despair, or change and hope. I figure that none of us needs me to confirm what we all know: our town is cash poor, and a whole lot of it—streets, sewers, parks, and schools—is simply falling apart. We already know that. What we hope to do in the course of the meetings that follow is not to wallow in the debt and despair, but discover the hope and the change. Ladies and gentlemen, *that* will be the theme of my remarks this evening, and it is my wish that the spirit of hope and change will motivate our discussions during the the next several days.

3   If I began my remarks to you this evening by asking the question *"What's the bottom line?"* the less tolerant among you would reach for the dial that regulates your attention span and set it to low. And you'd be right to do so. That question has become worse than a cliché. It's a knee jerk. Until you think about the definition of the "bottom line." There's the one that's all dollars and cents—and I'm not here to tell you that it's unimportant. But there's another bottom line that represents the sum total of our relationship to one another, to our col-

leagues, our clients, our competitors, and the community at large. It represents the net profit—or loss—of our ethics. And it is *this* bottom line on which our seminar series will focus.

SAMPLE SPEECH

In my grandfather's day, there was one question a man either dreaded or welcomed from his children. It was, "Daddy, what did *you* do during the war?" For the veteran of Europe or the Pacific, it was an opportunity to loom large and powerful in the eyes of one's children. But pity the poor father who served Stateside pushing papers on a desk or, worse, didn't serve at all. Never mind that the papers you were pushing helped to feed, clothe, and care for the troops at the front. Never mind that your civilian job kept those troops supplied with weapons and ammunition. You had an image problem.

So do we.

How many of us are really pleased and proud to answer our children when they ask, "Daddy—or Mommy—what do you do for a living?"

After all, Jimmy's mom is a doctor. She helps people by making them healthy. Sarah's father is a firefighter. He saves lives. Eddie's mother is a teacher. She shows kids how to read, write, add, and subtract.

You? You're a bill collector. You take people's money.

I'm glad you all can laugh about it. But, from up here, that laughter sounds just a little bit nervous, just a little bit weary.

Of course, *you* know that your job is not simply taking people's money. You help people, too. Merchants, credit and financial institutions, wholesale suppliers, hospitals, and professionals of all sorts—these are your clients. They aren't just "businesses." They are people, people who have worked and who expect and deserve to be paid for their work. Moreover, if they are not paid, sooner or later they go out of business. Families suffer, and a community grinds to a halt. Nobody is able to pay—or earn.

And what about the people you call, the folks from whom you attempt to collect money? *You* know that, while your primary responsibility is to the client who hired you, your job also involves *helping* the person on the other end of the phone. That person has financial problems and credit problems. He may be scared—or at the very least harried, anxious, and unhappy. Almost certainly, he feels embarrassed and powerless. *You* know that you are not the ogre who comes to shake him down. Your job is to help him settle the debt, to help him to see how he can resolve this particular financial problem.

Ladies and gentlemen, I hope that you realize that, as collection specialists, you are really in the business of creating win-win scenarios—establishing a relationship between your client and his debtor in which both gain something. Your client collects, and the debtor has the opportunity to resolve a financial problem.

It's easy for us in the business to forget these things. Deep down, you know that you are not the bad guys. You know that your job is not to "catch" or to "punish," but to help—to help your client collect, and to help the debtor settle his debt.

But, like the noncombatant grandfather of World War II, you've got— *we've* got—an image problem. And that is what this meeting will address: "Credit and Collections: Rehabilitating Your Image."

We will begin the program with you. We will break up into small groups to discuss our image problems from the only perspective that finally matters—yours. Then we will hear from three experts, who will analyze the problems—addressing in particular the issues you raise—offer strategies for working more positively with clients as well as debtors, and, finally, offer strategies for creating in you more positive feelings about what you do.

Ladies and gentlemen, it is the purpose of this meeting to help us serve our clients more effectively by improving our productivity. It is the conviction of the organizers of this program that we can improve our productivity dramatically by learning how to feel good about the important work we do—work that keeps cash flowing, not only to the firms and individuals who hire us, but, ultimately, to the individuals and families on whom we call. When your children ask you what job you do, I want you to be able to answer proudly and honestly: *I help mommies and daddies take care of their families.* Because, ultimately, that's what we do for a living.

Master of Ceremonies

At its simplest, the job of the master of ceremonies is to make a speech of welcome and brief keynote remarks, follow throughout the program with a series of introductions, and wrap it all up with a strong conclusion. Accordingly, the prospective MC should consult the sections on Welcomes, Keynote Speeches, and Introductions in this book. However, all this concerns only the speaking part of the MC's job. If you are lucky, that's about all that will be expected of you: a welcome, perhaps a keynote remark or two, introductions, and a conclusion. But, in many cases, the MC is required to do much more, serving as a hybrid cross between an air traffic controller and that plate-spinning juggler who was a fixture of the old Ed Sullivan TV show.

WHAT TO SAY (AND DO)

At many events, the MC is the person *in charge* and is expected to know, manage, and, if necessary, enforce a schedule of events. This is especially important in time-critical programs involving television or radio broadcast or rental of a hall, for instance. But even when time is not a crucial factor, overruns and delays have a way of mounting up until the attention span of even the most stalwart members of the audience is exhausted. Are you responsible for establishing the schedule? Or is somebody else? Will the program participants have printed copies of the schedule? Will they be thoroughly advised of the time allotted to them? Do they know that it is important for them to observe the time limits? Who will create these documents and inform the participants? You or somebody else? Better find out.

What is your role at mealtime? If the program includes coffee breaks, breakfast, lunch, or dinner, you may be responsible for directing the participants to the dining room and helping to see that the meal proceeds on schedule. If the meal is served in the meeting room, you may be responsible for helping to manage the waiters. This is especially important if food is to be served while you or someone else is speaking. Be sure to advise the waiters on the importance of doing their jobs as quietly as possible. Be aware, however, that an audience armed with food, dessert, or even just coffee can make some pretty irritating noises. Don't let the clink of plates—and the occasional shattering of same—rattle you.

Most programs involve at least rudimentary audio-visual equipment, such as microphones and P.A. systems. Many programs also require slide projectors, overhead projectors, movie projectors, videotape equipment, monitors, computers and computer video displays, and the like. Will somebody be in charge of these? That "somebody" might be you. Make sure the equipment is available and functioning properly. Even if you are not solely responsible for it, you should make certain that the equipment will be available and is in operating order before the program begins.

If awards, certificates, and the like are to be presented, ensure that they are delivered to the program site and that they are properly identified. Nothing sabotages a show more thoroughly than an MC having to fumble for awards. Make certain you know which award or certificate goes to what recipient. In case valuable prizes are awarded—from toaster ovens to the proverbial gold watch—make certain that someone is in charge of security. You wouldn't leave valuables unattended in a public place, would you?

Rehearse spontaneity. A good MC prepares ad libs *in advance*. To coin a cliché, expect the unexpected. Despite your careful checking, microphones will fail. Despite your careful scheduling, a featured speaker will be delayed in traffic or caught in an endless holding pattern around a busy airport. Despite your instructions to waiters, at least one of them will drop a stack of plates. Although your audience consists of intelligent, well-bred people, someone will have had too much to drink. Think beforehand about what might go wrong and prepare a plan of action. Most important, prepare a few "ad libs."

Get personal—in moderation. Depending on your relationship with the audience, a touch of personal banter can be quite entertaining. After all, if you are hosting a presentation to a group of sales personnel you have known for years, it is foolish to pretend you don't know them. Directing remarks from time to time at a member of the audience actually establishes a friendly bond between you and the audience, and it integrates the audience more fully into the program. But see the following "What Not to Say."

Give credit where credit is due. Acknowledge those who were instrumental in creating the program.

Devote planning time to your concluding remarks. You want to send your audience off with strong, positive feelings. You don't want them to feel that the program simply petered out.

WHAT NOT TO SAY

Avoid winging it. Don't depend on the inspiration of the moment to carry you through.

Be careful not to monopolize the program. Even if you are an entertaining speaker, running on takes time from other speakers and, even worse, gives your audience the impression that you are "stealing" time from others.

When things go wrong, avoid placing blame. Your audience does not want to bear witness to a squabble between you and the caterer, you and the A-V person, you and the hotel staff.

When things go wrong, refrain from making a lengthy apology. Devote your energy to correcting the situation or minimizing its impact, not to making excuses for it. It's bad enough if a microphone is faulty or slides are missing. Don't bore your audience with a long explanation, which, instead of gaining their sympathy, is apt to certify in their minds your incompetence. In the event of a snafu, apologize briefly then do what has to be done to get on with the show.

In making introductions, do not play favorites or give the impression that you are. Unless particular speakers are specially featured guests, strive to be even-handed in all of your introductions.

Avoid self-effacing remarks and remarks that denigrate the program or trivialize the proceedings. The role of master of ceremonies is no place for false modesty. Don't be obnoxious, but an air of self-confidence bordering on arrogance is quite appropriate.

Avoid lengthy dialogue with individuals in the audience. This does not mean you should avoid addressing an occasional remark to individuals, nor that you should altogether refrain from banter with individuals. However, you are "on stage," and you must not step down too far from that role. Nor do you want to give your audience the feeling that they are being ignored so that you can converse with a friend.

Words to Use

anticipate	glitch	prepared
anticipation	guests	presentation
applause	happy	prize
array	honor	produce
award	indulge	produced
celebration	indulgence	program
chock-full	instruct	prompt
create	interest	refrain
created	invitation	roster
creative	invite	schedule
dazzling	join	show
delighted	kind	showcase
eager	kindly	speakers
eagerly	learn	spectacular
enlighten	line-up	spontaneous
enlightenment	luminaries	stars
entertaining	meaningful	teach
entertainment	meeting	thrilled
enthusiasm	packed	thrilling
enthusiastic	patience	time
exciting	patient	urgent
fascinating	planned	valuable
feature	pleased	vital
featured	pleasure	welcome
gathering	positive	

Words to Avoid

amateur	flounder	sorry
Be quiet!	ho-hum	starving
blame	lecture	stupid
bored	lengthy	tedious
boring	long	tired
can't	mistake	unplanned
delay	oops	wait
errors	ringmaster	wing it
exhausted	sleepy	yawn
fault	so-so	

Phrases to Use

a lot in store for you

array of talent

ask speakers to adhere to the schedule

bear with us just one moment

best we have to offer

commands our attention

culmination of planning and thought

delighted to introduce

distinguished panel

enlightening program

extraordinary array of speakers

feast of information

feast of knowledge

full platter

full program

great deal of planning has gone into

greet all our good friends

happy to bring you

information you don't want to be without

in the interest of time

invigorating program

invite you to participate in

jam-packed schedule

join me in applauding

join me in welcoming

look forward to these gatherings

my pleasure to present

my pleasure to preside

promise some surprises

refrain from interrupting the speaker

richly deserving

save your questions until the end

star-studded roster of speakers

take questions from the audience

vital presentation

vote of confidence

we intend to move along smartly

withhold your comments and questions until the end

SENTENCES TO USE

Note: You will also find the chapters on Welcomes, Keynote Speeches, and Introductions helpful.

I am privileged to be your master of ceremonies for the evening.

I ask that you give your attention to James Montgomery, who will speak on "Retailing in the Smaller Community."

I trust that you will agree with me that today's program has stimulated thought, answered a few important questions, and raised many more worth thinking about.

It is my pleasure to welcome all of you to a program I am confident you will find informative and stimulating.

Our subject is options in elder care.

Our roster of speakers will offer information and insights we cannot afford to be without.

Our next speaker is a new member of our organization, and I ask that you make her feel very welcome.

The name of our next speaker is familiar to all of us.

Today's program concerns our collective future.

We have a rich harvest of hard information and sheer speculation to reap tonight, so I suggest we begin immediately.

We have heard a stimulating summary of the majority viewpoint, and now it is time for the minority report.

We have such a full program today that, in the interest of saving time, we will be serving coffee during the next presentation. Ladies and gentlemen, please sip quietly.

All of us at the dais appreciate your kind and careful attention and your stimulating comments and questions.

I thank you for your participation in what I consider a highly successful presentation.

SAMPLE PARAGRAPHS

Note: You will also find the chapters on Welcomes, Keynote Speeches, and Introductions helpful.

1   Welcome to the third annual Year End Review, in which representatives from each of our divisions report on the year's accomplishments and challenges. This is a unique opportunity for each of us to get a bird's-eye view of our company, and I find that I come away from this event impressed, overwhelmed, and generally buoyant. This year's program focuses more sharply than ever before on research and development, reflecting our heightened commitment in this area.

2   Ladies and gentlemen, it is my pleasure to welcome you to our program on strategies for community action. I am not telling you anything you don't already fiercely believe in when I say that most great social movements begin at the grassroots. But it is also true that too many grassroots organizations operate in isolation. This gives a group a certain freedom, of course, but the price of that freedom comes high. Operating in a vacuum limits our influence, our resources, and our power. Today's program is about clinging to our grassroots while, at the same time, growing together into a powerful union of cooperative action. Our program is divided into three parts: Pooling Resources, Cooperative Independence, and Toward an Effective Lobbying Union.

3   We have come to the conclusion of a most remarkable day. We have heard from a wide array of community organizers, separated by geography as well as constituency, but united by a single goal: to make democracy work for everyone by giving a voice to those whom

some fail to hear and others do not want to hear. We have answered many questions. We have outlined many strategies. But we have also opened up vast areas that demand further work. The challenges are formidable, but the task is not only rewarding, it is also urgent and absolutely necessary. I trust that, like me, you will return to your organizations invigorated and inspired, eager to meet the challenges we have identified and those yet to come. On behalf of the Coordinating Committee, I thank you for attending, and I hope to see all of you at next year's meeting.

SAMPLE SPEECH

I am pleased to greet you all at the opening of another Weekend Retreat. You know, ladies and gentlemen, I've never much liked the word "retreat." I know that it signifies the strategy of these meetings: to remove us for a time from the day-to-day pressures of our business so that we can glimpse the "big picture" and overall trends that are often obscured by the ringing of the telephone and the relentless pressure of daily deadlines. But "retreat," I can't help thinking, also implies surrender or withdrawal. And the one thing these convocations are not about is surrender and withdrawal. It is my hope that, by means of this "retreat," we will advance—advance the art and science of our industry, advance our bottom line, and advance the level of service we can provide our customers, our community, and, yes, our country.

So let us begin by stepping outside of the daily grind while doing our best to avoid any hint of withdrawal. Here in this beautiful mountain setting, let's do what the test pilots speak of doing: push the end of the envelope.

This is what our first round of speakers invite us to do, in a series of presentations that challenge virtually every principle of research and production most of us have become comfortable with. I suggest that we listen to these presentations with open minds, asking ourselves the question: "Have we become *too* comfortable?"

At the end of the day, after what promises to be a great dinner, we will divide into discussion groups to begin the work of evaluating, debating, and applying what our speakers have presented.

Day two will begin with the reports of these discussion groups and will conclude with a dialogue between the discussion groups and the featured speakers.

I have high hopes for this so-called retreat. These high hopes do not include finding answers to any particular question, but, rather, finding the questions themselves. Armed with these, I believe that we can return to our offices refreshed in spirit and intellect, fully prepared to lead this company in new and exciting directions.

Let us turn, then, to our first speaker. Bill Cornette has been director of solids research since 1988 and is about to tell you why he is (as the title of his speech puts it) "Fed Up with Project-Oriented R & D." Please join me in welcoming Bill to the rostrum.

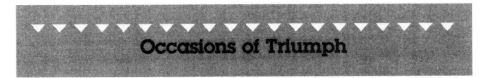

Occasions of Triumph

Any number of events can be occasions of triumph, including speaking situations treated elsewhere in this book, such as anniversaries, business meetings, charity events, dedications, inaugurals, and the like. This chapter will help you write an effective speech for an occasion of triumph regardless of the specific context.

Speaking at moments of triumph should be easy, and, indeed, it is easier to say something at times like this than on occasions of crisis. However, as the ancient Romans knew, it was precisely during occasions of triumph that one most needed to keep one's head. For the classical Roman, "triumph" meant a public celebration to honor a successful warrior, usually following some conquest. The central feature of the triumph was a public parade, during which the hero was transported through the streets by chariot. A slave or attendant held a laurel wreath over the hero's head, while repeatedly whispering in his ear: *sic transit gloria mundi*—all worldly glory is fleeting.

No, it is not your job to make a speech squashing the moment of triumph. But the Roman example is valuable to bear in mind. The great danger of speeches made on occasions of triumph is that they will encourage arrogance and complacency. The task of the speaker at moments like this is

- ▼ to acknowledge the achievement;
- ▼ to make the audience aware of the significance of the achievement;
- ▼ to acknowledge, praise, and thank those who contributed to the achievement;
- ▼ to foster a sense of community, cooperation, and teamwork, and
- ▼ to encourage further achievement.

The speech should, above all, make your audience feel good, but it should never imply that, victory having been achieved, work has now come to an end. An effective speech of triumph is open-ended. It fully acknowledges the present achievement, but also promotes further achievement. Such speeches should exalt many virtues and talents—hard work, faith, wit, resourcefulness, athletic prowess, intelligence, training, and so on—but the one quality that needs greatest emphasis is the importance of community, cooperation, and teamwork.

Most achievements are, in fact, the result of collaboration. Dr. John Doe may have received the prize for developing a new and improved widget, but he was backed by a strong team in R and D, which, in turn, received support, encouragement, and feedback from marketing, which relied on the expertise of customer service people and salespeople in the field—all of whom are supported by a fine management team. Even on occasions when the individual seems all-important—say a sports banquet honoring track-and-field champs—the speaker should make every effort to include trainers, coaches, administrators, parents, boosters, and fans. This takes nothing away from the individual's achievement, but it does allow others to share in the triumph. Why is this important? Obviously, it makes people feel good to be recognized and given credit for an accomplishment. Also, the more of your audience you include, the more successful your speech will be. But, more important than either of these things, by using your speech to create a sense of community, of participation, you create the conditions necessary for further achievement.

What to Say

Make sure your audience understands what happened: what has been won, what has been achieved, and who was involved.

Explain the significance of the victory or achievement.

Fully acknowledge the principals involved. This is particularly important if you are in a management or supervisory position, or if you are the principal "victor."

Say something about the kind and degree of work that was required for the achievement.

Use biography; say something about the life of the principal(s).

Emphasize the role of teamwork, community support, cooperation, and collaboration. Let as many of your listeners as possible share in the victory.

Use this sense of community effort to encourage further achievement.

WHAT NOT TO SAY

Avoid simple-minded arrogance, including such clichés as "We're number one!"

Avoid denigrating the competition.

Avoid inappropriately assigning credit or assigning credit to one individual at the expense of another. ("Sure Bob Dokes worked hard, but the *real* credit belongs to Sylvia Sasso.")

Do not exclude any of your listeners from sharing in the triumph. If you name names or list departments, make sure you include everybody, either by name or class. ("Let us acknowledge the remarkable work not only of Sarah Morris, but of everyone on the design team and in the marketing division, who gave 100 percent to this assignment.")

Don't minimize the achievement. Do not let your effort to avoid arrogance cause you to run down what has actually been achieved.

Don't be an ingrate. It is difficult to make your listeners feel bad at a time like this, but it *is* possible. One sure way is to say something like, "We've won this time, but we need to do even better next time," or "Don't be fooled into thinking this award means something. The real prize is the bottom line."

Don't upstage the heroes. This is their day, not yours.

WORDS TO USE

accomplishment	effort	raise
achievement	every day	recognize
acknowledge	enviable	role
acknowledgment	faith	share
additional	fantastic	spirit
again	foresight	staggering
assignment	further	strive
assisted	future	succeed
award	goal	success
celebrate	grateful	support
cheer	gratitude	supported
collaborate	hail	sweat
collaboration	honor	task
collaborative	imagination	team
colleagues	imaginative	teamwork
commitment	include	thank
communal	invent	tremendous
community	investment	triumph
concentration	job	uplift
contribute	kudos	victory
contribution	labor	vision
cooperation	lofty	visionary
cooperative	objectives	will
create	odds	win
creative	participate	winner
daily	praise	winners
devotion	prize	won
difficulty	progress	work

WORDS TO AVOID

alone	beat	defeated
annihilated	crushed	gutted

humiliated	minor	singlehanded
insufficient	next	solo
mauled	number one	trampled
meaningless	numero uno	trounced

Phrases to Use

advanced the state of the art

another success

beat the odds

celebrate this achievement

credit where credit is due

declined to take the easy way

excelled in this area

expect excellence

express our appreciation

express our pride

hard work and dedication

highly talented and absolutely committed

hope this will be the first of many

how proud we all are

impressive achievement

join our colleagues

made a genuine contribution

made the extra effort

magnificent accomplishment

magnificent job

many share in this achievement

mastered the details and big concepts alike

one more in a record of notable achievements

overcame each obstacle

path of excellence

pleasure to acknowledge

product of cooperation and collaboration

product of team effort

proud of our colleagues

proud to recognize

refused to accept pat answers

savor the moment

scored a triumph

scored a victory

share in this accomplishment

solved each problem

sweat and genius

terrific dedication

took risks

top-level performance

tradition of achievement

tremendous skill

Sentences to Use

We're proud to honor this year's winning sales team.

Thanks to the hard work, resourcefulness, and skill of everyone in marketing, Gisco Industries has enjoyed a banner year.

We owe a vote of thanks to Ginny Crofts and her research team, who have developed what promises to be a true breakthrough product.

This is about more than the triumph of one great department in this company.

Let's take a few moments to celebrate having achieved our goal.

Let's honor together what we have achieved together.

We are proud and grateful to have people like Jim Williams on our team, and let me say that James is fortunate to have such a team to support him.

I was delighted—but not surprised—to see that we have exceeded our goal for the quarter.

Your hard work and skill have paid off, and that means we are assured of a leadership position for this quarter.

You are building a record of achievement that—given the kind of people we have on our team—will inspire even greater achievements.

Reaching this goal hardly means that we can breathe easy, but it does mean that we can move ahead with confidence in our ability to work together to achieve tremendous success.

Let's savor this moment together, then prepare—eagerly—for the next triumph.

Perhaps you haven't achieved the impossible, but you have beaten the odds and set an example for all of us to follow.

As you know, our sales department, working with the finest products produced anywhere, has enabled us to set a new high for quarterly profit.

SAMPLE PARAGRAPHS

1.   I suppose most people would have said our soccer team was on a losing streak last year. Now that we've won the division championship, that "losing streak" looks like just what it really was: preparation. It is true that we didn't win a lot of games last year, but it is also true that we learned a lot. We learned to play together as a team. And now that has paid off. We played as a team, and we've won as a team.

2.   Nothing is more fun than savoring a victory. It's even more fun when the odds are stacked against us. Times are tough. Consumer confidence, all the reports tell us, is way down. But our product development team created a line of merchandise that has overcome all resistance. Our marketing team got that product into the spotlight. And our people in manufacturing and fulfillment got it out to the customers. Together, we've taken a bad time and turned it around 180 degrees. Let's celebrate—not just this particular triumph, but a timeless idea. That idea is teamwork, and we've just proven how well we can make it work.

3.   I've asked you to come together so that I could give you all some very good news. Thanks to Gerald Penderson and his "special task force" (Ben Harris, Clara Sharnhorst, and Liz Serious)—with strong support from the folks in the art department—our agency has bagged the Horton account. In the crudest (and, for many of us, most important!) terms, this means $375,000 in business over the next six months. It also represents the successful culmination of four months of constant labor. I don't think we've ever worked harder to attract a customer. At times, it has been frustrating for all concerned. But we are a team, and we support one another in pursuit of worthwhile goals. It's a gratifying strategy that is even more gratifying when it actually works!

SAMPLE SPEECH

    After a long, hard campaign, it is nothing less than a thrill to claim victory in this election. I'm not suddenly going to start playing modest. I worked very, very hard to achieve this goal, and I intend to enjoy this moment with you. But that "with you" is supremely important. For it was "with you" that *we* won this campaign. I worked hard, and so did every one of you on the campaign committee. This is not "my" victory, it is *our* victory.

You worked on this campaign because you knew that it was time for a change. You were tired of business as usual. Now that I have won, you have won. Because it won't be business as usual anymore. And as we won this election together, together we will work for change in the town council. Together, we will continue to win, point by point and issue by issue.

I know that this victory is just a beginning. It is the culmination of one phase of hard work and the start of another. But I embark on this work full of confidence, because I have ample proof of the power, skill, and effectiveness of the team that supports me.

I hope that you will congratulate one another. Each of you deserves to be singled out for special credit. But since it's more fun to stop talking and start celebrating, I'll confine myself to mentioning just a few names:

Howard Meacham, our general campaign manager, did an extraordinary job of coordinating a great many people, keeping their ample energies focused, and never faltering, even when our own polls were none too promising.

Catherine Littlefield, campaign treasurer, not only managed a complex and aggressive fund-raising program, she made each dollar count. There have been bigger campaigns than ours, of course, but none that made better use of what it had available.

Finally, I want to thank Claire Silverberg, volunteer coordinator, who forged an unpaid staff, most of whom were working on their first political campaign, into a very, very hot team. It's hard enough to motivate a work force when you're paying them a salary. But volunteers work because they believe in a cause—and when they believe in the people they are working with. Claire not only deployed our forces with supreme effectiveness, she constantly communicated her commitment to these fine people.

I wish I had time to mention more of you by name. But, different and diverse though you are, everyone who worked toward this victory has one quality in common: commitment. I promise you that I will do my best to live up to the example you have set for me in the course of this campaign. I will never forget that this is your victory—our victory— and that I owe you the same degree of commitment you gave to me.

Now, let's celebrate a moment that is both a culmination and a begin-ning—the most exciting kind of victory there is.

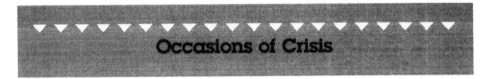

Occasions of Crisis

If you doubt the utility of words—the right words—in a crisis, ask anyone who lived through the Great Depression and World War II what the speeches of Franklin Delano Roosevelt meant to them. In England, during the dark early days of the war, it was the words of Prime Minister Winston Churchill that won the Battle of Britain as surely as the skill and courage of the pilots who flew for the RAF. Despite examples like these, most Americans, especially American men raised on the movies of Gary Cooper, John Wayne, Clint Eastwood, and Arnold Schwarzenegger, are contemp-tuous of words in a crisis. Many of us feel that difficult situations call for "deeds" rather than mere words. In a crisis, we look for "men of action."

Certainly, there are many crises that call for action rather than words. But these are, for the most part, situations of imminent physical danger. If your house is on fire, better not stand around talking about it. However, most of the crises we face from day to day are not physical. A project falls behind schedule. Money runs short. Our company loses a big contract. Membership in the organization falls off. In an anxious, complex civiliza-tion, such crises do, in fact, produce in us many of the same kinds of feel-ings we experience when physically threatened: anxiety, fear, panic, a pounding heart, sweaty palms, and a hollowness in the gut. "Don't just stand there," we want to shout, "*do* something!"

A moment's reflection, however, reveals that, in these situations, "doing something" begins with saying the right words, transmitting the effective message. All crises require planning and coordinated action to resolve. All crises produce negative feelings, ranging from low, morale, to anxiety, to out-and-out panic. Many crises, in fact, are entirely or in large measure the result of negative feelings. It is no accident that otherwise sober-sided financial analysts and commentators use such expressions as "the *mood* of Wall Street"; for even high-level and supposedly objective corporate financial decisions are to a great degree motivated by feelings. Produced by feelings, crises also generate powerful negative feelings that make planning and coordinated action difficult or impossible.

How does one change feelings? How can we replace negative emotions with positive feelings in order to create the kind of attitude required for the clear thinking necessary to resolve a crisis? The answer, of course, is with words.

Speeches in times of crisis *may* achieve two goals, but *must* achieve at least one. The effective speech may include a clear, well-reasoned outline of a plan for dealing with a given crisis. But that speech *must* first address, influence, and, if necessary, transform the feelings of your listeners. Whether or not a definitive plan is part of the crisis speech, you must at least make such useful, rational planning possible by creating in your listeners the right feelings.

WHAT TO SAY

Provide as much information as you can. The greatest fear in a time of crisis is of what one cannot see or understand. Without compromising sensitive information, let your listeners in on as much as you can.

Put yourself in your listeners' place. What information will they want? What do they need to know? What will make them feel better—or, more to the point, enable them to act most effectively? When you put together your speech, remember that your listeners have two overriding questions: What happened? and How will it affect me?

Try to define the extent of the crisis, especially in terms of time. What happened *when*. What will (or is likely to) happen *when?*

Address feelings. Telling your listeners to "cheer up" or not to worry is of little help. However, you need to counteract the feeling of loss of control. The most effective way to do this is to create a sense of community, of united, cooperative effort. United, your listeners will feel empowered and capable.

Put the crisis in perspective. Have you and your listeners dealt successfully with a similar situation before? What are the realistic limits of the likely damage? Crises tend to put people on a slippery slope, giving them the feeling that one misstep now will result in a bottomless plunge soon. Put the crisis in perspective by attempting to define—realistically—the worst-case and best-case scenarios.

If at all possible, outline an approach to the crisis. Enumerate, list-fashion, the steps you propose or the options available or under consideration.

Ask for help. Don't appear helpless, but don't hesitate to ask your listeners for help—in the form of suggestions and proposals, but also in the form of a willingness to work overtime, to hold out a little longer for that raise, to keep the lines of communication open, to project a calm and confident front to customers and clients, and so on.

Conclude by reiterating and reaffirming the need and the effectiveness of mutual commitment, of community, of united action.

WHAT NOT TO SAY

Avoid pronouncements of doom and phrases that make matters sound worse than they may be or that leave no room for hope and positive action. (Such phrases as "We're in for it now," "We've got BIG problems," or "We're in a serious tailspin" are counterproductive.)

Avoid pointing a finger and placing blame. These activities can only divide an organization. What you need now is unity, a sense of community, and a commitment to the common cause.

Avoid hollow exhortations to "stop worrying" or "keep your chin up." These will not help, and they make you sound feeble. Also avoid telling your listeners not to panic. Nothing is more conducive to panic than being told, "Don't panic!" Any serious dieter knows that the worst thing you can do when you are trying to lose weight is to think about *not* eating. It is a well-known principle of psychology that one tends to move toward what one has uppermost in one's mind. If one is thinking about *not* eating, one is also thinking about eating and will, therefore, tend to move toward food. If one is asked to think about *not* panicking, one will tend inevitably to move in the direction of panic.

Avoid expressing your personal fears. This won't do any good and may do a great deal of harm.

Avoid making predictions unless you have a strong, clear basis for them.

While it is helpful to keep a sense of humor in difficult situations, don't try to laugh off a crisis. Don't let humor trivialize the situation. Nero fiddled, the old saying goes, while Rome burned. Reliance on humor is a similar form of denial and, worse, will be perceived as such.

WORDS TO USE

act	faith	resolve
action	formulate	respond
address	goal	responsive
adequate	handle	rumor
adequately	historically	rumors
approach	method	safe
appropriate	methodical	safety
attend	morale	settle
calm	patience	solution
care	plan	strategy
caring	positive	strength
caution	precedent	strong
compassion	priorities	succeed
confidence	priority	survive
confident	proactive	tactics
contingency	procedure	team
contingent	proceed	teamwork
coordinate	protocol	think
courage	prudence	thought
cure	prudent	together
delay	rational	triumph
effective	reason	unite
effectively	reasonable	united
effort	reflect	work
emergency	reserve	
expedite	resolution	

Words to Avoid

abandon	failed	panic
abandon ship	failure	quit
bail out	fatal	run
bankruptcy	fate	scramble
broke	fault	scuttle
bury	helpless	s.o.s.
code blue	hide	surrender
condition red	inconsequential	trivial
dead	jobless	trouble
dead end	no problem	

Phrases to Use

approach this problem

best-case scenario

call on our contingency plans

cannot be defeated

come to a soft landing

confidence in our ability

continue to act prudently

damage assessment

determine priorities in this situation

develop a contingency plan

do not get discouraged

do not yield to the emotion of the moment

equal to the challenge

expedite the resolution

find a workable solution

formulate a plan

fully prepared to

go into it with belt and suspenders

handle this safely and quickly

importance of morale

limits of our liability

maintain a constructive attitude

maintain control

manage the situation

meet the challenge

navigate through the hazards

not let one another down

overcome this difficulty together

persevere through this crisis

reasonable projections

resolve this difficulty

responsible prediction

solve this problem together	weather the storm
stay together	won't get burned
take it step by step	work together
take the time necessary	work together toward a solution
take the safest, most direct course	worst-case scenario

SENTENCES TO USE

Make no mistake, we are in a tight spot, but we have successfully come through much tighter ones.

The time has now come for us to rely on one another and to work effectively as a team.

I am confident that, together, we will overcome this setback and still manage a highly successful year.

Our organization needs the combined effort of everyone here.

The present situation makes unusual demands on us all, but, knowing all of you as I do, I am confident that we are more than equal to the challenge.

We have a choice: to wait and react, or to take a number of proactive steps now.

Let me outline what I propose as the steps necessary for a speedy recovery.

The days and weeks to come will be demanding, but, by cooperating and collaborating, we can find satisfaction in resolving the difficult issues that confront us.

Let me begin by explaining the situation as I understand it.

I've found that I can't take three steps around here without tripping over a rumor.

I've asked you here to give you an answer to a very important question: What's happening?

It would be foolish to deny that we are facing difficult times, but it would be just as foolish to deny the tremendous assets—financial and intellectual—that we have at our command to cope effectively with these difficulties.

Whether we like it or not, we have been presented with an opportunity to exercise our resourcefulness, our collective wit, and our will to excel.

SAMPLE PARAGRAPHS

1   No method of communication is swifter in most companies than the grapevine, so I will not deceive myself into assuming that I'm delivering a hot news item when I tell you that we have lost the Jacobs account. Now, the grapevine is fast, but it is not terribly accurate, and it certainly does not give you the whole story and the whole story most cogently expressed. I propose to do just that right now. I will tell you what happened and why. I will tell you what it means to us as a company, and to you individually. And I will propose some steps for dealing with this unwelcome—but hardly tragic—turn of events.

2   We are likely to hear a lot of rumors, half truths, and untruths. We are likely to hear words—frightening words—such as *disaster, catastrophe, Chapter 11,* and the like. If we focus on such things, we will become paralyzed into inaction. Let us focus instead on evaluating reliable information, on finding solutions, and on working together toward a resolution of what, seen in perspective, are, after all, short-term problems.

3   After more than two decades with this organization, I have learned that teamwork makes "crisis," "problem," and "difficulty" synonymous with "challenge." Collectively, we have the talent to face any challenge, and, collectively, we also have the will.

SAMPLE SPEECH

I am here to speak to you about the annual membership report that each of you will be receiving soon in the mail. You will see a 24-percent decline in membership from last year. Over a five-year period, membership has declined a total of 43 percent. I am telling you this now not in an attempt to soften the blow of the report you will receive in the mail, but to start us all thinking about the choices this news compels us to make.

Here are the choices, as I see them. We can ignore the report and simply let membership levels settle wherever they will. The drawback of this approach is that we have no way of knowing just where the drift will stop. If membership falls below sustainable levels, we will be unable to pay our bills. We can try raising dues, but that, inevitably, will prompt more members to leave. If our numbers dwindle sufficiently, our only choice will be to disband.

We can take the report to heart, worry about it, make ourselves generally miserable, and devote the balance of our meetings to discussions of the Good Old Days.

Or we can take the report seriously, discuss it, think about what the decline in membership means, and formulate strategies for reversing the trend. It is this choice I want to prepare you for.

I ask that each of you think about what we offer and fail to offer. I ask that each of you ponder strategies for increasing enrollment and for retaining those who are currently members. Let's think about these issues individually, then come together at our next meeting to create an effective program for turning this situation around.

I have some suggestions to get us started. We need to assess the roster of special events we offer, with the object of broadening our traditional areas of appeal in the following ways: [list].

We need to reevaluate the extent of the financial commitment membership requires. I believe we might find a graduated schedule of dues useful. We might also consider adopting different levels of membership, since not everyone wishes to partake of everything we have to offer at all times.

We should look at our recruitment and induction policies. Is it too difficult to become a member?

Finally, we must take a hard, objective look at our image in the social and professional community.

One of the greatest features of this organization is that we tend *not* to think alike. We are founded on diversity. So I do not expect universal agreement on what we should do to reverse the present trend. What I do expect is that we will find answers and that we will unite to keep this organization active and healthy.

It is all too easy to let figures such as these erode our morale. But consider this: Why are we alarmed at the decline in membership? Because we all love this organization. We intensely feel that it is worthwhile and makes a valuable contribution to our community and to our lives. What this means is that we should be pleased and proud to be members of this organization—not depressed because some others have chosen to leave. Such an organization deserves everything we can do to preserve it and make it prosper again. Let's pool our collective diversity, then, to re-create this organization, to reverse the decline, and to bring about a new birth.

I look forward to hearing and discussing your ideas at our next meeting.

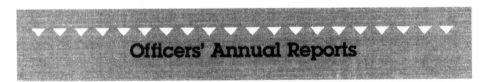

Officers' Annual Reports

Does the presentation of an annual report have to be numbingly dull?

If you take the pro forma nature of such speaking assignments as your guide, the answer is yes, and we might as well end the chapter here. But just because many corporate charters and organization by-laws mandate that officers deliver annual reports does not mean the reports must be inescapably boring. Think about it. You are reporting on activities that bear directly on the lives of your listeners. It is quite appropriate to transfuse more than a little life into the report itself.

How do you begin to do this?

Speak as if your life depended on your job. This should not be difficult since, to some degree, your life *does* depend on your job. The point is that, just because you are an officer of a firm or organization, you are not required to retreat so far into third-person pronouns and passive sentence constructions that you expunge any trace of personality expressed in "I," "me," "us," and "we." Personalize these pro forma reports, and they will suddenly seem to your listeners as important as they actually are.

WHAT TO SAY

Make sure the basics are covered. Be sure that you know what your corporate charter or organization by-laws expect you to cover. This can—and probably should—provide the skeletal structure of your speech.

Corporate audiences favor—both expect and are grateful for—well-ordered and crisply presented reports.

Raise reports above the routine by injecting something of your personality into them. Don't overdo it—your listeners have not come to hear about you—but remember that you *are*, after all, an integral part of the organization, and the organization is important in your life and in the lives of your audience. Remember that you are not merely the treasurer, or secretary, or comptroller, but a human being.

The most important element in humanizing your presentation is to use personal pronouns where appropriate and to favor active sentence constructions. Constructions such as "When I made my report last year" imply real *human* action: *I* made the report. In contrast, passive constructions suggest—passivity: "When the report was made by me last year." Not only is the second sentence wordier than the first, it puts an inanimate object in charge—the report—rather than a living human being. Active sentence construction can work real magic in a speech. Active construction compels the speaker to take responsibility for his statements and the actions they reflect. Passive constructions were suited to an era in business and institutional culture when it was desirable to hide behind a smokescreen of assumed objectivity, when we were supposed to believe that an abstract "organization" or set-in-stone "policy" was responsible for corporate actions. The reality is that *people* have always been responsible for these things. Nowadays, most firms and other organizations respect speakers who own up to this fact. Active sentence structure not only greatly simplifies presentations, it sets you center stage and puts you in charge.

Project enthusiasm—for your company or organization and for the task at hand.

WHAT NOT TO SAY

Avoid slavish adherence to the rules. The fact that reports are mandated by charters and by-laws does not mean they must *sound* pro forma.

Avoid passive sentence construction. See the aforementioned.

Avoid recitation of meaningless statistics and figures. Laundry lists of numbers are the bane of annual reports. Instead of droning on through such lists, hit the highlights and use handouts or visual aids (slides, overhead projector transparencies) to fill in the details. Note that the operative word here is "meaningless." Well-chosen, well-explained numbers in context are actually very powerful elements of a speech. Don't shy away from meaningful numbers or numbers meaningfully presented. Just don't smother your audience in figures that they could more effectively absorb in visual form.

Avoid a business-as-usual look. Don't ascend the podium as if you are setting about a distasteful, routine task, a ritual ordeal to which both you and your audience are annually subjected. Put on a show. Project an enthusiasm that tells your audience they are in for something special.

The following caution is probably unnecessary, but I'll issue it anyway. By all means, add a personal element to your report, but don't go overboard. You should amply demonstrate responsibility for the report, but it should not sound like your *subjective* opinion. Avoid sounding as if you are guessing or are intruding your opinions. Strike a balance between a personal and a businesslike tone.

WORDS TO USE

analysis	basis	decline
apply	course	develop
area	critical	development

disappointing	improvement	quantify
emerges	increase	reaction
encouraging	input	reading
estimate	lag	report
evolution	meaning	response
evolve	meaningful	result
examine	news	sensitive
exciting	numbers	shift
expand	optimistic	step-down
feedback	paradigm	step-up
figures	pattern	study
financial	phase	success
fiscal	picture	trend
graphic	potential	vital
important	profile	

WORDS TO AVOID

boring	pro forma	routine
guess	recite	suppose
guesstimate	rehearse	tedious
monotonous	ritual	

PHRASES TO USE

a significant pattern emerges

big picture

can learn a great deal from this

client base

client profile

continue to grow

continue to shrink

contour of our financial landscape

delighted to note that

exciting news from the front lines

facts and figures for the year

front lines

gratified to report

high profile

interpret the data

learning curve

look for trends

most useful approach

moving in a positive direction

offer an analysis

overall picture

phase in

phase out

pleased to report

pleasure to make this report

point out the significant features

present the most significant figures

raw data

reverse the trend

review the highlights

significant changes

strategic withdrawal

study the results

track the trends

SENTENCES TO USE

Each year it is my privilege and pleasure to report on the financial state of this organization.

This year's report reveals some very intriguing trends, which you will want to know about.

Allow me to point out the highlights of some very important statistics.

My approach to this data is from the perspective of discerning evolving trends.

I bring you the year's news from the front lines.

There are certain trends that are important to all of us.

I will take a few moments to explore these figures with you.

What do these numbers mean to us?

We need to see this short-term picture in the context of long-term trends.

My objective is to deliver these numbers in a meaningful way.

I find a great deal to be encouraged by in this year-end report.

Let me highlight the areas of greatest activity.

What do the figures in my report suggest about the coming year?

As you can see, our activities in this area have been extensive.

Sample Paragraphs

1   I must confess to you that I enjoy making these reports each year—not so much because I like to hear myself talk, but because there is pleasure in taking the pulse of a proud and successful organization. This year, although we have faced a number of economic challenges, the pleasure is undiminished. I think you will conclude, as I have, that there are a lot of positive indications and significant milestones in the following summary of our year's activities.

2   Nothing I do for this company is more important than my yearly visit with you. This is my opportunity to share with you my assessment of our financial profile. I always look forward to doing so, and I hope that my report will stimulate as many questions as it answers.

3   Financial folk are not supposed to like surprises. But I have more than a few in store for you in this year's report. A few are disappointing, especially the returns on our newest promotion program. However, most of the surprises are quite pleasant, and the trends they seem to forecast are highly promising. So, let us begin our journey back through the year together.

Sample Speech

It is always a pleasure to make my year-end financial report—even when the news is not uniformly good. I am convinced that our strength lies in unified, coordinated action, and this report is an important step in the process of achieving this kind of action.

Now, I began by cruelly letting slip that the news of this past year is not all good. Let's begin with the disappointments, then turn to the high points. I think you will agree with me that those bright spots vastly outshine the dull patches.

This year, we launched a new product line, the Turbomaster series. Our investment in the launch amounted to $400,000 (in round figures), which includes a $150,000 investment in special advertising. It is no secret that customer response to the product has been disappointing in all markets except the Southeast. Gross sales for the year amounted to $675,000, which nets out to a $145,000 loss. While we expected a very quick return on this product—which, obviously, we did not receive—the figures are more encouraging than mere year-end numbers would suggest. Sales picked up steadily in the last quarter and show signs of an increase. Looking at this trend, I am confident that we will see substantial profit from the Turbomaster line as early as the second quarter of this year.

So much for disappointment. The good news is that all of our principal lines—Electra, Hydra, and Hercules—set sales records in 199X. Total receipts amount to a most impressive $4,000,897, which is 14 percent above the year before.

These are the highlights. In addition, I ask that you review the printed reports that will be distributed directly after my remarks. In these you will find the details of our current financial picture.

I appreciate your kind attention this afternoon.

Patriotic Occasions

Our country celebrates relatively few national holidays, but most of them involve local ceremonies that call for speeches. Unfortunately, few Flag Day, Independence Day, or Memorial Day speeches are very memorable. Among the blessings Americans enjoy is the privilege of taking the blessing of liberty pretty much for granted. Patriotic speakers frequently talk about "our" having had to fight and die for "our" liberty, yet the happy fact is that most of "us" have neither fought nor died, but have simply enjoyed peace and plenty without having had to think very much about them. The result is that many patriotic speeches ring hollow and echo vaguely of dry-as-dust schoolbooks.

So what do you do when you are faced with the task of giving a patriotic speech?

I suggest you try talking about yourself. That's right. Patriotism is a theme that seems almost to demand vague—boring and hollow—generalities. Resist that demand by turning inward, by thinking about *your* feelings about America, by thinking about *your* definition of patriotism, by thinking about *your* experience of this nation. Are you an immigrant? Or were your parents or grandparents? Talk about that—about how you came to this country and what it meant for you to do so. Did you fight in a war? Or did your father? Or did you lose a loved one in battle? What did it all mean—to you? What opportunities has this country given you? What happens to you—inside—when you go to the polling place to vote your conscience? How about serving on a jury? Or even paying your income taxes?

What does it all mean *to you*?

I suggest you start this way, intimately, personally, and let your speech develop from an autobiographical core. Usually, it is most prudent for a speaker to anticipate the expectations of his audience and then aim squarely to satisfy these. Patriotic speeches are an exception. Your audience has come expecting the usual bland generalizations. A patriotic autobiography will be a most refreshing surprise.

WHAT TO SAY

Get personal. Begin by talking about your experience of America. Let the speech develop from this.

Develop the theme of patriotism itself. What does the word mean? Different things to different people and in different circumstances? Give examples. (You might begin with yourself—or at least speak from your own experience.)

Deliberately trigger controversy. Were the followers of Senator Joseph McCarthy patriots? They certainly thought they were. How about those who took the unpopular and even dangerous step of standing up to the senator? John F. Kennedy's *Profiles in Courage* is an excellent source of information about controversial patriots and acts of patriotism. The last thing your audience expects to do at a patriotic ceremony is think. Make them think, however, and your speech will be a success.

Turn to the flag and other national emblems. What, really, do they symbolize?

Celebrate peace, plenty, and liberty. What do these mean on a personal level?

Celebrate the beauty of your community.

Celebrate local history. What nearby events or personalities expressed the spirit of America?

Praise local patriots—local heroes that your neighbors may not even be aware of. What about an exceptional teacher at the local high school? What about a dedicated community leader?

Celebrate unity and the diversity possible within unity. A patriotic ceremony is no place for partisan politics. Avoid all electioneering.

Use well-chosen quotations, but avoid the old standbys. Look for the unusual. ("Winston Churchill once told the world: 'Democracy is the worst form of government that man has ever devised, except for all those other forms that have been tried from time to time.'")

What Not to Say

Avoid schoolbook history and civics lessons. It's hard, but avoid clichés.

Don't limit patriotism to the past—the world of Washington and Jefferson. Try to make your remarks directly relevant to the present.

Avoid invidious comparisons between "these days" and the "olden days."

Do not confuse jingoism with patriotism. Don't pit the United States against the world, but stress America's leadership position in the family of nations.

Avoid racism and ethnic slurs. Ours is a nation of immigrants.

Avoid sexist chauvinism. Too often patriots are perceived as strictly male. Avoid such clichés as "founding fathers." True, the signers of the Declaration of Independence were all men, but why not stimulate your audience to think about some "founding mothers"?

Avoid partisan issues.

Speak from emotion, but take care to avoid sloppy sentimentality.

WORDS TO USE

allegiance	endure	includes
America	equal	independence
battle	equality	initiative
belief	equitable	institution
better	experience	justice
blessed	fair	labor
blessing	fairness	land
blessings	family	legacy
capitalism	flag	liberty
celebrate	foresight	love
celebration	fortunate	meaning
ceremony	founded	pageant
choice	founders	parade
choose	founding	patriot
comfortable	freedom	patriotic
commitment	glorious	peace
committed	glory	peaceful
conceived	great	people
Constitution	greatness	personal
cooperation	healthy	plenty
creeds	history	popular
declaration	homage	posterity
dedicated	honor	pragmatic
dedication	hope	precious
defend	idea	pride
democracy	ideal	progress
discovery	idealist	prosperity
diversity	ideals	proud
elect	ideology	rainbow
emblem	immigrants	representative
embrace	improve	revitalize

riches	spirit	united
right	strength	United States
rights	strive	unity
sacrifice	struggle	unselfish
safe	suffering	vision
safety	symbol	visionary
secure	symbolize	vital
selfless	together	vote
self-reliance	tolerance	wealth
settled	treasure	welfare
settlement	tribute	work
spectacle	unbowed	
spectrum	union	

WORDS TO AVOID

alien	enemy	real American
compel	liberal	Republican
conformity	must	them
conservative	obedience	us
Democrat	radical	

PHRASES TO USE

ballots, not bullets	due process of law
beacon of democracy	evolutionary change
Bill of Rights	faith in our own ability to govern
blessings of liberty	family values
city on a hill	founding fathers and mothers
civic responsibility	Four Freedoms
civil disobedience	freedom from fear
compassionate government	freedom from oppression
Declaration of Independence	freedom from want
democratic process of debate and discussion	free enterprise system

govern ourselves

government of the people, by the people, and for the people

Great Society

healthy dissent

heritage of America

keep hope alive

land of opportunity

lessons of history

liberty within law

life, liberty, and the pursuit of happiness

melting pot

mutual good

my country right or wrong

my personal experience

nation of immigrants

New Deal

New Frontier

not died in vain

our strength is in our diversity

peaceful policies

peaceful revolution every four years

pledge our allegiance

preserve and perpetuate an idea

pride in America

protect our rights

religious freedom

religious tolerance

rule of reason and compassion

share a story with you

speak from my experience

standard of living

strength in diversity

take for granted

tolerance in all things

tolerance of dissent

tradition of dissent

what it means to me

working men and women

Sentences to Use

America is the biggest—and greatest—subject I can think of.

I asked my nine-year-old daughter what "patriotism" means.

If you want an education, ask your children what it means to be an American.

In a world full of images and symbols, I can think of none more powerful than the flag we love.

It is both a wonderful and dangerous thing that we take our many liberties for granted.

My father, like a lot of fathers, was killed fighting for this country.

My parents were immigrants, who became Americans by choice.

On this great public occasion, let me tell you about myself.

One of the greatest feelings I know comes when I step into that voting booth.

Our nation cares for the people and serves the people, but the idea of our nation is greater than any one person.

Ours is a neighborhood filled with patriots: the police officer, the fire fighter, the teacher, the shopkeeper committed to serving the community, the factory worker dedicated to doing a high-quality job—all are patriots.

The great English writer Samuel Johnson said, "Patriotism is the last resort of scoundrels," but let us realize that it is also the first resort of selfless men and women who care about the legacy they will leave their children.

The strength of our nation is in its diversity as much as in its unity.

Think about the phrase "land of opportunity."

What is a patriot?

No people on earth has ever been blessed with such diversity.

SAMPLE PARAGRAPHS

1   Looking out at this sunny day, looking across our well-manicured suburban lawns and the shops that line Main Street, hearing the cars go by, listening to the pleasant conversations of mothers and children, it is difficult to believe that this was the site of a struggle for liberty just over two centuries ago. Here a small, ill-equipped, but resolute and well-led group of farmers and merchants challenged the red-coated might of the greatest empire in the world. Why? There are many reasons, and, doubtless, each man and woman who was willing to die in the struggle against tyranny had his or her own reason. But they were united by a dream. Let's take a moment to reflect on that dream.

2   My parents came to this country from Italy. They were—and are—proud of their Italian heritage, but they knew that the United States offered something denied them in the Old World. It offered room to dream and the opportunity to realize whatever you dreamed. They knew that America meant hard work and struggle. But they also knew that it was a place where dreams were encouraged, where hope was possible, where aspirations were rewarded. It was a place to grow. It was a place to create a family whose members could fashion whatever roles they wished to play in the world. It was, to be sure, a place with faults and failings, but it was a place to be free.

3   Some people watch television. Some devour the newspaper every night, front to back. Others curl up with a mystery novel. Me, I love to read history. Sometimes I wonder why. After all, the history of the world is, by and large, depressing: war, struggle, starvation, misery, oppression, persecution, intolerance, and general folly. But then I think of our own nation. Yes, you don't have to look very hard to find plenty of oppression and trouble and stupidity in our own history. But, through it all, above it all, certain ideas and convictions shine like beacons. Ours is the first nation in the history of the world that has seriously sought to end the war, the struggle, the starvation, the misery, the oppression, the persecution, the intolerance, and the folly. It is a nation founded on hope. To me, all of world history adds up to what we are—or what, at least, we are always trying our best to be.

SAMPLE SPEECH

The Fourth of July has always been my favorite holiday. The weather is usually great, and it comes at a time of vacation—vacation from work and, of course, summer vacation from school. I have to confess that the holiday does not so much make me think of the Declaration of Independence and the American Revolution as it does my own childhood: carefree days of play and friends and fun.

I was thinking about all of this, as I usually do on the Fourth, when reality intruded. I started thinking about all the bills I have to pay this month: utilities, summer camp for my children, car payment, mortgage payment, credit card, food, food, and more food, doctors, this, that, and the other. The one thing I did *not* want to think about on the Glorious Fourth was the High Cost of Living.

The "high cost of living." Well, there it was, and I was thinking about it.

The United States *is* an expensive place to live.

Until you look elsewhere. How much does it "cost" to live in what used to be the Soviet Union? What do you have to "pay," each and every day, to live in South Africa? My grandparents fled Nazi Germany. What did that cost them? And what did it cost those who did not flee?

The cost of living is very high here. Some have paid with their lives. Many more have paid with hard work and sacrifice. Some of us are fortunate enough merely to pay with some portion of what is in our wallets.

Look at the rest of the world, however, and look down the corridors of history. Do some serious "comparison shopping." What you soon discover is that life here is a bargain—the greatest bargain ever.

Our freedom, of course, does not come free of charge. It requires material sacrifice and vigilance—not just against threats from the outside, but from within, especially from within ourselves. We must fight our own cynicism, our own short-sightedness, our own selfishness, and, above all, our own intolerance. The great bargain we enjoy cannot be maintained passively and without effort. On this patriotic holiday, we must all realize the necessity for universal patriotism. I don't mean that we need to wave the flag and march in a parade. But we must honor—in our hearts, in our minds, and in our actions—what our country means, what our country stands for.

We pay for everything in our lives. Maybe we don't like to think about these things on the Fourth of July: bills, bills, bills. But in a world of exorbitant costs and dubious deals, the United States, our country, is one value that is always at an all-time high. It is an investment, a demanding investment, but one that returns dividends unique in history and unique in the world. I am proud, pleased, and grateful to pay.

▼ ▼ ▼ ▼ ▼ ▼ ▼ ▼ ▼ ▼ ▼ ▼ ▼ ▼ ▼ ▼ ▼ ▼
PTA and Other Parents' Groups

Public speaking at PTA meetings and the like falls into two categories: either you are a featured speaker or you are a meeting participant who rises to make a point, ask a question, or raise an issue. Obviously, the two categories require different levels of preparation, but preparation is important in both cases.

Speaking at PTA and parent group events calls for observance of most of the same general principles as speaking at community meetings. You should state, outline, and review the issues clearly; create and appeal to a sense of community; demonstrate a willingness to listen, to hear all sides, and to entertain all points of view; and you should think of your speech both as an effort to communicate information and as an exercise in persuasion, much like an effective sales letter.

There is one very important difference between PTA and parent organization situations and general community meetings. As high as feelings may run at a community meeting, they are bound to run even higher at meetings concerning the present and future welfare of one's children. This is both a positive feature of such occasions and a challenge. The issue of children's well-being may serve to unite the group, focusing its energies and attention, thereby making for an extremely receptive audience. Differences of opinion concerning this same issue may, however, be intensely divisive. Where one's children are concerned, objectivity, rational discourse, and clear-headed argument may be rapidly overwhelmed by emotion and defensive anger. The task of the effective speaker is to keep energies and emotions focused on the issues, not on personalities and egos. Maintain a common ground by making it clear that, however those involved may differ on a variety of issues, all have the welfare of their children as the ultimate goal.

WHAT TO SAY

Whether you are the featured speaker or have risen to address a particular issue, begin by stating the issue clearly and outlining—in list fashion—the sub-issues and points involved.

As in a speech delivered to a community meeting, think about constructing your talk along the lines of an effective sales letter:

> Begin by *getting your listener's attention*. State the issue(s) simply, even starkly. Or ask a compelling question. ("Do we want the art education program to die in our school?")

> Identify a need—one that, despite differences, is common to the audience.

> Explain what you propose and show how it will fill that need.

> Persuade your audience by comparing and contrasting your proposition to others.

> Prompt action by telling your audience what their next step is. Don't leave them with a feeling that, yes, we *really should* do something about such and such. Give precise directions for action.

You may want to review the chapter on "Community Meetings" for additional details.

Try to use language that promotes unity and cooperation.

Invite comments and questions, but do not respond too quickly. Be sure the questioner has completed the question. Don't cut her off. Then take whatever time is necessary to consider your answer. It is perfectly all right to say, "Let me think about that one just a moment."

Acknowledge the faults in what you have to offer—but make it clear that the benefits outweigh any faults.

Give praise generously where praise is due: to parents' committees, to teachers, to the students, to the administration.

Dispute particular *policies*, but try to demonstrate confidence in *personalities*.

Know your options. Who has authority over the policies and issues under discussion? A teacher or teachers? The principal? District superintendent? The board of education? What legal and administrative procedures need to be followed in order to secure action? PTA and parents' meetings may degenerate into shouting matches and exercises in wheel spinning without this essential knowledge. Research is called for.

WHAT NOT TO SAY

Do not stress differences, and avoid appealing to factionalism.

Avoid attacking personalities. Address the issues, not the people behind them.

Avoid name calling.

Do not shout down opposing points of view. Allow all sides to be heard.

Stay off the horns of a dilemma. Most situations rarely come down to a simple either/or response. On the other hand, emotions often drive a group to act as if a situation calls for precisely such a response. Maintain your options, and look for alternatives. By the same token, avoid tactics that force your listeners into such simple-minded positions.

Avoid expressing issues in terms of "us" versus "them."

Avoid emotional responses to emotional assaults. Consider withdrawing from a discussion, at least for a time, if it begins to generate more heat than light.

WORDS TO USE

achievement	bolster	credit
address	calm	critical
admire	change	criticize
agree	children	critique
agreement	collaborate	cure
aid	confidence	debate
alternatives	confident	determine
ameliorate	consider	develop
analysis	constructive	discuss
appreciate	cooperate	education
approach	counsel	educator
assist	creative	effective
authority	creativity	evaluate

evolve	parental	solve
formulate	plan	strategy
freedom	planning	support
goals	praise	teacher
hear	principles	thought
hero	priorities	transform
improve	progress	understand
laud	rational	unhurried
laudatory	reasonable	valid
listen	regard	validity
message	resolve	values
objective	respect	welfare
objectives	responsibility	well-being
options	solution	workable

Words to Avoid

against	defeat	force
argue	demand	insist
battle	divide	showdown
conquer	either/or	ultimatum
crush	fight	

Phrases to Use

approach the task creatively

assess the impact of

atmosphere of cooperation

band together for our children

benefit our children

best for our children

can live with

combat this problem

consider all alternatives

constructive criticism

develop a united front

enlist the aid and cooperation
  of

fair to everyone

find a solution that will work
  for all our children

formulate a solution together

importance of these issues

jump to conclusions	thoughtful analysis
meet these challenges	use this as an opportunity to
most effective approach	build a stronger school system
points of view	vote of confidence
send a message	work together to achieve
sends the wrong message	work toward
take the time necessary	work with rather than against
take our time	work within the system

SENTENCES TO USE

Can we begin by agreeing that we all want a school system that will stop short of nothing less than excellence?

For each of us, our most precious asset is our children.

I suggest that we consider the following fund-raising options.

I am eager to hear your thoughts on these points.

I urge this meeting to come to agreement on the essential priorities we wish the teachers and administration to establish.

Let's not lose focus on the constant object of this discussion: our children and the education they are to receive.

Let's join together to protect our children's future.

Our schools face a great many challenges.

The teachers and the administration deserve our vote of confidence and our gratitude.

We must work together to create a school system that teaches compassion yet also prepares our children to compete successfully in an increasingly competitive world.

We have a healthy diversity of ideas and opinions, but we share a common goal: to provide the best educational experience for our children.

We have some difficult choices to make, but I want to stress that the choices are *ours* to make.

We need not confront this problem alone.

We are all agreed on the problem; now let's outline strategies toward a solution.

SAMPLE PARAGRAPHS

1   I am always disturbed when I hear someone say that "our children have great potential." Why does this bother me? Because it makes me nervous waiting for the "but" that is sure to follow. It's like waiting for the other shoe to drop. "Our children have great potential, but . . ." But what? But our schools lack the funding, lack the personnel, lack the specially trained personnel, and so forth. Isn't it about time that we took care of the part of the sentence that begins with "but"?

2   Any one of us could get up here and speak as an expert on what parents fear. It just so happens that I was given the opportunity to speak today. Well, it won't come as news to anyone here that we parents fear a great many things. But none of our fears is more intense—or, unfortunately, more justified—than the fear that our children will fall prey to the drugs that are so readily available even in this nice clean neighborhood of well-manicured lawns and pretty houses. We have a choice. We can live with our fears. We can deny and ignore the problem. Or we can admit the danger, give credence to our fears, and work together—as well as with the police and the Community Council—to formulate an aggressive program to protect our children from this terrible trap and tragic waste.

3   It's easy to become a fanatic about tests. We Americans test everything—especially our children. Well, I don't want us to fall into the trap of determining the course of a youngster's academic life on the basis of a test or two. But, ladies and gentlemen, we are talking about more than a test or two. The Texas Diagnostic Battery is a series of twelve diagnostic and achievement tests. Our sixth graders have performed 15 percent below the national average on these tests. Not on one test, or two tests, but on all twelve. So I do not think I am being rigid or fanatical in suggesting that we formulate a strategy for deter-

mining the implications of these results and dealing with them. Let me offer a few suggestions to start the discussion.

SAMPLE SPEECH

You'd think we would be complaining by now about being uncomfortable. I for one don't much like being stuck on the horns of a dilemma. But here we are: stuck.

We've got one group of parents who are concerned that our children are not performing well on basic tests measuring reading and math skills. I believe that we can all agree that this is alarming and cannot be ignored.

We have another group that is concerned about impending funding cuts in our school's art and music programs. This group argues that, without art and music, our children's educational experience is diminished, and their lives are to that extent impoverished. I believe we can all find merit in this assertion.

Now the problem is that we have somehow decided that it is a law carved in stone that the "back to basics" programs cannot coexist with a full program of art and music in our schools. So, we have two sets of parents, both committed to the well-being of our children and yet occupying opposing camps.

I propose that we find common ground.

Now, I'm not stupid. I realize that it will be difficult to *fund* both an extensive back-to-basics program and the full music and art program. Funding is a problem. But let's identify *that* as the problem rather than argue as if reading and math were incompatible with art and music. I suggest that we begin with the assumption that all these things—reading, math, art, and music—are essential to our children's education and that we don't want our children to do without any of them. Once we have decided this—established our common ground—we can stop attacking one another and go after the real problem: funding.

I have three suggestions for securing additional funds, funds that will enable the teachers and administration to develop and maintain excellent programs in all areas. Here are my suggestions: [list and outline].

I'm sure these are not the only options, but I offer them as feasible alternatives to a position that is most uncomfortable for us and certainly unfair to our children. Unless someone has an option at present to add to my short list, I suggest we begin discussing these alternatives, decide on a course of action, and work out the strategic details.

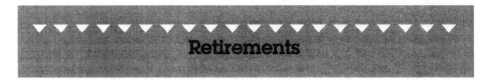

Retirements

Retirement speeches fall into two categories: either you are speaking as the retiree, or you are speaking to honor a retiree. In either case, you may want to look over the chapter on "Farewells," since such occasions are similar to retirement ceremonies. There is, however, an important difference between a farewell and a retirement. Both may be emotional occasions, but retirement has more of a finality about it and represents the definite culmination of a career—indeed, of a professional lifetime. It may be a bittersweet occasion. The retiree may think of retirement as a reward and welcome rest. She may be looking forward to spending more time with family, to traveling, or to volunteer or other work. On the other hand, many people dread retirement or at least fear it. Wherever the retiree falls along this spectrum, recognize that the event is a deeply emotional one. Nevertheless, keep your remarks upbeat and celebratory. If you are the retiree, express your appreciation for the ceremony and for years of association with the firm or organization. If you are honoring the retiree, acknowledge the achievement of a lifetime.

WHAT TO SAY

If you are the retiree:

Thank those who were thoughtful enough to organize the celebration.

Express thanks and affection for your colleagues and co-workers. Cite specific events: the extra effort that was devoted to making good on an important contract, the overtime everyone put in when flood waters made pulp of the files, and so on.

Be lavish in your praise.

Acknowledge those who brought you into the company or organization. Acknowledge your mentors.

Thank your family for their love and support.

Recall the past. Share some choice anecdotes. Humorous stories are fine on this occasion.

Did the company or organization grow and develop during your tenure? If so, describe the company or organization when you first joined it. Like it or not, you are an example of "living history." Share yourself as such.

Sum up your career with a brief, direct, dramatic statement: "I worked like hell and did the best I could."

Tell your listeners something of what you plan to do next. It is probably not a good idea to let them know you intend to vegetate in anticipation of the Grim Reaper's harvest. Instead, talk about your plans for the future. Retirements are very good occasions to speak about the future as well as to reflect on the past.

Announce your intention to stay in touch, and invite your colleagues to stay in touch with you.

Express your mixed emotions—but steer clear of melancholy.

Think about using an inspirational quotation.

If you are honoring a retiree:

Make sure your listeners know who is retiring.

Honor the retiree's achievements. Be specific, citing specific accomplishments.

Be lavish in your praise. Remember, what you say is supposed to characterize an entire career.

Express affection.

Share anecdotes. Good-natured humor is appropriate here, as is any-thing that will evoke fond memories.

Get personal. If you have had a special working relationship with the retiree, talk about it. Perhaps he has served as your mentor. Perhaps the two of you collaborated on some special project.

If you are presenting the retiree with some very special personal part-ing gift, discuss it. Perhaps her co-workers have assembled a scrap-book, a video or audiotape, some treasured item (the founder's per-sonal letter opener or the prototype of some best-selling product, for example).

What Not to Say

Whether you are the retiree or honoring someone else, avoid any-thing downbeat. It is fine to express your mixed emotions and to let your colleagues know that you will miss working with them, but don't make it sound as if it is the end of the world.

Don't skimp on thanks and praise. Now is the time to be fully gener-ous.

If you are the retiree, don't protest your unworthiness. Don't tell your colleagues that they should not have organized the send-off ceremony. Don't reflect on your achievements and conclude that what you've done hasn't amounted to a hill of beans. Just express gratitude.

Avoid dwelling on the past. By all means, reminisce, but, if you are the retiree, leave your listeners looking toward the future. If you are honoring a retiree, don't say anything that leads him to believe his best years are behind him. Look to the future.

Avoid speeches that sound canned. The best way to do this is to be as specific as possible. Mention specific events, and make use of anec-dotes. This is an occasion to get personal.

Words to Use

accomplishments	active	asset
achievement	admirable	begin

beginning	hail	praise
beloved	heart	profound
career	heritage	pursue
celebrate	honor	pursuit
congratulate	indelible	recall
creator	inspirational	record
culmination	inspired	remember
dedicate	inspiring	remembrance
devote	laud	renew
devoted	leadership	retirement
esteem	legacy	salute
example	lively	special
excellence	love	start
family	magnificent	thankful
far-reaching	memento	thanks
founder	memorable	tradition
future	mentor	tribute
grandchildren	momentous	unforgettable
grateful	motivate	vital
great	new	wonderful

WORDS TO AVOID

aged	infirm	step down
ailing	leave	tired
end	old	unworthy
finally	quit	vacation
goof off	rest	worn out
ill	sleep	

PHRASES TO USE

always available

always eager to help

always rely on

always remember you

always there when you needed him/her

astounding record of achievement

built our future

conscience of this company

contributed 100 percent at all times

contributed to the success of

culmination of a great career

dedication and hard work

extraordinary experience

for him, retirement does not mean taking it easy

gave me my start

go on to new activities

grateful for all you have done

heart of the organization

honor and privilege to work with

if ever you need a helping hand

indelible mark

I will continue to support the activities

I will miss each and every one of you

laid the foundation for

leave a monumental legacy

lifetime of achievement

list of achievements

look to the future

magnificent achievement

magnificent legacy

major accomplishment

my esteemed mentor

new fields of endeavor

one of the guiding lights

source of pride and satisfaction

this organization has been a big part of my life

unparalleled career

unwavering dedication

valuable contribution

we will miss

will figure in the history of

SENTENCES TO USE

If you are the retiree:

Each day—and, by my calculation, there have been 7,543 of them—working with you has been rich in challenges and rewards.

I knew the job was hard, and I came to work each day determined to give it 100 percent.

It has been my pleasure and privilege to serve this organization for the better part of my career.

Thank you, my friends, for this wonderful send-off.

The time has come to call it a career.

This job is the most difficult and demanding way I can think of spending twenty years of one's life—and I wouldn't have had it any other way.

This send-off is totally unexpected, and I am deeply moved by it.

Without the support of my colleagues and my family, I wouldn't have lived to reach retirement!

Working with all of you over the years has made each day an occasion of discovery and new pleasure.

If you are honoring a retiree:

Bill, you can't get away from us. We'll be in touch.

Knowing you, retirement is not the end of a career, but the beginning of some brand-new one.

Now that we're about to release you at last, I feel as if I should write a letter of warning to somebody.

Thanks in large part to you, we are all better prepared to face the challenges of the future.

We wish you very well, Sarah, as you embark on a new phase of your life.

Who would have thought that thirty years could seem so brief a time?

You may be leaving us, but your contributions to this organization will endure.

You leave this firm far stronger, smarter, and richer than it was when you joined it.

Sample Paragraphs

If you are the retiree:

1   June 6, 1959, was the proudest day of my life. That was when my son, Joshua, was born. April 5, 1963, was the second-proudest day of my

life. That was the day I joined Veeble and Fetzer as a junior account associate. It was the plum then. It is the plum today—a much bigger plum, in fact. When I joined the firm, thirty-three folks worked out of a suite of eight rooms in this building. Today, we own the building and have crammed 378 hard-working people into our offices. What an experience it has been, growing up with Veeble and Fetzer!

2   I made a good living here at Marsh and Mersh. That should be enough, more than enough to ask from any job. But, the fact is, I made much more than a good living during my three decades with this firm. I made a career, and I was given an extraordinary opportunity to help make this industry a better enterprise and this community a better place to live. Best of all, I made great friends.

If you are honoring a retiree:

1   I cannot bring myself to use the word "retirement" in connection with Edna Freebee. We cannot deny that, after thirty-six years, she is, in fact, leaving us. But *retiring*? Hardly. Let me read you a list of the associations to which Edna belongs and in which she will now be more active than ever.

2   It is fitting and proper at a retirement to rehearse the many accomplishments of the retiree. I intend to get around to some of that—although to list everything Pete Williams has given to this organization would take more time and patience than any of us could spare. I know Pete will find our tribute more endurable if I begin by telling you about what he plans to do now that he has the time to devote to some causes near and dear to him.

Sample Speeches

If you are the retiree:

My friends and colleagues—I am very proud to call you both—your send-off this evening, which is so kind and touching, makes it that much harder for me to leave O'Toole Tool and Die. Of course, I'm not yet quite ready to vanish off the face of the earth, and I can assure you that you'll be seeing plenty of me around here from time to time. But, it is true, I won't be working with you every day. And doing so, let me assure you, was a rare and wonderful privilege. O'Toole Tool and Die is a great company because it is made up of great people.

I think of "Old Man" O'Toole, who was what they call "my mentor." In truth, he did teach me everything I know about this business. I started on the lathe here in 1956. Those of you close to my age will remember how the "Old Man" used to spend a lot more time on the shop floor than up in the office. He was the only person I ever knew who could look over your shoulder without bothering you. That's because you never felt he was second-guessing you or criticizing you, but that he was teaching you to be your best. His first words to me on that shop floor were, "Don't do it faster than anyone else. Do it better."

That was my first lesson in quality control.

You know, I shouldn't have said that "Old Man" O'Toole taught me everything I know. What he taught me is to keep my eyes and ears open and learn from *everybody* here, because he knew that everyone at the firm had something of value to teach.

Jim Wilkinson, who came up from Florida to be here tonight, taught me more about marketing than I could have learned from a thousand books and from a hundred professors.

Fran Smith, one of the greatest customer service managers I have ever encountered, did as much as any human being could to educate me about dealing with customers. "No," she would tell me with infinite patience, "I don't think customers prefer being called 'knucklehead' over 'nitwit.'"

I am not "retiring" in the strictest sense of the word. I am joining the Senior Executive Corps, volunteering to work with young people who are interested in pursuing business careers. I am looking forward to the experience, and I expect to meet some very fine people. But I don't deceive myself into thinking that anyplace else on this planet is staffed by a crew quite like ours at O'Toole. I will miss you all, and I ask that you keep in touch.

If you are honoring a retiree:

We are here to celebrate the career of Henrietta Hornbeck. That's pretty much the same thing as celebrating the past thirty-eight years of the history and development of the ice cream industry, and it is precisely the same thing as commemorating the most significantly formative years in the history of Keen 'n' Kold Confections, Inc. Thanks to Henrietta, we are the third largest supplier of specialty ice cream products in the region.

And, also thanks in large measure to Henrietta, there is such a thing as "specialty ice cream" to supply.

She developed no fewer than forty-eight new confections, thirty-six of which are still being made—and, in turn, still making money—today. This includes our top-selling Whiz-Bang and Marshmallow Melted.

The truth is that most of us literally owe our jobs to Henrietta Hornbeck.

Now what do you give somebody like this as a retirement gift? The traditional gold watch?

Not a chance.

We are presenting Henrietta with the very ice-cream scoop that our founder, Benjamin P. Shamrock, used at the soda shop he opened on Fourth and Porter in 1887. This scoop has been in the company since Ben founded it in 1894. I know that he would want Henrietta to have it.

Henrietta Hornbeck is leaving us and the specialty ice cream industry, having made the world—what can I say?—a sweeter place. She has always been active in our company's community outreach program, to which she intends now to devote more of her time, thereby making the world an even sweeter place.

Henrietta, we are grateful for everything you have done, and while we will miss seeing you here on a daily basis, we look forward to working with you through the community outreach program.

Now come up here and get Ben Shamrock's old scoop!

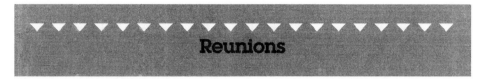

Reunions

Reunions of high school and college classes (or other organizations) have the potential for being joyous, emotionally rewarding, and just plain fun. All too often, however, for many people, reunions fall flat, fizzle, and become occasions of disappointment and discomfort. A good speech may not work the miracle of turning an assembly of duds into a roomful of live wires, but it can do much to set the tone for a successful reunion.

There are only five ingredients necessary for an effective reunion speech:

1. A warm welcome;

2. A few shared memories;

3. A heartfelt statement about what the school experience has meant to you (and, by implication, to the others attending the reunion);

4. An expression of thanks to those who worked to make the reunion possible;

5. Brevity. Unlike an anniversary celebration, which may call for a fairly substantial speech, the business of a reunion is simply to *reunite*: to see what your junior-year boyfriend looks like after five, ten, fifteen, twenty years, to talk to one another, to dance, to reminisce, and to remember where you've been and to say where you are now and predict where you'll be going. Your audience is probably anxious to do all these things and will not be very receptive to a longwinded speech. Let your audience get on with the reunion.

WHAT TO SAY

Welcome your classmates or former colleagues. Express your pleasure at seeing such a great turnout. If the turnout is, in fact, small, make a virtue of this fact by welcoming those in whom the spirit remains alive or in whom the memories burn brightly. If the group had a nickname, use it. My sister went to Chicago's Austin High. Students there were "Tigers." I went to Lane Technical High School, and I'm afraid we were called "Lane Brains."

Introduce yourself. If you had a special position in the class (president, valedictorian, etc.) or organization, mention it. Perhaps you had a nickname. Perhaps you had a certain reputation. Remind your listeners.

The body of your speech should be built of shared memories. In preparing for the speech, collect—either on your own or, preferably, with the help of classmates or colleagues—the momentous and touching events that everyone is likely to recall: the big game that was won—or lost; the blizzard that kept most everyone in school overnight and turned an ordinary schoolday into a mass slumber party; the retirement of a favorite teacher; graduation day; and so on. In addition, relate some anecdotes that single out a few memorable individuals: Marvin with his bewildering science fair projects; Zelda, whose story about a dedicated English teacher won a prize; Mary, who dyed her hair purple, persistently violated the dress code, and who today is an assistant district attorney. Then there was the time somebody liberated all the frogs in the biology class. Or Mr. Beezley, who always came up with just the wrong cliché: "I see the light at the end of the rainbow."

Recall the hit songs, the favorite books, the major issues of the old days.

Compare then and now: Petie Smith, once celebrated as the class clown, is vice president of the Third National Bank.

Conclude with a meaningful statement. Define the shared values and emotions of your school (or other group) experience. The danger here is that such a statement will come out as an abstract platitude or a preachy sentiment. You can avoid this by offering yourself—your emotions and conclusions—as representative of the group's. "It is true that Lankershim High did not make an Albert Schweitzer out of me. But I can tell you that the values I learned here, not just from the teachers, but from my classmates, from each of you, have made me a better, more caring dentist. I believe that, for most of us, whatever vocation we have chosen, this is true. To our years at Lankershim—and to one another—we owe some of what is best in each of us."

If appropriate, why not propose a toast?

Remember to thank those who made the reunion possible—usually the members of a special committee. Thank them by name. If their job involved extensive search efforts, acknowledge this. Maybe there is even a good story in one of the more difficult searches.

WHAT NOT TO SAY

Avoid highflown abstractions and platitudes. It is better to stay with emotions, genuine sentiment, and real memories.

By all means, poke gentle and affectionate fun at chosen individuals, but be careful not to embarrass, humiliate, mock, or belittle anyone.

Avoid all negatives. If, for example, the turnout is small, don't make your audience feel as if they are participating in a disappointment. Make a virtue out of the intimacy.

It is appropriate to remember classmates or colleagues who have passed on, but avoid reciting a litany of the dead or delivering lengthy eulogies. This is not the place for it.

Do not attack or mock anyone, including those who are absent. ("Remember how stupid Mel was? Always forgetting the combination to his locker.")

A tantalizing aspect of most class reunions is either to see one's old sweetheart or to recall who was dating whom back when. In general, the place for such talk is between and among friends, not up at the podium. Allusions to old flames may seem innocent enough, but, given public utterance, may in fact be embarrassing, painful, or even worse. (Irate wife: "Do you mean to tell me that you were dating Laura Swain when we were going steady?!")

Your audience will appreciate the genuine pleasure you take in delivering reminiscences, but keep them brief. By all means, get personal, but avoid making your speech a long and winding trip down your own private memory lane.

WORDS TO USE

celebrate	future	party
classmates	gift	pleasure
colleagues	golden	recall
courage	happiness	recollect
delight	inheritance	recollection
delightful	inspirational	remember
education	inspire	renew
educators	inspired	spirit
emotion	laugh	thrill
excited	laughs	toast
excitement	learned	value
faith	legacy	values
friends	loyalty	welcome
friendship	meet	yesterdays
fun	pals	

WORDS TO AVOID

bitter	grudging	outcast
cornball	homely	revenge
corny	mean	stupid
disappointing	misfit	ugly
dumb	odd	unpleasant
forgettable	oddball	unpopular

PHRASES TO USE

blessing of reunion	fond memories
bring us all together	good old days
can never forget	grateful for
celebrate the good times	great detective work
committee's hard work	great old days
depend on one another	lasting friendships

meant so much to us

put this event together

recall with one another

relive a few moments of the
  past together

savor these moments

school spirit

separated by time and space

shared our hopes

share our memories

share the moment

spirit of this organization

stop time

take a few moments

tears and laughter

those who made it possible

unforgettable events

unforgettable people

values we learned

what we did for each other

what we meant to one another

SENTENCES TO USE

Back in 1968 I had two things on my mind: ending the Vietnam War and getting a date for Friday night—not necessarily in that order.

Challenges, yes; heartaches, yes; but being there with all of you made it the best time of my life.

I am overwhelmed by the turnout this evening.

I am thrilled to see you all here; in fact, I know we're all thrilled to see each other.

I feel ten years younger already.

It is a rare treat to get together with so many friends and relive old times.

Let me share a story or two with you.

Let's rekindle our school spirit.

Two great burdens have been lifted since I left these hallowed halls: the Berlin Wall has crumbled, and I don't have to worry about Mr. Sarbane's calculus class anymore.

We were a close-knit class, who never let each other down.

We are fortunate in having an intimate group tonight.

We owe the Reunion Committee our gratitude for making this great time possible.

Welcome, friends and classmates, to the tenth reunion of the Western University Class of 19XX.

Welcome back to where we built our futures.

What did Branchburg High mean to us? Let me share my opinion with you.

What I remember most vividly is the way we used to work together to solve problems and reach common goals.

Who can forget the time Benny Harold and Ginny Ramos conspired to liberate the frogs from the Biology Department storage room?

You are the stars this evening.

What's become of us? Let me run down a few examples.

SAMPLE PARAGRAPHS

1   We used to think we were pretty hot stuff. Well, I've been looking at the questionnaires you all filled out and returned to us: doctors, lawyers, educators, mothers, fathers, construction engineers, a writer, an artist, and on and on. Let me tell you something. We were right. We *were* hot stuff—and, judging from where we are right now, we still are.

2   It is my pleasure to welcome you to the fifteenth reunion of the Glasshead College Class of 19XX. I am thrilled to see so many of you here—so many familiar faces that bring back the great times we had. Like you, I want to renew many old acquaintances; therefore, like you, I want me to shut up so that we can all start talking to one another. But let me just kick this evening off with a few memories—as far as I'm concerned, *choice* memories.

3   We have each other to thank for this evening, of course, but tonight would not have been possible without the hard work, dedication, diligence, and sheer inventiveness of the Reunion Committee: Dee

Walters, Sam Stropf, Perry Ellington, and Peggy Linton. I think it is pretty remarkable that one of us, Del Shattuck, came all the way from Cork, Ireland, to be with us tonight. But I think it's equally remarkable that the Committee managed to track Del down in the first place. There are any number of top-rate collection agencies that would pay very good money to have detectives like these on their staff.

SAMPLE SPEECH

Welcome, my friends—old, new, and rediscovered—to the tenth anniversary of the Newport High Class of 19XX. Since this is the Event of the Decade, I don't want to hold any of us back from it with a long-winded speech. But I do want to tell you how thrilled I am to see so many of you after all of these years. The dress code didn't allow beards back in 19XX—and, to tell you the truth, I'm not sure I could have grown one back then—so some of you may not recognize me in my present state. I am Joe Pearson, better known a decade ago as "Shorty." My chief claim to fame is, in four years, never having missed a Newport Falcons home game. In fact, it's my only claim to fame.

That's who I am—or was. Today, I sell insurance. But that's not all I am. I am—and I'm proud to say it—a graduate of Newport.

That means something to me, as I'm sure it does to you. The program at Newport was an academically demanding one. You could always tell a student who was facing one of Mr. Rooney's famous physics exams: eyes wide with terror, a tendency to reply to "hello" with a dissertation on the Second Law of Thermodynamics. But, hard as we had to hit the books, we always got the support we needed: from the faculty and, even more important, from each other. I'll never forget spending the night with Shirley Wilburs—no, no, not what you think. We *studied*. More accurately, she talked me through one Greek tragedy and two plays by Shakespeare, so that I was 100 percent ready for Mrs. Smith's essay exam the next day. That was typical. At Newport, we worked together.

Of course, we also played together. Who can forget the state championship that got away? Stolen from us in the last fifteen seconds of that knock-down, drag out match of June 3, 19XX. But we gave the team the biggest, best homecoming this school had—and, I bet, *has*—ever seen. That's the way we were.

We learned—a lot. Our diplomas meant something. We got into college. We got good jobs and rewarding careers. But it wasn't all facts and figures and history and concepts. We also learned about values like loyalty, compassion, optimism, and a willingness to pitch in and help. We learned what it was like to work hard and to play hard—together. We learned about teamwork, understanding, and mutual respect. These are the lessons we were taught, not from books and teachers, but from each other.

Before I close, let me acknowledge on behalf of all of us the superb work of the Reunion Committee. Not only did Dave Brower, Penelope Philpot, and Fran Torrington make all the arrangements for tonight, they sent out all the invitations—which more than once involved persistent detective work. Folks have come to us tonight from as far away as Bangor, Maine, Phoenix, Arizona, and Nice, France—that's *France*, ladies and gentlemen. The committee didn't just zip down somebody's address book. They cared. They cared enough to contact 579 out of our class of 640. But, then, you wouldn't expect less than maximum effort from a Newport Class of 19XX grad!

Sales Meetings and Presentations

In 1949, Arthur Miller wrote one of the most successful plays ever created by an American playwright, *Death of a Salesman*. There is a cast of unforgettable characters in this play, but one very important character never appears onstage. His name is Dave Singleman, and he exists only as a kind of legend that haunts the imagination of the central character, Willie Loman. Dave Singleman was the perfect salesman, a man who didn't manufacture or create anything himself, performed no service, didn't practice medicine or law, did not labor by the sweat of his brow, but nevertheless made a fine living and was accustomed to traveling from place to place, gorgeously attired in smoking jacket and slippers, in the luxury of a Pullman car on the New York, New Haven and Hartford Railroad. Beloved by all, Dave Singleman always made his sale. It was a charmed life: magic.

At first, it may seem odd that Arthur Miller would choose to write a major play on the subject of a salesman. But, like his character Willie Loman, who dreams of being another Dave Singleman, Miller knew that sales and selling is a subject immersed in mystery, myth, and legend. He knew that most of us regard the salesman (and, even as late as 1949, the typical sales*man* was male) with a mixture of suspicion and contempt but also with awe and envy. We know how a plumber makes money. He does *something* with *things*. He puts pipes together. He cleans clogs out of drains. He solders leaking joints. It's a combination of hard work, skill, and training.

But a salesman?

A salesman produces nothing and provides no tangible service. Nevertheless, as if by magic, a salesman persuades us to part with our money. Our *money*! In civilized society, money is life's blood. We need it to eat, to shelter ourselves, to put clothing on our backs. We need it to live. And here is a person who can persuade us to give up some portion of this most precious substance!

Arthur Miller understood that the salesman is at the very center of our society. No wonder he's an almost mythical figure, and no wonder no end of books have been written on how to sell—not just how to sell, but how to open a sale and how to follow up on the opening and then how to close the sale.

The existence of volume upon volume anatomizing every phase of the sales process has hardly dispelled the mystery and mystification. Sales remains, for most of us, a very intimidating area, a vitally important activity that is shrouded in mystery and full of "secrets"—the *Secrets of the Master Salesmen,* as one book title puts it.

The ideal of Dave Singleman, the perfect salesman who has achieved a way of life that amounts to simple bliss, remains a distant, elusive goal. Successful selling, we think, takes a talent that amounts to genius, to the kind of magic that animates the fingers of a virtuoso violinist, say, the kind of master who comes around once in a generation.

Now let's turn away from myth and face some realities.

First, it is absolutely true: Sales is at the heart of most of our activities. Even if your job does not directly involve selling item X to customer A, you are always selling something: an idea, a concept, a service, even a feeling of confidence in yourself. It is possible to look at all important human transactions as a form of selling.

Second, it is absolutely true: The ability to sell is enhanced by learned skills and, quite probably, natural talent.

Third, it is absolutely true: Those who know how to sell most effectively make more money than those who do not.

Fourth, it is absolutely true: You are already an effective salesman or saleswoman. This proposition is true because the first proposition is true. The fact that you have gotten through some schooling, that you have a job, that you deal with people each and every day means that you are doing some form of effective selling. The only real "secret" here is to take what you already do and make it work on a conscious, more systematic level. Sales is not magic. It is a deliberate, thoughtful extension of what you already do—and have done—virtually every day of your life. Aptitude, natural talent, and a willingness to learn can make you that rare being: the Great Salesperson. But everyone sells, and even if you do not aspire to be the Great Salesperson, you can be a more consistently effective one.

Let's begin by reducing the sales presentation to its essentials. Whether you realize it or not, almost any time you succeed in selling something to someone—whether it is an actual product, or an idea, or a proposal, or your point of view—you take your "customer" through five essential steps:

1. You establish that your "customer" has an urgent need or problem.

2. You offer a way to satisfy the need or solve the problem.

3. You overcome the "customer's" objections to your offer of a solution. The "customer" may actually state these objections, or, more often, it is up to you to anticipate unspoken objections and, in effect, preempt them.

4. You underscore, reinforce, restate, and reiterate the need or problem.

5. You urge the "customer" to act. If this is an actual sales situation, you ask the customer to place an order. If you are selling an idea, you might (for example) ask the "customer" to back you up when you make the pitch to the boss.

The effective sales presentation begins by systematizing these steps. But the point to remember is that there is nothing special or mysterious about them. You go through them, repeatedly, every day, whether you think about them or not.

So much for the basic structure of the sales presentation. But there is more to the selling process than structure.

First, prepare for the sales presentation by convincing yourself that selling is not a mystery. You do it every day. You can, therefore, do it now.

Second, it helps—it helps a great deal—to believe in what you are selling. Most of us (thank goodness!) object to selling what we know to be faulty or inadequate. That is, few of us aspire to be cheats and con men. Whether you are selling a product, a service, or an idea, make it your business to learn as much about the "merchandise" as possible. Get yourself hyped on what is good and valuable about it. Your genuine enthusiasm will be contagious. If you find that you cannot believe in the "merchandise," well, maybe you should try to get out of having to sell it. In any case, you'll have to face the fact that selling something about which you have doubts is much more difficult than promoting a "product" in which you have confidence.

Third, while you cannot escape the fact that belief in the "product" is invaluable in helping you to sell it, any experienced salesperson will tell you: *You are not selling a vacuum cleaner (or a set of encyclopedias, or a cleaning service, or whatever). You are selling yourself.* The five-part structure outlined here is the rational part of the sales presentation. It is the logical argument, and it is essential. But, operating simultaneously with this argument—this logical journey from need/problem to product/solution—is an emotional process of selling yourself, that is, of building within the "customer" confidence in yourself.

Perhaps this is the real source of the mystique that envelops the art of selling. For this process is difficult to reduce to an outlined formula. It is in part nonverbal—a function of body language and *tone* of voice as well as *rhythm* of speech—and in part a function of choosing a vocabulary that conveys the right shades of meaning. It is a process of bonding with the "customer," of establishing a commonality of interest. We will now explore this process.

WHAT TO SAY (AND DO)

Prepare by learning as much as you can about the audience ("customer") you will address and the "merchandise" you will sell.

Structure your presentation to include all five steps of the selling process:

1. Establish a need or problem.

2. Offer the means/merchandise to satisfy the need or solve the problem.

3. Address and overcome objections. Think about this beforehand so that you can anticipate likely objections ("It's too expensive," "It's too cumbersome," etc.) and preempt them before they are even raised.

4. Restate the urgency of the need or problem.

5. Move your audience/customer to act. Sign up now. Place your order today. "Why wait?"

Interact with your audience/customer in a controlled way by asking rhetorical questions—that is, by posing questions to which you and your audience both know the answer. "Are you interested in saving money?"

Handle any questions straightforwardly and honestly. If you don't know the answer to a question, say so—and promise to research an answer and get back to the person who asked it. (Be fully prepared to make good on your promise.)

Identify with your audience/customer. In the 1980s, Victor Kiam took a faltering manufacturer of electric razors and turned it around by appearing on television and announcing that he was so impressed with the Remington electric razor that he decided to buy the company. This pitch operates on two powerful levels. First, it is a dramatic (as well as humorous and hyperbolic) demonstration of absolute confidence in a product. Second, it is a dramatic gesture of identification with audience and customers. *Like you*, Kiam is saying, I needed a really good shave. (The implications of this are many: A good shave makes you look good, makes you look clean, civilized, refined, and successful; most of all, it is one of those everyday activities that can either be an annoying—even painful—chore, or can be quite satisfying and make you feel good about yourself). Kiam's unspoken argument continues: I *found* a really good shave—and I invested in it ("I bought the company!"). Now I'm willing to share my discovery with you. The object is not to convince your audience/customer to buy something from you, but to avail himself of your offer to share something good, great, exclusive, and/or beneficial.

Sell yourself. Communicate confidence. This means that you should think about your body language. Make frequent eye contact with your audience. This suggests honesty—that you have nothing to hide. In contrast, looking down or aside suggests shiftiness and evasion. Use open gestures. Avoid touching your face; this suggests that you have something to hide. Avoid crossing your arms or putting your hands on your hips; such gestures communicate resistance and defiance. When you speak, open your mouth and take your time. Mumbling suggests evasiveness, and rapid speech is synonymous with the stereotype of the "fast-talking salesman." Both will evoke resistance in your audience/customer. See the section on "Body Language" in Part Three of this book.

Think about what you will wear. The section on "Clothes" in Part Three gives some good general advice, but for specifically sales-oriented occasions you should dress on the conservative side, with an eye toward looking at most a notch above the level of your audience/customers. If you are selling securities, the finer the clothes the better. If you are selling vacuum cleaners, a $1,200 suit or a $5,000 designer ensemble will seem out of place. Worse, it will tend to price you out of your customers' league. Wear clothes that identify you with your audience/customers. Of course, whatever you wear, make sure it is crisp, well-laundered, and in perfect repair. A casual look may well be appropriate in certain selling situations, but never look sloppy or shabby.

Visual aids and other props can be very effective in sales presentations. If possible and appropriate, exhibit and demonstrate the product itself. Otherwise, use *graphic* and *simple* charts, photographs, and the like to help make your point. "Before" and "After" exhibits are time-tested sales aids. Remember, the point of the visual aid is to convince your audience/customer that "seeing is believing." Your audience/customer does not have to take your claims unsupported, but can see and judge the value of what you are selling for himself. Therefore, do not bully your audience/customer into drawing a conclusion.

WHAT NOT TO SAY (OR DO)

Avoid disorder. Make sure you have a clear sense of the five-point structure of the sales presentation before you begin.

Avoid negativity. Don't argue the case *against* your sale, unless you are doing so for carefully planned rhetorical reasons. If you are playing devil's advocate for the purposes of preempting your audience/customer's objections, make very sure that the case in your favor is unmistakably stronger. Trial lawyers hold as sacred the principle that you should not ask a witness a question to which you do not already know the answer. Similarly, don't play devil's advocate unless you are absolutely certain that, like you, your audience/customer will reject the negative point of view.

As in most speaking situations, humor can be useful. But avoid pointless jokes, which tend to stereotype you as a "typical" polyester-and-plaid salesman.

Avoid bullying your audience/customer. You must create a feeling in your listeners that they are being *offered* an *opportunity*, not being *handed a line*. Your audience/customer must feel that he is in control, that the choice is his.

Avoid pleading, begging, and anything else that smacks of desperation.

Don't lie. Don't exaggerate.

If you don't know the answer to a question, neither evade it nor make up an answer. Admit that you don't know the answer off hand, but that you will try to get an answer.

Do not rely on demonstrations of the merchandise unless you are confident that the product will perform as promised. Nothing will kill a sale faster than a public demonstration that fails.

See "What to Say (and Do)" for cautions regarding body language and clothing.

Words to Use

act	evaluation	prudent
action	examine	reasonable
additional	exceptional	reliability
advanced	exciting	reliable
agree	exclusive	rely
agreement	extra	resolve
answer	facts	results
assurance	features	reward
bargain	finest	safe
benefits	free	safety
best	fussy	savings
breakthrough	gift	secure
choice	guarantee	security
choose	indulge	serve
choosy	investigate	service
client	investment	settle
confidence	lasting	share
confident	luxurious	solution
convenient	luxury	solve
customer	move	sophisticated
deal	need	special
decision	needs	spectacular
demonstrate	negotiate	substantial
demonstrated	offer	support
depend	opportunity	technology
dependable	option	terms
deserve	particular	treat
discerning	pledge	trial
discovery	practical	unconditional
durable	premium	urgent
enduring	problem	value
engineering	promise	warranty
ergonomic	proposal	
evaluate	proven	

PHRASES TO USE

about time you treated yourself to

act now

avoid obsolescence

be assured

buy with confidence

check out the features

client support

client-oriented

compare the features

complete satisfaction

count on it

customer support

cutting edge

decide for yourself

don't you deserve

evaluate the proposition

exclusive benefits

exclusive features

find out for yourself

guarantee of satisfaction

hear me out and decide for yourself

indulge yourself

indulge yourself with

isn't it about time

look at the facts

luxuriate in

make a move

make it easy for you

move in the right direction

move up to

my word on it

no strings attached

peace of mind

proven technology

relax with

rest easy

reward yourself with

see for yourself

share this opportunity

simple steps

special benefits

special opportunity

state of the art

take action

take decisive action

take this important step

time-tested

top of the line

treat yourself to

try it out

user friendly

weigh the options

what you deserve

win-win proposition

without obligation

SENTENCES TO USE

Could you use some extra money right now?

How long do you propose to wait before you give yourself something you really want?

How much would you pay for genuine peace of mind?

I understand your problem completely.

I make my living sharing new and exciting discoveries with folks like you.

I am confident that I can help you solve your maintenance problems.

I am going to ask *you* to tell *me* how I can serve *you*.

I don't spend my precious time talking to just anybody.

I am proud to offer this opportunity.

I believe that we are thinking along the same lines.

I am pleased to offer this opportunity to you.

I am pleased to share this discovery with you.

I'll lay it out for you so that you can judge for yourself.

If not now, when? If not you, who?

Imagine the following situation.

Isn't it about time you treated yourself to something special?

Isn't it about time you had some relief?

Let me outline the possibilities.

The fact that you are here this evening is proof that you have an open mind.

The decision is yours to make.

This is an exciting opportunity.

This is an exceptional offer.

We are agreed that you need affordable life insurance.

We're all in the same boat, but I can tell you how to reach shore.

What would it take to make it possible for you to say "yes"?

What is security worth to you?

You have not gotten to this stage in your career without being able to recognize opportunity.

You have a wide variety of options open to you.

You can't afford to keep putting off your investment decisions.

SAMPLE PARAGRAPHS

1   Let me begin by telling you two things you already know. First: your home is your biggest investment, almost certainly the biggest personal investment you will ever make. Second: Your home is your single greatest liability—if you can't sell it when you want to. What happens when you've got a half-acre, $250,000 albatross around your neck? Well, you all know better than I do. That's why you've come to hear me tonight. Let me ask you to face reality. If you think I can unload that albatross for you, you're mistaken. I can help you do much more. I can show you how to sell that home you've worked so hard for not at a loss, but at the handsome profit you deserve to make from it. I can show you how to turn that albatross into a treasure.

2   You are special. Let me tell you why. "The mass of men," Thoreau said, "lead lives of quiet desperation." They play by all the rules, as they understand them. They go to school, they learn a job, they get a job, they go to work, they earn a salary, and, if they are lucky, they get by. But you are special. You deserve more. A salary is for survival. Wealth, real wealth, the kind of wealth you want and deserve, will never, ever come to you as a result of putting in time at the office—no matter how hard you work and how much of yourself you give to your job. Once you admit that, you are ready to hear about the variety of opportunities I am in a position to share with you.

3   How long do you intend to wait? How long will you put off rewarding yourself for all the hard work you've done? You've served your company. You've made your boss look good. You've helped your customers. You've paid your taxes. You've raised a family. You've worked and worked and worked—for everyone except yourself. Isn't it about time you seized the moment, grabbed that brass ring, and

took something for yourself? Let me ask you to give up just one more thing—ten minutes of your time—before you start digging in and getting some pleasure, satisfaction, and relaxation for yourself.

SAMPLE SPEECH

Everybody wants something—a great many things, a great variety of different things. But everybody wants one thing for sure. [Fan out a sheaf of currency.]

Money. That is why you have come here, and that is why I am talking to you. I am here to offer you an opportunity to make money. That's the bottom line. But what's even more exciting is that I'm here to offer you an opportunity to make money by offering people a chance to *protect* and *save* the money *they* have.

Let's start with you.

I was, not too long ago, in exactly the position you are now in. Literally and exactly. I was sitting in the audience listening to some guy in a blue suit tell me that I was about to be given an opportunity to make money. Now, like many—maybe most—of you out there, I was very skeptical. But I was also broke, and I was ready to give anything a good shot.

Or almost anything. I was a lot like you. I knew I could get a part-time job in a convenience store or at a gas station or stuffing envelopes and answering telephones. But, I thought, no, I'm better than that.

Let me tell you something—and you know this already—you don't make any real money in most spare-time jobs. A hundred a week take-home? Two hundred? Maybe. Okay, that's survival. But if you really are like me, survival isn't good enough. You want to *live* a little. Maybe more than a little.

Now, there's one need. You *need* money.

Here's another need.

Nationwide, one out of five homes is burglarized each year. Let's bring it even closer to home. Last year, in this neighborhood, 674 burglaries were reported to the police. This is not a poor neighborhood or a bad neighborhood. It is an ordinary neighborhood. It is your neighborhood. And I can tell you this, your neighbors are scared. They should be. They need protection.

I'm going to give you the opportunity to furnish them the protection they need.

I'm going to offer you the opportunity to become a GuardsAll Home Security sales representative. This means I'm going to give you the opportunity to provide your neighbors with something they desperately need and desperately want.

How desperately? In one community we serve, six out of every ten households our representatives called on purchased a home security system from us. Ripe. The market is ripe.

How ripe? Give us fifteen hours a week and you'll make—$200? $300? $400? Try $600 to $800. And that's for fifteen hours a week. If you can give us more, and if you are willing to expand the territory, well, I have representatives who make $3,000 a week.

How do you do it? The need, I've just told you, is there. You're not selling freezers to Eskimos. You're selling security to folks who need and want it.

But let me tell you first what's wrong with most home security systems. Three things. First, they are expensive. Second, they are disruptive to install—drilling, snaking wires through the house, wrecking the homeowner's woodwork. Third, they are a pain in the neck to use—so they don't get used.

Now let me tell you why the GuardsAll System practically sells itself. First, it costs up to 50 percent less than other systems that give comparable coverage. Second, it is wireless and requires no drilling. In fact, you give the customer the option to install all or part of the system himself—or to leave the installation (which rarely takes more than a single day) to our professionals. Third, they are easy to use.

But don't take my word for it. We've set up a demonstration. [Present demonstration and explain, in simple terms, the special technical features of the GuardsAll System.]

As I said, don't take my word for it. And just as you see the GuardsAll System in action for yourself, so will your customers. This is the same demonstration kit we'll equip you with.

Ladies and gentlemen, I am very happy in my work. It is not every business person who can offer a win-win proposition. If you take this opportunity, I win, you'll win, and the friends and neighbors whose homes you make safer will win. But I'm going to be making this presentation in your area only once--here and now--and it is here and now only that you have the opportunity to sign this employment guarantee. Sign up now, show up for a training session tomorrow, Friday, or Saturday, and you can be making the money you need starting Monday.

Thanks

Various chapters in this book treat words of thanks on special occasions— accepting an appointment, accepting an award, thanking a retiring colleague for years of service, paying tribute to a distinguished individual, and so on. This chapter deals with more general occasions for thanks and includes such things as thanking sponsors for supporting a program, thanking colleagues for making a project a success, thanking constituents for support, thanking customers and clients for patronage, and so on. By themselves, such speeches are generally very brief. Oftentimes, thanks are a part of longer remarks or an entire program.

At first glance, the task of thanking an individual or a group seems simple and pleasant. Pleasant it is, and simple it can be. How simple? Just tune into the Academy Awards show or the Grammys or the like. For most of the speakers, thanks is no more complicated than reciting a list of names.

And—unfortunately—no more interesting.

It is all too easy to get away with reducing a speech of thanks to a laundry list of deserving names. True, publicly acknowledging people who deserve thanks makes those who hear their names feel good. And that *is* something. But such speeches bore everyone else. It looks as if it comes down to a sorry dilemma: either make your colleagues feel good and bore everyone else, or skimp on the praise and get through the speech fast.

There *is* a better solution. And, surprisingly, the answer is *not* to make the speech shorter. What's tedious about the laundry list approach is not the length of the list, but the fact that it is a mere list—names without any meaningful context. You are losing your audience because you are not giving them any real information. Instead of a series of names, then, attach some pertinent information to the names. Explain *why* you are thanking Joe Blow. What did he do? You might go even further than this. Think of one or two things to say about Joe—a couple of quick, deft brushstrokes—that suggest what he's like as a person. Do the same for at least some of the people you have to thank.

WHAT TO SAY

Bear in mind that your task is twofold: You want to make the folks who deserve acknowledgment feel good, *and* you want to engage your general audience in your remarks.

Prepare in advance by making an exhaustive list of those you should thank. Next, pare the list down, if possible, without leaving out anyone essential.

Using your list, write beside each name precisely what it is you are thanking him or her for. How did that individual contribute to the project, program, or enterprise in question?

For at least a selected number of the individuals whom you are thanking, think of one or two things you might say that suggests character or personality. A meaningful phrase or two is sufficient.

Address a quick remark directly to the person you are thanking.

If time permits, ask the person being thanked to stand up or to take a bow.

Invite your audience to join in the thanks.

To whatever extent you can, show how the work of the individual(s) being thanked has benefited everyone, especially those in the audience. Make your thanks as relevant to as many people present as possible.

WHAT NOT TO SAY

Avoid meaningless laundry lists of individuals you are "obliged" to thank.

Avoid a perfunctory tone.

Avoid such dismissive phrases as "too numerous to mention."

Don't try to wing this. Prepare a list of whom to thank and why to thank them.

Humor is fine, but don't let it become sarcasm. Say nothing that might mitigate the sincerity of your thanks.

WORDS TO USE

accomplish	explain	profound
accomplishment	fruition	reach
acknowledge	goal	respect
appreciate	grateful	sacrifice
appreciation	gratitude	scope
character	heartfelt	selfless
commitment	honor	sincere
contribute	inestimable	sincerity
contribution	invaluable	stretch
cost	labor	succeed
culmination	magnitude	success
dedication	motivate	successful
deed	motivated	thanks
deepest	motivation	tremendous
depth	pleasure	unselfish
duty	praise	work
effort	priceless	
excellence	privilege	

WORDS TO AVOID

crew	gang	obliged
crowd	gophers	peons
faceless	must	remiss
forget	nameless	

PHRASES TO USE

acknowledge the hard work and dedication of

always reliable

badly needed support

can't thank him/her enough

caring, compassionate contri-bution

dared to dream with us

example of what is best in this community/profession/industry

express our collective thanks

fortunate to have had the ser-vices of

generosity unbounded

guiding genius

helped make our dream come true

helped make this a reality

helped us help ourselves

helped us reach our goals

helped us realize our goals

inexhaustible generosity

inspired us all

invaluable contribution

made it all possible

my pleasure to thank

opened her heart and her checkbook

our good fortune to have worked with

patience of a saint

performed an admirable ser-vice

performed a priceless service

priceless contribution

proud to acknowledge

proud to thank

refused to accept limitations

share in this achievement

thank you for

thanks for

too numerous to mention

unstinting effort

unwavering support for us

went above and beyond the call of duty

what's-his-name

with deepest gratitude

without whom this would not have been possible

without whom we would have failed

SENTENCES TO USE

Debts are not usually very pleasant, but I am delighted to acknowledge all that I owe to Peter Haines, Benjamin Poston, and Sarah Smith.

Each of the wonderful people I am about to thank made an essential contribution to the success of our program.

I could not have done my job without the help of a lot of great people doing *their* jobs so well.

I would like to give you a glimpse into the world behind the scenes in order to acknowledge the many professionals who played indispensable roles in the successful completion of this project.

It is a pleasure to thank a team that gave us so much.

It is my pleasure to thank Fred Silverberg for his expert advice, which proved invaluable in completing this project on time and *under* budget.

Let me tell you a little bit about each of the extraordinary experts who have contributed to this enterprise.

Not only was I fortunate enough to have worked with the following people, I now get the great pleasure of thanking them.

One of the joys of a project such as this is working with so many fine people, then getting to dispense the thank you's at the successful completion of the job.

SAMPLE PARAGRAPHS

Note: In many thanking situations, a single paragraph is all that is required.

1   A project like this is the result of work by many hands, heads, and hearts. The following fine people gave unstintingly of all three: Fran Torpington contributed many extra hours each week to fund raising. Betty Bowler did what every administrative assistant secretly longs to do with her leisure time—she entered data into our contributor data-

base. Fred Molineux shared with us his expertise and fine eye to create great graphics. Paul Singleman took a busman's holiday from his prosperous ad agency to write dynamite fund-raising copy for us. And Ed Lalo performed the delicate job of running interference with the city authorities. You couldn't *pay* for a great team like this. In any case, *we* certainly couldn't pay for them. They contributed—free of charge—their time and energy and talent, for which we are tremendously grateful.

2   In a world of more perfect justice and stronger *sitzfleisch*, I would be able to thank each of you by name. But this enterprise has involved the combined talent of more than five hundred of you, so I must content myself with acknowledging the contribution of the R & D team, led by Paul Williams; the Division of Manufacturing Engineering, headed by Patricia Smithson; Marketing and Market Research, Bill Franks, director; and the Corporate Allocations Committee, chaired by Sara Beth Gallup.

3   You know, It's really not all that easy to thank your boss. People get the wrong idea, and a lot of ugly phrases involving the aftermost portions of the human anatomy come to mind. But, hard as it may be to believe, bosses sometimes really do deserve—earn—our thanks. Without the vision and support and confidence of Alice Nardine, there would be no such thing as the Inca Incubator. Yes, it is the product of the talent, work, and skills of many. But the initial push and the many nurturing shoves that followed originated at the top corporate level.

SAMPLE SPEECH

As project director, I must confess that I am sorely tempted to grab for myself and myself alone every last bit of credit for what has been accomplished here. After all, I'm only human.

The fact is, however, that nobody would ever believe that such a complex undertaking could have been the work of a single person. So I had better give credit where credit is due.

But I think you'll *still* have a hard time believing me. I've talked to people who assume that I worked with a staff of a dozen or more people. Actually, my team consisted of three—three very dedicated and multitalented individuals, the sum of whose efforts far exceeds what anyone has the right to expect from two *dozen* first-class researchers, engineers, and managers.

Henry Milton had charge of Phase I of the project, which included acquisition of rights and properties and the negotiation of long-term licenses. Henry goes after red tape like a bull after a red cape. But then—and it is a beautiful thing to watch—he cuts through it with the finesse and precision of a master surgeon.

Charlotte Gorham took us through Phases II and III, preliminary and final design. One can only stand in awe of an imagination like hers.

Then Karl Schmidt launched the final phase, fabrication. No firm has ever had a more efficient, dedicated, and resourceful engineer.

Those of you who have the pleasure and privilege of knowing Henry, Charlotte, and Karl are well aware that these are uncompromising individuals. What you don't know until you have worked closely with them for an extended period is how wonderfully they work together. I am very thankful to them individually and as a team. In every sense and on every level, they made this project a success.

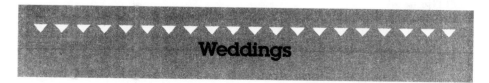

Weddings

Much speechmaking at weddings is confined to a few toasts, for which you should consult "Toasts" in Part Two of this book. However, nowadays, many couples feel that the ceremony prescribed by church or state is insufficiently personal, and they ask a good friend to "say a few words," usually at the reception. Sometimes this speaking assignment is actually a reading or recitation task. Your role may be to choose an inspirational text, usually a favorite poem, and read it. But what do you do when the bride or groom or both ask you to address friends and family with something more elaborate than a toast and more original than a quotation?

WHAT TO SAY

Prepare for the speech by thinking about the couple, about your relationship to them, about what they mean to you. Begin your remarks by establishing this relationship for your audience. Share past moments, an anecdote or two.

Talk about what the couple means to those assembled for the ceremony. They are good friends, loving family members, and so on.

Talk about what the newlyweds mean to one another; emphasize commitment and caring.

Express your good wishes for their future and your confidence that, in a world of flux and changing commitments, their love and loyalty will endure.

By all means, strike a lighthearted, joyous tone. Humor is fine, but see "What Not to Say," below.

Don't be afraid to strive for the inspirational.

Generally, be brief.

WHAT NOT TO SAY

Avoid preaching.

Avoid platitudes about the Institution of Marriage.

Avoid issuing advice.

Avoid pessimism, telling the couple that "marriage is hard work," that many marriages end in divorce, that wedded life requires patience and compromise, that raising a family entails great responsibility. All of this is true enough, but nobody needs to hear about it now.

This is a happy occasion, and humor is quite appropriate to your speech. However, avoid vulgarity, sexual innuendo, and anything else that might embarrass the couple. Nor should your humor verge on or cross the line into sarcasm. If you have bitter feelings about marriage, either keep them to yourself or politely decline the invitation to speak.

WORDS TO USE

bless	enrichment	lifetime
blessing	faith	love
care	faithful	loyalty
caring	family	mates
celebrate	friend	meaning
challenges	friends	meaningful
comfort	future	mutual
commitment	happiness	pledge
companionship	happy	prayer
comrade	harmonious	promise
confidence	harmony	rewarding
confident	help	share
cooperation	helping	support
covenant	honor	tolerance
discovery	journey	trust
ecstatic	joyous	union
enjoy	joy	years

WORDS TO AVOID

advice	fail	reality
argue	fight	work
cheat	infidelity	workaday
divorce	lesson	
dreary	poverty	

PHRASES TO USE

building a new family

celebrate the marriage of our
   two friends

cold, cruel world

commitment to one another

commitment to sustain their
   love and regard

confident of their future
   together

continue to build a relationship

demonstrate their love

embark on a great adventure

founded on trust

friends and lovers

gift of faith in one another

gift of love

gift of trust

grim reality

if two people ever deserved happiness together

lifetime together

look forward to a great life together

look forward to the coming years

offer our congratulations and best wishes

send them our best wishes for the present and future

share in their joy

sharing a lifetime together

testament to their love

they deserve one another

true to themselves and one another

union founded on caring

we wish them every happiness

willingness to accept the rewards and challenges alike

Sentences to Use

I have known Bill all of my life and Susan for less than a year, but I am thoroughly convinced that they are perfect for one another.

I know that there are at least two people here who are as happy as I am on this occasion.

I can't tell you how honored and pleased I am to say a few words on this very happy occasion.

If marriage is a great journey, these two are in for the ride of a lifetime.

It is a great thing to see two people you care about care about each other.

It is far more exciting to anticipate spending the future with someone you love than it is to march into it alone.

It is our job to celebrate with Mary and John and to send them on their way with our love and best wishes.

Jean and I have been like sisters, and now I feel as if my family is adding a brother.

Join me in celebrating the union of Ed and Mary and sending them off on their new life together with our prayers, hopes, and best wishes.

On behalf of all us married types, welcome to the club.

We are here to celebrate the union of two people we dearly love.

SAMPLE PARAGRAPHS

Note: Being asked to "say a few words" at a wedding may be taken literally; a single paragraph is often speech enough.

1   It makes me very happy that two of my best and dearest friends, Ed and Betty, have been united in marriage. The world is a better, brighter place for having in it the likes of these two. So much the better that they have chosen to live their lives together. Not the least of the benefits the world will derive from this union is the fact that I'll always have a place to go for a great meal. As most of you know, both Ed and Betty are gourmet cooks. For this—and other reasons—I ask that you join me in wishing Ed and Mary Smithson a long and happy life filled not only with great food and drink, but all the best things life has to offer.

2   Nobody can tell you how to live your lives. In any case, I don't think that's why you honored me by asking me to say a few words on this wonderful day. No, I won't tell you how to live your lives. I will just give voice to my wish that the future will make it easy for you to continue to love, honor, and cherish each other—just as you do now.

3   It's no wonder that so many folks get married in June, deep in the heart of a spring full of promise. My wish for you is that, through the more difficult and demanding seasons, you hold this first spring in your hearts and remember always the renewal it embodies. May each day of your lives together begin with a renewal of the vows you have made on this beautiful afternoon.

SAMPLE SPEECH

I had the rare privilege of being present when Jerry and Sandy first met. It was a double blind date. Now, let me tell you, *my* date and I hit it off great right from the start. But Jerry and Sandy—well, it was pretty lively. I can't hope to re-create the conversation, but I can, I think, reduce it to a kind of list.

Jerry ordered a French red wine. Sandy remarked that California reds seemed more interesting to her.

Jerry let it be known that his taste ran to jazz of the Pacific Coast "cool school." Sandy thought such music was "a little pretentious."

Jerry confessed he was a liberal. Sandy was a card-carrying Young Republican.

Jerry ordered something with tofu. Sandy had a blood-rare sirloin.

My date and I agreed on just about everything. Strange, though: That was our first and last date. Jerry and Sandy—well, we just bore witness to how far they have taken things.

I know that these two will remain individuals. Neither will change just to please the other. And neither would have it any other way. Sandy and Jerry have discovered in each other something that goes beyond the superficial level of this or that taste in drink, music, politics, or food. I believe they are a very rare and fortunate couple who have quickly discovered a core of absolute love and respect and compassion. It's like a precious nugget they share.

So what more can I add on this very happy day? Only my sincere wish that they never let anything come between them, that they always see, as they do now, beneath the surface, and that they always remember that however much they may differ on this or that, they share a deep love and an abiding commitment.

Jerry and Sandy, may the wind always be at your backs, and may God hold you in the hollow of his hand!

Welcomes

Speakers are often called on to welcome new staff members, volunteers, new club members, a new class of students, and so on. It doesn't take much effort to call to mind any number of dog-eared clichés about the importance of first impressions. But, like many clichés, these are well worn because they are true. First impressions *are* important indeed. How you welcome a group can affect a day or even a working lifetime. You have the opportunity to set a tone that will help a new group operate most effectively together, with you and with your organization.

WHAT TO SAY

Greet your audience warmly, making sure that you mention the full name of what you are welcoming them to. (You want to ensure that everyone in your audience is where they expected to be!)

Encourage your audience to make themselves at home, to get comfortable.

Convey your enthusiasm through your tone of voice and through an upbeat vocabulary.

If appropriate, tell you audience about your organization at this point. At least give them an overview.

Outline what's ahead in the program. Who will speak? What will be covered? What will be accomplished? What is expected of your listeners?

Encourage active, alert attention.

Ask your listeners to roll up their sleeves and plunge into the program.

Outline goals—for the day, for the year, for the organization as a whole.

Outline responsibilities, expectations, and benefits.

Underscore the key values of the organization.

What Not to Say

Avoid anything perfunctory.

Avoid anything downbeat. Don't mislead your audience into over-looking challenges that may await them, but put these in the most positive light possible. No one enjoys being welcomed to a wake.

Avoid threats and warnings.

Avoid telling your audience how they should or will feel. ("You will find this material technical and dull.")

Use a tone that is appropriate to your audience. If you are welcoming fellow professors to a symposium, better not greet them with "Howdy, folks."

Words to Use

absorbing	exciting	invitation
ahead	explore	invite
aid	fascinating	navigate
ask	foundation	orient
assist	fundamental	orientation
attention	fundamentals	participate
base	future	plan
challenging	glad	planned
comfortable	goals	pleased
cordial	grateful	program
delighted	groundwork	query
eager	group	question
effort	guide	questions
enjoy	happy	relax
establish	help	stimulating
excited	inquire	team

thrilled	variety	welcome
together	warm	

WORDS TO AVOID

crowd	formidable	thankless
crowded	grim	tired
difficult	hopeless	toil
dreary	impossible	wait
dull	jammed	warning
fail	task	chores
failure	tedious	

PHRASES TO USE

appreciate your close attention

chomping at the bit

dig right in

eager to get started

explore the many possibilities

find this enjoyable

get comfortable with

get in on the ground floor

get your bearings

get you started

give you a very warm welcome to

glad to see so many of you here

great-looking group

hope you'll find beneficial

in store for you

let me welcome you

look forward to what is to come

look forward to working with you all

make yourselves at home

no end to the potential

no time like the present

now you're part of the team

open attitude

point you in the right direction

positive attitude

rarin' to go

ready, willing, and able

remarkable opportunity

roll up our sleeves

select group

share this opportunity with
  you

spirit of teamwork

start at the beginning

thank you for coming

trust you will find rewarding

welcome aboard

welcome to our program

SENTENCES TO USE

I am happy to welcome you to the first session of the Associated Publishing Seminar.

I promise that you will not leave this initial meeting confused, but, if we are successful, you *will* leave it full of questions.

I am here to answer the one question I'm sure you all share: What's ahead?

I invite you to get comfortable, to keep your minds open, and to ask plenty of questions.

I invite you to roll up your sleeves and dig into the task at hand.

I am delighted to see so many of you here this morning.

I suggest that we devote this first session to getting better acquainted with one another.

It is my pleasure to welcome you aboard an organization I believe you will find consistently innovative and challenging.

Let's begin by outlining our goals and the process through which we will achieve them.

We have a great many choices to make, and I will begin by outlining them for you.

Welcome to the opening session of the Fat No More Weight Control Program.

Welcome to the first in a series of what I am confident you will find stimulating and rewarding sessions.

The business we transact here could very well change our lives.

You will encounter plenty of challenges in this program, but I promise that you will receive all the support you need to help you meet those challenges successfully.

SAMPLE PARAGRAPHS

1   Welcome to the first session our three-week seminar in writing more effective advertising copy. I am assuming that I understand your goal—to hone your copywriting skills and set yourselves on your way to becoming truly satisfied with every piece of copy you write. To reach this goal, we will write copy, we will analyze copy, and we will creatively criticize—and just as creatively praise—one another's copy. The only ground rules in all this will be to approach the work with enthusiasm and in the spirit of learning from one another. I will be doing a good deal of talking, at least at first, but I invite your comments and questions in profusion.

2   I am delighted to welcome you to the staff of Beltway Industries. The purpose of this morning's program is to acquaint you with the policies and procedures that, we believe, make Beltway a rewarding, pleasant, and productive place to work. In the course of the program, you will also be introduced to the heads of our major departments, who will tell you something about their responsibilities. In this way, we aim to give you a bird's-eye view of the company. All this is very important, of course, but the most important part of the program comes at the end, when you are invited to participate in an open question-and-answer session. At Beltway, we have no silent employees. We ask that you join the team *and* remain an individual who speaks his or her mind.

3   It is always a great pleasure to welcome a new group of members to the Castle Club. Of course, you are already thoroughly familiar with our programs, and you have met—many times—the principal officers. This evening, then, is just for fun. It is an opportunity for us to continue to get to know one another and to get a taste of one of the two things this organization is all about: friendship. I hope, too, that in the course of the evening you will find ample time to discuss your role in achieving our organization's other purpose, service to this community. I am looking forward to a meeting that I hope will open new horizons of fellowship and service for us all.

Sample Speech

The banner outside reads "Welcome Freshmen." I could simply repeat that message here—using a few more words, of course, if only to give the impression that I am earning my salary. But the problem is that the phrase "Welcome Freshmen" is utterly one-sided. Of course, your faculty, your fellow students, and I are very eager to welcome you.

But that is not enough.

We ask that you welcome us as well.

We are not so arrogant here at Horkum College to believe that the experience you are about to begin is some mechanical process, like developing photographic film, where *we* welcome *you*, induct *you*, and transform *you*. It is true that your faculty and fellow students have much to offer you. You *will* learn here, and we will do our best to facilitate your learning.

But, in reality, we don't teach you. You learn for yourselves, you learn from one another, you learn from us, *and* we learn from you. Therefore, I ask that, as we welcome you into this mutual learning experience, you welcome us. For you have not wandered into an educational processing plant, but have entered into an educational contract in which all of us must give and take as liberally as possible.

I hope that you will take the word "liberally" very much to heart. We don't have a lot of rules here. We believe that too many rules get in the way of learning. We do ask two things, however. We ask that you offer one another a very special courtesy—the courtesy of an open mind, a willingness to listen, and a willingness to discuss. We also ask that you engage *actively* in learning. Take nothing on faith. Accept nothing as true merely because one of the faculty members tells you it is true or because you read it in a textbook. Question everything. If a question does not immediately occur to you, work at thinking of one. Keep your eyes and ears open. Report what you see and hear.

Do you think you have nothing valuable to contribute?

Consider that education is not a search for truth, but a journey to gather truths. There are many truths, at least as many as there are human perspectives on so-called reality.

I remember reading a news story about a semi-rig that got stuck under a low-clearance viaduct. Emergency workers were called in. There was talk about using jackhammers to chisel out space under the viaduct. There was talk about dismantling the truck's trailer. There was a plan to use a crane or special jack to raise the viaduct. There was talk about hewing out grooves in the pavement under the truck's wheels.

At first, nobody paid much attention to one earnest young lad—he was eleven or twelve—who had another suggestion. After all, here was a man's job, a job for experts.

But the boy persisted, and what he suggested made so much sense that even these experts had to listen.

He told the men to let the air out of the truck's tires.

Fortunately for the truck company and the taxpayers, the boy's advice was heeded, and the truck, of course, was extricated.

Doubtless, most, if not all, of the plans offered that afternoon were "true" in that they would have gotten the truck out of its predicament. But the boy's perspective on the problem was the most useful truth in that particular situation. The story is amusing, but we should not laugh at the experts for failing to see what the boy saw. We should admire them for ultimately listening to the boy and for recognizing the usefulness of his truth, even though the source was neither expert nor, for that matter, fully grown.

We welcome you in this spirit. We recognize that you come to us in search of truths. We promise to offer what we can. But we also promise to look to you for what truths you offer. So let us welcome one another at the start of a great enterprise and adventure in learning together.

PART TWO

▼

▼

▼

Special Subjects

▼ ▼ ▼ ▼ ▼ ▼ ▼ ▼ ▼ ▼ ▼ ▼ ▼ ▼ ▼ ▼ ▼ ▼ ▼
Featured Speaker

Part One of this book covers a great many speaking situations, but it hardly hits every conceivable venue and kind of speech. After all, the range of human interest and endeavor is very wide, and the forums for public speaking plentiful. What happens when you are asked to give a speech on no particular occasion—it's not a sales meeting, not a holiday, and nobody died—and the choice of topic is left entirely up to you?

What do you do when you are the Featured Speaker?

The obvious answer is to begin by coming up with something to talk about.

There are two components in this process: you and your audience. If you are well known as an authority in a certain field, your choice of subject, at least in the broadest sense, is probably obvious. The same holds true if you believe passionately in some issue. However, if choosing your topic is not self-evident to you on the basis of knowledge or belief, try asking yourself this question: Why did they ask *me* to speak? What do they expect of me? The answer may well yield your topic. These questions will probably also lead you to the second component in the process of "invention" (as classical rhetoricians called the act of coming up with a topic): the audience. Who are they? Why are they interested in hearing me? What brings them to the meeting room, classroom, lecture hall, or auditorium? What interests do they have in common?

Those of us who grew up on television shows like *Leave It to Beaver* and *Father Knows Best*—and maybe even *The Brady Bunch*—are probably pretty familiar with the Junior Achievement program: You make a product, then try to sell it.

Well, that's not quite right. One of the valuable lessons JA taught was that, before you make a product, you had better learn everything you can about the available market for that product—the potential buyers. With the knowledge of your market firmly in mind, you go about creating the product and then selling it. Heed the lesson of Junior Achievement. Unless your knowledge, interests, and/or passionate convictions make the choice of topic a foregone conclusion, it is best to begin the process of "invention" by learning everything you can about your audience.

Does this mean that you are expected to read their minds?

In a sense, yes. But no telepathy is required. This kind of mind reading you do every day. "By their works you shall know them," the Good Book says. What people do for a living says a lot about what they're interested in. If you are asked to speak to an association of supermarket executives, for example, you won't talk about how to sell shoes. Nor—unless you are an expert on the subject—do you need to talk specifically about how to sell food. But you might instead speak about the ways in which supermarkets can build closer relationships with the communities they serve. You might take a softer approach and talk about what the corner grocery store once meant to a neighborhood (using your own childhood recollections as an illustration) and how, even though it's big and corporate, a supermarket can make itself a similar focal point for the community.

You don't have to engage in a lot of guesswork, either. By way of preparing for the speech, ask questions in order to learn everything you can about your audience. Begin by asking whomever it was who invited you to speak:

1. Who will be listening to my speech?

2. What will they expect?

3. What do they want to hear?

4. What interests do they share?

5. What do they care about?

6. What do they love?

7. What do they hate?

8. What are special topics of current concern?

9. What would you like me to talk about?

10. What would *you* talk about if you were asked to speak to this group?

11. Is the audience predominantly male or female? Young, old, or middle aged? Predominantly white, African American, Hispanic, ethnically mixed? Does any particular religion predominate among them? Are they white collar or blue? Democrat or Republican? Conservative or liberal?

Finally, why not come out and ask it—"Why did you invite *me* to speak?"

Now probe a little deeper: What does the audience know (or believe they know) about me? About the organization I represent? About my topic (if one has been chosen)?

Once you've learned all you can about your audience, turn back to yourself—and start talking. Not to your audience—not just yet—but to yourself. Open up a dialogue, a kind of self-interview.

I used to make my living as a non-fiction book editor. Part of my job was to "acquire" new books. The first step, usually, was to review the heaps of proposals that came in from hopeful authors and their even more hopeful agents. These proposals arrived in all shapes, sizes, and degrees of finish. The roughest—vaguest and least focused—I usually rejected out of hand. But not always. The proverbial diamond in the rough is not just a cliché turned myth. Sometimes you really do find one. But you've got to dig for it.

When I came across such a proposal, I'd try to get the author to come in for a conference. I'd begin by telling him or her what I liked and did not like about the proposal. Then I would ask a question: "What do you want to achieve with this book?" It is a very hard question, but as basic as a foundation is basic to any building.

Some initial answers were quite direct and honest, if superficial: "I want to make money." "I've always wanted to write." "I want people to admire me."

These are not *wrong* answers. They are *personal* answers; that is, they define (however vaguely) what the author wishes to achieve personally. So I'd go on to the next question: "How do you propose to get people to buy your book?" Or, "How will you get your reader to admire what you've done?"

The authors who had a prospect of panning out finally got down to a response something like: "I will give my readers something they want—even if they never realized they wanted it." "I'll teach my readers something they'll find valuable." "I'll make this the most entertaining read anyone has ever had."

Now we were progressing from *personal* goals—what the author wanted the book to do for himself—to *communication* goals: what the book will do for the reader. This gave us the *what*. Next, we had to consider the *how*. How would the author reach these goals? "I'm going to write the best photography how-to ever."

Fine, but how will you go about it?

"I'm going to target a certain audience. Not the would-be professional. Not even the dedicated amateur. I'm going to concentrate on how to photograph your kids. But the book won't just consist of advice. I'll put in interactive exercises—make it very practical and very 'hands-on.'"

Soon, if the budding author had any real potential, he was conducting the dialogue entirely with himself, posing questions and then answering them. In this way, he arrived at the subject of his book and his approach to it.

Conducting a similar self-dialogue is a very useful way of defining the subject and approach to your speech. Jeff Scott Cook, in *The Elements of Speechwriting and Public Speaking* (Collier, 1989), defines what he calls "the five kinds of speeches commonly recognized by veteran speech makers." Some speeches (Cook points out) are intended *to stimulate*; some *to inform*; some *to persuade*; others *to activate*; and still others *to entertain*. Of course, any single speech may combine more than one of these elements, but a good way to begin to define the goals of your speech is to ask yourself what the *primary* purpose of your speech is.

Do you want primarily to stimulate certain emotions? Sympathy for the underprivileged? Patriotism on a national holiday? Outrage at an injustice? Pride in your company during a difficult and demanding period?

Do you want—again, primarily—to inform? This is the most common kind of speech. You are in possession of a certain body of (presumably useful) knowledge, which you want to impart to your audience. You are a frequent business traveler and have learned valuable secrets of traveling efficiently and securely. Or you have just managed the installation of your company's computer network and have discovered all the pitfalls as well as the shortcuts from firsthand experience. Or you have just taken your small business public and are now addressing a gathering of entrepreneurs with similar ambitions.

Do you want primarily to persuade? This is probably the second-most common type of speech. Persuasion is not to be confused with the bullying, soft-soaping, or silver-tongued oratory of the nineteenth-century politician. The task of the persuasive speechmaker of today is to recognize a need, articulate it, and demonstrate that need to others. State your point of view directly and back it up concretely.

> Can I have a show of hands of all those in favor of generating as much unnecessary paperwork as possible?
>
> Don't be shy. There must be plenty of you out there who are enthusiastic about generating paper. Last year, you see, American business used 775 billion pages of paper. That's enough to make a stack 48,900 miles high.

We love paper. In fact, we're crazy about paper. *Crazy.*

Now, don't you think it's time the madness stopped?

Do you want primarily to activate? Perhaps you want to go beyond stimulating, informing, and persuading in order to move your audience directly to action. This type of speech is appropriate when you know precisely what you want your audience to do. Let's say your community has experienced a dramatic upsurge in drug use among teenagers. If you are speaking to a community group, you may be in a position to *stimulate* emotions about this crisis, thereby bringing it to the attention of your audience. Or you may want to *inform* your audience about the nature and extent of the problem, using information provided by the police, social workers, teachers, and the children themselves. Perhaps you want to give a speech to *persuade* your audience—all too prone to deny the problem—that a drug crisis indeed exists and that something should be done about it. All of these are legitimate approaches to the subject.

But what if you are prepared to offer a *solution* to the drug problem in your community? In this case, your speech should activate your audience to do whatever needs to be done.

> Of course, we can *talk* endlessly about what a great thing it would be to build a youth community center in this town. Or we can *do* something. We can raise the necessary funds through the following means:
>
> First: . . .
>
> Second: . . .
>
> Third: . . .

Do you want primarily *to entertain*? If so, you've chosen the most difficult kind of speech to write and to deliver. Usually, such speeches are humorous—or, at least, are supposed to be. Stand-up comedy is a high-risk business, as attested to by the vocabulary of comics. It's either "I *killed* the audience" or "I *bombed*" and "I *died*." No book can tell you how to be entertaining, let alone funny. A humorous speech is not just one joke after another, any more than a great symphony is one tune after another. It is a structured, carefully modulated, skillfully told narrative that builds to one humorous climax after another. If you can tell a good story well, you have a shot at making a good *entertaining* speech. If not, stick to the other types of speeches.

While it is essential that you decide what you want to accomplish with your speech, there is no hard-and-fast rule that says you must make this decision before or after you decide on your topic. Whether you determine your overall goal first, followed by your topic, or whether you hit on your topic, then decide on your approach to it, you should be careful to choose a topic appropriate to the occasion and appropriate to yourself.

As suggested earlier, ask questions before you accept the invitation to speak. Learn as much as you can about your audience and what they will expect from you. Not only should the topic you choose be appropriate for this audience, it should suit *you*. This means, first of all, that you should command sufficient knowledge and authority to speak on the topic. Ideally, it should be something you really care about. Passion is hard to fake, but genuine passion about a subject is infectious and helps immeasurably in "selling" the speech to your audience.

Let's face it: The suggestions in the previous paragraph are pretty self-evident. Less obvious is the drawback of speaking on a subject with which you may be *too* familiar. *You* may be tired of it, and, if you are, your audience is bound to fall under the spell of your somnolence. Yawn in a roomful of people, and, before you know it, you have a roomful of yawners. The same principle applies to delivering a speech on a topic you're tired of.

Combat this by deliberately choosing a subject you may not be quite so thoroughly familiar with. Or go out of your way to find a fresh approach to what is (at least as far as you are concerned) a tired topic. Let's go back to the teenage drug-use problem in your community. Unfortunately, your audience is probably numb from listening to anti-drug pronouncements. What would happen if you gave a speech telling your audience how to *ignore* the drug crisis in your community (after all, it will never affect *their* family)?

Finally, remember that even the featured speaker is featured for a limited amount of time. Of course, there is no absolute and universal time limit for a speech, but a good rule of thumb is to limit yourself—as a featured speaker—to about twenty minutes. This means that you should choose a topic and an approach to it that can be handled adequately within that span of time. In general, remember that a speech is *not* the appropriate medium for an exhaustive treatment of a subject. If you were writing a marketing textbook, you might list fifty *specific* points concerning consumer-research techniques. In a speech about how the independent entrepreneur can make effective use of market-survey techniques, you might outline at most four or five *broad* principles.

Children's Groups

The idea of making a speech to a bunch of squirmy kids is, for a fact, appalling. So don't try it.

Don't make a *speech* to them. *Talk* to them. And don't just talk to them, put on a show—or, more precisely, a show and tell.

Actually, any good talk, whether delivered to an audience of adults or of children, contains plenty to touch, see, smell, and hear. In speaking to adults, it is an effective strategy to employ language rich in verbs and nouns that denote real actions and real objects. *Dull:* "Imagine what it would be like to have a lot of money." *Effective:* "Picture yourself in a tropical garden, bathed in sunlight and the fragrance of gardenias, listening to the call of exotic birds, and free from the tyranny of an alarm clock, traffic on the Interborough, your windowless office with the buzzing fluorescent light, and the heavy breathing of a boss who hasn't brushed his teeth in years."

This approach is good for talking to children as well, but you need to do even more. Don't just use words to evoke sights, smells, and sounds. Whenever you can, use the actual objects themselves.

If you are a physician, bring your stethoscope. If you work with computers, better bring one along with an appropriate demonstration program. Let's say you are a firefighter or an insurance broker, and your topic is fire prevention. Bring a charred and melted toy to show what happens if you don't use the other prop you've brought with you: a smoke detector.

Show and tell.

This means, of course, that you should choose a topic that lends itself to the use of such simple props. In fact, this is a good way to test the appropriateness of your topic. If you cannot find props to suit your topic, it is almost certainly inappropriate for children under the age of ten. Find another topic.

In addition to props, use simple language, but do not patronize your audience. If you keep your talk as concrete as possible and explain any difficult words, you won't have to resort to gross simplifications or, worse, lame phrases such as "This may be hard for you to understand" or "You'll understand when you get older." You should also exercise caution in using the language of the children themselves. It is risky to make liberal use of slang in any speech. If you use vocabulary exclusively associated with children, you will almost certainly sound ridiculous or, at best, patronizing. Restrict your use of slang to terms that have entered the general vocabulary. "No, it is *not* true that only nerds obey traffic regulations when they cross the street." But be sparing even with such common terms as *nerd*. Don't be afraid to serve as a role model—that, after all is what adults are supposed to be—and this applies to the example you set by the language you use. Standard English, very lightly peppered with appropriate slang or simply taken straight, is fine.

While it is good to interact with your audience, it is patronizing *and* tedious to ask a lot of rhetorical questions. You're that insurance broker, and you hold up a smoke detector. You have a choice. You can ask, "Can anyone tell me what this is?" Or you can talk about *what* a smoke detector does, *how* (in basic terms) it works, and *why* it is important. Most adults speaking to a group of children will tend to ask the rhetorical question. But think about it first. Today, most children know what a smoke detector is. If you ask them what it is, they will either assume that you are awfully stupid yourself or that you are playing dumb—that is, patronizing them. If you don't want to cut to the chase and start talking about smoke detectors directly, why not start by asking for a show of hands of the kids whose homes have smoke detectors. Then ask for a show of hands of those whose homes contain *working* smoke detectors with fresh batteries. These are legitimate questions. They are still easy enough to answer, but they mean something and naturally lead into the main part of the talk.

Now, having said this, I don't want to overlook the importance of questions. Leave plenty of time for them—not for *your* questions, but for the kids'.

As in any good speech, speak slowly and clearly. But—especially if you are a man—don't boom and bellow at your audience. This will intimidate them. Speak loudly enough to be heard, but speak gently, make eye contact, and smile. And don't sugarcoat your voice unnaturally. To hold your listeners' attention, try speaking with *less* or even *decreasing* volume. This tends to draw your young listeners in and naturally quiets them down. Try this technique if you sense restlessness among the youngsters.

What happens if things get too rowdy? Do not try to speak above the din. Stop speaking. That alone may serve to quiet your audience down. If this fails, tell the children that it is now your turn to talk and that they will have their turn—a chance to speak and ask questions—in just a few minutes. Finally, restlessness may well indicate that it is simply time to wrap the speech up. Do so.

Many supposedly knowledgeable folks will tell you that, in speaking to kids, you cannot hope to compete with television. In fact, television cannot hope to compete with *you*, a live speaker. It is true that you don't have a cast of characters—live and animated—at your command. You don't have elaborate sound effects. You don't have stunt men and women. You don't even have fuzzy puppets.

What you *do* have is your approachable humanity, live and in person. Don't stand behind a desk or a lectern. If at all possible, arrange your listeners in a circle with you as part of it, not in the center, but, like everyone else, on the circumference. If you must speak in a more rigid classroom situation—where the chairs and desks are arranged in rows or even bolted to the floor—try walking around the room and among the children as you speak. Always begin by telling your audience your name and letting them know—directly—the subject of your talk.

SAMPLE SPEECH

My name is Mr. Johnson, and I'm here to talk to you about recycling.

How many of you sleep in a bed? Can I see a show of hands?

Good.

Now how many of you would *like* to sleep on a heap of garbage?

I don't see any hands.

Look, I've brought along a bucket of garbage [show garbage]. This happens to be pretty clean garbage. It doesn't smell too bad. They wouldn't let me come here to talk to you if I were carrying a mess of really smelly garbage. But it looks nice and dirty and disgusting anyway. Are you *sure* you don't want to live on top of it, sleep on it, eat on it?

Of course not. Nobody does.

But in our country there are more than 250 million men, women, girls, and boys. Every year, each of us throws away six tons of garbage. Your family's car is very heavy. It weighs about two tons. So that means that if you saved all the garbage you threw away for a whole year, put it in a pile, then weighed it, it would be as heavy as *three* cars!

Your teacher says that you're real wizards at math. What happens if we multiply six by 250 million? We get a *very* big number: one billion, five hundred million. Each year, in our country, we throw away one billion, five hundred million tons of garbage!

All that garbage! Where do we put it?

We bury some of it. We burn some of it. We take some of it and dump it into the ocean.

But even though the earth is very big, we'll run out of room before too long. So now, all over our country and all over our world, we're trying something new. We are recycling garbage instead of throwing it away.

Recycling means reusing. Old paper can be thrown away, piled up, and wasted. Or it can be turned into new paper. Used plastic bottles can be tossed out or they can be made into new plastic bottles. Aluminum cans can be heaped into big, ugly metal mountains, or they can be turned into new aluminum cans.

Not only does recycling help keep us from being buried in our own garbage, it makes sure that we'll all have plenty of the paper, the plastic, the aluminum, and the other things we need.

But recycling doesn't just happen all by itself.

I'm going to ask for volunteers. Raise your hand if you would like the job of sorting through one billion, five hundred million tons of garbage in order to separate the paper, the glass bottles, the plastic bottles, and the aluminum cans into nice neat piles.

No volunteers?

Well, I don't blame you. It would be an impossible job.

But what if, each and every day at home, you put your glass bottles in one bin, your old newspapers in another, plastic in another, and aluminum cans in another? If everyone did this, a whole lot of that one billion, five hundred million tons of garbage would end up completely sorted and could be sent to the proper factory for recycling instead of being thrown away and wasted.

How hard is it to do?

I'm going to so something fun right now. I'm going to take this can of garbage I've brought with me, and I'm going to dump it out—right here in the middle of your classroom! Here goes. [Dump garbage can.]

Now here are bins labeled GLASS, PLASTIC, ALUMINUM, and PAPER. Come on up here and let's see how fast you can sort this big pile into the bins. I'll time you with this stopwatch.

Go!

[Children sort trash.]

Eighty-six seconds flat! You've done a great job! Now you don't have to go home and sleep on top of a pile of garbage!

You know, it's even easier to sort your garbage if you and your parents do it every day. Don't toss that empty glass bottle in the trash can. Put it in the GLASS recycling bin. The plastic bottle? First crush it, to save space, then put it in the PLASTIC bin. Help mom and dad tie up their newspapers into bundles. Have a soda, rinse out the can, and then put it in the ALUMINUM bin. Someday, it will be another can—or maybe part of a car.

Remember, nobody wants to live on top of a world that's a heap of garbage. And, if we all recycle, nobody will have to.

You have been great listeners—and recyclers! Thank you for letting me talk with you.

Now, would any of you like to ask me any questions?

The Impromptu Speech

I've heard teachers call it the Teacher's Nightmare and actors call it the Actor's Nightmare. You find yourself in front of a classroom in the middle of a course on astrophysics. The trouble is that you know nothing about astrophysics because you're an English teacher. Or you're onstage playing Hamlet. The trouble is, you've never studied the part.

Those are dreams. Nightmares.

Then there is this scenario: You're at a product-development meeting and the subject of widget marketing comes up. The division vice president looks at you.

"How would you approach retailing this widget?"

You've been concentrating on framisses and have barely given widgets a passing thought. If you had a day, you could come up with something convincing. But what you have is a matter of seconds. The really bad news is *this is no dream.*

The truth is that if you occupy a position of any authority or even limited public visibility, you will probably be called on to make an impromptu speech from time to time.

What can you do about it?

The first step is to minimize the "impromptu" element of the impromptu speech. It is perfectly true that you might go into a meeting, expecting to be nothing more than a listener, only to be asked to make some remarks. But you need not be taken completely by surprise. Being asked to make a speech is not a wholly random event, like getting mugged on the street or struck by lightning. If you are about to attend a PTA meeting and have spoken up in the past concerning the cost and content of school lunches, you should prepare in advance to say something on this or a related subject. Jot down three or four major points—perhaps a relevant statistic or two as well—on a 3" × 5" card, just in case.

Before any public appearance or participation in any meeting or forum, think carefully: Is there any possibility that I may be called on to speak? If the answer is yes, find out everything you can about the meeting or event:

- ▼ *Who* will be attending?
- ▼ *What* will be on the agenda?
- ▼ Who is *scheduled* to speak?
- ▼ What *issues* are likely to come up?
- ▼ What areas of *controversy* are likely to emerge?
- ▼ What do I *know* that is relevant to any of the above?
- ▼ What do I know that *nobody* else present is likely to know?

Jot down the answers to these questions. Then list some appropriate topics, together with one or two remarks about each. A cold, hard fact—an impressive statistic or two—goes a long way toward gaining credibility for you in an impromptu speech.

Is it possible to be overprepared? Strange as it may seem, the answer is yes. Don't try literally to memorize an impromptu speech. Your response will seem "canned," like the feigned expression of astonishment uttered by one who has walked into a surprise party he knew all about weeks ago.

Even if your response is a thoughtful one, your audience will tend to equate its canned quality with a *thoughtless* "stock" answer. It's like anticipating a home-cooked meal and instead being fed out of a plastic tray hot from the microwave. Political candidates in particular are compelled to tread a very narrow line between being so spontaneous as to appear unprepared on the one hand, and being so thoroughly prepared as to appear programmed on the other.

Undesirable as it is to sound as if you're flying on automatic pilot, by far the worse alternative is to flounder in total unpreparedness. Go into the meeting or event adequately—not overly—prepared. Then, if you are asked to speak, react:

▼ There is a saying among Chicago drivers that the briefest span of time measurable by humankind is the interval between the appearance of the green traffic signal at any intersection and the blast of the first car horn behind you. An immediate response may be required on the streets of Chicago, but the same is not true when you are suddenly asked to say a few words. Take a few seconds to collect your thoughts before you step on the gas. You may think that your audience will be satisfied with nothing less than an immediate response, but, in fact, they are just as likely to distrust a "quick answer" as a glib shot from the hip. Take those few seconds in thoughtful silence. Do not fill them with such unintelligible sounds as a protracted *ummmmmmmmmmmmm-mm, duhhhhhhhhhhh,* or *hisssssssssss.*

▼ Need even more time? Stall, but stall creatively. You can begin with a very general statement, the equivalent of the "topic sentence" your high school English teacher drummed into your head. "A good school lunch program is vital to the well-being of our children. It is, in fact, a very important part of the school day." Alternatively, repeat and rephrase the question you've been asked. "You want me to list some ways in which we can improve the school lunch program?" The creative aspect of these stalling tactics is genuinely creative.

Astronomers know that when you want to look at a faint and distant star with the naked eye, it is best to glimpse it with your peripheral vision rather than try to see it straight on. Peripheral vision is less sharp than center vision, but it is much more sensitive to faint light. Analogously, creative stalling allows you to look away from your topic for a moment in order to glimpse those faintly forming ideas and bring them into sharper focus. It is also helpful just to begin *talking,* to get over the blank inertia that tends, for a frightening moment, immediately to follow a question or a request that you "say a few words." Finally, making a general statement or repeating a question serves to focus your audience's attention and to help ensure that they understand what you are responding to.

▼ Seize a topic, then don't let it go. Once you've hooked an idea, play it out. Thinking on your feet will tempt you to stray to other topics. Resist the temptation.

▼ Keep it simple. There may, in fact, be a lot to say on a given subject, but don't try to say it all. Make two to four clear points, then stop.

▼ Even if your "speech" consists of a brief answer to a specific question, direct your response to the entire audience, not just the questioner. Play the entire house.

▼ Just as you should attempt to begin decisively, try to come to a solid conclusion. Once having reached your conclusion, stop.

▼ Partake of the milk of human kindness. Unless you are selling yourself to the crowd as a political candidate, audiences tend to be very forgiving of an impromptu speaker. They do not expect the Gettysburg Address. However, beware of coaxing your audience into undervaluing what you do have to offer. If you are apologetic or self-denigrating, you are, in effect, telling your listeners to disregard or at least discount what you are about to say. "Gosh, I really haven't thought much about this, but . . . here goes nothing!" An audience would be foolish to take seriously anything that followed a foot-scraping statement like this. The bottom line: Don't apologize. Your listeners realize that you are speaking off the cuff, and they have unconsciously adjusted their expectations accordingly. Nothing is needed to prompt additional readjustment.

▼ As your flight attendant says, *please familiarize yourself with the location of the emergency exits.* If you are thoroughly stuck, reply with: "I don't know. I'll do some research on the topic and get back to you with what I find." Or: "A responsible answer to that requires more thought than I've given it at this point. Let me get back to you on it." Or: "I don't have a ready-made answer for that one. Let me reflect on it, research it, and get back to you."

SAMPLE SPEECH

Question:

"You've had experience with off-the-shelf software versus custom programming. Can you talk to us about the benefits of one over the other?"

Impromptu speech:

Let's compare off-the-shelf software to custom-developed software. First, the features of off-the-shelf software.

Off-the-shelf software is always going to be less expensive than custom-developed software, at least in a company such as ours, where we need to purchase licenses for approximately ten PCs. The best commercial programs are also well-documented, well-tested, and, in varying degrees, adequately supported. You have an "800" number to call if you need assistance—although that line is sometimes very busy.

Custom programming is like a tailor-made suit. It will fit us precisely to our specifications. We won't have to make any compromises. Of course, it is also more expensive—by about a factor of ten. The fee, however, should include unlimited support, including the services of the developer, who will come out to us and personally iron out any problems.

Ordinarily, the sad fact is that the more money you can afford to throw at a problem, the better the solution you can come up with. In this case, however, I don't believe that the extra expense of a custom-developed accounting program is justified. A tailor-made suit is nice, but if you happen to be a perfect size 40 regular, why not buy off the rack? Our operation is not particularly unusual, let alone unique.

Therefore, mainstream commercial software off the shelf should be quite adequate for us. My principal caution is that we be certain to invest a little extra in going with a product that will guarantee superb and timely over-the-phone customer support.

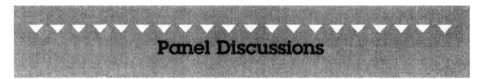

Panel Discussions

Your role in a panel discussion may be either as the moderator or as a panelist.

The moderator's role is governed by a few simple-sounding rules, but the job is a demanding one that calls for a combination of judgment and firmness tempered by courtesy. It also requires many of the same qualities found in any good host, including concern for the comfort of the panel and the audience.

The moderator should prepare the panel discussion by ensuring that the room is comfortable, well-lighted, and well-ventilated. She should be certain that the audience as well as the panelists are provided with adequate seating. As to the panelists, they should be supplied either with large name tags or bold place cards at the conference table. Each panelist should be supplied with a glass of water. Do not seat the panelists more than a few minutes before the discussion begins. They should have a moment or two to collect themselves, arrange notes, take a drink of water, but they should not be given the opportunity to settle in, slouch, or fidget. Start out fresh.

Don't insult your panelists by giving them gratuitous advice concerning public speaking; however, you might suggest to them that they relax and enjoy the session by thinking of it not as a debate, but as a spirited conversation among colleagues. "I hope that you will think of this event as a kind of conversation among yourselves—but one that we are giving the audience an opportunity to eavesdrop on."

In most panel discussions, time is particularly important. Often, participants are assigned to speak in a given order and each is permitted a certain amount of time to speak as well as an additional span for rebuttal. Make certain that any ground rules are clearly understood by the participants before you begin. It is especially important that panelists have an adequate view of an accurate clock and that you establish a discreet way of signaling each speaker when his time is about to elapse. A small index-size cue-card is appropriate; hold it up as a thirty-second warning.

Since time is of the essence in panel discussions, set a good example by beginning the discussion precisely on schedule.

In the presence of the audience, your first act should be to introduce yourself in the context of the discussion. "Good evening. I'm Sarah Sertin, vice president of Veeble Enterprises, and it is my pleasure to moderate our panel discussion entitled 'The Commission Broker: Whose Side Are We On, Anyway?'" Go on to say a word or two about why you are serving as moderator, then define the purpose of the discussion. What do you want your audience to leave with?

Next, introduce the panelists. Begin by characterizing the group as a whole. What qualifies them? How are they distinguished? Why should we listen to them? What *range* of opinion do they represent? (Note: If you are responsible for choosing panelists, ensure that they are indeed qualified, will impress your audience as credible, and that they represent a legitimate range of opinion.) After characterizing the group, introduce the individuals by name, giving affiliations and qualifications (see "Introductions" in Part One of this book). Try to use each panelist's name two or three times in the course of your introduction.

Before the discussion began, you ensured that the panelists understood the session's ground rules. Now explain those identical ground rules to your audience, specifying speaking order, time allotments, rules for rebuttal, and provisions for audience questions.

Ideally, the moment has now come for you to turn the event over to the panelists, who will conduct their "spirited conversation" in the assigned speaking order, each holding religiously to her allotted time. Each will speak clearly, and all will understand one another perfectly.

Sure.

More likely, you will be called upon to enforce the panelists' time limits. Many moderators find this difficult, but you must be firm—in fairness to the other panelists and to the audience, who has a right to hear all points of view. Use your 30-second warning card. If this fails to elicit a wrap-up from the speaker, then, at about the ten- or fifteen-second mark, pipe in: "Mr. Johnson, you have fifteen seconds." *Precisely* at the moment a speaker's time expires, thank him, but tell him that his time is up. It is not necessary for you to apologize ("I'm sorry, but your time is up"); after all, the speakers were advised of the ground rules, and they agreed to them.

You may also think of your role, in part, as similar to that of a Greek chorus in a classical tragedy: that is, as a kind of stand-in or spokesperson for the perceived point of view of the audience. If something a panelist says is grossly unclear to you, you must assume that it will be similarly obscure to your audience. Judiciously ask for a clarification: "Ms. Gerhardt, I'm not sure I follow you. Are you saying that . . . ?" But be careful not to disrupt the speaker's train of thought or to usurp her precious time.

As you began the session, so it is your job to bring it to a conclusion. Do so on time. If there is to be a question-and-answer period, make the transition to it by thanking the panelists for their presentations, then invite questions. Do your utmost to call on as many people in as many parts of the room as possible. As you near the end of the allotted time, point out that only a few minutes remain. In a question-and-answer format, it is always advisable to avoid locking yourself into a potentially disappointing finale by saying something like, "We have time for one last question." If that question turns out to be a dud, you've forced yourself to end the entire program on a flat note. As you near the end of the question-and-answer period, say something like, "Our time is almost up." If the subsequent question and answer will end the session on a high note, call it quits with, "Our time is up." If the question or answer misfires, take another.

At the end of the entire program, thank the speakers (for a second time, if you have already thanked them in making the transition to the question-and-answer period) and make some statement of finality that does not, however, tell your audience what to think. "I want to thank the speakers once again as well as the audience for their most challenging questions. I trust that, like me, you have found this discussion stimulating, exciting, and useful."

If you are a panelist, prepare as you would for any important speech, paying particular attention, however, to the time limits imposed. If the format allows, this means that you should write out your opening remarks, keeping in mind that the style of a panel presentation is more conversational than oratorical. Remember, you will be *sitting* with other panelists rather than *standing* alone at a podium.

Perhaps more difficult than composing your opening remarks is the task of anticipating the additional issues, controversies, and questions that may be raised in the course of the discussion. It is important that you do try to anticipate these and jot them down, together with possible responses to rebuttals that are likely to be directed against you.

Assert yourself in the matter of the order of speakers. If you have a preference, state it. Generally, it is best to go first and least desirable to be last up—especially if the program runs long. Even if you really have no particular preference, it is a good idea to voice one anyway. This will give the moderator the message that you are thoughtful and anything but passive. Of course, your request should be framed within the confines of courtesy. It does not pay to alienate the moderator by coming on like gangbusters with a string of ultimatums.

One final word regarding preparation: Do not assume that your moderator is experienced (or has even read a book like this one!). Not everyone takes the assignment seriously, and many moderators go into the task with the intention of winging it and hoping for the best. Of course, as a panelist, you are in no position to take over the moderator's duties, should he fail to discharge them adequately. But you can and should assert yourself, if necessary. First, make sure the moderator knows how to pronounce your name. If he mispronounces it (or fails to introduce you at all), begin your opening remarks by *re*introducing yourself, starting out with something like, "Good afternoon. I'm Walter von der Vogelweide." Just as it is your responsibility to provide the moderator with the proper pronunciation of your name, it is also up to you to furnish, at minimum, a condensed resume or curriculum vitae listing your credentials; better yet, write out a very brief, ready-to-read introduction. If, despite these measures, the moderator gives short shrift (or no shrift) to your background and credentials or has committed a significant error concerning them, make up the deficiency in your opening remarks.

The area in which the moderator is most likely to falter is in enforcing the time limits agreed upon. If a panelist significantly or repeatedly exceeds his time limit, and the moderator does nothing about it, don't sit passively by and take the abuse. Slip the moderator a note. If that fails, slip the longwinded panelist a note. If neither of these expedients prevails, speak up. Avoid anger, and direct the appeal away from yourself. Don't say, "You're cutting in on my time" or "You're being unfair to me." Instead, refer to the schedule and the best interests of the audience: "Pardon me, but we are running seriously overtime. In consideration of our audience, can we try to get back on schedule?"

The most dispiriting and deflating panel experience is to be caught on the tail end of a badly run program that has gone overtime. Unfair though it is, you may be allowed in this circumstance less time than was agreed upon. Even if the moderator is willing to permit you your full time, *you* may want to give a shortened version of your presentation if you sense that the program has dragged on so long that the audience is restless. To be sure, in either case, you will feel offended and cheated. That's because you *have been* offended and cheated. But take the opportunity to turn this unhappy situation to your advantage. Don't cast blame on anyone, but do let your audience know that, out of consideration for them, you will make your remarks briefer than you had planned. Tempering the announcement with a touch of humor will also earn points with a weary audience: "In the interest of getting you all back to the loved ones you left anxiously waiting at home, I'll make my remarks more mercifully brief than I had originally intended."

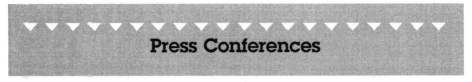

Press Conferences

It is well beyond the scope of this book to detail the ins and outs of setting up and running a press conference. Indeed, no book can tell you in very specific terms how to deal with the media. Media practices and contact persons vary from place to place. If you need to call a major press conference, you should secure the services of an experienced press relations consultant who knows the local media very well and has a full list of solid contacts. If you were hiring a sales rep to vend a new product in, say, the Southeast, you wouldn't seek out a rookie from Seattle. You would look to employ a veteran salesperson who is on intimate terms with the territory in question, a person who knows the accounts, who knows the folks to call on, and who has a proven track record with those accounts. The same holds true for setting up a significant press event. Call on someone who knows the territory, who can summon the media people with the clout you need. If you don't, at the very least you run the grave risk of throwing a party that hardly anyone will attend. The worst disaster that can befall a press conference is an empty room. Correction: The *worst* disaster is an *almost* empty room. If you've managed to snag one or two reporters, they may well dutifully report to their readers or listeners that your press conference was greeted with thunderous indifference.

Most of us are naive enough to believe that news personnel simply go out and find news. Well, sometimes they do just that. More often, however, news is "sold" to them by a good media relations person who successfully convinces those who have the public's eye and ear that your "product"—what you offer at your press conference—is worth retailing to their audience.

Having duly issued this very necessary warning, let's get on with the chapter.

For all its potential complexities and pitfalls, the actual press conference is structurally quite simple. It usually begins with a brief speech—the "statement"—that in all essential points duplicates a written press release distributed to the audience. (Note: If you distribute the release too far in advance of the conference, you run the risk of discouraging attendance—unless the subject of the conference is so manifestly newsworthy and potentially controversial that the advance statement entices reporters to attend in order to ask questions.) Following the statement comes a question-and-answer period.

We have all heard about the "ten-second sound bite." What this means to you is that your twenty-minute press conference, if it receives any air play at all, will be distilled to a ten-second snippet. Even in the print media, what you say will be subjected to drastic truncation. If the media will take at most only a bite of the banquet you offer up, better serve that banquet in bite-size pieces. Make your statement clear, direct, and unambiguous. Lace it with self-contained sentences that can stand on their own and that cry out to be quoted. (Professional speech writers call these "focus statements.") Be aware that you *will* be quoted out of context, so avoid any ambiguous statements that, out of context, will have you saying something you never intended.

With work and careful attention to detail, you can adequately control the statement portion of the press conference. The question-and-answer session presents more risks but also, potentially, greater rewards—an opportunity for genuine communication.

If the press conference is your show, you should establish some ground rules for the questions. This can be a delicate matter, since you do not want to appear to be dictating to the press. However, you can make it clear from the outset that the conference will be restricted to such-and-such a subject area and that you will entertain questions relating to that subject area exclusively.

Depending on your personality, position, and the subject of your press conference, handling questions can be an exhilarating challenge or an intimidating ordeal. There are steps you can take to maintain at least a modicum of control.

1. Prepare. Anticipate likely questions and be ready with solid answers.

2. Listen to the question. This may seem too obvious even to mention, but it is actually all too easy to concentrate so intensely on your own anxiety that you block out the question. Listen.

3. While listening, avoid reacting. Don't telegraph your answer or display your feelings through grins, nods, frowns, or grimaces. Keep your eyes fixed on the questioner, but remain impassive until you actually give your response.

4. Be conscious of your body language. Not only should you avoid reacting to a question while it is being asked, you should also beware of fidgeting with your clothing, the microphone cord, a stray pencil, what have you. Avoid folding your arms across your chest, which tends to signal resistance and closed-mindedness. Avoid placing your hands on your hips, which conveys defiance. Avoid covering your mouth, which not only suggests evasion and a sense of shame, but makes you difficult to understand. Avoid bringing your hand to your forehead or other parts of your face, which conveys evasion. Avoid biting your lip, which suggests anxiety. While you should strive to look emotionally neutral while listening to a question, do not hesitate to use positive gestures when answering. It's okay to talk with your hands—though you should avoid fist pounding and continual or distracting motion. The world still remembers when Nikita Khrushchev pounded the podium with his shoe during the course of a United Nations speech. The world remembers it, but that crude and blustering gesture did nothing to enhance the premier's image as a world leader.

5. Begin your response to a question by making firm eye contact with the questioner; then, as you develop your response, look around the room, making eye contact with others, just as you would in the course of a regular speech.

6. The more directly you can respond, the better. Get to the point. Unless doing so serves a definite purpose, do not spin out your answers at great length. Don't turn an answer into a dissertation.

7. Be fair. Make a very deliberate effort to take questions from all parts of the room.

8. Be gracious. Avoid patronizing questioners. Avoid clichés such as "Good question" or "Gee, that's a good one." Just answer the question.

9. Most of the time, you and your audience will find it useful if you begin your response by repeating the question. This is especially important if the question is one that you have a strong, positive answer for and that you wish to emphasize.

What can go wrong in a question-and-answer session? Plenty. But, if you keep your head, you can turn a negative situation to your advantage.

10. A questioner attempts to poison the well. You know that classic question: "When did you stop beating your wife?" Unscrupulous—or merely provocative—media folk are not above asking others like it: "Why does your organization discriminate against women?" Do not simply repeat this kind of question. Not only will you needlessly underscore a negative remark (at *your own* press conference, no less!), but in a universe of disjointed sound bites, the negative remark you repeat might even get attributed *to* you. Try to rephrase negative questions: "What can we do to avoid all discrimination? Let me tell you about some steps we have taken."

11. A questioner attempts to lead you into a mine field. Combat this by refusing to follow him. If you try to answer the following kinds of questions *in the terms presented by the questions,* you are likely to be blown to bits:

   ▼ *You are asked a hypothetical question.* Beware of any question that begins with "What if." These are excursions into a fantasy realm of the questioner's own creation, and she can easily get you lost in it. Respond by rejecting the question as hypothetical and then bring the questioner and the audience back to reality. *Question:* "What if the unions reject the salary offer?" *Answer:* "The unions have given no indication that they will reject the offer—nor should they. It is a very fair offer and one that we can all live with."

   ▼ *You are handed an invitation to exclude and offend.* Don't accept it. Beware of questions that force you into an absolute and finite answer. *Question:* "What are the three greatest dangers our community faces today?" *Answer:* "A number of issues deeply concern me at the present time, among them . . ." Avoid yielding to the demand for an answer in the superlative degree (*best, biggest, most important, favorite,* etc.). These slam the door, locking you *in* and lord knows how many others *out*. At most, venture a response in the comparative degree (*among the more important issues are,* etc.).

▼ *You are offered a seat on the horns of a dilemma.* Remain standing. *Question*: "Is your firm going to emphasize productivity or protection of the environment?" Why fall for a gambit like this? Why concede a situation of mutual exclusivity if such a situation does not exist? *Answer*: "Our firm intends to emphasize both productivity and environmental integrity by developing programs that allow us to attain optimum productivity while achieving the greatest possible level of ecological responsibility."

▼ *You are targeted for extortion. Question*: "Will you vote in favor of increased taxes—yes or no?" A press conference is not a court of law. No one present has the right to extort from you a "simple" yes or no or any other one-word answer. *Answer*: "The issue is complex and does not admit of a simple yes or no. Let me outline for you some areas in which I believe we should increase tax revenues and other areas that would benefit from significant tax rollbacks."

▼ *You are asked to speak for another.* As Pilgrim Priscilla admonished Mr. Alden, "Speak for yourself, John." *Question*: "Why does your opponent take such a dim view of Ms. Peterson's knowledge of the subject?" *Answer*: "You will have to ask *him* that one. As for myself, having examined her report, which is the product of six months' study, I am confident that Ms. Peterson speaks with great authority and that what she has to say is worth considering very carefully."

▼ *You are given a blank check.* Make sure you've brought along your pen. The one question that will stop me cold at a cocktail party is, "I hear you're a writer. Tell me all about it." It's like being shown a pile of iron rods and then being told, "Go ahead. Build the Eiffel Tower." You hardly know where to begin and, for that matter, you hardly have any desire to begin. Wide-open questions look easy, but they invite a blank mind and total silence. Better anticipate the kinds of open-ended questions you are likely to be asked and simply memorize some good responses to them.

▼ *You are "asked" a statement.* Questions end with question marks. Statements are punctuated with periods or exclamation points. If you are "asked" something that ends in one of the latter, it's not a question. "I can't see how the stockholders would benefit from expanding our present customer service operation." It is difficult to respond to a nonquestion such as this without coming off as argumentative. Nor can you reject the statement and refuse to respond because it is not a question. Your best alternative is to convert the statement into the question you *want* to answer. "Well, what you are asking is very important: How will the stockholders benefit from an expanded customer service operation? Here's how . . . ."

▼ *You are "asked" a speech.* This is unlikely at a professional press conference, but it is not impossible: A question turns into a longwinded speech. Don't let it happen. In a civil tone, jump in, ask the "questioner" to ask his *question*—in the interest of saving very limited time.

▼ *You are stumped.* If you really are at a loss, admit it, but promise that you will look into the subject and comment on it later.

What else can go wrong?

12. *Someone asks you something you've already covered in your opening statement.* You can't simply assume the questioner is a blockhead (though she may be); it is possible that you failed to make this point clear in the first place. Answer the question, if possible taking a somewhat different tack from the one you took originally.

13. However, *if someone repeats a question you've already answered*, reply, "That question has already been asked and answered" or "Mr. Harris already asked me that one, and I believe I've said all I have to say on it." Then just move on.

14. *Someone asks a meaningless, irrelevant, or vacuous question.* It is quite difficult to respond to nonsense. If possible, give a brief answer and then quickly move on. Your audience will understand. If you cannot muster a brief answer, respond with something like, "I cannot even begin to tackle that one." Again, your audience will understand and will be very happy to move along. If the problem is not so much that the question is dumb, empty, or inane, but simply irrelevant, respond by invoking your ground rules: "That's not what we're all here to discuss."

15. *Someone turns a question into a personal attack.* Again, this is not likely to happen at a gathering of professional journalists. But it is possible.

Bear in mind that, by launching into a personal attack, the "question-er" has made a serious rhetorical blunder. He (or she) may be big, bad, and loud, but he (or she) is at an argumentative disadvantage. Your first task is to keep cool enough to avoid being sucked into the same trap. While your questioner targets a *personality*, your job is to keep the focus on the *issues*. Ignore the attack. Ignore the emotions. Highlight the issues.

Anything else? Oh, yes.

16. *No one asks any questions.* In a professional press conference, this is highly unlikely. It is possible, though, that there will be a paucity of questions. If this happens, don't just stand there, stand *in*. Ask *your-self* some questions. "I am a little surprised that none of you has chal-lenged me on . . . ." Or: "Just the other day, Ms. Perkins from the *Sun* asked me about . . . ."

Then there is the final trap, which is particularly frustrating because it is of your own making. In your anxiety to assert control over the press confer-ence or simply to get the thing over with, you may be tempted to declare with firmness and finality that "This will be the last question." This is harmless enough, if that final question happens to be a good one. But what if it is dumb, a dud, negative, hostile, nasty, or dull? You will be stuck with *that* as the final chord to your symphony. Better to leave yourself some-thing to fall back on by wrapping things up with a less final remark: "We have a few moments left. Are there more questions?"

Radio

In a nation seemingly glued to a hundred million television sets, it is easy to think that radio is dead. That, however, is anything but true. There are about 800 commercial broadcast television stations in the United States, but ten times that number of AM and FM radio stations. The burgeoning segment of this huge broadcast base is not music, but talk. And radio talk is indeed cheap. If you're dealing with a local station, they'll probably have you drop by the studio for an interview. If you are in Chicago and the station is in Los Angeles, well, maybe they'll spring for airfare and a modest hotel room, but it is just as likely that the interview will be conducted by a long-distance telephone call. (Yes, they'll pay for it.)

What can you expect on a radio date? It is highly unlikely that you will be asked to make a formal presentation. Shows are customarily either in an interview format or in some combination of interview and listener call-in. You can handle the interview using many of the techniques appropriate to panel discussions and to press conferences (see the appropriate chapters in this section); however, one important difference is that, usually, the host—the interviewer—is entirely on your side. Her job is not to stymie you, embarrass you, or even challenge you, but to facilitate conversation. Radio is a blind medium. All it has is ears, and the one thing a talk show host cannot afford is dead air. She wants you to keep talking.

Still, it is possible that you will encounter a less-than-skilled interviewer who will fire one dud after another. Even good interviewers treasure what they call "self-starters," guests who get on a roll and keep going on their own. Make yourself into a self-starter by preparing "spontaneous" conversation in advance. Arm yourself with sharp anecdotes and startling statistics, all bite-sized and easily digested. You should also consider furnishing the interviewer with some questions you have prepared in advance. Make certain that your interviewer understands that you do not intend to force these down his throat, but that you offer them in order to make his job easier. Busy talk show hosts or producers, responsible for preparing five or six shows a week, are almost universally grateful for this kind of help.

Convince yourself that you are the star of the show and that you are in control. Don't be afraid to dominate the conversation. If you are coming into the studio for the interview, why not impress the staff with your professionalism by requesting a puff guard? This is a gauze disk placed in front of the microphone or a foam cover placed over it for the purpose of diminishing the annoying effect of a speaker's "explosive P's." Not only will a puff guard make you sound better, asking for it will make your host and the studio personnel feel that they are dealing with a seasoned performer.

How do you get booked on a radio show? You may be working through your company's publicist, part of whose job is to get you on such programs. If, however, you are on your own, try calling local stations about two weeks before you'd like to appear. Ask to speak to the program director and, as concisely as possible, pitch him your story. You've just written a new book on stock options strategies for the nonprofessional investor. "I believe your listeners will be interested in hearing how they can profitably become players in the market without buying or selling a single stock and using only a fraction of the money required to trade stocks." Formulate a hook, cast your line, then shut up and wait for a bite.

If there is immediate interest, fine. More likely, a positive response will be manifested not as an invitation to appear, but as a request for more information. Send whatever relevant material you have: a book, magazine articles you have written, a speech you have given, and so forth. Include a cover letter alluding to your telephone conversation and prominently giving your daytime and nighttime phone numbers. A few days after mailing the letter, follow up with a second phone call.

Television

As I write this chapter, I imagine my reader to be a sophisticated individual of some authority. Who else would have use for a book on speech making? I imagine, then, that a significant number of my readers, business, political, educational, or social leaders, have already appeared on television. But I am also sure that probably an even greater number of my readers are casting an eye on this chapter and thinking, "TV. *Me? Yeah, sure.*"

There are one-tenth the number of broadcast television stations across the United States as there are broadcast radio stations, and it is true that television is a far costlier medium than radio and is, naturally, more visually oriented—which tends to mean more celebrity oriented. However, currently some 5,000 cable stations operate in addition to the roughly 800 broadcast stations. Some of these cable stations are local in nature, community-access stations that highlight issues at the level of the community—almost at the level of the neighborhood. If broadcast radio and TV are media of mass communication, many cable stations are, in effect, community forums. And these forums are open to you.

You can approach local television, including cable, much as you would a radio station, by contacting the news manager or, if it is a very small station, the station manager. (See the "Radio" chapter in this section.) Do what you can to include visual material in your pitch—slides, video, film footage, or other visual aids—and you should also furnish a good photograph of yourself.

As with radio performances, most of the principles of the panel discussion and the press conference apply to television interviews as well. You should also be aware of the requirements of working in as intimate a visual medium as television. Much of the time, you will be seen rather tightly framed, from the shoulders up. This will tend to magnify what on the podium would be quite subtle elements of body language. If you grimace or bite your lip, a lot of people will see it—and close up, too. On the other hand, the camera's tight focus will, most of the time, render invisible any hand gestures that aren't within about ten inches of your face. Occasionally raising a thoughtful finger to your lips is effective television body language, but beware of other hand gestures near your face: the hand over the mouth, the hand brought to the forehead. These suggest evasion.

Give extra thought to how you will dress for the camera. That tired cliché about the camera adding ten pounds to a person is, alas, all too true. If you are svelte and fine-featured, more power to you. If, on the other hand, you can afford to lose a few pounds, you might gravitate toward darker colors in your choice of clothing and avoid large, light patterns, especially florals. Regardless of girth, men and women should avoid small, intricate patterns such as checks and hound's-tooth zigzags. These produce a "strobe" effect on camera, seeming to vibrate and wiggle, imparting to your wardrobe an unwanted life of its own. Also avoid highly reflective jewelry, which creates a video "burn" onscreen. If you can get along without eyeglasses, take them off in order to avoid problems with glare. Television hates bright white shirts and blouses. Best to wear grays, tans, or light blues. Adjust your clothing to smooth out any wrinkles or awkward folds that result from sitting. Men wearing suitcoats or sport jackets should pull down on the tail of the coat or jacket and sit on it. This tends to keep the collar from riding up. For additional advice on dressing for a public appearance, see "Clothes" in Part Three of this book.

Experienced television performers learn how to play to the camera. They also learn how to turn from one camera to another when the director varies the shot. In the case of an interview, however, unless the host or director tells you differently, it is best simply to make eye contact with the interviewer. The intimacy of the television medium calls for a conversation rather than an oratorical performance.

▼▼▼▼▼▼▼▼▼▼▼▼▼▼▼▼▼

Toasts

The word *toast* is an etymological puzzle. No one is quite sure how it came to denote the ceremonial act of raising one's glass in honor of or to the health of a person, institution, or enterprise. The best guess I've been able to find is that the word used in this sense derives from a former custom of flavoring drinks with spiced toast. Thus the verbal toast we offer is meant to add spice to the drink we enjoy and, by extension, seasoning and flavor to the special occasion on which we enjoy it. A toast, then, should be a dash of flavor, a delightful seasoning that may be savored at the moment of tasting it.

Any celebratory occasion at which drink will be served is likely to summon a toast from somebody. If you have even the vaguest reason to believe that you will be called on to offer a toast, it is a good idea to come prepared with a few appropriate ones. One word of caution: If you are asked to make a toast, even if you are caught by surprise (and shame on you for that!), don't demure. Begging off will have the effect of stepping on a good time. It's also insulting to the person, institution, or enterprise being honored. To paraphrase the advertising slogan of a well-known manufacturer of sports shoes, if you are asked to make a toast, *just do it*.

Toast-prone occasions include:

Anniversaries

Birthdays

Christmas

Gatherings of good friends

Inaugurations and Launches

New Year's celebrations

Newborn celebrations

Retirements

Reunions

Weddings

The following suggests a few guidelines, together with some sample toasts, classics you may want to quote as well as more contemporary models. Many more toasts can be found in the books listed under "Toast Collections" in the Appendix.

ANNIVERSARIES

The anniversary toast honors the couple (if the occasion is a wedding anniversary), individual, or institution for having passed some temporal landmark: one year, five, ten, and so on. You might make specific mention of the time elapsed, and if the anniversary is evidence of impressive longevity, mention that. It is always appropriate to express a wish for many more years of happiness, joy, success, devotion, and so on.

Classics

(To mother and father on their wedding anniversary)

> *We never know the love of our parents for us till we have become parents.*
> —Henry Ward Beecher

> *Here is to loving, to romance, to us.*
> *May we travel together through time.*
> *We alone count as none, but together we're one.*
> *For our partnership puts love to rhyme.*
> —Traditional Irish

Contemporary

Here's to fifty years of joy (service, dedication, etc.). May we all enjoy another fifty.

May each new day bring added joy.

May tomorrow be even more splendid than today.

Let your coming years together be outnumbered only by the pleasures and joys they bring.

Our enterprise has survived and prospered through one year. May this be the first of many.

BIRTHDAYS

Offer congratulations on a long, prosperous, joyous, and useful life that has blessed all who know the honoree. Look toward the future.

Classics

May you live a hundred years with one extra year to repent.
—Traditional Irish

God grant you many happy years,
  Till, when the last has crowned you,
The dawn of endless days appears,
  And heaven is shining round you!
—Oliver Wendell Holmes, Sr.

May the wind be always at your back,
And may the Lord hold you in the hollow of his hand!
—Traditional Irish

Many happy returns of the day of your birth:
Many blessings to brighten your pathway on earth;
Many friendships to cheer and provoke you to mirth;
Many feastings and frolics to add to your girth.
—Robert H. Lord

Contemporary

To your first XX years—and your next!

Drink up and cheer up! I'm *still* older than you.

We thank you for the pleasure your years have given us, and we greedily beg you for many more.

To your continued health and happiness!

XX years! If this party doesn't finish you off, nothing will!

We offer you gifts on *this* day in feeble token of the many gifts you have given us *every* day.

May each of your days be a celebration equal to this.

CHRISTMAS

A Christmas toast should be an invitation to bask in a holiday that summons the feelings of family, friends, and childhood wonder.

Classics

Apple pie and Simon Beer,
Christmas comes but once a year.
   —Traditional Southern

At Christmas play and make good cheer
For Christmas comes but once a year.
   —Thomas Turner

God bless us every one!
   —Tiny Tim in Charles Dickens's *A Christmas Carol*

Holly and ivy hanging up
And something wet in every cup.
   —Traditional Irish

May your sheep all have lambs, but not on Christmas night.
   —Traditional Irish

Christmas is here,
Merry old Christmas,
Gift-bearing, heart-touching, joy-bringing Christmas.
Day of grand memories, king of the year.
   —Washington Irving

Joy to the world!
   —Traditional

Peace on earth. Goodwill to men.
   —Traditional

As fits the holy Christmas birth,
  Be this, good friends, our carol still—
Be peace on earth, be peace on earth,
  To men of gentle will.
    —William Makepeace Thackeray

Contemporary

Here's to the best Christmas gift of all—good friends and great family!

May the joy of tonight linger through each day of the coming year.

No matter how cold it gets outside, here's to the knowledge that we will always find plenty of warmth with one another.

Let's drink to this Christmas together and look forward to many, many more.

Take a moment with me to reflect on the meaning of this season: Peace on earth and joy to the world!

GATHERINGS OF GOOD FRIENDS

Toasts to friendship provide a valuable opportunity to express feelings of gratitude and affection that would otherwise go unexpressed. If the drink of the evening is fine wine, comparison between the beverage and friendship is virtually inevitable.

Classics

To your good health, old friend, may you live for a thousand years,
and I be there to count them.
    —Robert Smith Surtees

Here's to you, as good as you are,
And here's to me, as bad as I am;
As bad as I am, as good as you are,
I'm good as you are as bad as I am.
    —Traditional Scots

A day for toil, an hour for sport,
But for a friend life is too short.
  —Ralph Waldo Emerson

Don't walk in front of me,
  I may not follow.
Don't walk behind me,
  I may not lead,
Walk beside me,
  And just be my friend.
  —Traditional Irish

Here's all that's fine to you!
Books and old wine to you!
Girls be divine to you!
  —Richard Hovey

May the hinges of friendship never rust, nor the wings of love lose a
feather.
  —Dean Ramsay

Pour deep the rosy wine and drink a toast with me:
Here's to the three: Thee, Wine, and Camaraderie!
  —Tom Moore

Were't the last drop in the well,
  As I gasp'd upon the brink,
Ere my fainting spirit fell,
  'Tis to thee I would drink.
  —Anonymous

Contemporary

Good friends, like good wine, grow better and better with age.

May this drink loosen our tongues sufficiently for us to declare full
and loud tonight the love and friendship we feel for one another.

Here's to the friends of today, tomorrow, and yesterday.

Here's to the friends gathered with us, and to those now absent.

Here's to friendship—in the flesh and in the heart.

To our best friends, who know us well, yet love us nevertheless.

To our best friends, who tell us the truth about ourselves, but not too loudly.

To friendship and to life, which are one and the same.

INAUGURATIONS AND LAUNCHES

When a ship is launched, it is traditional to christen it by breaking a bottle of champagne across its prow. A toast offered at the outset of a project or enterprise or in celebration of an individual's inauguration as head of a corporation or organization performs much the same function: a traditional anointment for good luck.

Classics

As you slide down the bannister of life
May the splinters never face the wrong way!
—Traditional

When Napoleon was asked whom he deemed his favorite troops, he replied, "Those who are victorious." At the outset of this enterprise, I propose a toast: To the victors!

If at first you don't succeed, try, try again—then give up. There's no use being a fool about it.
—W.C. Fields

I greet you at the commencement of a great career.
—Ralph Waldo Emerson in a letter to Walt Whitman

Good luck till you are tired of it!
—Traditional

Let us toast the fools; but for them, the rest of us would not succeed.
—Mark Twain

Contemporary

To your success!

May you always be confident in the knowledge that you have our support and faith.

Here's to the triumph of [name of project], which we launch today!

Let's drink to fame and fortune, which, let us face facts, is what we all want out of this new project.

NEW YEAR'S CELEBRATIONS

New Year's Eve festivities are customarily associated with much drinking and mindless merriment. Look a little below the noisy surface, however, and you will find a bittersweet core—hope for the future, but anxiety as well; fond recollection of the past, tinged, perhaps, with regret for the bygone.

Classics

Happy New Year!
—Traditional

Here's wishing you the kind of troubles that will last as long as your New Year's resolutions!
—Traditional

A song for the old, while its knell is tolled,
  And its parting moments fly!
But a song and a cheer for the glad New Year,
  While we watch the old year die!
—George Cooper

As we start the New Year, let's get down on our knees to thank God we're still on our feet.
—Traditional Irish

Be at war with your voices, at peace with your neighbors, and let every new year find you a better man.
—Ben Franklin

May the New Year bring summer in its wake.
    —Traditional Irish

In the New Year, may your right hand always be stretched out in friendship, but never in want.
    —Traditional Irish

Ring out the old, ring in the new,
Ring happy bells across the snow;
The year is going, let him go.
    —Alfred Lord Tennyson

We'll tak' a cup o' kindness yet,
For auld lang syne.
    —Robert Burns

May the New Year grant you the eye of a blacksmith on a nail, the good humor of a girl at a dance, the strong hand of a priest on his parish.
    —Traditional Irish

Contemporary

Old Ambrose Bierce defined a year as 365 disappointments. Let's drink to the coming one as 365 great possibilities!

Whatever comes in this new year, I am grateful for the fact that it will come in the presence of all of you.

Let's drink to our past mistakes, our present forgiveness, and our future triumphs.

Here's to facing the challenges together!

To your health, happiness, and a speedy recovery from tomorrow's hangover.

To the old year—let it go. To the new one—embrace it.

To our old friends, and to those we are about to make.

NEWBORN CELEBRATIONS

Toast the child's health, happiness, and future. How about paying tribute to the parents and grandparents as well? The essence of this occasion is hope, perpetuation, and affirmation.

Classics

Every baby born into the world is a finer one than the last.
—Charles Dickens

A generation of children on the children of your children!
—Traditional Irish

May he (she) grow twice as tall as yourself and half as wise!
—Traditional Irish

We haven't all the good fortune to be ladies; we have not all been generals, or poets or statesmen; but when the toast works down to the babies we stand on common ground. We've all been babies.
—Mark Twain

Grandchildren are gifts of God. It's God's way of compensating us for growing old.
—Traditional Irish

Babies bring luck.
—Traditional Yiddish saying

To life. The first half is ruined by our parents and the second half by our children.
—Traditional

Contemporary

To the parents: Congratulations! To the grandparents: Rejoice in your pride! To the new one: Welcome to the family!

Welcome to the planet, little one. Use it well, and make it better.

Here's to your present joy and your future happiness, pride, and fulfillment.

Welcome, stranger. You have found a good home. Best of health and fortune to you.

On behalf of the federal government of this great republic, I congratulate you on your new deduction.

God grant you the year of persistence needed to get this girl (boy) to stand up and talk, and the eighteen years of patience required to get her (him) to sit down and shut up!

May the love among you all be continuous, without interruption, misunderstanding, or condition.

RETIREMENTS

The best retirement toasts acknowledge the honoree's contributions and career, providing, as it were, a punctuation to them. They also express affection for the honoree, tinged with regret at his departure.

Classics

To a job well done.
—Traditional

'Tis grievous parting with good company.
—George Eliot

Must we part?
Well, if we must—we must—
And in that case
The less said the better.
—Richard Brinsley Sheridan

The pain of parting is nothing to the joy of meeting again.
—Charles Dickens

Parting is such sweet sorrow.
—William Shakespeare

Everyone has his day, and some days last longer than others.
—Winston Churchill

One generation plants the trees; another sits in their shade. Here's to you, [Name], for planting those trees.
—Adopted from a traditional Chinese proverb

Contemporary

A toast to you on your retirement: The greatest tribute we can offer is the knowledge that your going makes us miserable.

Here's to the legacy of service you leave to us.

Let's drink to your busy future as a so-called retiree.

I propose a toast to the future you have helped create for us all.

REUNIONS

The reunion toast serves to reaffirm old ties and to establish a toehold of stability in a changing and changeable world.

Classics

Here's to all of us!
For there's so much good in the worst of us
  And so much bad in the best of us,
That it hardly behooves any of us,
  To talk about the rest of us.

Here's to us that are here, to you that are there, and the rest of us everywhere.

Some among many gather again,
A glass to their happiness; friendship,
Amen. . . .
The Survivors.
—James Monroe McLean

Here's a health in a homely rhyme
To our oldest classmate, Father Time;
May our last survivor live to be
As bold and as wise and as thorough as he!
—Oliver Wendell Holmes, Sr.

To the Good Old Days. We weren't so good, because we weren't so old.
—Traditional

I drink to the general joy o' the whole table.
—William Shakespeare

Contemporary

Here's to the fact that so many of us are still alive and kicking.

Let's take a drink to melt the years away.

Let us quench the drought of years spent in the absence of one another.

It has been a long time—too long a time—between drinks together. Bottoms up!

To those of us here—again—and to those of us who are not—and cannot be.

I propose a toast to Alma Mater, to all that she has given us, and for the opportunity now to celebrate her gifts.

WEDDINGS

If you're invited to a wedding, you run a high risk of being asked to propose a toast. Wedding receptions are great opportunities for sincerity, and even better ones for good-natured humor. Just be certain that your humorous toast does not veer into genuinely bitter or abrasive sarcasm.

Classics

Grow old along with me!
The best is yet to be.
—Robert Browning

Here's to the groom with bride so fair,
And here's to the bride with groom so rare!
 —Ralph Waldo Emerson

Here's to the happy man: All the world loves a lover.
 —Ralph Waldo Emerson

Look down you gods,
And on this couple drop a blessed crown.
 —William Shakespeare

Let's drink to Ambrose Bierce, who defined marriage as "A communi-
ty consisting of a master, a mistress and two slaves—making in all,
two."

Here's a toast to Groucho Marx, who once said that "marriage is a
wonderful institution, but who wants to live in an institution?"

May you have many children
and may they grow as mature in taste
and healthy in color
and as sought after
as the contents of this glass.
 —Traditional Irish

Never above you. Never below you. Always beside you.
 —Walter Winchell

Hail to the bridegroom—hail the bride!
Now the nuptial knot is tied!
 —Rudyard Kipling

Contemporary

Let nothing come between you.

Go forth, be thou fruitful, and file a joint return.

Here's to a thrilling journey and a blessed haven in a happy home.

May your joys be boundless and your sorrows few and of brief duration.

To the happily-ever-after that begins right now!

May your wedding days be few and your anniversaries many.

PART THREE

▼

▼

▼

The
Nuts
and
Bolts

Architecture

Most books on writing and on that special application of writing called speech writing begin with a prescription for structuring the composition of the piece. After all, you can't build a house without working from a plan.

But a speech is not a house. Really, it is an extension of something that we human beings do every day: communicate. So I began this book not with abstract instruction on the theory and practice of speech architecture, but with the real occasions that demand real speeches. Now that you've—presumably—plunged into at least some of those examples, you might find it helpful to step back and look at the principles that guided the construction of the speeches.

Veteran speechwriter Joan Detz, in her *How to Write and Give a Speech* (St. Martin's Press, 1984), boils the process down to two pairs of principles. Want to write a good speech?

1. Make it simple.

2. Make it short.

Want to write a *great* speech?

1. Make it simpler.

2. Make it shorter.

Not all good speeches, let alone great speeches, are simple and short. But you can't go wrong if you at least begin the process of planning and writing your speech from these principles. I'd alter Ms. Detz's advice this way:

1. Make it as simple as an enlightening treatment of the subject will allow.

2. Make it as short as an enlightening treatment of the subject will allow.

The same writer also introduces a time-honored "formula for a successful speech," the origins of which have been attributed to a wide variety of speakers and speech writers:

1. Tell them what you're going to tell them.

2. Tell them.

3. Tell them what you've told them.

Unfortunately, if you try to follow this formula literally, you will create a very boring speech. You also run the risk of sounding as if you are *telling* your audience what to think. A good speech does, of course, inform, persuade, move to action—in short, create thoughts or a certain mind set. But it does not *dictate* thought. It guides your listeners. It makes it possible for your audience to think the thoughts you want them to have, to reach the desired conclusion for themselves. It is no accident that, when we are particularly impressed by a speech, we use a metaphor so commonplace that we no longer think about what it really means. We say that the speech *moved* us.

An effective speech *moves* us to a desired mental or emotional place. It does not thrust that "place" upon us or force us, kicking and screaming, to it. It moves—motivates—us to that place seemingly of our own volition.

With this caution in mind—move, don't shove—the simple formula given here is nevertheless a good point from which to start thinking about your speech. Be aware that the spoken word is the most ephemeral of all communication. A speech consists of sound waves that move through the air only to vanish as soon as they are produced. In a speech, you cannot develop the subtlety and complexity of exposition available to the writer of a printed text meant to be read, reread, studied, underlined, and consulted again as often as necessary. Make the simplest points your subject will allow. Make them as simply and as directly as your subject will allow. Begin as clearly as you possibly can. Develop the subject as clearly and as unambiguously as possible in the body of the speech. Then conclude as definitely as your subject will allow, taking the opportunity to underscore your point of view.

In 1687, Sir Isaac Newton formulated the First Law of Motion, the principle of inertia, which holds that a body at rest remains at rest and a body in motion remains in motion at a constant velocity as long as outside forces are not involved. An analogous principle seems to apply to human behavior. Just as an extra effort is required to coax a still body into motion or to alter the motion of a moving one, so the beginning of a speech is the most difficult part of the talk, both for the speaker and the audience. An extra effort is required to overcome the mental and emotional inertia that affects the speaker as well as the audience. How do you get into a speech? I won't presume to say that there are x number of ways, because somebody more creative than I will always be around to think of a dozen more. However, here are some opening strategies that have proven effective:

1. *Jump right in with a declaration of your subject*: "Tonight, I will speak to you about . . . ." Assuming your subject is of interest to your audience, this no-nonsense approach is quite effective.

2. *Jump right in with an offer.* The benefit—and the risk—here is that this approach is, quite frankly, a sales pitch. "I am here to tell you how to improve your life by at least 60 percent."

3. *Start with an anecdote.* The illustrative story is at least as old as Aesop. It works best when it is personal in origin; just think about how much money Andy Rooney of TV's *60 Minutes* makes with his autobiographical fables. Generally, the anecdote should be short and sharp. Avoid beginning with a shaggy dog story.

4. *Come clean.* Admit something about yourself or your qualifications. "I hate motivational speakers—people who get up and give you a pep talk—so, let me admit to you that what I'm about to say is very difficult for me." This approach involves risk, but if you use common sense it can be an effective attention getter. Obviously, if you've come to address a gathering of dermatologists on the subject of acne cures, you should not begin by declaring your ignorance of skin disorders.

5. *Throw down a gauntlet—sort of—by challenging a common misperception or cherished belief.* "Ladies and gentlemen, I know that the Constitution guarantees the right to bear arms. But this does not make gun control unconstitutional." As with the "come clean" approach, this one requires careful judgment. You do want to shock your audience into "motion," at least mildly, but you do not want to begin by offending them or turning them off. The late movie director Sam Peckinpah was widely admired (and in some circles reviled) for the masterful way in which he orchestrated the violence of his often quite violent movies. Why go through the trouble of making an *art* out of violence? Because ultrarealistic violence would, according to Peckinpah, incite an audience revolt. "If I send them running out of the theater, I've failed," Peckinpah observed. Don't begin so outra-

geously or offensively that you drive your listeners (figuratively or literally) from the room.

6. *Bond with your audience.* You are speaking to the Irish Cultural Club and you begin, "I'm proud to be Irish." What if you're not Irish? "My mother's father was Polish and my father's people all came from Russia, but right now, standing before all you lovely people, I wish to hell I were Irish."

7. *Turn the preceding strategy up a notch by beginning with an outright compliment.* "It is not every day that the most prestigious retailer's association in the state asks you to address them." The danger here is that audiences are likely to see through a phony compliment. Better be sincere.

8. *Start with a relevant bit of humor.* "There is a tombstone in a little cemetery in Georgia that bears a very interesting epitaph. It says: 'I *told* you I was sick.' I want to talk to you tonight about what it means to be right at the wrong time."

9. *Conjure with the title of your talk.* "I've titled my talk 'Three Bags Full.' You have every right to ask: *full of what?*"

10. *Promise brevity.* Hard as it may be on your ego, there is no surer way to win the heart of your audience than to promise them imminent release—especially if your talk is only one part of a lengthy program. Just make sure that, having promised to be brief, you are.

After the beginning comes—what else?—the middle. There is more than one effective way to organize this, the body of your speech. The most useful methods tend to be the most natural.

- ▼ Chronology (a narrative of events from first to last)

- ▼ Cause and effect, or before and after

- ▼ Need and fulfillment, or problem and solution

- ▼ Emotional order—from what your audience will find most acceptable to what will most challenge their beliefs

▼ Dramatic order—from least intense to most (think of this in musical terms as building to a crescendo)

▼ From smallest or least to biggest or most

If your speech is primarily descriptive, figure out a logical way to break up your subject. For example, if you are talking about the results of a national sales survey, you might divide the nation into regions (Northeast, Southeast, Middle West, Middle South, and so on) and work from east to west and north to south. If you are describing an airplane, you might naturally start from the nose and end up at the tail. All else being equal, there is also that old standby, alphabetical order.

Whatever method of organization you use, you might also find it helpful—especially in a heavily descriptive speech or report—to begin the body of your talk by providing a verbal outline. "I will approach the subject in three parts: origins, development, and consequences." Then announce each part as you come to it. "First, to origins . . ." "Now we move on to development . . ." And so on. Unless you are a very skilled speaker, it is a good idea to telegraph these *transitions* from one part of your speech to another. Let's say you're presenting a problem-solution speech. You've explained the problem; now it's time to get to the solution: "This, then, is the problem. Now let's move on to the solution." Or perhaps you've structured the body of your speech in emotional order: "Up to this point, I've been covering pretty familiar territory. Now, if you will, let's venture into the extraordinary, an area that may well strain your willingness to believe." Or you've gone from smallest to biggest: "These problems are significant, but by far the biggest problem facing us is . . . ."

A special method of organizing a speech is the extended metaphor. This takes skill on your part and a certain mental agility on the part of the audience. Furthermore, inappropriately used, an extended metaphor quickly becomes strained, cloying, and unintentionally comic. But it can be a very useful device for explaining the unfamiliar in terms of the familiar—which is, after all, the primary purpose of a metaphor. For example, I had an English teacher who made crystal clear the very difficult and arcane distinction between ordinary language and the language of poetry. He explained that ordinary language was a match. It is struck, illuminates, then burns out and disappears. Having served its purpose, it is given no further thought. If someone asks you to "bring the cup, please," you do not stop to admire or ponder the language of the request. The words motivate action as the match creates light, but once the action has been performed, the words burn out and are—mentally—discarded. Poetic language, in contrast, is a gorgeous chandelier. Like the match, it also produces light. But it is treasured and admired for itself as well. John Keats's "Ode on a Grecian Urn" provokes much thought and invites admiration of its beautiful language.

More famously, philosopher-designer-ecologist R. Buckminster Fuller wrote and lectured on what he called Spaceship Earth, developing the metaphor of our planet as a spaceship, self-contained, self-sustaining, but vulnerable and finite. Using this metaphor, he counseled ecological and political responsibility. Another thinker of the period, media and communications theorist Marshall McLuhan, spoke of how television was transforming the world into a "global village." In many of his writings, McLuhan effectively developed the implications of this metaphor, speculating on what it means to live in such a village.

My English teacher's metaphor, like those of Fuller and McLuhan, was not only extremely helpful in communicating a complex idea by making an abstraction more concrete and explaining the unfamiliar in terms of the familiar, it also made an idea easier to retain and remember. That English class took place years ago, and it has been a long time since I read Fuller or McLuhan. The details of what they said and wrote are lost to me, but their metaphors remain vividly in my mind.

Beyond the very real danger that you or your audience can easily get lost in the metaphor ("can't see the forest for the trees," to cite a familiar metaphor), there is also the hazard of falling into what rhetoricians call the metaphorical fallacy. During the 1950s, for example, Red-baiting American politicians often said that Communism was a "cancer" on this country. This is a most compelling metaphor. Cancer is universally dreaded, crippling, and deadly. It spreads insidiously, takes over the body, then kills it. The cure? No halfway measures: major surgery. Extirpate it. Cut it out.

The trouble is that political beliefs and the human beings who hold them are *not*, in fact, cancers. But if you are swallowed up in the metaphor, it is all too easy to see them as such and to lose sight of their rights as human beings and as citizens of a democracy. Doubtless, the Nazis found it convenient to think of those individuals they condemned to death camps as mere cancers on the Third Reich. Particularly in ideological speeches,

organization through extended metaphor is powerful—and very dangerous—medicine.

For many speakers, conclusions are almost as tough as beginnings.
One reason for this is faulty reasoning in the body of the speech. Ideally,
your speech should "add up" to a logically justifiable conclusion. If the
logic fails, it is time to rethink your assumptions.

Beyond the logical component of the conclusion is a small arsenal of
rhetorical methods for ending the speech:

1. *End by referring to your opening.* "I began by stating such and such. I
   would like to conclude on the same note."

2. *Review the main ideas of your speech.*

3. *End with an anecdote or story that illustrates your main point(s).*

4. *End with an inspiring quotation.*

5. *End with a rhetorical question.* "Is this the kind of school board we
   want? Are we satisfied that we have the best school system possible?"

6. *End with a dose of reality.* "Nothing I've said here is the magic bullet
   that will cure all of our ills. But I know that, together, we can *significantly* improve the situation—now—and *vastly* improve it within five
   years."

7. *End with hope and optimism.*

8. *End with a call for unity and cooperation.*

9. *End with a call to action or thought.*

In addition to these strategies for bringing a speech to a close, bear in
mind two principles that are important enough to be called rules:

1. *End briskly.* Once you've announced or rhetorically signaled that you
   are about to conclude, get on with it. Don't leave your audience waiting for the dropping of the proverbial other shoe.

2. *Summon up and concentrate whatever eloquence you have within you and
   use it here.* Use strong, direct language—and this, above all others, is
   the place for deliberately quotable phrases.

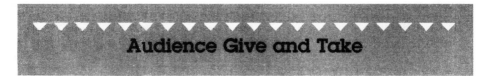

Audience Give and Take

I am a music lover, and I have been most fortunate to have heard over the years some of the greats (as they say) Live and In Person. Two performers stand out: Vladimir Horowitz and Luciano Pavarotti. Well, why *shouldn't* they stand out? These are two of the greatest musicians of our time—of *all* time. But, when I think of the experience of having heard them in performance some fifteen years ago now, it is not so much their exquisite music making that comes to mind, but that difficult-to-define quality called *stage presence*. Both of these musicians, in personality and performance style quite different from each other, had in common a certain magical rapport with the audience.

A kind of special aura, is, to be sure, a gift. I don't know that it can be learned, at least not fully. But once you become aware of the existence of such a thing, an ability to create a unique bond with an audience, you can begin to practice it in an effort to cultivate it within yourself.

Don't regard your audience as a mass, a screen of blank faces. They are people who want to hear you, to make contact with you, to communicate with you. Performers regularly speak of deriving energy from an audience. Tune in to your listeners as human folk, and you, too, can draw on this power.

It's not as mystical as it sounds. Begin by taking some practical, deliberate steps:

1. Use the first person: I, me.

2. Along with using the first person, adopt the active voice and eschew the passive. "I wrote the report" is a good, strong statement in the active voice. "The report was written by me" is a weak statement in the passive voice. The next step into the swamp of total anonymity would be to say "The report was written." Using the active voice puts you and your listeners in a world populated by living, breathing, *doing* humanity. The active voice makes people more important than actions or things. In contrast, the passive voice alienates listeners by serving up a murky world of beings whom we glimpse at best dimly, if at all. People take a back seat to acts and things. At its worst—as in the last example—people disappear altogether. Active voice not only

greatly simplifies your sentence structure (passive constructions are more awkward and require more words and more complex syntax than active constructions), it builds a rapport between you and the audience, an "I" and "thou."

3. While using the first person in reference to yourself, address the audience as "you."

4. Snuff out stale and overblown oratorical phrases such as "I am honored to have been chosen," "Unaccustomed as I am to public speaking," "Let us address the major issues of the day," and anything else that smacks of artificiality.

5. Don't make your audience conscious of passing time. "I have three minutes left" will drive your audience to concentrate on their watches and the clock on the wall rather than on what you have to say in those precious three minutes.

In addition to these means of establishing warm relations with your audience, please consult "Body Language" and "Getting Personal" in this section.

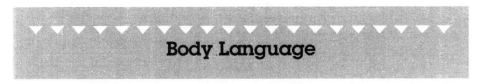

Body Language

A speech is speech, right? That's why they call it a *speech*.

This is true enough for a tape-recorded discourse, but one presented in the flesh is a live performance, consisting of words as well as actions. It hardly comes as news nowadays that the body speaks its own language, and many books have been written on the subject since Julius Fast published *The Body Language of Sex, Power and Aggression* in 1977. Fine. Most of us are willing to admit that body language—our visible gestures and expressions—have some effect on how our verbal messages come across.

Some effect? A 1971 study by psychologist Albert Mehrabian (cited in Jeff Scott Cook's *The Elements of Speechwriting and Public Speaking* [Collier, 1989]) reveals this startling fact: When listeners judge the "emotional content" of a speech, they give greatest weight to facial expression and body movement (55 percent), followed by vocal qualities (tone of voice, etc., 38 percent), and only then to the words themselves (a mere 7 percent). It behooves the effective speaker, therefore, to devote some attention to his or her body language, at least to the extent of ensuring that facial expressions and bodily gestures are in harmony with the verbal message.

The one thing everybody knows about body language and speech is the importance of eye contact. We speak of a dishonest person as "shifty-eyed," and when we doubt someone's veracity, we'll ask him to "look me in the eye and say that." Obviously, then, it is important to maintain good eye contact during the course of your speech if you want your remarks (as that most revealing and relevant phrase puts it) to be taken at face value. This shouldn't be too difficult, but, unfortunately, it often is. Why? There are mechanical, logistical, and psychological reasons.

Mechanical: Many of us find it difficult to read from a manuscript without taking our eyes off it. We fear we'll lose our place. Two things can help us get over this hurdle. First, make sure that you type the speech neatly and legibly. See "Typing the Speech" later in this section for details. Another factor that contributes to legibility is adequate lighting at the podium; consult "Lighting" in this section for a brief discussion. Also make certain that your microphone, if you are using one, is positioned comfortably—neither so low that you feel compelled to look down at it, nor so high that it interferes with your field of vision. Finally, even if you have completely written out your speech, rehearse it, practice it so that it becomes familiar; see "Reading, Memorizing, Rehearsing, and Winging It." Practice the technique of glancing down at your speech, absorbing a phrase or sentence, then looking up. The more familiar you are with what you have written, the more legibly you have typed it, and the better lighted it is, the easier it will be for you to look down, absorb, and look up with a natural, graceful rhythm.

Logistical: Even shy folk can train themselves to make eye contact in the course of one-to-one conversation. But how do you make simultaneous contact with twenty, fifty, a hundred or more pairs of eyes in a meeting room?

The answer is, you can't and you don't. Experienced speakers learn not to gaze out into a shifting—and highly distracting—sea of faces. Instead, they talk to one person at a time, making eye contact with that one person for a few moments—five to fifteen slow beats is a good measure—then moving on to another. This will have the effect of visually underscoring your credibility, enlivening the speech (nobody wants to hear a reader, head down, drone on and on), and establishing a bond of intimacy with the audience, who will, quite accurately, get the feeling that you are speaking to them personally and as individuals.

I wear eyeglasses, and I can tell you that they do present a potential obstacle to maintaining eye contact. I make certain they are clean and tight fitting. Glasses that slip down your nose are annoying and distracting to you—and even more so to your audience, who has to watch the ticlike lifting of hand to face and who must anxiously anticipate the spectacles' falling to the podium or the floor (thinking, perhaps uncharitably, Well, at least, *that* would bring an end to this irritating speech). Don't do without glasses if you need them. Whatever problems they may cause are far less significant than the consequences of not being able to read your speech easily and smoothly. Nor should you be reluctant to wear your eyeglasses because you think they make you look old, infirm, or like a nerd. Most audiences do not equate glasses with age or infirmity, but with wisdom—a plus. As to looking like a nerd, it certainly is possible to select eyewear clumsy enough to match that ink-stained plastic pen protector you wear in your wrinkled white shirt—the one that has the little notches in the short sleeves. But there are a lot of other, quite fashionable eyeglass styles available as well.

There are two types of eyeglasses speakers should avoid. Bifocals (or trifocals) and half-frame reading glasses force you literally to look down your nose at your audience, giving your listeners the uncomfortable feeling that you hold them in contempt. Purchase full reading glasses at least for speech-making purposes.

Of course, you can sidestep the entire issue of eyeglasses by wearing contact lenses. But many people—myself included—cannot stand the thought (let alone the deed) of poking themselves in the eye with a piece of plastic.

Let's move out from the eyes to the face. The great silent film actor Lon Chaney, Sr., was billed as the "Man with a Thousand Faces." This instance of Hollywood hyperbole was actually an understatement. It has been calculated that each of us exhibits a range of at least *seven* thousand facial expressions. The difference between us ordinary folk and a Lon Chaney is that he, like other gifted and well-trained actors, learned how to command—consciously and at will—a wealth of the expressions available to him. Alas, few of us possess the natural ability to do the same; nor can we afford to invest the time and cash necessary to secure professional training.

This does not mean that you should neglect the matter of facial expression. The simplest positive step you can take is to smile more often than you are accustomed to doing. Obviously, this is not called for if you are delivering a eulogy on a dear departed friend or a report on your firm's impending bankruptcy. But, in most speaking situations, a pleasant smile is appropriate and certainly preferable to a grimace or a hard-set frown.

Beyond this, if you will be speaking regularly, you should consider videotaping some of your performances or, at least, your rehearsals. Take the tape and view it—alone—once with the sound on and again with the sound off. Make careful note of any repetitive or distracting gestures or expressions. Work on ridding yourself of them.

Now, from the face to the body. Except for the middle period in the history of rock 'n' roll and the heavy-metal headbangers of today, it has always been possible to distinguish dance from random motion. In varying degrees, dance consists of prescribed or choreographed steps coordinated to music. Similarly, the experienced speaker learns to choreograph her movements to suit her message in order to facilitate communication. She retains only those gestures that are useful, while suppressing any that are random, nervous, distracting, or ticlike.

It is generally easier to take away than to create and cultivate. So begin by ferreting out any nervous gestures that afflict you and that you, in turn, inflict on your audience. Most common among the purposeless distractions are continuous hand motions, face rubbing, shoulder shrugging, adjustment of clothing, pacing, and, most prevalent and most distracting, habitually shifting weight from one side to the other. Using a videotape, identify any of these and work on eliminating them. Once you've established a more or less clean slate by getting rid of what you don't want, think about developing some purposeful gestures. The goal, after all, is not to learn how to stand stock still and function as the human equivalent of a loudspeaker, but to use gestures to underscore, propel, and energize verbal language.

There is a long way and a shorter way to accomplish this coordination. The long way involves close observation of effective public speakers and even seeking professional speech coaching or acting lessons. I don't offer this alternative as a rhetorical extreme, but as a very reasonable option, especially if your livelihood requires frequent speaking. For most of us, however, the shorter course is the more practical. Most of us use our hands in conversation, especially when we are making an emphatic point.

Moreover, we don't gesture idly, but purposefully, though without thinking about it. Try to achieve the same level of emotional commitment to what you are saying in a speech as you feel when you are talking to a good friend about something that has genuine meaning for you. Then let yourself gesture naturally and emphatically.

Elsewhere in this book, I have pointed out some basics of body language. They bear repeating here.

Adopt a firm but comfortable stance at the podium. (If you are short and the podium is tall, stand on a box or step to the side or in front of the podium.) Practice good posture: stand upright. Be aware that crossing your arms in front of you suggests a closed attitude, as if you are resisting input from the outside. Placing your hands on your hips, in the manner of Benito Mussolini, communicates defiance. Avoid bringing your hands to your mouth; this conveys evasion. Running your hand across your forehead not only conveys evasiveness, but anxiety as well. While you should freely, naturally, but purposefully use your hands to underscore the verbal points you make, beware of pounding the podium or clenching your fists. Such gestures are not 100 percent taboo, but they must be used very, very sparingly. For gesturing purposes, it is generally better to keep your hands open or to make an open fist, in which only the thumb, index finger, and middle finger make contact at their tips.

Clothes

This is not the place to present a dissertation on "dressing for success." (As I type this, I'm dressed in blue jeans and a T-shirt—though, admittedly, there's no one else in the room.) But there are a few points universal enough to be made here.

1. Be yourself—unless you are (frankly) a slob or very, very strange.

2. Learn from the well-dressed sales executive, who aims to dress *just a little more* expensively than his client. You don't want to dress so

impressively that you impress your audience as a "fat cat" or a "snob," in short, someone from an alien culture. The exception to this is if you are an investment broker (or the equivalent) speaking about or promoting investment. In this case, by all means, dress expensively, impeccably, but conservatively. In a money game, the proper clothes communicate confidence.

3. Avoid the bizarre or *outré*.

4. Avoid loud patterns and jarring color combinations. This is always important, but particularly crucial if you are appearing on television. Video equipment has a tough time digesting sharp contrasts, loud patterns, small patterns (checks, hound's-tooth zigzags, etc.), and bright whites. For television, wear a light blue, light gray, or light tan (khaki) shirt in preference to white.

5. More important than the style of your clothing is its condition. It should be spotless, shirts freshly laundered and suits and skirts dry cleaned especially for the occasion.

6. Avoid wearing elaborate jewelry. It is visually distracting, and it gets in the way of the podium and the microphone. Lapel mikes are notorious for picking up the jingle-jangle and click-clack of pendulous jewelry. Shiny jewelry also reflects the bright lights of television, creating a distracting video "burn" that is the bane of studio engineers and viewing audiences alike.

7. To pick up on the first point, be yourself. Wear what makes you feel good about yourself. If that means going out and buying new clothes, a speaking engagement is a better excuse than most for doing just that. If it means donning something old and familiar, well, just make sure it's clean and pressed and in tip-top repair.

Comfort

Let's face it. It may not be possible for you to get comfortable facing a hundred or more strangers and semi-strangers whose collective attention is focused on you. We'll deal with nerves under its own heading later in this section; however, here is a checklist of steps to take to ensure as much comfort as possible:

1. Prepare. Nothing will make you more comfortable than adequate preparation.

2. Get a good night's sleep.

3. Don't go to the podium hungry (positioned low enough, a good lapel mike will pick up gastric rumblings very nicely), but don't fill up on unfamiliar food, either.

4. Limit your intake of coffee and sweets. If you are accustomed to having a cup of coffee to wake up, don't choose the occasion of your speech to break that habit, but don't load up on caffeine or processed sugar. These will raise your anxiety level. Drink too much coffee and you may actually feel buzzed, tipsy, and disoriented.

5. Wear clothing as comfortable as the situation permits. Avoid anything constricting—trousers, jackets, shirts, and skirts you've "outgrown," or tightly tied neckwear. Feeling neat and natty—feeling that you look your best—will also increase your level of comfort.

6. Go to the bathroom before you venture onstage.

7. See that you are provided with a pitcher of water and a glass. Fill the glass before the program begins.

8. To the degree possible, familiarize yourself with the lecture hall or meeting room. Make sure you know how to work all audio-visual equipment, including microphones and slide projection equipment. By all means, try to check out the podium lighting beforehand.

9. If it is within your power to do so, adjust the climate of the room for optimum temperature and ventilation. In a room that will hold fifty to one hundred persons, a temperature of 68 to 70 degrees is about right.

10. In general, do what you can to ensure the comfort of your audience: provide the proper climate, glare-free lighting, minimize extraneous noise, and furnish comfortable seating. The more comfortable your audience, the more comfortable you will be.

Diction, Pronunciation, and Grammar

If you must make your living in significant measure through public speaking, you should, as I suggested earlier, consider investing time and cash in professional coaching, both acting and voice. When the Warner Brothers' *Jazz Singer* sounded the death knell for silent films in 1927, Hollywood rushed its hitherto mute actors and actresses to diction coaches. After all, it wouldn't do for the Count of Monte Cristo to sound like one of the Lords of Flatbush. Similarly, I taught for some years at a small southern college specializing in preparing students for law and business administration. In the neighborhood of the college, a private diction coach prospered by promising to teach students how to overcome "talking southern."

It is commonly believed that a flat, "neutral" midwestern accent is best for the public speaker. "Least offensive, most desirable," diction experts say. I believe, however, that, regardless of your region of origin, the really important thing is to speak clearly, giving full value to each of your words and to each syllable within those words. To my ear, regional variations are not only permissible, they are even attractive; I don't go to New Orleans to eat the Styrofoam-packaged fast food I can get in New Jersey. It is possible, though, that your audience will equate some geographically influenced features of diction as evidence of poor education or lower economic origin. Nothing wrong, of course, with wearing a blue collar—unless you are speaking to a white-collar audience. Our democracy proclaims equality for all, but ours is hardly a classless society. Remember the lesson of George Bernard Shaw's *Pygmalion* (or its musical incarnation as *My Fair Lady*) if you doubt that diction greatly affects how you—and your message—will be perceived.

This is not the place to make a complete list of regional and socioeconomic habits of diction that will load you down with negative freight, but here are some of the more common locutions most likely to work against you:

ax for "ask"

d for *th* (dis for "this," etc.)

failure to pronounce the entire word ('n for "and," woulda for "would have," etc.)

heighth for "height"

in for *ing* (nothin' for "nothing," etc.)

pixture for "picture"

t for *th* (boat for "both," etc.)

Contractions (don't for "do not," etc.) make some speakers uptight. I don't object to them, because they lend a conversational touch to any speech. However, when you want to underscore a point, use the long form. "Merely hoping for the best isn't enough" is not as effective as "Merely hoping for the best is not enough."

In a single sentence, here is what you should do to ensure effective diction: First, purge your speech of the habits of diction that work against you, then take the more positive step of opening your mouth and slowing down.

Closely related to diction is pronunciation. Speakers of languages other than ours often express amazement at the range of pronunciation English allows as "correct." Modern dictionaries have given up much of their traditional prescriptive role as arbiters of correct pronunciation and, instead, "report" a range of pronunciation for a given word, even telling us that the order in which these pronunciations are listed is not intended to reflect a judgment as to which pronunciation is "preferred." Despite all this, it is certainly still possible to mispronounce an English word, and, let's be frank, doing so can make you sound dumb. Look up any word or proper name of which you are unsure. In your typescript, spell it out phonetically and, if necessary, indicate the accented syllables. If you are introducing other speakers, make certain you pronounce their names correctly. Check it out with them personally.

The harsh fact is that as an audience will not forgive poor diction or obvious errors of pronunciation, neither will they excuse grammatical clinkers. I don't have the space to provide a guide to grammar, but, fortunately, I don't have to. An excellent, concise, painless, and even pleasurable one exists that will give you all the guidance you're likely to need. *The Elements of Style*, by William Strunk, Jr., and E. B. White, published in paperback by Collier Books and universally known to writers and writing teachers simply as Strunk and White, is justly considered a classic.

If you use a computer to write your speeches, you might find some of the currently available grammar-checking software useful. These programs comb your manuscript, ferreting out and flagging any questionable sentences. Some of them even give you stylistic comments ("too wordy," "confusing," etc.). The flaw in some of these programs all the time and all these programs some of the time is that they flag *too many* sentences as questionable. If you are in a hurry, this can really try your patience. If you already lack confidence in your writing, this can shake you up even more. (The stylistic function of these programs is particularly finicky. If most of this software would choke on the likes of Faulkner, Fitzgerald, Mailer, and Styron, what will it do to you and me?) I suggest that, if you do use such programs, you use them in conjunction with Strunk and White or another solid guide to grammar and style.

Finally, a word on spelling. Who cares, you say, as long as *you* can read it?

True enough, if you are sure that nobody else will ever see your manuscript. But what if you give your manuscript to a local newspaper for publication or to *Vital Speeches of the Day* or any of the other journals that regularly publish speeches? (See "Publicizing and Publishing" later in this section.) It is best to take the time to proofread your spelling. For those who compose on computer, I can unreservedly recommend the "spell-checking" software that is usually a part of the most widely used word-processing programs. These programs have gotten very good at finding errors. Otherwise, consult a good modern dictionary.

Getting Personal

Most novice speechwriters do everything they can to stamp out every last trace of humanity that may stray into their presentations. They avoid speaking in the first person, substituting "one" or, perhaps, the imperial "we" where "I" is called for. They use complex and tiresome passive sentence construction where the active voice would greatly simplify and vitalize their message. They never address the audience directly. They avoid all reference to themselves.

Throughout this book, I have suggested a strategy of getting personal—that is, speaking as yourself and speaking directly to your audience, communicating as one human being to another.

I have very little fear that my advice to get personal will result in a wave of shocking confessional speeches sweeping across the nation's

Kiwanis clubs. However, do exercise common sense. By all means, whenever appropriate—by which I mean whenever it is genuinely meaningful to do so—speak from your own experience. Nothing is more powerful and commands more attention than one human being reaching out in direct communication to another. But beware of irrelevant personal details. Don't spill your guts when what's really required is the Annual Treasurer's Report.

The same principle holds true in addressing members of the audience. Beware of directing your speech to this or that individual or to a clique of friends. To be sure, you need not ignore audience members you know. If it is relevant to your message, you may even make special reference to someone present. But don't turn your talk into a personal dialogue that excludes the majority of your listeners. Also avoid embarrassing individuals in your audience by making revelations about them they may not want to share or by coaxing them to say something they may not want to say or for which they may be unprepared. If you plan to call on Joe Blow to give an "impromptu" report on the progress of a project, work it out with him well in advance of your speech. Don't put anyone on the spot. It will be awkward for that person (who will hate you for it), for your audience (who will fear that they, too, are at risk), and for yourself (who will look sadistic and silly).

Hecklers

Relax. This is largely a nonproblem. Hecklers are, fortunately, a very rare breed. Most speaking situations do not lend themselves to heckling, anyway. If hecklers are to be found anywhere, they are liable to show up at controversial or strongly partisan speeches or where liquor is served (nightclub comics *do* regularly contend with this sort of person).

Okay and great. But what if the unlikely does happen. What if you are beset by a heckler?

If the heckling is relatively innocuous—a hand upraised and waving as if the audience member is undergoing a flashback to his days as a second-grader—ignore it. Chances are, the hand will come down.

If the heckler is or becomes more insistent, especially if he speaks up, do not try to outshout him. Stop speaking, look him in the eye, and politely *ask* him to hold his question until after the speech. Most of the time, this will prove effective.

If the heckler persists, stop again, and speak to him again. This time, however, assert more control by framing what you say as a declaration rather than a request: "As I said, I will be happy to take questions *after* I have concluded my remarks."

Escalation at this point is unlikely, but it is possible. Now is the time to put the heat on the heckler. "I have been invited to speak here. *My* name is Mary James from Gordon and James, Inc. Suppose you tell us *your* name." Most hecklers crave anonymity and will back down. If, however, the heckling continues, it is time for you to stop, step away from the podium, and look at the person who invited you to speak. Let him deal with the heckler. Failing that, look out at your audience. Let them apply the necessary pressure. If everything fails, leave quietly and without demonstration.

Humor

To paraphrase Dr. Samuel Johnson's remark on patriotism, humor is the first resort of nervous speakers. Don't get me wrong, genuine humor is welcome in virtually any speech. Audiences love to laugh, and we all crave amusement. The trouble is that many speakers equate *humor* with *joke*, and, in the manner of the old-fashioned traveling salesman, hamhandedly graft a "good one" onto the head end of a speech to "soften the audience up." Irrelevant humor culled from joke books and "speaker's handbooks" instantly turns off any audience that possesses an ounce of sophistication.

Here are some serious rules for using humor in a speech:

1. Make sure it is relevant to your message—not just an add-on to kill time.

2. The more original the material, the better. Avoid canned jokes and off-the-shelf humor.

3. Avoid humor that offends, embarrasses, hurts, or humiliates anyone.

4. Avoid sexist, racist, or religious humor.

5. Avoid using humor to make a serious situation seem less serious. By all means, a speech delivered in or about a crisis should help put that crisis in a perspective that will allay panic and promote effective action. But an attempt to laugh off a problem or make light of a grave situation is not only ineffective, it is irresponsible, and it will certainly backfire on you.

6. If you are not adept at telling a story, you should probably avoid humor altogether. It will fall flat.

7. Unless you are a good comic storyteller, don't base your speech on laughs.

Lighting

You may not have a great deal of control over the lighting that will be provided at the site of your speech, but try to ensure that:

▼ *You as well as your audience have adequate light.* If you were a pop star or a rock act, darkening the hall and putting the spotlight on you would be a good idea. Unfortunately, in a speaking situation, a darkened room invites audience somnolence. It also prevents your listeners from taking notes, if they so wish.

▼ *The podium is provided with adequate light.* If you can't see your script, you can't read your speech.

▼ *Glare is minimized.* Close any window curtains behind you.

▼ *Lighting on you is flattering and comfortable.* Don't let spotlights blind you, making it difficult for you to read your speech or to make eye contact with the audience.

▼ *The room can be darkened adequately if you are going to use slides or overhead transparencies.* In this age of media saturation, the projection of still images is not very exciting. If slides and overheads are truly relevant to your talk, by all means use them. If, however, they are marginal, minimize their use. The less time you keep your audience in a darkened room, the less incentive you give them to drift into semiconsciousness or, indeed, a profound (and perhaps highly audible) slumber.

Nerves

The best advice I can give on the subject of nerves is just to get used to feeling scared. The butterflies in the stomach, the sweaty palms, the feeling of dread—the whole nine yards: just get used to them. These things are, after all, only feelings. Feel them, and get on with the speech.

You can also take steps to minimize the unpleasant aspects of anxiety. Read the chapter on "Comfort" in this section. Prepare and rehearse; nothing allays anxiety like confidence, and nothing builds confidence more effectively than competence born of preparation and rehearsal. Beyond this, understand that anxiety and the unpleasant sensations that accompany it are perfectly normal. Then sit down and make a list of what you fear. What are the worst things that are going to happen to you when you get up to speak? Look at the list, then evaluate it realistically. Your list may include:

▼ *The audience will laugh at me.* Why? What's so funny about you?

▼ *The audience will discover that I know nothing.* In twenty minutes? Anyway, if you know (or learn) enough about your subject to talk for twenty minutes or so, you've acquired a great deal of knowledge. If someone asks you a question to which you don't have the answer, tell him that you don't know, but that you'll look into it.

▼ *The audience will be bored.* Create a speech that interests *you*, and it is likely that most of your audience will be interested as well.

▼ *I'll freeze up or make a big blunder.* Prepare. Arm yourself with a good script or thorough notes. You may as if you're freezing up, but, unless you've made the mistake of trying to wing the whole affair, you have simply to remember how to read. This should give you the push you need, if you need it.

▾ *My voice will fail.* Have a glass of water ready. If you voice does crack, flash a knowing smile to your audience. It will endear you to them in all of your humanness.

▾ *I'll get sick or wet myself.* If these things happen to you with any frequency, consult a physician; there are medications to help. If such accidents have not occurred to you in the past, they're not likely to occur now.

After realistically appraising your fears, try some of the following to reduce the physical sensations of anxiety:

1. Understand that you will feel uncomfortable, but that such adrenaline-related sensations as sweaty palms; tight, dry throat; rapid heartbeat; weak knees; flushed face; and butterflies will recede or pass altogether once you are into the speech.

2. Take a walk before your speech. If possible and practical, step outside into the fresh air and the "real world."

3. Take a few deep, cleansing breaths.

4. Stretch and move.

5. If you have heart palpitations, try forcing a yawn or a few vigorous coughs. This often helps.

6. Mouth dry? Have some water or chew some gum. (Remove it before you speak, of course).

7. As soldiers obliged to stand at attention in the hot sun quickly learn, don't stand with your knees locked. Flex them slightly.

8. Avoid unusual quantities of coffee and food containing large amounts of processed sugar. These things may help to get you "up" for a speech, but a little too much will significantly raise your level of anxiety and reduce your ability to concentrate.

9. Avoid alcohol or (except on the advice of a physician) tranquilizers. These may or may not calm you. (Indeed, alcohol may have the opposite effect.) What they will almost certainly do is make you less alert,

which definitely will not improve your performance. You are better off enduring some discomfort and, in fact, learning to use it to help you hone what athletes call their "competitive edge." (A note of extra caution: In your anxiety, do NOT be tempted to self-medicate by mixing prescription—or even nonprescription—drugs. And remember, combining alcohol with tranquilizers can put you to sleep, maybe even permanently.)

10. Bear in mind that, unless you are addressing a meeting of Sadists International, the overwhelming majority of your audience wants your speech to be a success. They are on your side. Really.

Off-Color Language, Remarks, and Stories

Little needs to be said on this subject, but that little does need to be said. Whatever your feelings about the First Amendment to the United States Constitution (as a writer, my sentiments on this topic are particularly strong) and regardless of your attitude toward acts of communication between and among consenting adults, off-color language, remarks, and stories have no place in any speech you are likely to give.

You are not a nightclub—or cable TV—comic. As far as smutty stories are concerned in public speaking, just say no. It is not only that you risk offending someone and thereby turn off part or all of your audience, but that, in imposing off-color material on your listeners, you risk treading on *their* rights. Sure, you have a right to free speech. But your listeners have a right not to be offended or embarrassed.

The question of what constitutes obscenity is subject to endless debate. One Supreme Court justice threw up his hands and simply declared that he couldn't define obscenity, but he knew it when he saw it. I would argue that there is one area of obscenity that, in a democracy, we cannot afford to dispute. Avoid language, remarks, and stories based on sexist, racist, or ethnically denigrating assumptions and ideas. These are obscene without question and, beyond question, absolutely unacceptable.

Publicizing and Publishing

The chapters on "Radio" and "Television" in "Part Two: Special Subjects" discuss how to bring your speech to the attention of radio and television program directors. Here are some additional ideas for getting the most publicity mileage out of your speech:

▼ Give serious thought to a provocative title. The title should offer your audience (as well as the greater audience of TV viewers, radio listeners, and newspaper readers) something of value to them: "Talking Yourself into a Better Job," "It's 10 A.M.: Do you Know Where Your Children Are?" and so on.

▼ Make copies of your presentation available to your audience. Unless your talk is of a highly demanding technical nature, make sure you distribute the copies *after* your speech. You don't want a lot of people noisily fumbling through papers when they should be listening to you.

▼ Make use of your company's public relations office or the publicist associated with the organization that has invited you to speak. Give the appropriate person or persons a copy of your speech, together with an abstract and a resume. *Do not count on these folks coming to you.* Go to them with the material.

▼ Identify specialist and trade publications that will be interested in the topic of your talk. Invite representatives to the speech itself. Send them an abstract of the talk in advance. Immediately before or after the event, send a copy of the complete text. Take time to highlight with a bright transparent marker anything especially germane or quotable. Unless you know of a specific contact person, address the material to the editor or managing editor.

▼ Prepare a press release, which amounts to a strong abstract of your speech, and distribute it to the media, including community newspapers, local media, and local college newspapers. Try to get coverage of the speech itself. Immediately before or after the event, send a highlighted copy of the complete text to the appropriate editors or reporters.

Even after the immediate newsworthiness of the speech has faded, you can extend its life by distributing a self-published version of the text to key individuals in your field. With the availability of desktop publishing and inexpensive laser printers, you can make the document attractive and professional looking. You should also consider sending a copy to *Vital Speeches of the Day* (City News Publishing Company, P.O. Box 1247, Mount Pleasant, SC 29465), which reprints current speeches on a wide variety of topics. The newsletter-style publications is issued twice a month and is in the periodical collection of all major and many moderate-sized libraries, including school libraries. Other reprint outlets worth tapping are *Speechwriter's Newsletter* (407 South Dearborn Street, Chicago, IL 60605) and *The Executive Speaker* (P.O. Box 2094, Dayton, OH 45429).

Whenever you offer your speech for publication, make sure you send a clean and thoroughly proofread manuscript. These days, if you can, offer a keyboarded manuscript on computer diskette in addition to the "hard copy." This will save the publisher the labor of typesetting it from a manuscript, will minimize errors, and may serve as an added enticement to publish. You should also offer to read galleys or proofs—but you should not demand to do so.

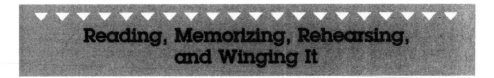

Reading, Memorizing, Rehearsing, and Winging It

I was trained as a college instructor at a time when the emphasis was so heavily on spontaneity in the classroom that *lecture* became a dirty word. Once I actually started teaching, I soon discovered that students are not, in fact, turned off by lectures. What turns them off are poorly written, tedious, droningly delivered lectures. And this is not the only thing that turns them off. Misguided and ill-prepared stabs at spontaneity—*at winging it*—deeply offend students, especially those who are paying their own way through college. Confronted by a professor spouting random remarks, they feel cheated—and for very good reason.

I believe that my experience as a teacher applies to public speaking in general. Give up the idea that audiences are turned off by a well-written speech well read, that what they crave is unbridled spontaneity. Few of us have the gift of delivering spontaneity in a consistently interesting and informative manner. Why, then, expose our listeners to what we cannot do exceptionally well?

Unless you are a brilliant impromptu speaker, write your speech and read it.

Read it well, however. Writing out your speech does not absolve you from the responsibility of rehearsing it any more than possessing the score of a Mozart piano sonata absolves a concert pianist from practicing the work before performing it in public. Rehearsal will accomplish six things:

1. It will give you an opportunity to *hear* your speech before you commit it, irretrievably, to the public ear. Don't read it aloud for the first time with the purpose of congratulating yourself. Listen for anything that sounds awkward or that falls short or wide of the target. Make the necessary revisions—now. You should NOT attempt your first trial reading immediately after you have written the speech. Let the completed manuscript "cool" for at least a day—preferably two—before you try it out on yourself.

2. It will give you an opportunity to indicate points that should be verbally and/or visually emphasized. Mark these, just as a pianist would mark special places in his score.

3. It will identify any words you have a tendency to stumble over. If possible, substitute other words. If this can't be done, provide yourself with appropriate phonetic clues.

4. It will make you aware of the logical and dramatic rhythms of your speech. You'll appreciate where to slow down, where to pause, where to speed up, where to increase volume, and where to reduce it. Mark these places.

5. It will give you an accurate idea of the length of your speech. The rule of thumb is that each typewritten page consisting of about 300 words takes two minutes to deliver. But you never know for certain until you actually read the speech aloud.

6. It will get you accustomed to the piece, so that you will, to a degree, commit it to memory. This will make it easier for you to read with conviction and enthusiasm and without having to keep your gaze glued to the page under your nose rather than the audience in front of you.

Should you rehearse in private, in front of a friend, or before a small "rehearsal audience"? The easy answer is to do whatever you are comfortable with. My personal preference is to rehearse entirely in private. (Certainly, your first read-through should be done in solitude.) If I want the opinion of a friend or two, I give them the manuscript to read for themselves, since I find it unnatural and awkward to deliver a speech to one or two people sitting across a table from me. If you can gather together a rehearsal audience, you might try that technique. But I have never had the luxury of drawing on such a group, and I don't know any speaker who has.

There are wonderful speakers who insist on memorizing their entire speech rather than reading it. Garrison Keillor, the writer and host of Public Radio's "Prairie Home Companion" and other shows, delivers marvelous, elaborate, and lengthy monologues that he fully writes out and then fully commits to memory. If you possess a talent for memorization, by all means a well-delivered speech spoken without script or notes will greatly impress your audience. It's up to you. Just remember: there is no dishonor in reading a speech, as long as you read it well.

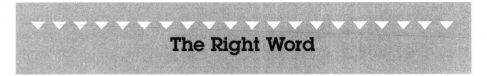

The Right Word

The great French novelist Gustave Flaubert, author of *Madame Bovary* and a handful of other masterpieces, was famous for the slow and meticulous pains he took in order to find what he called *"le mot juste,"* the right word. *Madame Bovary* was the product of seven years' labor. The American librettist Oscar Hammerstein II, collaborator with Richard Rodgers on such musicals as *Oklahoma!* and *The King and I*, was similarly obsessive. It is said that he pondered a full two weeks over whether to begin the song that opens *Oklahoma!* with or without the "Oh" ("what a beautiful morning").

Few of us can afford to invest the kind of time available to Flaubert or Hammerstein, but any time we do invest in finding what Mark Twain called "the right word, not its second cousin" will be amply repaid.

There are no absolute rules for finding the right word, but, usually, the simplest term, the most concrete, the most vividly appealing to the senses is the strongest and best choice. Minimize the use of adjectives and various qualifiers while emphasizing solid verbs and nouns. Not "he shouted loudly," but "he roared." Not "they objected violently," but "they rebelled." Did she *win, triumph, conquer,* or *overcome*? I *understand* or I *grasp*? He *likes, loves, admires, appreciates, is fond of,* or *has an affection for*?

You will certainly find it helpful to consult a good dictionary in your search for the right word. You will probably also find a thesaurus of some value.

Slang

For linguists and etymologists, professional students of language, slang is a topic of endless fascination. It is difficult to define slang precisely (indeed, a symposium held in Paris during 1989 for the specific purpose of arriving at a definition broke up after several weeks without having reached a consensus), but the poet Carl Sandburg called it "language that rolls up its sleeves, spits on its hands and goes to work." At its best, this is certainly the case. For instance, the word *skyscraper* started out as slang, and the language offers no term more vivid to describe a building so sharp and tall that it seems to abrade the very heavens. The trouble is that it's difficult to tell in the heat of the present moment which slang terms will live long and prosper, moving from the periphery of generally accepted vocabulary to its mainstream, and which will wither and die or merely degenerate into quaintness. (Groovy, man. Like, far out.)

Slang can enliven a speech or can date it—and, if you're not sufficiently hip (hep?) to the jive—it can date the speaker as well. Some rules of thumb:

▼ All else being equal, if you can find an effective, vivid word in "standard" (that is, mainstream) English to say what you want to say, use it in preference to slang.

▼ If you are comfortable with a slang term, chances are your audience will be as well. If the term makes you uncomfortable, why use it?

▼ Observe decorum. Don't appeal to diners at a $5,000-a-plate charity gala to "lay some more bread on us."

▼ Beware of ethnic slang. You run a very real risk of appearing to mock the group whose language you are borrowing. If you yourself are a member of that group, you run the risk of alienating those in your audience who are of different ethnic background.

▼ Slang is by no means synonymous with smut. However, as language "at an extreme position on the spectrum of formality" (to borrow the definition Tony Thorne gives in his marvelous *Dictionary of Contemporary Slang* [Pantheon, 1990]), slang does often encompass sexual and scatological taboos. Usually, these have no place in a speech that readers of this book are likely to give. (See "Off-Color Language, Remarks, and Stories" earlier in this section.)

▼ Slang is best employed sparingly, like a dash of tabasco, not served up as a main course. It can be very effective, especially to make a strong point in a speech otherwise framed in mainstream English.

Surviving Mistakes

One of the most moving piano recitals I ever heard was by the late Rudolf Serkin, who delivered a luminous performance of the Beethoven *Waldstein Sonata* and the Schubert *Wanderer Fantasy*. During one of the innumerable virtuoso runs that make up the Schubert work, Serkin's fingers became audibly tangled, but he went on. When he rose from the bench at the conclusion of the piece, he acknowledged his error by good naturedly shaking his fist at the piano, evoking laughter from the audience, who, I can assure you, were nonetheless moved by the performance as a whole. It was a more revealing, more beautiful rendition of this piece than many other "perfect" versions I have heard played by other musicians before or since. The lesson is obvious: Deliver a good product overall, and you will be forgiven an error or two, even an obvious one. Moreover, just as Rudolf Serkin's audience did not attend his recital for the purpose of catching him in a blunder—as if waiting to pounce on that wrong note—so it is highly unlikely that your audience will have gathered for the express purpose of hearing you make a mistake. And if you do err, well, we all do. Acknowledge the gaffe and get on with the show.

Broadly speaking, there are three kinds of mishaps that may befall you when you speak.

1. Your tongue may trip. Don't try to cover this up. Doing so usually results in compounding the gaffe. Instead, pause. Smile. Start the sentence again and proceed.

2. You may experience "technical difficulties." A microphone may fail. A slide projector may break down. A guest speaker due at the dais may be stuck on the Turnpike. Again, don't try to cover up. Explain to your audience what has happened and what you are doing to remedy the situation or how you plan to carry on despite the problem. Do whatever you can to avoid making your audience wait, and don't blame anyone ("The audio-visual person should have . . ."), including yourself ("This wouldn't have happened if I had only . . ."). The best strategy, of course, is to take to heart that hoary old law of Murphy and assume that, if anything *can* go wrong, it will. Try to anticipate and prepare for technical difficulties: Have on hand extra projector bulbs and even a spare projector. Tell your guest speaker to arrive at 9 A.M., even though he won't go on until 10:30.

3. You may commit an error of fact. World War II veteran George Bush embarrassed himself early in his term as president when, in a speech, he gave the date of the Japanese attack on Pearl Harbor as *September 7, 1941*, and Mr. Bush's vice president erred so frequently that a small magazine was started just to publicize Dan Quayle's latest howler. If, in mid-speech, you realize that (as Mr. Bush put it) you "misspoke yourself," stop at a convenient point and correct your error. Don't try to cover it up, hoping no one will have caught it. And don't try to ignore it yourself. It will irritate and distract you throughout the balance of your presentation, prompting you into additional errors.

What if an audience member challenges a point of fact during a question-and-answer session? You should not react defensively, but neither should you plunge blindly into admitting an error. You should pause to hear your questioner out. If you are not convinced that you are in error, tell him and your audience that your sources indicate a different conclusion and that you would be interested in discussing the matter further with the questioner at the end of the program; alternatively, promise to investigate the matter further. If it seems likely to you that you are, indeed, mistaken, admit it—with an explanation: "You know, it is perfectly possible that you are correct. I was using figures based solely on the February study. You have had access to some additional information. I think this bears further investigation and discussion."

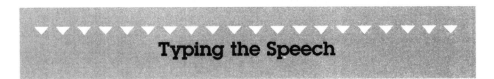

Typing the Speech

I knew a man who used to deliver sales presentations twice a year. He wrote out his speech, which is, of course, just fine, except that he really did *write it out*: in longhand, in pencil, on yellow legal paper. Up on the podium, the document was barely legible, and he would stumble through it in a manner both excruciating to watch and tedious in the extreme to hear.

Type your speech. At minimum, use a new, clean ribbon (preferably a black acetate ribbon rather than one made of fabric) and a clean typing element. Triple space the copy, leaving plenty of room at the top, bottom, and sides for margin space. Put four spaces between paragraphs.

Better than this is to use a typewriter equipped with the "speechwriter" typeface, a very large and very legible typeface designed expressly for speakers.

Better still, compose the speech on a computer and print it out on a laser printer using a 14-point sans-serif font. Always use upper and lower case.

Some additional pointers:

▼ Put your name at the upper right- or left-hand corner of each page, together with the name of the group to which you are speaking, the location of the speech, and its date.

▼ End each line with a complete word. Don't hyphenate, especially at the end of a page.

▼ Keep numbers together on a single line:

Six hundred dollars   *not*   Six
                               hundred dollars

▼ Spell out numbers, especially large numbers: Five billion, not 5,000,000,000. Never use Roman numerals.

▼ Best to end each page with a complete paragraph or at any other point where a natural pause occurs. In this way, shuffling a page won't cause you to introduce an awkward and purposeless pause.

▼ Number the pages clearly and boldly. (What if they fall to the floor?)

▼ Write out abbreviations with hyphens: PhD becomes P-H-D.

▼ Spell out difficult words and proper names phonetically, using a phonetical system that has meaning for you.

▼ Underline words you wish to emphasize.

▼ Use an ellipses (. . .) to mark brief pauses. Use # or // to indicate a longer pause of three or four beats. This is appropriate after a punchline or conclusion, to remind you to allow your audience a few moments to react.

▼ Do not staple your speech together. Hold it together with a paper clip, which you remove when you read the speech.

▼ Carry the speech in a folder so that it will stay crisp.

▼ Prepare two or three spare copies. Carry at least two with you in separate places (say a suitcase and a briefcase). If possible, deposit one copy with a trusted friend who will be present in the audience.

Using Facts and Figures

If you think that statistics appeal only to nerdy number crunchers, think again. We are a nation of number junkies perpetually hungry for statistics. This does not mean that your speech should indiscriminately reel off an endless stream of facts and figures. Use them selectively and in vivid context, but by all means, *use* them.

Just as you should choose your words with the goal of making your message as real, as concrete, and as appealing to the senses as possible, so you should use numbers in a way that maximizes their reality. What, you may ask, could be more real than numbers? Consider this statement, quoted in Jeff Scott Cook's *Elements of Speechwriting and Public Speaking*: "1988 inflation in Nicaragua has been 10,000 percent." Pretty impressive. But, as Cook pointed out, TV newsman Garrick Utley made it even more real in a report he delivered from Managua: "If America had inflation at the same rate as Nicaragua this past year, this pineapple that costs fifty cents would instead cost fifty dollars." Activate the numbers you use. Put them to work—instantly and dramatically.

Whenever possible, provide a context for facts and figures. If you declare that inflation is running 8.5 percent this year, point out that it was 7.5 percent the year before and has averaged out at 8.3 percent for the decade. Better yet, talk about what your dollar will buy today, compared to what it bought last year or ten years ago.

Where figures are likely to be controversial, cite your source—and make sure that it is, in fact, up-to-date and authoritative. If timely figures are unavailable, explain why. ("Since the Communist unification of North and South Vietnam, accurate figures on birth rates have been virtually impossible to obtain.")

To bolster your interpretation of statistics, you might draw on expert testimony. "What does a 10 percent rise in the rate of violent crime mean? Police Captain Rod Stark of the Village Police Department told me that his officers have investigated 230 more muggings, assaults, and rapes this year than they did last year, but that they have been able to solve only 1,850 cases this year as compared to 2,105 last year. More crime makes the police work harder, but less efficiently, and it leads, inevitably, to even more crime."

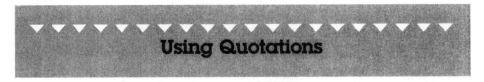

Using Quotations

A true story from my days as a college instructor: A student handed in a term paper on the philosopher Friedrich Nietzsche. I awarded it an F accompanied by the following comment: "This paper consists of approximately 1,800 words. Of these, some 250 are yours and the rest are Nietzsche's. Nietzsche passes. You don't."

Intelligently used, quotations are valuable adjuncts to a speech, extending its authority well beyond yourself and demonstrating that you are not shut up in an ivory tower, but that you are alive to the world around you. It is all too easy, however, to let quotations usurp your speech. Remember, it is *your* speech, and the words of others should be subordinated to yours. Beyond this caution, observe the following guidelines:

1. Keep the quoted material brief. Be selective. Don't distort the quotation, but do paraphrase the marginally relevant or dull parts and cut to the chase.

2. Work the quoted material organically into your speech. Not:

   President Dwight Eisenhower once said, and I quote "Farming looks mighty easy when your plow is a pencil and you're a thousand miles from a cornfield," unquote.

   But:

   President Dwight Eisenhower put it well by observing that farming "looks mighty easy when your plow is a pencil and you're a thousand miles from a cornfield."

   Use nonverbal cues or marginally verbal ones—a significant pause or a drop in the tone of your voice—to signal the beginning and end of a quotation.

3. If you use more than two or three quotations in a speech, make sure you draw from a variety of sources, especially if you are quoting material concerning a single subject. Not only will overuse of a single source bore your audience, they will come away feeling that they should be in the library reading your single source rather than listening to you give it to them secondhand.

4. Make certain you are quoting accurately and in context: "As Winston Churchill declared, 'Democracy is the worst system devised by the wit of man.'" Nope! "Democracy is the worst system devised by the wit of man, except for all the others."

5. Sure, we all use books such as *Bartlett's Familiar Quotations*, but be advised to gain at least a modicum of familiarity with the actual

source of any quotation you use. At least make sure you can correctly pronounce the name of the sage in question. (In my hometown of Chicago, everybody pronounces Goethe Street Go-ee-thee. But that doesn't make it right.)

Visuals

Technical talks, speeches involving numbers, and discussions involving geography (for example, a presentation concerning zoning) greatly benefit from visual aids. These do not have to be elaborate. Third-party presidential candidate H. Ross Perot made a strong impression during his 1992 campaign by appearing on television with simple but effective hand-drawn bar graphs and pie charts. The object is not to impress your audience with audio-visual hardware (in this age of big-screen televisions, VCRs, and high-resolution color computer monitors, that's pretty difficult to do in any case), but to subordinate the visuals to the speech, using them only as a graphic underscore to your words. When you are talking about market share, for example, a handy pie chart gives added meaning to the figures you're rattling off.

The visual aids you are most likely to use are flip charts, overhead transparencies, slides, videotape presentations, and visual handouts.

Flip charts are the simplest. Unless you are a quick-draw artist, prepare your illustrations in advance, using the best-quality and biggest flip chart you can find. And note that these really _should_ be illustrations, not just figures. Use graphs, pie charts, and the like to help make numbers come alive. Here are some additional guidelines:

▼ Make sure the lecture hall or meeting room will be equipped with an appropriate stand for your flip chart.

▼ Limit yourself to one graphic per page.

▼ Arrange your graphics in the precise order your speech requires.

▼ Leave a blank page between graphics. Do not flip to the graphic until you discuss it. Then cover it with the intervening blank page until you get to the next point requiring a graphic. You want your audience paying attention to you, not studying an out-of-synch illustration or anticipating what you're going to say next by examining the graphic for your upcoming point.

▼ Stand to one side of the chart and do not fall into the trap of directing your speech at *it* rather than the audience.

▼ Make sure that the terms you use in your speech are the terms that are written on the chart.

Overhead transparencies serve a function similar to that of the flip chart. The transparencies are easy to prepare and have the virtues and vices of the flip chart's graphic simplicity. What can go wrong?

▼ As with any projector, the bulb can burn out. Make sure spares are available.

▼ Unless they are clearly numbered, the transparencies can easily get out of sequence.

▼ The machine, which is equipped with a fan, may make a loud and distracting noise.

▼ The light from the overhead projector may be irritatingly bright, especially if your graphics are very simple. Dim the room lights only as much as is necessary for legibility on the screen. Usually, an overhead projector does not require a significantly darkened room—unless you are trying to project the image from too great a distance. Turn off the projector between transparencies, especially if there is a long pause between them.

▼ As with a flip chart, show your graphic only when you have reached the appropriate point in your talk. Do not keep the image on screen after you have finished discussing it.

Preparing good slides used to require the work of a professional. To be sure, professional photographers and graphic artists can still be employed effectively to produce top-quality slides, but if you are a good amateur photographer or know how to make use of computer graphics programs to create material that a specialized service bureau can transfer to slides, you can produce excellent 35-mm visuals on your own.

▼ Carefully coordinate the choice and order of the slides with your talk. You will be tempted to choose more slides than you need in a mistaken belief that the audience will find them entertaining. In fact, even very good slides cannot compete with the other kinds of graphic stimulation readily available to your audience in the form of television and movies. Use the fewest slides you need to get your message across.

▼ Even though the slides for a presentation are usually arranged in a "carousel" tray, number each of the cardboard mounts, just in case they fall out of the tray.

▼ As with flip charts and overhead transparencies, do not project the slide until you are ready to discuss that particular image. Unless the projector has a blackout feature, include opaque blanks in the carousel between each image so that you can remove the image from the screen when you have finished discussing it.

▼ Make sure that the room can be darkened adequately. Slides that are barely visible or washed out because of room light make for a most irritating and tedious presentation. Also make sure that the projector bulb is of sufficient wattage to cover the distance between the projector and the screen.

▼ Although slides do demand a darkened room, minimize the amount of time during which your audience is plunged into darkness. Depending on the time of day or evening (and, perhaps, the blood alcohol level of your listeners), a darkened room may well induce slumber.

Although presentation-quality video is expensive to produce, some speeches benefit from it and others virtually require it. Training seminars, documentary progress reports, and the like may consist of your live introduction, the presentation of the video, then your conducting a question-and-answer period. In general, it is difficult to subordinate a video of more than fifteen minutes' length to your talk.

Handouts can reproduce material presented visually during the speech or may include additional, supplementary graphic material. Usually it is best to distribute handouts at the conclusion of your speech rather than before beginning to speak. If you distribute the handouts early, you are inviting your audience to look at them instead of giving their full attention to you. It is very difficult to talk to a crowd of bowed heads and against a noisy background of shuffling, shifting papers.

In addition to two-dimensional graphics, you may find three-dimensional props quite useful. If you are demonstrating a new product or if you are speaking to children, a prop may be an absolute requirement.

▼ Hide it until you are ready to use it.

▼ If the thing has working parts, make sure they work. This is especially true if you are demonstrating a product you are trying to sell.

▼ If possible and appropriate, make the prop available for hands-on audience examination at the conclusion of the speech.

Volume, Tone, and Pace

Oratory is by its very nature louder than normal conversation. Even if you are using a microphone, you must speak up and project your voice. The goal is not to shout, but to bring your voice up from a place inside you that feels deeper than the origin of ordinary conversation. How do you know if you are speaking loudly enough? You should feel that your voice is resonant and sustained when you speak. It should not sound strident, but verge on the musical. It should sound and feel impressive to you.

Anxiety tends to work against volume. When you are scared, your breath comes faster and more shallowly. Sustained speech at higher than normal volume requires measured and deep breathing. So what do you do when you are nervous? Will your voice come out thin and squeaky? Not necessarily. It has been my experience—and other speakers have shared similar experiences with me—that if you force yourself to begin at the required volume, the demands your voice makes on your heart and lungs and nerves will help these systems work for you. The great American psychologist William James once declared that we do not run because we are afraid, but that we are afraid because we run. The nasty thing about an attack of nerves is that it feeds on itself. You feel anxious, so your heart starts to beat faster, your palms sweat, and the pit of your stomach is invaded by butterflies. In turn, these physical sensations make you feel more anxious. But just as the physical aspects of anxiety can increase the emotional intensity of anxiety, so the physiological changes brought by oratory at a sustained and substantial volume actually reduce those physical and emotional symptoms. In short, yes, your anxiety may make it more difficult for you to speak loudly and evenly, but exert the effort to speak at the required volume and the sensations that accompany anxiety will likely be reduced.

Tone of voice is harder to control than volume. Some of us have smooth voices, others harsh. Some speak in the lower registers, others up high. If you feel that the quality of your voice presents a problem and you plan to do a good deal of public speaking, it might be advisable to look into professional voice training. But almost anyone can make some improvement on his own.

▼ Unless you have a deep voice to begin with, pitch your voice slightly lower than normal. Listeners tend to associate credibility and authority with a relatively deep voice. This is true whether you are a man or a woman.

▼ Unless the sentence is a question, do not end on a rising note. Many speakers (more women than men) end declarative sentences on an up-pitch, as if the statement were meant to be interpreted tentatively. This undermines your authority and, over the course of a speech, is also quite irritating. Try to end declarative sentences on a low tone without, however, trailing off in volume.

▼ Audiences find prominent nasality very annoying since, over the course of a speech, it begins to sound like whining. Speaking slowly and consciously lowering the pitch of your voice should minimize an unwanted nasal quality. If you suffer from allergies or chronic breathing problems, consult a physician.

Finally, the matter of pace. Ninety-nine percent of the time this can be addressed in two words: *slow down.*

Anxiety, a desire to get the speech over with, and a benevolent inclination to avoid boring an audience all tempt you to deliver your speech at the rapid conversational rate of about 200 words per minute. This is much too fast for public speaking. True, it will get you through the speech faster—though you are also much more likely to trip and stumble over words and sentences. Rapid reading will not make the speech more interesting, however. Your audience will find your words more difficult to follow and almost impossible to enjoy. Speak fast enough, and they will be downright irritated, offended by what strikes them as an unprofessional and even impolite presentation—as if you don't even want to give them the time of day.

Slow down. The maximum rate of speed you should reach is about 150 words per minute. This means that it should take you about two minutes to get through a conventional, double-spaced, typewritten page of manuscript. (If you type the manuscript as recommended in "Typing the Speech"—using 14-point type and triple spacing—you will get through a single page in one minute.)

To be sure, don't slow to a crawl that your audience will find excruciating. And be aware that a faster pace is appropriate to some kinds of speeches: a sales *spiel* should proceed at a livelier pace than a funeral oration. But if, like most of us, you tend to rush through a speech, inscribe in large letters on each page of your manuscript a self-instruction to "slow down."

Appendix

▼ ▼ ▼ ▼ ▼ ▼ ▼ ▼ ▼ ▼ ▼ ▼ ▼ ▼ ▼ ▼ ▼ ▼ ▼ ▼
Sources of Anecdotes

Unless you've done a protracted stretch in solitary confinement, by far the best source of anecdotes for *your* speech is *your* life and *your* experience. Such stories are the freshest, most original, and are most likely to make the greatest impact. If you choose to relate a story someone else told you, make sure you check out the details with your source and secure her permission to use the material.

Another excellent source of relevant anecdotes are the journals and professional publications in your field. As long as you give full credit to the publication and author, you do not need special permission for a brief quotation or paraphrase of *published* material. If you plan to use a substantial amount of the material verbatim—more than about two hundred words—you should write to the publisher to secure permission to quote. If you have access to an article prior to its publication, you definitely should not quote or use the material without very explicit permission. Most journals, quite rightly, will strongly object to your scooping them—especially with their own story. Unpublished manuscripts are automatically protected by common law copyright and must not be quoted without permission. Secure all permissions in writing.

Finally, think about your own reading. If you will be speaking regularly, you should set aside ample time to read the literature relevant to your field, including more general works (especially biographies) that may be counted on to offer a rich harvest of anecdotes and stories. Use index cards to make note of any potentially useful items you encounter, and put these cards in a file, perhaps arranged alphabetically by subject. Be sure to include the quotation and the source (author, title of book, publisher, date of publication, and page number) on the index card.

If firsthand sources are unavailable or insufficient, you may consult any number of anecdote collections especially designed for public speakers. Remember, these books contain, in effect, secondhand material. Use them with caution and only when something fresher is unavailable.

Fadiman, Clifton, ed., *The Little, Brown Book of Anecdotes* (New York: Little, Brown, 1985). An excellent, comprehensive general source.

Gilbert, Michael F., *The Oxford Book of Legal Anecdotes* (New York: Oxford University Press, 1989).

Hall, Donald., *The Oxford Book of American Literary Anecdotes* (New York: Oxford University Press, 1981).

Hastings, Max, ed., *The Oxford Book of Military Anecdotes* (New York: Oxford University Press, 1986).

Hay, Peter, ed., *The Book of Business Anecdotes*. (New York: Facts on File, 1988).

Henning, Charles, *The Wit and Wisdom of Politics* (Golden, CO: Fulcrum Press, 1989).

Johnson, Paul, ed., *The Oxford Book of British Political Anecdotes* (New York: Oxford University Press, 1989).

Langford, Elizabeth, ed., *The Oxford Book of Royal Anecdotes* (New York: Oxford University Press, 1989, 1992).

Morris, Desmond, *The Book of Ages* (New York: Penguin, 1983). A volume of birthday-related anecdotes.

Prochnow, Herbert V., *The Toastmaster's Handbook* (Englewood Cliffs, NJ: Prentice Hall, numerous editions).

Prochnow, Herbert V. and Herbert V. Prochnow, Jr., *The Toastmaster's Treasure Chest* (New York: Harper & Row, 1979).

Sutherland, James R., *The Oxford Book of Literary Anecdotes* (New York: Oxford University Press, 1987).

Tomlinson, Gerald, ed., *Speaker's Treasury of Political Stories, Anecdotes, and Humor* (Englewood Cliffs, NJ: Prentice Hall, 1990).

Tomlinson, Gerald, ed., *Speaker's Treasury of Sports Anecdotes, Stories, and Humor*. (Englewood Cliffs, NJ: Prentice Hall, 1990).

Van Ekeren, Glenn, ed., *The Speaker's Sourcebook* (Englewood Cliffs, NJ: Prentice Hall, 1988). Another excellent general source.

▼▼▼▼▼▼▼▼▼▼▼▼▼▼▼▼▼▼▼▼
Sources of Facts, Figures, and Statistics

As with anecdotes, the best source of "hard facts" is your own research. Make liberal use of the most reliable journals and newsletters in your field. For more general information, your first stop should be one of the major encyclopedias. The universally acknowledged standard among these is the *Encyclopaedia Brittanica*, with the *World Book* coming in a respectable second. Make certain that you check the annual supplements to these works for updates. Other general sources of facts, figures, and statistics include any book that contains the word *Almanac* in the title. Your library will have a slew of these. The best-known general almanacs are:

> *Congressional Quarterly Almanac*. (Washington, DC: Congressional Quarterly, published annually).

> *Information Please Almanac*. (New York: Houghton Mifflin, published annually).

> *Reader's Digest Almanac*. (Pleasantville, NY: Reader's Digest, published annually).

> *World Almanac and Book of Facts*. (New York: New York World, published annually).

These are also great sources of up-to-date information:

> *Facts on File World News Digest with Index*. (New York: Facts on File, updated weekly).

> Martin, Frederick, *Statesman's Year-Book: Statistical and Historical Annual of the States of the World for the Year*. (New York: St. Martin's Press, published annually).

> United States Bureau of the Census. (*County and City Data Book*. Washington, DC: Government Printing Office, series).

United States Bureau of the Census. *State and Metropolitan Area Data Book.* (Washington, DC: Government Printing Office, series).

United States Bureau of the Census. *Statistical Abstract of the United States.* (Washington, DC: Government Printing Office, series).

United States Government Manual. (Washington, DC: Federal Register, annual). An indispensable guide to and through the federal bureaucracy, including contact persons, addresses, telephone numbers, and fax numbers.

In addition to these formidable tomes, there is the authoritative and endlessly amusing Guinness series, inluding:

Dunkling, Leslie, *The Guinness Book of Names* (New York: Facts on File, 1991).

Dunkling, Leslie, and Adrian Room, *The Guinness Book of Money* (New York: Facts on File, 1990).

Greenberg, Stan, *The Guinness Book of Olympic Records* (New York: Bantam, 1992).

The Guinness Book of Records (New York: Facts on File, published annually).

The Guinness Book of Sports Records (New York: Facts on File, published annually).

Hindley, Geoffrey, *The Guinness Book of British Royalty* (New York: Facts on File, 1994).

Porter, Valerie, *The Guinness Book of Marriage* (New York: Facts on File, 1991).

Robertson, Patrick, *The Guinness Book of Movie Facts and Feats* (New York: Abbeville Press, 1991).

You should also become familiar with a monumental series in your local libary's reference section called *The Reader's Guide to Periodical Literature.* This remarkable work, continuously updated, allows you to look up a subject (say "Fishing") and find the location of recent magazine articles on it. In a world overflowing with ephemeral information, *The Reader's Guide* is invaluable. For information on relevant newspaper articles, the best place to start is *The New York Times Index*, which is updated quarterly.

If you have access to a computer with a modem, consider a subscription to one or more "on-line" sources of information. By far the largest and most comprehensive on-line service is CompuServe, based in Columbus, Ohio. A start-up kit for this service is available in most computer software stores or by calling 1-800-848-8199. CompuServe offers some 1,400 databases, including demographic statistics, bibliographies in many fields, government reports, and financial information. Similar to CompuServe and less expensive, but also offering less depth, is Genie, which can be reached at 1-800-638-9636. More expensive than either of these services, but of very high quality is Dow Jones News Retrieval, which is especially strong in the financial area. It can be reached at 1-609-452-1511. Other, smaller on-line services may also prove useful. The single best guide to them (as well as to many other aspects of PC communications) is *Dvorak's Guide to PC Telecommunications* by John C. Dvorak and Nick Anis (New York: McGraw-Hill, 1992).

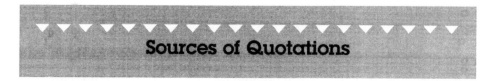

Sources of Quotations

Need I say it again? For good quotations, begin with *your* experience, *your* colleagues, associates, and mentors. And don't overlook *your* family, especially your kids! Beyond your immediate experience, cultivate the habit of reading greedily in your field, snatching up whatever looks quotable. As with anecdotes, copy the good stuff onto 3" × 5" cards, identifying the author, source, date, and relevant page numbers. File the accumulated cards alphabetically by subject.

Secondhand sources of quotations exist in abundance, many of them quite good—so good, in fact, that you may be tempted to drown your speech in these *bon mots* much as you would ladle gravy over a slice of Thanksgiving turkey. Resist the temptation, and use quotations sparingly.

The venerable standard in the field of general quotation collections is:

Bartlett, John, *Bartlett's Familiar Quotations* (Boston: Little, Brown, 1980).

Other useful collections include:

Augarde, A. J., ed., *The Oxford Dictionary of Modern Quotations* (New York: Oxford University Press, 1991).

Bettmann, Otto L., *The Delights of Reading* (Boston: Godine, 1987).

Camp, Wesley D., ed., *What a Piece of Work Is Man!* (Englewood Cliffs, NJ: Prentice Hall, 1990). This is especially valuable in that it deliberately concentrates on *unfamiliar* quotations not found in other collections and that are therefore likely to strike your listeners as fresh.

Charlton, James, ed., *The Executive's Quotation Book* (New York: St. Martin's Press, 1983).

Edelhart, Mike, and James Tinen, eds., *America the Quotable* (New York: Facts on File, 1983).

Eigen, Lewis, and Jonathan Siegel, eds., *The Manager's Book of Quotations* (New York: AMACOM, 1989).

Frost, Elizabeth, ed., *The Bully Pulpit* (New York: Facts on File, 1988). A collection of presidential quotations.

Marsden, C.R.S., ed., *Dictionary of Outrageous Quotations* (Topsfield, MA: Salem House, 1988). A lot of fun, but use with care!

Mencken, H. L., ed. *A New Dictionary of Quotations* (New York: Knopf, 1987). A reissue of a classic by one of the nation's most distinguished authors and most celebrated curmudgeons.

Partnow, Elaine, ed., *The Quotable Woman* (New York: Facts on File, 1985).

Patington, Angela, ed., *Oxford Dictionary of Quotations* (New York: Oxford University Press, 1992). A major new work.

Safire, William, and Leonard Safire, eds., *Words of Wisdom* (New York: Simon & Schuster, 1990).

Sampson, Anthony, and Sally Sampson, eds., *The Oxford Book of Ages* (New York: Oxford University Press, 1988). A small book of quotations geared to the "ages of man."

Simpson, James B., and Daniel J. Boorston, eds., *Simpson's Contemporary Quotations* (Boston: Houghton Mifflin, 1988).

Telushkin, Joseph, ed., *Uncommon Sense* (New York: Shapolsky Publishers, 1987). Penetrating religious and philosophical quotations.

Thomsett, Michael C., *A Treasury of Business Quotations* (New York: Ballantine, 1990).

Wells, Albert M., Jr., ed., *Inspiring Quotations* (Nashville: Thomas Nelson, 1988). A collection of quotations from a noted publisher of religious books.

In addition to these books, the collections listed under the preceding "Sources of Anecdotes" are replete with quotable sentences and paragraphs. And don't forget that special species of quotation known as the proverb or aphorism. You'll find some of the most beloved and sharpest in any good anthology of the writings of Benjamin Franklin. You'll find hilarious—if snide, sarcastic, and bitter—aphorisms in the works of Mark Twain (consult Bernard De Voto, *The Portable Mark Twain* [New York: Viking, 1968]) and in the *Devil's Dictionary* of Ambrose Bierce (a good edition was published in paperback by Dell in 1991, but several others are currently available as well). General collections of aphorisms and proverbs include:

Auden, W. H., and Louis Kronenberger, eds., *The Viking Book of Aphorisms* (New York: Penguin, 1966).

Fergusson, Rosalind, *The Penguin Dictionary of Proverbs* (New York: Penguin, 1983).

Gross, John, comp., *The Oxford Book of Aphorisms* (New York: Oxford University Press, 1987).

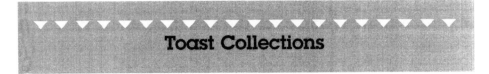

Toast Collections

Hard-pressed for something original? Consult one of these:

> Dickson, Paul, *Toasts: The Complete Book of the Best Toasts, Sentiments, Blessings, Curses, and Graces* (New York: Delacorte, 1981).

> Garrison, Robert L., *Here's to You!: 354 Toasts You Can Use Today for Parties, Holidays, and Public Affairs* (New York: Crown, 1980).

> Pasta, Elmer, ed., *Complete Book of Roasts, Boasts and Toasts* (West Nyack, NY: Parker Publishing, 1982).

In addition to these, consult the two Prochnow volumes listed under "Sources of Anecdotes."

There remains one other little-tapped source of good toasts. We tend to look down our noses at greeting-card sentiments, but, actually, much greeting-card verse is quite good: concise, musical, touching, and/or clever. Need to prepare for a toast at a birthday party? Go to your local drug store or card shop and peruse the birthday card section. You may be surprised.

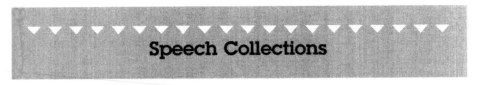

Speech Collections

Classic speeches are available in a range of collections, including:

> Copeland, Lewis, and Lawrence Lamm, *The World's Great Speeches.* (New York: Dover, 1973).

> Hobbs, H. Herschell, comp., *Welcome Speeches and Responses* (New York: Baker, 1987).

> Parrish, Wayland M., and Marie Hochmuth, eds., *American Speeches* (Westport, CT: Greenwood Press, 1969).

> Peterson, Houston, *A Treasury of the World's Great Speeches* (New York: Simon & Schuster, 1965).

Safire, William, *Lend Me Your Ears: Great Speeches in History* (New York: W. W. Norton, 1992).

Spinrad, Leonard, and Thelma Spinrad, *Speaker's Lifetime Library* (Englewood Cliffs, NJ: Prentice-Hall, 1979).

If you wish to locate a particular speech by a well-known orator, consult Charity Mitchell's *Speech Index: An Index to Collections of World Famous Orations and Speeches for Various Occasions,* available in library reference collections. (The most recent supplement was published by Scarecrow Press in 1982.)

You may also find it inspiring to look for collections of speeches by the great orators, including Abraham Lincoln, Winston Churchill, Martin Luther King, Jr., and the like.

The single most current source of *contemporary* speeches is *Vital Speeches of the Day,* a twice-monthly newsletter that reprints current speeches in many fields (business, industry, politics, education, and the like). Published by City News Publishing Company (P.O. Box 1247, Mount Pleasant, SC 29465), *Vital Speeches* can be found in the periodical collection of most public libraries as well as those of high schools and colleges. Owen Peterson is the latest in a series of compilers of *Representative American Speeches,* which has been published annually by the H. W. Wilson Company of New York since 1883.

Other sources of contemporary speeches include: *Speechwriter's Newsletter* (407 South Dearborn Street, Chicago, IL 60605) and *The Executive Speaker* (P.O. Box 2094, Dayton, OH 45429).

With Alice Marks, I am co-editor of *The Business Speaker's Almanac,* a collection of business-related speeches published annually by Prentice Hall (Englewood Cliffs, NJ) beginning with a volume for 1994.

How To's

This isn't the only book that can help you write and deliver better speeches. The following provide valuable insight:

Cook, Jeff Scott, *The Elements of Speechwriting and Public Speaking* (New York: Collier, 1989).

Detz, Joan, *How to Write and Give a Speech* (New York: St. Martin's Press, 1984).

Detz, Joan, *Can You Say a Few Words?* (New York: St. Martin's Press, 1991).

Ehrlich, Henry, *Writing Effective Speeches* (New York: Paragon House, 1992).

Fletcher, Leon, *How to Design and Deliver a Speech*, 4th ed. (New York: HarperCollins, 1990).

Hoff, Ronn, *"I Can See You Naked": A Fearless Guide to Making Great Presentations* (Kansas City and New York: Andrews and McMeel, 1988).

Humes, James C., *Standing Ovation: How to Be an Effective Speaker and Communicator* (New York: Harper & Row, 1988).

Ott, John, *How to Write and Deliver a Speech* (New York: Trident, 1970).

Reager, Richard (revised by Norman P. Crawford and Edwin L. Stevens), *You Can Talk Well* (New Brunswick, NJ: Rutgers University Press, 1960).

Sarnoff, Dorothy, with Gaylen Moore, *Never Be Nervous Again* (New York: Crown, 1987).

Tarver, Jerry. *The Corporate Speech Writer's Handbook: A Guide for Professionals in Business, Agencies, and the Public Sector* (Westport, CT: Greenwood Press, 1987).

Tarver, Jerry, *Professional Speech Writing* (Richmond, VA: The Effective Speechwriting Institute, 1982).

In addition to these books devoted to speechmaking, you will also find the following helpful:

Strunk, William, Jr., and E. B. White, *The Elements of Style* (New York: Macmillan, 1979). The best concise guide to grammar and "correct" usage.

And here are two good guides to research:

Felknor, Bruce L., *How to Look Things Up and Find Things Out* (New York: Morrow, 1988).

Madsen, David, *Successful Dissertations and Theses* (San Francisco: Jossey-Bass, 1983).

Index

A

After-dinner speeches, 8-14
    phrases to use, 11
    sample paragraphs/speeches,
       12-14
    sentences to use, 11-12
    what not to say, 10
    what to say, 9-10
    words to avoid, 10-11
    words to use, 10
Anecdotes, sources of, 321-22
Anniversaries, 14-19
    phrases to use, 17
    sample paragraphs/speeches,
       18-19
    sentences to use, 17-18
    toasts, 261-62
    what not to say, 15-16
    what to say, 15
    words to avoid, 16
    words to use, 16
Appointment, acceptance of, 3-8
    phrases to use, 5
    sample paragraphs/speeches, 6-7
    sentences to use, 5-6
    what not to say, 4
    what to say, 3-4
    words to avoid, 5
    words to use, 4-5
Audience:
    give and take, 284-85
    identifying, 200
Audio-visual equipment, 37
Awards/tributes:
    acceptance of, 19-24
       phrases to use, 22
       sample paragraphs/speeches,
          23-24
       sentences to use, 22-23
       what not to say, 21
       what to say, 20
       words to avoid, 21
       words to use, 21
    presenting, 24-29
       phrases to use, 27
       sample paragraphs/speeches,
          28-29
       sentences to use, 27-28
       what not to say, 25-26
       what to say, 25
       words to avoid, 26
       words to use, 26

B

Birthdays, 30-35
    phrases to use, 32
    sample paragraphs/speeches,
       33-35
    sentences to use
       at party for another, 32-33
       at your own party, 33
    things to say
       at party for another, 30
       at your own party, 31
    toasts, 262-63
    what not to say, 31
    words to avoid, 32

words to use, 31
Body language, 201, 285-89
    logistical, 286-87
    mechanical, 286
Body Language of Sex, Power and Aggression (Fast), 285
Business meetings, 35-44
    phrases to use, 41-42
    sample paragraphs/speeches, 43-44
    sentences to use, 42
    what to say/what not to say, 36-40
    words to avoid, 41
    words to use, 41

C

Charity events, 44-49
    phrases to use, 47
    sample paragraphs/speeches, 48-49
    sentences to use, 47-48
    what not to say, 45-46
    what to say, 45
    words to avoid, 46-47
    words to use, 46
Children's groups, 237-41
    rhetorical questions, asking, 238
    rowdiness, controlling, 238-39
    sample speech, 239-41
    speech characteristics, 238
Christmas, toasts, 263-64
Clothing/dress, 201, 289-90
    for television interview, 259
Comfort, 290-91
Commencements, 50-59
    phrases to use, 55
    sample paragraphs/speeches, 56-59
    sentences to use, 56

speech preparations, 50-51
    what not to say, 53
    what to say, 51-53
    words to avoid, 55
    words to use, 54
Commercial clubs, *See* Fraternal organizations/commercial clubs
Community meetings, 59-67
    phrases to use, 63-64
    sample paragraphs/speeches, 65-67
    sentences to use, 64-65
    what not to say, 61-62
    what to say, 60-61
    words to avoid, 63
    words to use, 62
Congratulations, 67-72
    phrases to use, 70
    sample paragraphs/speeches, 71-72
    sentences to use, 70-71
    what not to say, 68-69
    what to say, 68
    words to avoid, 69
    words to use, 69
Crises, 150-58
    phrases to use, 154-55
    sample paragraphs/speeches, 156-58
    sentences to use, 155-56
    what not to say, 152-53
    what to say, 151-52
    words to avoid, 154-55
    words to use, 153
Customer, identifying, 200

D

Dedications, 73-78
    phrases to use, 75-76

sample paragraphs/speeches, 77-78

sentences to use, 76-77

what not to say, 74

what to say, 73-74

words to avoid, 75

words to use, 74-75

Diction, 292-94

Dictionary of Contemporary Slang (Thorne), 306

Disorder, 38-39

E

Elements of Speechwriting and Public Speaking, The (Cook), 285, 310

Elements of Style, The (Strunk/White), 293

Equipment checks, 37-38

Eulogies, 79-87

phrases to use, 83-84

sample paragraphs/speeches, 85-87

sentences to use, 84-85

what not to say, 81

what to say, 80-81

when words fail, 82

words to avoid, 83

words to use, 82

Extended metaphor, 281-83

Eye contact, 201

Eyeglasses, 287

F

Facial expressions, 287-88

Facts/figures:

sources of, 323-25

using, 309-10

Farewells, 87-94

phrases to use, 90

sample paragraphs/speeches, 92-94

sentences to use, 91

what not to say, 89

what to say, 88

words to avoid, 89-90

words to use, 89

Featured speaker, 231-36

audience identification, 232-34

self-dialogue, conducting, 234-36

topic selection, 231-32

Flip charts, 313-14

Fraternal organizations/commercial clubs, 94-101

phrases to use, 98

sample paragraphs/speeches, 99-101

sentences to use, 99

what not to say, 96

what to say, 95-96

words to avoid, 97

words to use, 96-97

G

Gatherings of good friends, toasts, 264-66

Gestures, 288

Grammar, 292-94

H

Handouts, 314

Hecklers, 295-96

How-to books, 329-31

How to Write and Give a Speech (Detz), 277
Humor, 296-97

words to avoid, 120
words to use, 120
Issues, defining, 39

I

Impromptu speech, 241-46
  minimizing impromptu element of, 242
  preparing for, 243-45
  sample speech, 245-46
  statistics, using, 243
Inaugurals, 102-11
  phrases to use, 105-6
  sample paragraphs/speeches, 108-11
  sentences to use, 106-8
    as featured speaker, 107-8
    as inauguree, 106-7
  toasts, 266-67
  what not to say, 104
  what to say, 103
  words to avoid, 105
  words to use, 104-5
Introductions, 111-17
  phrases to use, 115
  sample paragraphs/speeches, 116-17
  sentences to use, 115-16
  what not to say, 113
  what to say, 112
  words to avoid, 114
  words to use, 114
Invocations, 117-23
  phrases to use, 121
  sample paragraphs/speeches, 122-23
  sentences to use, 121-22
  what not to say, 119
  what to say, 118-19

K

Keynote speeches, 123-33
  phrases to use, 129-31
  sample paragraphs/speeches, 131-33
  what not to say, 126-27
  what to say, 125-26
  words to avoid, 128-29
  words to use, 127-28
Kiam, Victor, 200-201

L

Launches, toasts, 266-67
Lighting, 297-98

M

Master of ceremonies, 134-42
  phrases to use, 138-39
  sample paragraphs/speeches, 140-42
  sentences to use, 139-40
  what not to say, 136-37
  what to say (and do), 134-36
  words to avoid, 138
  words to use, 137
Meetings:
  scheduling, 36-37
  site, 37
Memorizing, 302-4
Mistakes, surviving, 306-8

Moderators, panel discussions, 246-50
Mumbling, 201

N

Nerves/nervousness, 298-300
Newborn celebrations, toasts, 269-70
New Year's celebrations, toasts, 267-68
Nouns/verbs vs. adjectives, 39-40

O

Occasions of crisis, *See* Crises
Occasions of triumph, *See* Triumphant occasions
Off-color language/stories, 300
Officers' annual reports, 158-64
    phrases to use, 161-62
    sample paragraphs/speeches, 163-64
    sentences to use, 162-63
    what not to say, 160
    what to say, 159-60
    words to avoid, 161
    words to use, 160-61
Organization of speech, 38-39
Overhead transparencies, 313-14

P

Pace, 315-17
Panel discussions, 246-50
Patriotic occasions, 164-72
    phrases to use, 168-69
    sample paragraphs/speeches, 170-72
    sentences to use, 169-70
    what not to say, 166-67
    what to say, 165-66
    words to avoid, 168
    words to use, 167-68
Personal touches/references, 294-95
Persuasion, 234-35
Practice, importance of, 39
Press conferences, 250-56
    negative situations, turning around, 253-56
    preparing for, 252-53
    questions, establishing ground rules for, 251
    structure of, 251
Pronunciation, 292-94
PTA/parents' groups, 173-80
    phrases to use, 176-77
    sample paragraphs/speeches, 178-80
    sentences to use, 177-78
    what not to say, 175
    what to say, 173-74
    words to avoid, 176
    words to use, 175-76
Publicity, 301-2

Q

Question-and-answer sessions, 40
Quotations:
    sources of, 325-27
    using, 310-12

R

Radio, 256-57
    control, maintaining, 257
    formats, 257

getting booked on, 257-58
Rapid speech, 201
Rehearsals, 302-4
Retirements, 180-88
    phrases to use, 183-84
    sample paragraphs/speeches,
        185-88
    sentences to use, 184-85
    toasts, 270-71
    what not to say, 182
    what to say, 180-82
    words to avoid, 183
    words to use, 182-83
Reunions, 189-96
    phrases to use, 192-93
    sample paragraphs/speeches,
        194-96
    sentences to use, 193-94
    toasts, 271-72
    what not to say, 191
    what to say, 189-91
    words to avoid, 192
    words to use, 192

S

Sales meetings/presentations,
    196-209
    phrases to use, 204
    sales presentation, basics of,
        198-99
    sample paragraphs/speeches,
        206-9
    sentences to use, 205-6
    what not to say (or do), 202
    what to say (and do), 199-201
    words to use, 203
Scheduling meetings, 36-37
Self-dialogue, conducting, 234-36
Selling yourself, 201
Slang, 305-6

Slides, See Visual aids
Speeches, sources of, 328-29
Speech writing, 277-83
    body of speech, organizing,
        280-81
    ending the speech, 283
    extended metaphor, 281-83
    opening strategies, 279-80
    principles of, 277-78
    verbal outline, 281
Spontaneity, 39
"Spontaneous" rambles, 39
Stance, 289
Statistics:
    sources of, 323-25
    use of, 39

T

Television, 257-59
    dressing for the camera, 259
    interview, handling, 258-59
    stations, number of, 258
Thanks, 209-15
    phrases to use, 212
    sample paragraphs/speeches,
        213-15
    sentences to use, 213
    what not to say, 210-11
    what to say, 210
    words to avoid, 211-12
    words to use, 211
Three-dimensional props, use of, 315
Toasts, 260-61
    sources of, 328
Tone, 315-17
Tributes, See Awards/tributes
Triumphant occasions, 142-50
    phrases to use, 146
    sample paragraphs/speeches,
        148-50

sentences to use, 147
what not to say, 144
what to say, 143-44
words to avoid, 145-46
words to use, 145
Typing the speech, 308-9

V

Visual aids, 40, 201-2, 312-15
equipment, 37
Volume, 315-17

W

Weddings, 215-20
phrases to use, 217-18
sample paragraphs/speeches, 219-20
sentences to use, 218-19
toasts, 272-73
what not to say, 216
what to say, 216
words to avoid, 217
words to use, 217
Welcomes, 221-27
phrases to use, 223-24
sample paragraphs/speeches, 225-27
sentences to use, 224-25
what not to say, 222
what to say, 221-22
words to avoid, 223
words to use, 222-23
Word selection, 304-5

How to Say It®

When You
Don't Know
What to Say:

The Right Words for Difficult Times

ROBBIE MILLER KAPLAN

PRENTICE HALL PRESS

For my husband, Jim, and our daughters, Sam and Julie,
with all my love

And in loving memory of Aaron and Amy

Acknowledgments

No book is written without assistance. I am deeply grateful to a group of special people who helped me through some daunting experiences, and I owe them a debt of gratitude: my husband, Jim, who loves and supports me every step of the way, and wonderful friends and family members whose support and love helped me heal: my mom, Jean Miller; my sister, Judy Barclay; Dot Dance; Stephanie Eckert; Dr. Helene Gayle; and Rabbi Mindy Portnoy.

To the memory of both my grandmother, Mollie Weil, and my mother, Jean Miller, who passed along a deep commitment to family and the importance of caring and supporting those in need.

Many thanks to my daughters, Sam and Julie, for their contributions.

A special thank you to my agent, Andrea Pedolsky, who always brings out the best in me.

And to my childhood friend, Stephanie Tesone Palmer, whose supportive conversation sparked the idea for this book.

And to my editor, Michelle Howry, for her belief and enthusiasm in this book.

A special thank you to Dr. Alan Dappen, Rabbi Rosalind Gold, and Betsy Giller, for their expertise and review of the manuscript.

And a bouquet of thanks to many friends and contributors whose personal stories and wisdom helped shape this project: Hope Avery, Jill Avery, Stephanie Barclay, Ellen Blalock, Elissa Buie, Sandy Corish, Christina Davis, Lia Denson, Carroll Ellis, Mary Fairchild, Janice Farr, Elyse Fischer, Maureen Gallagher, Heidi Graff, Sara Grasman, Caitlin Hilber, Robin Joseph, Mara Kamen, Margie Kaplan, Joan Lisante, Susan McCullough, Betty McManus, Mark Ouellette, Nicole Ouellette, Kim Palmer, Ritchie Palmer, Stephanie Palmer, Heidi Poza, Judy Reinecke, Beth Remick, Leslie Rose, Brette Sember, Alissa Shubar, Patty Spencer, Katie Sternberg, Nancy Sullivan, Tina Tessina, Angie Walker, Mike Walker, Dianna White, and Jennifer Willoughby.

Introduction

A beautiful baby boy was born to a couple who had been married ten years. Their joy knew no bounds, but the euphoria was short-lived. Just a few hours after birth, the baby developed breathing difficulties and was moved to the neonatal intensive care unit. The doctors were certain something was wrong with his heart but were unable to make a diagnosis.

The next morning the baby was sent by ambulance to Children's Hospital. The dad went along, and in the early afternoon the mom got the horrifying diagnosis; the baby was not going to live. The cardiologist explained he had been born with hypoplastic left heart syndrome, a congenital heart defect for which there was no repair. The baby was expected to live just a few days, and he died when he was seven days old.

The chief cardiologist and the geneticist at the hospital told the grief-stricken couple that the birth defect was not genetic and it was not something they did or could have prevented.

Just eleven weeks later, the couple was both surprised and elated to learn they were expecting another baby. But this second pregnancy held none of the anticipatory joy. This was long before the proliferation of support groups—it was difficult to find families with similar experiences, and their story was a conversation-stopper. They made many people uncomfortable, and worse, there were new and old friends they never heard from again.

In December of that same year, a beautiful baby girl was born. A neonatologist assisted in the delivery room, and she knew immediately that something was wrong. It was quickly decided to send the baby to Children's Hospital. Despite the astronomical odds against it, she was immediately diagnosed with hypoplastic left heart syndrome. They had never known another family to have two children born with this birth defect. The bereaved parents were told that she, too, wouldn't live for more than a few days. But the hospital offered them some hope the next morning. This baby's heart was slightly more developed, and they wanted to try to reconstruct it into a three-chambered heart. They performed her first heart surgery when she was a day old. But after three surgeries, the surgeon told them the baby's heart was too damaged to repair. She died in the operating room at just eleven weeks.

This is a true story, and those babies were my children, Aaron and Amy, and they were both born in 1981. Their deaths were traumatic, but they taught me how important it is to provide support when someone is dealing with loss, no matter what that loss might be. Research tells us that individuals heal and bounce back faster if they can voice their feelings and feel the support of caring souls. Communications need not be elaborate; notes, visits, and phone calls can help someone through a difficult time. An offer of nonjudgmental listening will ease anyone through the healing process.

Like you, I often hear of family members, friends, co-workers, neighbors, and community members who are dealing with difficult and challenging times. I know firsthand how much they need support, but I also find it tough to say and do the right thing. I have written this book for everyone who has been at a loss for words when they need them most. *How to Say It When You Don't Know What to Say* is an outgrowth of my experiences and the experiences of many others who shared their personal stories. I've gathered constructive verbal, nonverbal, and written communication strategies to help you and those in need work through some of life's most daunting experiences. I've spoken to professionals, experts, and individuals who have gone through these losses themselves. From my discussions I have gathered tips and suggestions on what to say and do, how to say it, what not to say and do, how not to say it, and hundreds of resources to learn more about grief, communications, and every type of loss.

I've organized this information into five sections. Because all difficult experiences involve loss and grief, Part One provides an overview of the process of grief and mourning and details how you can help someone who is coping with loss.

Communications are crucial to the healing process, and Part Two details communication strategies you can use to foster healing. And because it is sometimes best to say nothing at all, you will find dozens of listening techniques and suggestions that will help you encourage grievers to articulate their feelings.

Parts Three, Four, and Five provide specific insight into illness, death, suicide, miscarriage, pet loss, mental illness, nonviolent crime, violent crime, sexual assault or rape, domestic violence, natural disasters, terrorism, legal or criminal problems, infertility, adoption, baby or child with special needs, physical disability, separation, divorce, job loss, financial troubles, caregiver responsibilities, and personal disappointment. Each chapter lists emotions and feelings to anticipate so you'll be aware of a range of responses to each loss. The chapters also offer models of appropriate sentences, letters, and e-mails, as well as what *not* to say to the bereaved. The "Special Situations" sections provide productive suggestions on handling specific "real-life" problems you might encounter. You'll find these in all the chapters except Eleven through Eighteen, which involve criminal, legal, and medical issues. Beyond basic support, these experiences require assistance from professionals.

You have the power to make a difference in someone's life. I continually hear personal stories of how one small act of kindness warmed someone's soul. The memory of that kindness acts like a talisman they reach for time and time again during the grieving and healing process.

You can make a difference, and you can start right now.

Postscript

My life had a happy new beginning—my husband and I had the good fortune to adopt a baby girl born in Korea, and she arrived just six months after our daughter Amy's death. She was a vibrantly happy and healthy baby and the tonic we so desperately needed. She continues to bring us sunshine and brighten our lives. Two years later, we adopted another baby girl born in Korea, and finally this precious jewel made our family complete. Our daughters have been the joy of our lives, and despite the terrible pain and loss, it is hard to imagine a day without them.

PART ONE

COPING WITH LOSS

✧

Loss is an inevitable part of living, and at some point in our lives, we all experience loss. Even if we anticipate loss, whether from illness, death, or job termination, it is still shocking and traumatic, releasing powerful emotions and feelings that compromise our coping skills.

And yet we need to cope if we are to heal. That's where loved ones, friends, colleagues, and community play a crucial role. They provide the short-term and long-term support that will initiate healing and help in reestablishing healthy living patterns.

Part One provides general guidelines on grief and the mourning process, emphasizing dozens of strategies you can use to comfort and help the bereaved. More targeted advice on how you can help others cope with specific difficult experiences is offered in Parts Three, Four, and Five.

ONE

What Is Grief?

UNDERSTANDING THE PROCESS OF
MOURNING AND HOW YOU CAN HELP

∞

"O, grief hath changed me since you saw me last,
And careful hours with time's deformed hand
Have written strange defeatures in my face."

—William Shakespeare,
The Comedy of Errors, Act V, Scene I

GRIEF is a normal and healthy response to loss. Individuals experience grief when something is taken away from them such as a physical loss (death of a parent or a chronic illness) or a symbolic or social loss (bankruptcy or employment termination). Mourning is our reaction to grief; it is the painful process we go through to work through our grief and adapt to the loss. We grieve not just for the death of someone we care deeply about, but for any loss we experience, whether it is our health, a marriage, a relationship, financial stability, a job, or a dream. We mourn for what was and what will never be.

Grief is a numbing ordeal; it might seem surreal to those grief-stricken that the sun continues to rise each morning, it sets every night, and the world goes on about its daily business despite their personal upheaval. The world of the griever has changed, and they will need support to find their place in a new world. This is where you can help.

It is helpful to understand how grief can manifest itself and the negative impact it can have on our physical, emotional, spiritual, and social well-being. It is common for grievers to respond:

- **Physically:** Changes and difficulty in sleeping, eating, taking care of one's health, energy, and one's overall well-being.

- **Emotionally:** Feelings of sadness, anger, guilt, anxiety, confusion, and despair.

- **Socially:** Inability or unwillingness to see family, friends, and other acquaintances; go back to work; look for work; or assume responsibilities for the care of others.

- **Spiritually:** Understanding of the world and their place in it, belief in God, religion, and the possibility that prior spiritual beliefs may have lost their meaning.

The Stages of Grief

There has been extensive research on the stages of grief and mourning and the emotional response to loss. We know grief takes over the body, leaving the griever with a host of troublesome feelings that occur in different stages; response and emotions can be so intense that the griever might feel as if they are going crazy.

Emotions tend to cluster in different stages during mourning. The stages are a normal part of grief, but they are not predictable and individuals do not necessarily go through them in order or experience them just once. Individuals can go backward and forward through the different stages; once one emotion is finished, it's not gone for good. It's important to understand the types of emotions and feelings that might occur; if we know it is normal for the griever to feel different emotions, we take the power and fear away from it.

> ↬ There is no "right" way to grieve.

Dr. Elisabeth Kübler-Ross, an expert on grief, conducted extensive research into death and dying. She described five typical stages of grief people go through following the diagnosis of a terminal illness. Her landmark work has been used and adapted to demonstrate the stages of grief people go through following a serious loss.

STEP 1: DENIAL AND ISOLATION

Immediately after a loss, the body becomes numb, as if it just can't fathom or believe that the loss has occurred. A feeling of serenity or a sense of shock, disbelief, denial, and disorientation occur, protecting the body from a huge emotional upheaval while the loss is being processed.

STEP 2: ANGER

Anger over the loss can be uncontrollable and frightening. The anger can be directed anywhere and at anyone as the griever vents the emotion. The bereaved often question "Why me?" or "Why are others allowed to escape this?"

STEP 3: BARGAINING

For certain types of loss, the bereaved tries to bargain, promising to do something in the future to prevent the loss. They might bargain: "If you let my wife live, I promise to go to church every Sunday" or "If you let me conceive, I promise I will never ask for anything else."

STEP 4: DEPRESSION

Once the bereaved accepts that the loss has happened, the acknowledgment of the loss initiates depression. The bereaved relives the experience over and over again, trying to make sense of it and find an answer to the question, "Why?"

> ✒ When individuals are feeling very down, they tend to isolate themselves. If you are out of touch with a loved one who is going through the grieving process, make a point of reaching out to them; they might be unable to reach out to you.

STEP 5: ACCEPTANCE AND HEALING

Acceptance and healing come months or years after the bereaved is no longer haunted by the loss. With time, most bereaved accept the reality of the loss and heal.

Although everyone grieves in their own way and their own time, many find grief to be a frightening and overwhelming process. They might experience feelings of high anxiety, depression, sleeplessness, exhaustion, loss of concentration, and a host of responses. Many report raw emotions that feel toxic and foreign, unlike anything they have felt before. The griever wonders, "Will I ever get over it?" or "Will I ever be normal again?"

> ॐ We don't ever get over loss; what we do is work through it. We must do our "grief work," and eventually, many grievers accept their loss.

How We Can Help

It is extremely important that we provide emotional support to individuals experiencing loss. They need us not only during the initial period of loss but also over the duration of the grieving process, which can last anywhere from months to years. And yet many individuals reveal that when they need support the most, they often find themselves alone.

The bereaved report that sharing their loss is particularly difficult when some friends, family members, co-workers, and acquaintances withdraw from them. In the case of a death, loved ones and the community rally around the bereaved in the initial days after the loss, but when the bereaved are in the throes of working through their grief in the months afterward, they find themselves without vital support when they need it most. This feels like yet another series of losses.

Sometimes, even caring and well-intentioned individuals shy away from the bereaved because they feel uncomfortable and don't know what to say or do.

The most important thing we can do for someone suffering a loss is to be there for them, just as we will need help someday when we experience loss.

Why is it so tough to help someone else with loss? It might be that:

- Grievers, those experiencing loss, remind us of life's fragilities.

- We fear that these frightening types of losses could happen to us.

- It can be downright scary to be in the presence of someone grieving who has such powerful emotions.

■ We have unresolved feelings of loss, and experiencing the feelings related to loss with someone else takes us right back to our own personal loss.

It's helpful to understand that different stimuli trigger varied responses in the bereaved. It doesn't really matter what causes the trigger, the bereaved has little control over their response to it. But this in no way implies that the bereaved no longer have responsibility for *any* actions.

Reactions to loss are very personal and quite different for each of us. Over the course of our lives, we will each be challenged by different types of losses.

> ↜ The bereaved have very basic needs: companionship, a willing listener, and the privacy to say what they feel without fear of judgment or embarrassment.

It is sometimes hard to comprehend and put into perspective the terrible sadness and loss of someone who has been laid off from a job when you or someone you care about is dealing with the death of a loved one. And yet we can't begin to compare one person's loss to another's—and we shouldn't. Each of us must express our emotions to heal from our losses, and we deserve the respect, understanding, and support to do that.

It is difficult for anyone to understand a specific loss unless you have experienced it yourself. Even if you have experienced the same event, the meaning of it is unique to each one of us. If you have experienced something different, you can't compare or judge others based on your own experience.

We should encourage the bereaved to articulate their feelings; those who repress and keep their feelings and emotions bottled up might prolong and exacerbate their grief. No matter how raw or painful, it is crucial that we encourage the bereaved to fully experience

> ↜ Always remember that each person is unique and will express themselves in their own way and in their own time.

grief and the resulting emotions, mourning fully the loss. It is only through the experience of grief that we can eventually come to accept our loss.

The Anger Backlash

Although anger is a normal response to grief, when someone is grieving, their anger can be misdirected. It is important to understand that if someone directs their anger at you, you are not at fault. Yet it can be hard not to personalize it.

Realize that there is an underlying cause for their anger, and it is not always evident in how it is expressed. Try to encourage someone who is grieving to vent and redirect their anger in safe ways.

- Suggest they scream or yell in a secure environment.

- Recommend they practice sports and physical movement such as aerobic exercise, kickboxing, and martial arts, as these affect mood and help deal with biochemistry gone amuck; but realize that everyone is different and each person needs to find what works best for them.

- Encourage them to explore the arts such as reading poetry and books, playing or listening to music, or writing a journal or other written form of expression.

- Recommend punching a pillow or putting on boxing gloves and punching a bag to let off steam.

- Encourage them to eat well and take care of their physical well-being.

Above all, the bereaved will need to tell their story over and over again. Your gift of patient listening is what they need to facilitate the healing process. In the next chapter, we'll discuss specific words you can say and ways you can communicate that comfort and heal those going through difficult times.

For further information:
Attig, Thomas. *How We Grieve: Relearning the World.* New York, NY: Oxford University Press, 1996.

Canfield, Jack, and Mark Victor Hansen, eds. *Chicken Soup for the Grieving Soul: Stories About Life, Death, and Overcoming the Loss of a Loved One.* Deerfield Beach, FL: Health Communications, Inc., The Life Issues Publisher, 2003.

Cobb, Nancy. *In Lieu of Flowers—A Conversation for the Living.* New York, NY: Pantheon Books, 2000.

Deits, Bob. *Life after Loss: A Personal Guide to Dealing with Death, Divorce, Job Change, and Relocation.* Tucson, AZ: Perseus Publishing, 1999.

Hickman, Martha Whitmore. *Healing After Loss—Daily Meditations for Working Through Grief.* New York, NY: HarperCollins Publishers, 1994.

James, John W., and Russell Friedman. *The Grief Recovery Handbook: The Action Program for Moving Beyond Death, Divorce, and Other Losses.* New York, NY: HarperCollins, 1998.

Kübler-Ross, Elisabeth, and David Kessler. *Life Lessons: Two Experts on Death and Dying Teach Us About the Mysteries of Life and Living.* New York, NY: Touchstone Books, 2002.

Mabey, Juliet, comp. *Words to Comfort, Words to Heal—Poems and Meditations for Those Who Grieve.* Oxford, England: Oneword Publications, 1998.

Moody, Raymond, Jr., M.D., and Dianne Arcangel. *Life After Loss—Conquering Grief and Finding Hope.* New York, NY: HarperCollins Publishers, 2001.

Prend, Ashley Davis, A.C.S.W. *Transcending Loss: Understanding the Lifelong Impact of Grief and How to Make It Meaningful.* New York, NY: The Berkley Publishing Group, 1997.

American Association of Retired Persons (AARP) Grief and Loss, a collection of resources, a community of care
www.aarp.org/griefandloss/

GriefNet.org is an Internet community of persons dealing with grief, death, and major loss with forty-seven e-mail support groups and two websites.
www.GriefNet.org

Especially for children:

Doka, Kenneth J., ed. *Living with Grief—Children, Adolescents, and Loss*. Washington, DC: Hospice Foundation of America, 2000.

Emswiler, Mary Ann, M.A., M.P.S., and James P. Emswiler, M.A., M.ED. *Guiding Your Child Through Grief*. New York, NY: Bantam Books, 2000.

See also: WHAT CAN I SAY? COMMUNICATIONS THAT COMFORT and WHAT CAN I DO? HOW TO LISTEN.

PART TWO

BASIC COMMUNICATIONS

☙

Your instinct might be to avoid someone who is experiencing loss because you fear you'll say the wrong thing. But loss can be very isolating, and if you stay away, you will compound the loss and the pain.

Communications can be the tonic individuals need when experiencing loss, and comforting communications can play a vital role in the healing process.

But words alone won't help those experiencing loss. Their complicated and sometimes contradictory feelings must be articulated if they are to work through their grief. In addition to comforting, you can help in another way, too—by listening.

Part Two gives general guidelines on verbal, written, and nonverbal communications that are sure to comfort. It offers models of what to say as well as what not to say to the bereaved. You'll also learn techniques for listening, which is sometimes the most effective communication of all. More fine-tuned advice is offered in Parts Three, Four, and Five as it relates to specific difficult experiences.

TWO

What Can I Say?

COMMUNICATIONS THAT COMFORT

∞

*"Our words are useless unless they come from
the bottom of the heart."*

—Mother Teresa

WORDS are powerful, and we are often unaware of the consequences our words can have on someone experiencing or suffering a traumatic event. Despite intentions to comfort or console, we might inadvertently say something that truly hurts or angers someone we care about. No matter how well meaning we are, we can easily increase someone's suffering by thoughtless and inappropriate statements and actions. How we communicate with those around us experiencing difficulties or tragedies can positively or negatively impact the individual's recovery as well as make or break the future of our relationship with them.

Individuals experiencing trauma must deal and react to myriad emotions. They are feeling overwhelmed and frightened. It is possible that they themselves don't understand what they are going through. In this state, it is normal to suffer conflicting emotions and easy to feel isolated.

Medical and mental health professionals use timetables to predict healing stages. These might be useful clinical guidelines, but in truth, they are just that—guidelines. We all have our own timetables—life is lived outside a textbook, and stages are not always predictable. It is essential that we not judge others by their ability and timeliness in coping and healing.

The greatest gift you can give someone experiencing a trauma is love and acceptance, no matter what they might be feeling. Everyone responds to traumatic situations differently; whatever they feel or do is the right thing for them.

Despite your best intentions, you might shy away from supporting someone who is dealing with a situation that is beyond anything you have personally experienced. You might be afraid to communicate, fearful that you might hurt rather than help. Don't allow your lack of experience to suppress your good intentions. Just be honest and tell them, "This is a journey I have yet to take or understand. I want to be there for you, and if I say something inappropriate, you can let me know."

Keep in mind that even the simplest words and gestures bring solace. You'll find inspiration in the dozens of potential words and phrases that follow, along with plenty of ideas and specific tips for crafting written, spoken, and electronic communications that are sure to comfort.

WHAT TO SAY AND DO

- *Become a sympathetic ear.* Be willing to listen attentively, without giving advice or opinions.

- *Be a support system.* Let the speaker know that you will be available to support them through this difficult time.

- *Time your communication.* Choose a time to interact that is private.

- *Be specific in asking what you can do and offer to help.* Clearly state what you would like to do to help, such as taking over the carpool for the week or bringing over a dinner on Thursday. Don't wait for them to come to you for help. When you say "Call me if I can do anything," you are transferring the burden to someone who is having difficulty coping. When you offer, you accept the burden, and the recipient will be most grateful.

> ✍ If you are at a loss for what to do or say, you can simply say "I am so sorry for your loss" or "I am so sorry this has happened."

- *Be persistent, but not annoying, in offering help.* Some folks are so afraid of being a burden or appearing needy that they refuse offers of help even when they need it. Don't worry about rejection, and continue to keep in touch and remain a presence in their life.

- *Listen without judging.* Foster an atmosphere that promotes understanding and open communication.

- *Don't be afraid to touch.* Touch is therapeutic, but before touching, take your cues from the person experiencing the loss. A light touch on the arm or hand can comfort without infringing on the recipient's personal space.

- *Find common ground.* You might have been through something similar that you rarely share that might make the individual feel less isolated and more hopeful of healing. Share your personal journey, but be careful the dialogue doesn't shift the focus to you.

- *Be in attendance—at the hospital, wake, funeral, or at home.* Your physical presence is a comfort and support.

- *Write notes and send cards.* Notes and cards become personal keepsakes, and many recipients reread them when their spirits sag.

- *Bring a meal.* It's okay to bring comfort foods, even if you are told nothing is needed. Bring something that can be placed in the freezer for a future date.

- *Be there and support the person when they need to cry.* Don't be intimidated by tears—they are a healthy response to grief and loss.

- *Allow yourself to cry with the person.* You have feelings, too, and it's okay for you to express them.

- *Keep in touch by phone, mail, and e-mail.* And *stay* in contact—most contact is made at the beginning, but you will be needed for the long term.

- *Remember important dates.* Recipients will be most appreciative if you remember them at significant anniversaries such as the date of birth, death, or surgery, as well as holidays.

- *Listen attentively, even if you have heard a story a dozen times.* Talking is essential to the healing process, and individuals need to share their story again and again. This is one way to try and make sense of what has occurred.

- *Offer to do specific tasks.* Individuals might be so overwhelmed it may be impossible for them to single out specific chores. If you take the initiative it will significantly lighten their burden.

WORDS TO USE

Brave	Heartfelt	Remembrance
Cherish	Heartrending	Respect
Comfort	Heartsick	Saddened
Compassionate	Honor	Share
Condolences	Hurt	Shocked
Console	Inspirational	Sincere
Courage	Keepsake	Solace
Courageous	Lasting	Sorrow
Ease	Legacy	Sorry
Embrace	Loss	Spiritual
Enriched	Memorial	Strength
Eternally	Memories	Sustain
Eternity	Miss	Sympathy
Everlasting	Mourn	Thoughts
Faith	Offer	Touched
Forever	Pain	Tribute
Friendship	Painful	Understanding
Grieve	Peace	Unforgettable
Hardest	Prayers	Uplifting
Heart	Praying	Weather
Heartbroken	Regard	

PHRASES TO USE

Deeply saddened	My heart aches
Ease your pain	Our thoughts are with you
Left their mark	Remembered with love
Made a difference	Sending loving thoughts
May love sustain you	Thinking of you
May you find peace	This difficult time
May you gain strength	This sad time

We share your grief

We share your sadness

We will always remember

We will never forget

With deep sympathy

Words are inadequate

Words cannot express

Words escape me

Your great loss

HOW TO SAY IT

How very sad I was to hear that you are going through such a difficult time.

How very sad we were to hear of your loss.

I am here, and I want to listen.

I am here to listen if you want to talk.

I am sad for you.

I am so sorry you are faced with such sorrow.

I am sorry.

I know how it feels to have no one know how you feel.

I will never forget her.

I would like to bring you lunch; which is better for you, Monday or Tuesday?

I would like to pick you up and take you out to lunch.

Is there something I can read so I can understand what you're facing?

It must be difficult to go through this.

May your fondest memories of her comfort you always.

May your memories be everlasting.

May your memories be sweet and everlasting.

May your memories fill your heart with love and peace.

Memories of our friendship have flooded my thoughts and touched my heart.

My heart aches for you.

My love and prayers are with you.

My sympathy and thoughts are with you.

My thoughts are with you during this difficult time.

My thoughts are with you during your time of sadness.

Our hearts go out to you.

Our thoughts and hearts are with you in your great sorrow.

Our thoughts are with you.

Please accept my sincere condolences.

Please know how much I care.

Please know that our sympathy and thoughts are with you.

Take all the time you need.

There might not be a reason we can understand for everything that happens, but if we look carefully, whatever happens is generally full of meaning.

We hope you will feel some comfort knowing your grief is shared by so many friends.

We share your loss and grief.

We will always remember him with happy memories.

We will keep you in our thoughts and prayers.

Words cannot express how sad I feel for your loss.

You continue to be in my heart and prayers.

Your loss is unimaginable.

WHAT NOT TO SAY AND DO

- Don't force your religious views or opinions about afterlife on the ill or bereaved person.

- Avoid inappropriate statements such as "It's a blessing in disguise."

- Don't give your unsolicited opinion on what they should do, such as "You have no choice but to have the surgery."

- Don't downplay the severity of their illness or their feelings.

- Don't try to change their feelings.

- Don't try to lighten the mood when someone is crying by saying something to initiate some laughter. Although laughter might feel good for the moment, the individual who is crying might think you are uncomfortable with their crying and prefer that they stop.

- Don't think you are commiserating by sharing your own aches and pains.

- Don't compare your pain and experience to the person who is grieving; you can't possibly know what this person is experiencing, and they need your comfort, not a comparison.

- Avoid any statements that minimize the problem such as "You must be relieved it is over."

- Don't use judging statements such as "It's time to be over this."

- Avoid any statement that makes them feel guilty for feeling so bad, such as "Other people have it worse than you."

> ↗ Pay special attention to individuals who are not crying or demonstrating emotion. Just because they are not articulating their grief doesn't mean they are okay. Everyone who experiences loss needs our support, especially those who keep their emotions to themselves and have difficulty vocalizing their feelings.

- If you have listened, said, and done all the comforting things and the person opens up and shares their experience and feelings, don't ignore or avoid them in the weeks ahead. If you do, it will embarrass them and make them feel that they made a mistake by trusting and confiding in you.

HOW NOT TO SAY IT

I really believe things happen for a reason.

If something had to happen, this isn't so bad.

It could have been worse.

It won't happen again.

It's all for the best.

Look on the bright side.

Maybe this is the way it's meant to be.

Perhaps it is better this way.

Put it behind you.

How to Communicate in Writing

It's sometimes hard to speak with family members, friends, neighbors, colleagues, or acquaintances when we learn they are experiencing adversity. It's not that we don't care, but we might be afraid we'll say the wrong thing and hurt, rather than help. Or someone we care about might be too difficult to reach or a phone call might be inappropriate.

If you are uncomfortable or unable to place a call, a personal message in the form of a card, note, or letter is an excellent way for you to communicate and let them know you care. Electronic mail is another option. Although it is less personal than a letter, its rapid delivery and around-the-clock accessibility make it a perfect match for individuals too busy to call or write, users seeking frequent contact, or those who fear phone calls might disturb the recipient. It's particularly appealing for those located out of town, as electronic mail is free to send and an easy way to keep in touch.

Here are some tips and suggestions to help you craft thoughtful electronic and written messages:

- It is best to compose your electronic message and let it sit for a short while to ensure it conveys what you would like to say. It is very tempting to draft your message and press the "send" key, but once it is sent, it is too late to make any changes.

- Personal written messages should include the date, salutation, paragraphs, complimentary close, and your signature.

- Most personal notes are handwritten, but if you are more comfortable writing at your computer or your handwriting is difficult to read, it is also fine to send a typewritten message. Just be sure to sign your name at the end.

> ⚑ Sympathy notes are treasured remembrances and are often saved. They become tangible reminders of how others care for us, and they often help us deal with loss.

- If you are writing to a colleague who might not know your home address, include it on the outside of your envelope so they can reach you if they desire.

- It might be helpful to draft your message first, edit and make changes, then write your final note or e-mail.

- You might want to wait a day or more before drafting your message to digest the news and collect your thoughts; it is helpful to have time to process the loss or difficulty and decide what you would like to say.

> ⚑ The individual or family will most likely be distracted and taking care of the business at hand. They will not be upset if they don't hear from you immediately. In fact, they might get a lot of mail initially. They'll have more time to read a note from you a few days later, and they might appreciate the distraction.

- If you do choose to write immediately, let your note or message sit overnight and read it again before mailing it to ensure it makes sense and communicates the message you would like to convey.

■ Use postcards for quick communications when you just want to keep in touch. They are easy to collect in your daily travels and are a terrific and easy way to reach out to someone whose life has turned upside down. A short note such as "I hope this is a good day for you" or "Thinking of you and sending some sunshine your way" will brighten the recipient's day.

■ If your brain goes numb when you attempt to write, purchase thinking of you or sympathy cards; but a card with just your signature is so sterile that you'll add more meaning with a handwritten line or two.

Special Situations

When something bad happens to someone I care about, I say nothing because I am afraid I will say the wrong thing.
If you say nothing, you send a message that you don't care or the experience makes you so uncomfortable you'd rather stay away. It's important to be in touch with people you care about, and it's better to just let them know you care and are thinking about them than to avoid contact.

A friend of mine suffered a terrible loss. I made contact with her initially, but I have not heard from her since and am very afraid that I might have said the wrong thing.
Your friend might be overwhelmed with her grief and unable to respond to you. It is appropriate to follow up either by a note to let her know that she is in your thoughts or with a telephone call. She might respond or not, and either is okay. When you reach out to someone suffering a loss, you are giving them a gift of yourself and you should expect nothing in return. So don't take a lack of response personally; they received your message of your caring and concern, and that was your purpose. If at some point you learn that you said something that hurt her, just move on. Relationships are ongoing, and you get a chance to do it again; just continue to maintain contact, and keep the door open for when she is feeling better.

For further information:
Baugh, L. Sue. *How to Write First-Class Letters*. Lincolnwood, IL: NTC Publishing Group, 1994.

Bridges, John, and Bryan Curtis. *A Gentleman Pens a Note—A Concise and Contemporary Guide to Personal Correspondence*. Nashville, TN: Rutledge Hill Press, 2003.

Kushner, Harold S. *When Bad Things Happen to Good People*. New York, NY: Avon Books, 1997.

Maggio, Rosalie. *How to Say It*. Paramus, NJ: Prentice Hall Press, 2001.

Olen, Dale R., Ph.D. *Communicating—Speaking and Listening to End Misunderstanding and Promote Friendship*. Holmes Beach, FL: Learning Publications, 2002.

Sell, Colleen. *A Cup of Comfort*. Avon, MA: Adams Media Corporation, 2001.

———. *A Cup of Comfort for Inspiration*. Avon, MA: Adams Media Corporation, 2003.

Shepherd, Margaret. *The Art of the Handwritten Note*. New York, NY: Broadway Books, 2002.

Spitzman, Robyn Freedman. *When Words Matter Most*. New York, NY: Crown Publishers, Inc., 1996.

Venolia, Jan. *The Right Word! How to Say What You Really Mean*. Berkeley, CA: Ten Speed Press, 2003.

American Self-Help Group Clearinghouse
www.selfhelpgroups.org
A keyword-searchable database of more than 1,100 national, international, model, and online self-help support groups for addictions, bereavement, health, mental health, disabilities, abuse, parenting, caregiver concerns, and other stressful life situations.

Especially for children:
Coleman, Dr. Paul. *How to Say It to Your Kids*. Paramus, NJ: Prentice Hall Press, 2000.

See also: WHAT IS GRIEF? UNDERSTANDING THE PROCESS OF MOURNING AND HOW YOU CAN HELP and WHAT CAN I DO? HOW TO LISTEN.

THREE

What Can I Do?

How to Listen

∽

*"Wisdom is the reward you get for a lifetime of listening
when you'd have preferred to talk."*

—Doug Larson,
United Press International

IN the last chapter, I discussed some general techniques for talking with someone who has faced a loss—words you can use, phrases you can express, and
thoughts you can communicate to ease their pain. But often, saying absolutely
nothing—just being there to listen—is the single most important thing you can
do to help.

Most of us yearn to share our feelings and thoughts with someone who will
really listen, and yet we are often disappointed. When someone is troubled and
experiencing difficult and challenging times, they want someone to understand
and appreciate what they are going through. Their needs are really quite simple;
they are just looking for comfort.

When we listen, we give the speaker something quite special—a gift of our
time and attention. Listening allows the speaker to vent feelings and emotions.
By giving a voice to their problems and difficulties, the speaker can sort through
issues, challenges, and alternatives, often discovering answers and potential solutions by themselves.

Difficult experiences can leave us feeling lonely and isolated. An effective listener can ease someone's suffering and promote healing. The best listeners are
empathetic or have prior experience with similar grief. They have the unique

ability to put themselves into someone else's shoes and experience so they appear to know how that person truly feels. An empathetic listener is the first aid someone needs while dealing with a difficult and challenging situation.

How Do I Listen?

Listening is neither innate nor automatic. It is both a skill and a discipline, and it must be learned. Like any skill or discipline, it takes practice and self-control to become proficient.

Although listening is the most frequently used form of communication, you won't find it taught like reading, writing, and speaking. Listening is the primary key to effective communications, but you'll need to be self-motivated to develop your own techniques to acquire, practice, and master this skill.

Many people think that "hearing" is the same thing as "listening," but it's not. Hearing is the physical part of listening, when your ears first sense sound waves. After we hear, we interpret what is being said. Next, we evaluate the information, and finally, we react to what has been said. This interaction is essential to listening. Good listeners foster the silence necessary to encourage speech.

It is easy to find talkers—everyone seems to have something to share and wants to be heard. But if we are continually talking, we can't possibly be listening. And when we do take the time to listen, most folks act like it is something for them to do while waiting their turn to speak.

When someone thinks enough of you to share their burden, they are seeking an outlet to articulate their feelings and troubles. This is referred to as cathartic communication. You are being asked to listen and nothing more; no one expects you to have the answers, and no one wants you to judge.

Your job as a listener is quite simple: You are to listen and allow the speaker to feel, whether it is anger, pain, or fear.

> ⊁ Listening is not a passive activity; it takes energy, and it is hard work.

It is not your job to teach, to influence, to direct, or to correct; it doesn't matter how you think or feel. What is important is to allow the speaker to vent. Whatever emotions the speaker experiences are normal. Emotional release is a good thing and vitally important in the mourning and healing process.

> ↣ Don't take anything personally. This is not about you but about the person who is hurting.

There are a number of things you can do to show that you're an active, engaged listener.

WHAT TO SAY AND DO

- Choose a setting that is quiet; one that is comfortable and private is even better.

- Look directly at the speaker.

- Tilt your face toward the speaker.

- Lean toward the speaker.

- Use body language.

- Mirror the body language of the speaker.

- Make eye contact.

- Employ facial expressions.

- Restate words and messages when appropriate.

- Open your posture.

- Be calm.

- Be patient.

- Demonstrate warmth.

- Disregard your own needs, and concentrate on the speaker.

- Allow the speaker to experience their feelings rather than you anticipating or guessing what they are feeling and putting words in their mouth.

- Train your eyes to look for nonverbal signals.

- Send out your own nonverbal signals, such as nodding your head, that indicate you are actively listening.

- Stop talking.

- Avoid interruptions.

- Open your mind to concentrate so you can hear what the speaker is conveying.

- Allow the person to talk as much as they need to, even if they ramble and don't make sense. It is the telling and retelling that will enable them to discover for themselves what is going on in their life and the meaning of those experiences.

- Change the way you are sitting if you feel yourself begin to slip away during the conversation.

- Encourage the person to talk more by asking open-ended questions, one at a time.

- If you are reaching out to them by telephone, make sure you have enough time to listen before placing the call.

- Graciously accept their appreciation by telling them it makes you feel good to be able to help in some way.

> ⌁ Ending an emotional conversation can be awkward. Wait until there is a real lull in the conversation and say, "I'm really glad we had this chance to be together. Is it okay if I visit you again soon? (or call you again soon?)"

- If the person cries or has no words, just listen. Assure them that they should take all the time they need before continuing the conversation.

HOW TO SAY IT

I can see that you feel strongly about that.

I can understand how you can see it like that.

I can understand how you might feel that way.

I can't be in your shoes, but I can be by your side and listen.

I can't say I've been there, but I've been in the neighborhood.

I see.

I understand.

If you want to talk, I'm here for you no matter how you need me.

Thank you for trusting me enough to share your feelings.

Would you like to talk about it?

WHAT NOT TO SAY AND DO

- Don't assume that you know what the speaker thinks or feels.

- Don't multitask—save the knitting or mail-sorting for later.

- Don't look away from the speaker.

- Avoid crossing your arms or legs.

- Don't roll your eyes.

- Avoid tapping your fingers, cracking your knuckles, or cleaning your fingernails.

> ✌ Turn off your cellular phone; a ringing phone will interrupt the speaker's thoughts and might conclude the conversation.

- Don't interrupt.

- Don't take it personally if anger is expressed.

- Don't abandon someone because they are angry and need to vent their emotions.

- Don't yawn or nod off.

- Don't shake your head.

- Don't rush the speaker.

- Don't get ahead of the speaker and finish their thoughts.

- Don't ask questions about the details; allow them to express and share that information with you if or when they are ready.

- Don't cut them off before they have finished expressing themselves.

- Don't tell your own stories; this is not about you.

- Don't tell stories about people you know or things you have read or heard about; their story is unique and all their own.

- Don't change the subject when the speaker takes a pause.

- Don't judge them for what they have expressed.

- Don't tell them what to think or feel.

- Don't try to solve their problems.

- Don't offer advice.

HOW NOT TO SAY IT

I know just how you feel.

If you think that's bad, wait until you hear . . .

I'm sorry you feel that way.

My sister (mother, father, brother, cousin, neighbor) had the same thing happen.

So what are you going to do about it?

That reminds me of . . .

That's nothing, let me tell you about . . .

You should be happy; things could be a lot worse.

You shouldn't feel like that.

For further information:

Barker, Larry, Ph.D., and Kittie Watson, Ph.D. *Listen Up: How to Improve Relationships, Reduce Stress, and Be More Productive by Using the Power of Listening.* New York, NY: St. Martin's Press, 2000.

Burley-Allen, Madelyn. *Listening: The Forgotten Skill: A Self-Teaching Guide.* New York, NY: John Wiley & Sons, 1995.

Kratz, Dennis M., and Abby Robinson Kratz. *Effective Listening Skills*. New York, NY: McGraw-Hill, 1995.

Nichols, Michael. *The Lost Art of Listening: How Learning to Listen Can Improve Relationships*. New York, NY: The Guilford Press, 1996.

Shafir, Rebecca Z. *The Zen of Listening: Mindful Communication in the Age of Distraction*. Wheaton, IL: Quest Books, 2000.

International Communication Association
1730 Rhode Island Avenue, NW, Suite 300
Washington, DC 20036
(202) 530-9855
www.icahdq.org

International Listening Association
(800) ILA-4505
(715) 425-3377
www.listen.org

See also: WHAT IS GRIEF? UNDERSTANDING THE PROCESS OF MOURNING AND HOW YOU CAN HELP and WHAT CAN I SAY? COMMUNICATIONS THAT COMFORT.

PART THREE

COMMUNICATING IN TIMES OF ILLNESS AND DEATH

Illness and death bring unwanted change—change that shakes an individual's confidence, disturbs their life, interrupts their routines, and leaves them feeling vulnerable. And in this state of confusion and vulnerability, they must make major decisions while taking care of their lives and their households.

You can play a major role in helping your loved one, friend, coworker, or community member cope with illness and death. Your presence and support can guide and lead them through this traumatic period.

Part Three provides specific insight into illness, death of an adult, death of a child, birth of a stillborn or death of a newborn baby, suicide, miscarriage, pet loss, and mental illness, with guidelines on verbal, written, and nonverbal communications you can use to comfort.

FOUR

Illness

∞

"Happiness, grief, gaiety, sadness, are by nature contagious. Bring your health and your strength to the weak and sickly, and so you will be of use to them. Give them not your weakness, but your energy, so you will revive and lift them up. Life alone can rekindle life."

—Henri-Frederic Amiel

A T some time, we all encounter a sick or ailing family member, friend, neighbor, colleague, or acquaintance. When someone we care about is in physical and emotional pain, we suffer along with them. Whether the illness is acute (short term), chronic, or terminal, it takes a physical and emotional toll. You can't fix the physical, but your words and nonverbal actions can significantly aid the emotional recovery and healing process.

Each of us is unique, and we each deal with diagnosis and treatment in our own way. The person you care about can be experiencing a variety of emotions at any given time. Diverse stimuli, encounters, and experiences trigger these responses, and during the course of recovery and healing, one can succumb to and resolve these feelings any number of times.

Your personal experience with illness, hospitalization, or similar situations will influence your feelings and emotions—and impact your ability to help and support others in need. If you've had a bad experience and find going to the hospital to visit a friend a hard thing to do, it's okay if you don't go—but plan to make contact in another way. Use past experience as a guide to extend comfort; offer what made you feel better or things you wished others had done for you in a comparable situation.

No matter what you choose to do, keep in mind that different people need different things. Some folks like to be fussed over, and others prefer to be left alone. It will be your job to discover what works for each person.

THINGS TO CONSIDER

- Whether the illness is acute, chronic, or terminal.

- The person's physical condition and ability to communicate.

- Their emotional well-being.

- Their desire to interact.

- Whether they have family or loved ones living with them or nearby.

EMOTIONS AND FEELINGS TO ANTICIPATE

- Anger
- Devastation
- Disorientation
- Fear
- Frustration
- Grief
- Guilt
- Helplessness
- Loss
- Paralysis
- Self-blame
- Self-devaluation
- Self-pity
- Shame

GUIDELINES FOR VISITING SOMEONE WHO IS ILL

- Direct the conversation to focus on the patient; it is not appropriate to discuss your personal or health issues.

- Limit your hospital or home visit to ten to fifteen minutes. Patients might not have the energy for a longer visit in the early stages of illness but might appreciate more of your time as they convalesce. Take your cues from the patient to determine if they are up to a longer visit.

- Don't ask intrusive questions about their prognosis, treatment, or frailties.

- Do ask questions that show interest and leave the door open for the patient to share their health situation with you such as "How are you?" or

"How are you feeling?" If the patient is in the hospital, ask, "What are they telling you about when you'll get to go home?" or "How long will your hospital stay be?"

- Bring something for them that requires little attention, such as a potted plant, flowers in a vase, a cheerful helium balloon, a framed photo, a stuffed animal, a book on tape or CD, or a book to read. Only bring a spiritual item if you know this would be appropriate.

- Don't bring cut flowers that need to be arranged or a fussy plant that requires special attention.

- Do take your cues from the patient in conversing.

- You can ask "Is there someone you would like to see?" and you can make the contact.

WHAT TO SAY AND DO

- Ask if you can set up a phone tree to update family and friends so they won't barrage the household with extensive phone calls.

- Offer to accompany the patient to the doctor and be the one who takes the notes.

- Offer specific assistance in the way of grocery shopping, meals, errands, and transportation to physician appointments, physical therapy, or the pharmacy.

- Call at a time when you know the answering machine will pick up and leave a message that you are thinking of them and not expecting a return call.

> ↝ Give the patient a call before you leave for the grocery store, the mall, or the pharmacy; let them know where you are going and volunteer to pick up something for them. Ask before you set out if they will call ahead and pre-charge or whether they will reimburse you.

- Suggest that the pharmacist at the patient's pharmacy be advised about the illness and potential patient needs.

- Inquire if there are special needs such as a hospital bed, plastic mattress cover, or other equipment. Families are often under so much pressure they might gratefully accept your offer to do some comparison pricing, put an item on hold, or do the shopping.

- If the illness and/or convalescence falls during a holiday period, offer to contribute to holiday preparations. You can bake and decorate Hanukkah or Christmas cookies, prepare Easter baskets, cook a pot of chicken soup and matzo balls, wrap holiday presents, or select and address greeting cards. Bringing the holiday spirit to someone who is ill will surely bolster their spirits.

- Encourage the person to speak.

- Be an active listener.

- Think carefully before you speak.

- Give your full and undivided attention when listening to them.

- Restrict conversations to short periods so you don't tire the patient.

- Choose words and actions that express compassion.

- Be careful in offering advice, even if you are asked; they are the ones who will live with the consequences of the decisions they make.

- Reassure them that whatever they are feeling is normal.

- Encourage them to share their feelings when they are ready.

- Recommend they explore support groups. Many people find it comforting to interact with others who are experiencing the same problems, and they can be especially helpful if they are feeling isolated. Support groups can be found in diverse settings; some hold meetings, and others are online discussions or forums.

> ↷ If you would like to buy or loan a book on tape or CD, make sure they have a player (and batteries) so they can listen.

- If someone is well enough to read, send them a book to read rather than recommending one.

HOW TO SAY IT

Are you up to a visit?

Can I take the children to a movie?

How are you doing with all of this?

I am here for you.

I am here to listen.

I am on my way to the grocery store; what can I pick up for you?

I am thinking of you.

I am willing to help in any way I can. (Ensure that you follow through.)

I have a free hour tomorrow afternoon. I can run an errand for you or do some of your housekeeping—your choice.

I will be at the pharmacy this afternoon; let me know if there is something you need that I can pick up.

It is so good to see you.

It must be difficult to go through this.

Let me take care of that for you.

What can I do to help you?

Would you like some company?

WHAT NOT TO SAY AND DO

- Don't change the subject or end the conversation if they are frightened. If they tell you "I'm afraid," you can ask them "What are you afraid of?" Or you can ask them "Is there anything I can do to make you less frightened?" or "Is there anyone I can talk to to help minimize your fear? Your doctor? Your clergy?"

- Don't excuse yourself if they are angry and need to vent. Anger is part of the grief and healing process, and they need to release their feelings.

- Don't use a statement that minimizes the situation, such as "You are lucky that . . ."

- Don't compare their experience or the way they are coping to another person's, such as "My co-worker didn't miss a beat and was back to work after a week."

- Don't find something good in it, such as "If you had to get (a disease), this is a good one to get."

- Don't deliver unrealistic or false assurances, such as "You'll be as good as new."

- Avoid statements that imply they are responsible for their problems, such as "I wish you hadn't . . ."

- Don't tell them "You don't deserve this." Realistically, who does? But it is okay to empathize with their possible feelings, such as "This is *so* unfair!"

- Avoid any message that expresses pity or increases a person's sense of helplessness or victimization, such as "I wouldn't wish this on my worst enemy."

- Don't interrupt. Avoid any conversation or thoughts, no matter how important you think they are, that break their train of thought or speech.

- Avoid messages that infer that it is "God's will" or they somehow deserve what has happened.

- Don't use sentences that begin with "You should," as it appears as if you are imposing your views, opinions, or advice.

- Don't share pessimistic opinions, such as "He won't live long."

HOW NOT TO SAY IT

At least it isn't life-threatening.

Being so sad isn't going to help you recover.

Don't be scared.

Don't worry.

I'm sure everything will be okay.

It says in the book you gave me that you can live a normal life.

Lying around isn't going to make it better.

The diagnosis could have been a lot worse.

This is so sad. Let's talk about something positive.

You shouldn't be angry.

You shouldn't be sad.

You're being a worrywart.

NONVERBAL STRATEGIES

Beyond being supportive through words, your help can come in the form of action. Each of us has an expertise, one thing that seems to come easier than anything else and that we are always good at. You might have a recipe for a soup that is your signature dish—one that you always prepare or keep in the freezer in case someone is in need. Well, now someone is. Offer to bring some over. Or you might be a whiz on the Internet, always locating information and resources that seem to elude others. See if you can help out with some online searching.

Take a look at the following list of ideas and helpful actions. Don't be overly ambitious and promise what you can't deliver. You can offer to help in any of these ways, but realize that someone might already have chosen their physician, surgeon, or course of action. If your initial offer is refused, choose something else and offer again.

- Conduct research on medical tests and potential treatments.

- Conduct research on specialists and surgeons who have an expertise in the illness or problem.

- Conduct a search for current and future clinical trials.

- Search for medical facilities that have an expertise in the illness, problem, or procedure.

- Conduct research on surgical options.

- Investigate pharmaceuticals and holistic treatment options.

- Conduct a search for medical literature.

- Identify appropriate support groups and include information on when and where they meet.

- Offer to act as an advocate.

- Offer housekeeping help in the way of vacuuming, dusting, food shopping, or laundry.

- Provide needed transportation, whether it is for physician appointments, children's carpools, or after-school activities.

- Volunteer to watch the children or keep the children at your home.

- Offer to prepare meals or organize neighbors or friends to sign up to deliver meals.

- If you are skilled in organization or bookkeeping, offer to track, reconcile, and organize health insurance invoices and bills.

Special Situations

A relative called with the news that a cousin has been diagnosed with a chronic illness, and I have never heard of it. I have no idea what to do or say.
It's okay to do nothing for a few days until you learn more about the illness and the diagnosis. It would be helpful to do a little research to understand the illness, symptoms, and treatment options—not to give your cousin advice but so you can listen and better understand your cousin's situation. Begin online or at your public library. Once you are familiar with the illness, either write your cousin a note and express your concern or give them a call. We expect more from our families, so be sure to make some contact, even a greeting card that says you're thinking of them.

An acquaintance called to tell me they heard my co-worker was in a car accident while on vacation and is in bad shape. The co-worker is in the intensive care unit, and I don't know what to do.

Immediately contact your supervisor and let them know what has happened. There are other ways to support the family, but further interaction might depend on how close you are to the co-worker. You can contact the hospital and get an update on their condition. The hospital can tell you how to reach family members. You can speak with a social worker to learn the seriousness of the injury and get any suggestions on what you or the office can do to help. You can ask for donations from the office and send flowers or arrange meals for the family members. The family might welcome help in researching information or resources or relieving them of some duties you can do from your home location. You can offer to notify people. If you are a close friend, you might request permission from the family to join them at the hospital.

A colleague has taken a leave of absence while undergoing chemotherapy. How can I stay in touch and show my support?

It's very isolating changing daily routines and support systems while dealing with illness and treatment. You can help your colleague feel less isolated by keeping in touch and helping others in the office do the same. A short note can make a tough day seem less so. Because many people are willing to help but are unsure of what is appropriate, you could circulate a memo that provides your colleague's mailing address and a suggestion that co-workers send cards and notes to keep in touch, too. Meals are often welcome, but some treatments alter taste and impact the digestive system. Ask what foods are welcome and if there are any allergies, restrictions, or preferences. If you are willing to be a coordinator, you can initiate a sign-up sheet for others in the office to take a turn and communicate the food requirements. Check with your colleague's supervisor to coordinate any other outreach effort. You could also make a donation to a charitable organization in honor of your colleague and in hope of a speedy recovery. This gesture might bolster your colleague's spirits and make them feel good knowing that your remembrance will also help someone else in need.

A friend's newborn baby is having serious problems and has been transferred to a children's hospital.

Ask your friend if you can visit at the hospital and if so, what would be a convenient time. It might be comforting for you to bring the parent(s) lunch or take them out for lunch. Hospital food can be unappealing, so anything homemade or purchased from a favorite food outlet is always appreciated. Offer to keep them company while the baby is having a procedure or for a set period of time. Bring along a magazine or novel to distract them. Inquire if they need items purchased for themselves or the baby. They might need transportation for friends or relatives arriving from out of town. Let your friend know you'd like to support them in any way you can, and make yourself available if they need to talk or require assistance.

A family member shared that she has a potentially debilitating chronic illness. I did some research and tried to ask her how she is doing, but she shrugs it off and changes the subject. Should I continue to follow up with her or just forget it?
Chronic illnesses are tricky; there are times when someone feels really sick and needs help and other times when things are in control and the individual just wants to be like everyone else and go about their business. It might be that your family member's illness is under control and they would rather not talk about it. Keep in touch and let them know that you think of them often. You might want to be honest and tell them you would like to be there for them but don't know what kind of a role they would like you to play. Let them know that you want to help in any way you can, and they should let you know what would be most helpful.

SAMPLE LETTERS/E-MAILS

To a friend recently diagnosed with a serious illness.

January X, 2XXX
Dear Wendy:

You've been in my thoughts all day. I have been trying to think of something I could say that would help you through this difficult period, but all I could think to tell you is how much I care about you.

I promise to support you in any decision you make. I will call you in a week so we can talk about your needs and what I can do to help in the days ahead. You are in my heart and prayers.

Love,
Nancy

To a friend whose mother had cardiac surgery.

October X, 2XXX
Dear Heather:

Dan's been keeping me posted on your mom's recovery. I was so sorry to hear about the surgery but pleased your mom continues to make progress. It's tough to deal with all this away from your support system, but I know it means the world to your mom to have you with her.

I miss you and look forward to your mom's recovery and your return. If there is anything you need done while you're away, I would be happy to help.

Sending all good thoughts your way.

Love,
Sharon

To a neighbor recovering from surgery.

April X, 2XXX
Dear Malcolm:

I've been getting reports from Peter, and it sounds like you are on the mend. He tells me you can even take the stairs each day—what good news!

I think of you every time I pass your house. I will call next week to see when it's convenient to make a short visit.

Get well soon!
Luke

To an elderly friend or family member who has just returned home after recuperating in a nursing home.

March X, 2XXX
Dear Paul and Mary:

It must be wonderful to be home and back to your routine. I often think of you and hope that you are both doing well.

I bet the views from your window with all the snow must be lovely. I enjoy looking at the snow from inside where it is warm and cozy; shoveling it and driving in it are another matter!

The crocuses should be up by now, and I checked my garden journal the other day to see when they normally appear. Not only should the crocuses be up but the primrose, too; right now those beds have about six inches of snow. My garden journal tells me spring is just around the corner. I wonder if anyone told Mother Nature.

Sending warm thoughts your way. Be well.

Love,
Amanda

For further information:

Albom, Mitch. *Tuesdays with Morrie.* New York, NY: Broadway Books, 1997.

Babcock, Elise NeeDell. *When Life Becomes Precious.* New York, NY: Bantam Books, 1997.

Callanan, Maggie, and Patricia Kelley. *Final Gifts: Understanding the Special Awareness, Needs, and Communications of the Dying.* New York, NY: Bantam Books, 1997.

Doka, Kenneth J. *Living with Life-Threatening Illness: A Guide for Patients, Their Families, and Caregivers.* San Francisco, CA: Jossey-Bass, 1998.

Doka, Kenneth J., ed, and Joyce Davidson. *Living with Grief: When Illness Is Prolonged.* Washington, DC: Hospice Foundation of America, 1997.

Kabat-Zinn, Jon. *Full Catastrophe Living: Using the Wisdom of Your Body and Mind to Face Stress, Pain and Illness.* New York, NY: Delta, 1990.

Kane, Jeff, M.D. *Be Sick Well: A Healthy Approach to Chronic Illness.* Oakland, CA: New Harbinger Publications, Inc., 1991.

American Cancer Society
1599 Clifton Road, NE
Atlanta, GA 30329-4251
(800) ACS-2345
www.acscsn.org

American Heart Association
7272 Greenville Avenue

Dallas, TX 75231
(214) 373-6300 or (800) AHA-USA1
www.americanheart.org/presenter.jhtml?identifier = 1200000

American Lung Association
1740 Broadway
New York, NY 10019-4374
(212) 315-8700 or (800) LUNG-USA
www.lungusa.org

American Parkinson Disease Association, Inc.
1250 Hylan Boulevard, Suite 4B
Staten Island, NY 10305-1946
(718) 981-8001 or (800) 223-2732
www.apdaparkinson.org

Hospice Foundation of America
2001 S Street, NW #300
Washington, DC 20009
(800) 854-3402
www.hospicefoundation.org

The Leukemia and Lymphoma Society
1311 Mamaroneck Avenue
White Plains, NY 10605
(914) 949-5213 or (800) 955-4572

Multiple Sclerosis Association of America
706 Haddonfield Road
Cherry Hill, NJ 08002
(800) 833-4672

National Association of People with AIDS
1413 K Street, NW
Washington, DC 20036
(202) 898-0414
www.napwa.org

National Cancer Institute
9000 Rockville Pike, 31 Center Drive
MSC 2580
Bethesda, MD 20892-2580
(301) 496-5583 or (800) 422-6237 or TTY number (800) 332-8615
www.nci.nih.gov

See also: WHAT IS GRIEF? UNDERSTANDING THE PROCESS OF MOURNING AND HOW YOU CAN HELP, WHAT CAN I DO? HOW TO LISTEN, WHAT CAN I SAY? COMMUNICATIONS THAT COMFORT, and CAREGIVER RESPONSIBILITIES.

FIVE

Death of an Adult

∞

"Some people live in our hearts forever."

—Anonymous

DEATH is a natural and inevitable part of life and something we all have to deal with at some time. Although the cessation of life is a familiar concept, it is impossible to comprehend the permanence of a loved one's death unless you have personally experienced it. None of us can anticipate how we will react to the death of someone we care about or even someone we might not know well. The nature of our relationship—parent, grandparent, sibling, spouse, child, friend, cousin, neighbor, or co-worker—and the circumstances of the death both play a part in our personal response.

The finality of death brings on a tremendous sense of loss. The deep feelings of sorrow caused by the loss are expressed in grief, and this period is called bereavement. Mourning is the painful process of working through the grief, and it is through this process that we learn to live with our loss.

Grieving is not like any other experience. No matter how often you do it, you never get better at it, and even if you have done it before, it doesn't make the process any easier. You never get used to grieving, and the process can and is different with each death you experience because every relationship is different.

Most of us relish our routines and personal rituals because they bring order and pleasure into our daily lives. Death triggers personal chaos, and the ordered world the bereaved lived in no longer exists. Many find that participation in traditional mourning observances restores some order to the chaos and brings a spiritual and emotional strength.

Mourners should be encouraged to express their grief. Held inside, grief will fester over time, eventually surfacing in destructive ways. Grief does not go away on its own.

Much has been written about the stages of grief (see Chapter One), described as periods of denial, anger, guilt, bargaining with God, depression, and acceptance. But grief manifests itself in many emotions that make it hard for others to interact with the bereaved. Some of the stages can be strange, very strong, and frightening.

Many books provide guidelines for the stages of grief along with timetables predicting the duration of the stages. It must be remembered that these truly are guidelines. Individuals grieve in their own way, and stages can last anywhere from one day to weeks or months. It might take the bereaved one to several years to fully accept their loss.

If you are like many folks, you might fear death and have yet to come to terms with your own mortality; don't let this fear keep you away from the bereaved. Death and bereavement are not contagious, and the experience of grief and mourning won't make you more susceptible to it. Your care and concern, expressed through verbal, nonverbal, and written communications, makes you an essential link in the healing process.

THINGS TO CONSIDER

- The circumstances of death, whether unexpected, from a long illness, or an accident.

- The nature of your relationship with the deceased.

- The personal requests of the family.

- The religious or cultural beliefs of the bereaved.

- The customs, rituals, or words of comfort in the faith tradition of the bereaved.

- Death changes the identity of the bereaved; they are no longer a husband, wife, partner, mother, father, sister, brother, daughter, or son.

- The bereaved must redefine their role, priorities, and place in a world that is quite different since their loss.

EMOTIONS AND FEELINGS TO ANTICIPATE

- Anger
- Depression
- Disorientation
- Fear
- Forgetfulness
- Guilt
- Isolation

- Loneliness
- Overwhelmed
- Panic
- Rage
- Relief
- Sadness
- Sense of futility

WHAT TO SAY AND DO

- Accept that you are an integral part of the grieving process. Mourners must have a strong support network to cope with the death of a loved one.

- If you are close to the bereaved, there are some difficult tasks that someone should not do alone. You can offer to notify other people, accompany the bereaved to the funeral home, help them choose the casket, or order/arrange food for the post-funeral reception.

- Do make sure the family's religious leader and congregation are aware of the death; the congregation often has resources in place to provide bereavement support.

> ↝ You might be needed for the short term, but you might also be needed for the long term in handling carpools or child care.

- If there are children among the bereaved, offer concrete ways to help. They might need to shop for appropriate funeral attire, make arrangements for school absence, or pick up homework assignments. Try to anticipate ordinary activities that need to be handled, such as carpools.

- Offer to provide transportation for family or friends coming in from out of town.

- Offer to stay at the house and answer the phone.

- Keep a record of who called, what has been delivered, and by whom.

> ☞ **Think of concrete and specific ways to help.**

- Volunteer to stay in the house while the bereaved is running errands, attending responsibilities at the funeral home or house of worship, or during the funeral or memorial service.

- Offer to bring over a large-capacity coffeemaker, a large can of coffee, and perishable food necessities.

- Share in the traditional funeral and mourning observances of the bereaved.

> ☞ **The bereaved family of a co-worker might not be up to facing the crowds at the office, but there are ways co-workers can help. Offer to sort office belongings into boxes labeled personal and business-related. If the bereaved is uncomfortable coming to the office, suggest a co-worker deliver the boxes. Recommend that a human resources staff member visit the bereaved at home and review benefits paperwork that require a signature.**

- Offer to help with correspondence. The task might be less painful if you organize a small group to write and address notes together.

- Allow the bereaved to talk about the deceased as often or for as long as they would like.

- Encourage the bereaved to face and express their feelings.

- Provide an outlet for the bereaved to voice their feelings.

- Offer a shoulder to cry on.

- Cry with the bereaved.

- Share your special memories of the deceased.

- Make a quick phone call just to say hello and let them know you are thinking of them.

- Call on the spur of the moment and invite the bereaved out; you can say "I've made dinner—nothing fancy—won't you please join me?" or "We are going out to get a casual dinner in about an hour; can we pick you up?"

- Offer transportation for a social outing; they might be uncomfortable driving by themselves, especially at night.

- Be there for the duration. Most folks feel they are most needed for the funeral and immediately thereafter, but you are needed from the first two weeks onward.

- As the months pass by, so do calls and invitations. They will really appreciate a call and an invitation for lunch.

HOW TO SAY IT

Could you use some help with your correspondence?

Do you want to talk about it?

How are you doing with all this?

I am glad to see you.

I am so sorry for your loss.

I have some free time on Sunday. Why don't I come over, and you can give me your grocery shopping list.

I think of you often.

I will miss (Mary) very much.

Thank you for sharing your feelings with me.

This must be terribly difficult.

What can I do for you?

Why don't I come over and we can make a list of what needs to be done.

WHAT NOT TO SAY AND DO

- Don't avoid the bereaved. Silence can be isolating and will only add to their pain.

- Don't tell the bereaved not to cry. Mourners need to cry and express their anger as part of the grieving process.

- Don't think talking about the deceased will be upsetting to the bereaved; they will need to talk about their loss again and again as part of their grieving.

- Don't compare someone's loss to anyone else's—each person's grief is unique.

- Don't judge them. Each person grieves in their own way and in their own time.

> ✍ Don't be alarmed or angered if the bereaved behave in peculiar ways. They are not being disrespectful but absorbing and processing the loss. They will grieve in a way that is appropriate for them and in their own time.

- Don't offer quick solutions.

- Don't compare the death of a loved one to your divorce or your pet's death. Even if you have the best intentions and are trying to demonstrate your personal experience with loss, you can't equate your situation to anyone else's.

- Don't assume the bereaved is okay because they have transitioned back into their familiar roles and daily activities. They still need your support.

- Don't show up as a guest, even if you are a family member, without an invitation.

- Don't expect to be entertained when you visit. It would be appropriate to bring something to eat; their bodies as well as their souls need some nurturing.

HOW NOT TO SAY IT

Death is a part of life.

Death was a blessing.

Give me a call if you need anything.

He (she) is in a better place.

He (she) led a full life.

I know how you feel.

I understand how you feel.

If there's anything I can do, just let me know.

It was God's will.

It's part of God's plan.

Keep a stiff upper lip.

Oh, you poor thing.

Something good comes out of everything.

Spare me the details.

Was it expected?

Were they ill?

You look great.

RELIGIOUS AND CULTURAL DIFFERENCES

Funeral and mourning customs are influenced by cultural and religious rituals. It is helpful to understand how different religions and cultures mourn and cope with loss prior to interacting with the bereaved.

It is often appropriate to bring food, and you'll find this information under the following "What to Bring" section. It is important to ask first if the family observes special dietary laws or if there are special dietary needs based on food allergies.

Respect the family's wishes, particularly regarding flowers. Flowers are not sent at all in some faiths, and some families prefer their loved one be remembered with a donation rather than flowers.

The following guidelines provide basic information on how different religions deal with death and mourning. This section will help you understand what to expect, but since there are many different branches, sects, and denominations, it is important that you personally check with the funeral home, religious institution, or bereaved family to clarify their preferences.

BUDDHIST

What to Expect

- There are different sects of Buddhism, and their traditions for memorial services vary. They all share a great respect for the dignity and eternity of each human life.

- There is no one prescribed order of funeral services for all Buddhist sects. Funeral services can be held at a funeral home, the home of the bereaved, a community center or at a temple.

- A post-memorial service might be held ninety days after the death.

- Close family members and friends observe the first anniversary of death, and subsequent anniversaries are observed in private.

What to Wear

- Subdued, modest clothing appropriate for funerals; you should inquire, as dark dress is appropriate for some sects and light dress for others.

- Call ahead for seating details if the service is held in a temple. You might be sitting on meditation (floor) cushions and need to dress appropriately.

What to Do

- Pay respects to the family prior to the start of the funeral service.

- View the body, bowing slightly.

- Make a charitable donation if the family chooses a charity or cause in memory of the deceased.

What to Bring

- Send flowers to the funeral.

- Check first to see if food gifts are appropriate; if so, bring a vegetarian dish.

What Not to Do, Say, or Bring

- Avoid wearing the color red.

CHINESE

What to Expect

- Chinese funerals can be made up of a combination of Christian, Buddhist, Confucian, and Taoist rituals, depending on the family's beliefs.

What to Wear

- Modest and conservative dress.

What to Do

- Attend and stay for the entire service. It might be long—up to two hours in duration.

- Walk around the coffin for a final viewing after the service.

- If given a small packet of candy and a red lucky money envelope at the funeral, eat the candy immediately and spend the money on a small treat.

- Turn away as the coffin is lowered into the grave, as it is considered unlucky and impolite to watch.

- Attend the funeral meal after the burial.

- Visit the family during the month of mourning.

What to Bring

- Flowers in colors of white or yellow only. Chrysanthemums are very popular.

- Gifts of food when visiting the family during the mourning period.

What Not to Do, Say, or Bring

- Do not bring flowers with thorns, especially roses in any color.

HINDU

What to Expect

- Hindus believe in reincarnation and cremation, and the funeral service is both a celebration and a remembrance. The funeral ritual frequently includes noise, usually horns and bells, and flowers and sweetmeats might be passed around as offerings.

■ The eldest male or the oldest son in the family is the chief mourner and will represent the family in saying good-bye. Male family members might shave their heads to show their respect.

■ The family gathers for a meal and prayers afterward.

■ The mourning period might last ten to thirty days, the family might observe "shraddha"—an eleven-day ritual that liberates the soul so it can descend to heaven.

What to Wear
■ White is a traditional mourning color, but funeral attendees should inquire what is appropriate attire.

What to Do
■ Visit the bereaved at home.

What to Bring
■ Visitors should check before bringing anything when making a post-funeral visit.

What Not to Do, Say, or Bring
■ Do not bring food.

ISLAMIC

What to Expect
■ Muslims believe the soul departs at the moment of death, and immediate burial usually takes place, often within twenty-four hours.

■ Funerals are simple and respectful, and cremation is forbidden.

■ Official mourning period is three days but might be longer for a remaining spouse.

■ There might be a special meal to remember the deceased.

What to Wear

- Dark and modest dress; women should wear a dress and cover their heads and the lengths of their arms.

What to Do

- Usually only men attend the burial.

What to Bring

- Baked goods, fruits, or simple meals.

What Not to Do, Say, or Bring

- Do not send flowers to the funeral.

- Shoes are not permitted if the service is held in a mosque.

JAPANESE

What to Expect

- Japanese traditions are a blend of Buddhist and Shinto influences.

- The family might observe Shojingyo, a forty-nine-day period of mourning, or they might observe a longer period, depending on their religious beliefs.

What to Wear

- Simple and conservative black clothing; dark blue is acceptable. No one should wear shiny black shoes, and women should wear dark tights.

- Women should refrain from wearing jewelry; a strand of pearls is acceptable, as it resembles a tear.

What to Do

- Attend the funeral.

- Be prompt.

- There should be a table set up at the entrance with someone to greet visitors. Sign your name in the registry, and present a monetary gift called "koden" to defray the funeral costs.

- Put crisp, new bills in a clean, new, white envelope (a supply of envelopes may be available at the funeral home or can be purchased at Japanese bookstores). Traditionally, if you could not get brand-new bills, the bills were ironed. This is no longer required if you do not have the time.

- You may write a check, but it does not convey the same courtesy as cash bills.

- If you pay a condolence visit and a salt shaker is provided prior to entering the home, sprinkle salt on yourself outside the home to purify yourself before entering the house.

What to Bring
- Flowers in shades of white and yellow, white being the most desirable; chrysanthemums are most frequently given, as they are an important flower and represent the emperor.

What Not to Do, Say, or Bring
- Do not wear red to the funeral or give red flowers, as red represents blood.

- Do not give flowers with thorns.

- Do not give money gifts in increments of four or containing four because the pronunciation of the word *four* is the same as the word for death.

JEWISH

What to Expect
- The burial must take place as soon as possible—within twenty-four hours after death but no more than two days after the death. Burial may be delayed if the immediate family must travel long distances.

- Funerals are not held on the Sabbath, Rosh Hashanah, Yom Kippur, Festival of Tabernacles (Sukkot), Passover (Pesach), and Feast of Weeks (Shavuot).

- There is no wake.

- There is no viewing; the casket remains closed.

- Mourners may have a symbolic small tear—keriah—made to their clothes, which represents a broken heart.

- Family observes shiva for seven days—the Hebrew word for *seven* is "shevah," and *shiva* is taken from *shevah* to mean there are seven days of mourning after the funeral.

- Family continues to observe mourning during sh'loshim (Hebrew for thirty) for twenty-one days, the three weeks following shiva. The family returns to work but does not usually attend social functions.

- Families observe yahrtzeit, the annual anniversary of a loved one's death.

What to Wear
- Dark and conservative clothing.

What to Do
- Family members and friends, regardless of their religion, gather at the home to comfort the mourners during shiva. Visitors are not expected to cheer up the mourners—they should follow the lead of the mourners and be either silent or listen to the mourners speak of the deceased.

- It is appropriate to make charitable contributions in memory of the deceased.

- Visits from friends are especially appreciated during Sh'loshim, as condolence visits have usually slowed down and mourners might feel especially isolated.

What to Bring
- It is customary to provide food to the mourners during the shiva week.

- Bring baked goods, fruit, or meals (without pork or pork products) that need only to be reheated.

What Not to Do, Say, or Bring
- Do not send flowers, as all aspects of the funeral are to be as simple as possible.

PROTESTANT

What to Expect

- Some Protestant denominations have established rituals which would include three parts of the funeral service—the visitation, church service, and graveside service. Other denominations are less structured. The family usually notifies you of their plans and expectations through a published death notice in the local newspaper.

- Death notices usually indicate visitation hours and the family's request for flowers or donations. If a notice is not published you can check with the funeral home.

What to Wear

- Dress in a respectful manner, usually in dark colors.

What to Do

- Pay your respects to the deceased at the visitation. Approach the casket or urn, either say a brief prayer or observe a moment of silence, and offer your condolences to the family.

- Sign the guest register at the funeral home.

- Make a charitable donation in memory of the deceased; check the funeral notice for the family's preference.

What to Bring

- Many families prefer that flowers be sent to the funeral home before the funeral or to the church, unless otherwise indicated.

What Not to Do, Say, or Bring

- You are not expected to attend all three parts of the funeral service—the visitation, church service, and graveside service—unless you are a very good friend or family member.

- Do not wear red or bright-colored clothing.

ROMAN CATHOLIC

What to Expect

- There might be three distinct parts to the funeral service—the visitation, funeral mass, and graveside service.

What to Wear

- Black, brown, or dark blue colors are appropriate; jacket and tie for men and dress, suit, or skirt and blouse for women.

What to Do

- Pay your respects to the deceased at the visitation. Approach the casket or urn, either say a brief prayer or observe a moment of silence, and offer your condolences to the family.

- Sign the guest register at the funeral home.

- Make a donation in memory of the deceased; check the funeral notice for the family's preference.

- Visit the family at home.

What to Bring

- Flowers may be sent to the home before or after the funeral or to the funeral home.

- Send a mass card. Contact the Catholic Church office, either a local parish or the parish of the deceased. The office assistant will explain how to obtain mass cards at the parish.

- Send food to the home of the bereaved.

What Not to Do, Say, or Bring

- You are not expected to attend all three parts of the funeral service—the visitation, funeral mass, and graveside service—unless you are a very good friend or family member.

- Do not participate in the communion wine or wafer unless you are Catholic.

- Do not wear red or bright-colored clothing.

Special Situations

I recently learned that a friend from high school was killed in an accident. It has been more than ten years since I was in touch—is it appropriate to write to his parents?

A letter will bring great comfort to your friend's parents, and it is something they can read over and over again. You may share the story of how you met, a memorable experience from your high school days, and reflections on your friendship. It would be thoughtful if you could make a copy of a photo of your friend or one of the two of you from your high school days. Your letter and any memorabilia will be a wonderful keepsake, something they will greatly appreciate, and will help your friend's parents cope with their loss.

My co-worker's mother just died. He asked our supervisor to let the staff know but requested no one speak to him about it so he wouldn't risk breaking down at the office.

You should honor his request not to speak to him at work about his loss, but there are a number of ways you can let him know that you are sorry for his loss. You can send him a condolence card or a written note. If you can't locate his home address, you can leave it for him on his desk or in his mailbox. You can make a donation in his mother's memory; other co-workers might wish to contribute as well, and you can organize a group. If you don't know what specific charity to donate to, contribute to a local group that helps the community.

I learned a year ago that a friend's wife died. I didn't know what to say, so I said nothing and stayed away. I have been thinking a lot about him recently and would like to reconnect.

It is never too late to get in touch with someone you care about. You could break the ice by sending a plant with a note that says "You are often in my thoughts. I would like to see you and will call soon." Or it might be easier to approach him with a letter or note. Be honest, and tell him you are sorry you have been out of touch. You were upset to hear his wife died and unsure how you could help. You have really missed his friendship and would like to rekindle the relationship. You might invite him to be your guest at lunch, dinner, or a movie. Let him know you will call him in a few days to schedule a date, and follow up with a phone call.

My estranged friend's mother just died.
Let your friend know that you are so sorry for his loss and he has your deepest sympathy. If you would like to open the door to renew the relationship, communicate that you would like to be there for him and are ready to help. If his response is receptive, plan to help him in ways that are comfortable for you.

SAMPLE LETTERS/E-MAILS

To a good friend/colleague whose husband died after five years in an incapacitated state.

> January X, 2XXX
> Dear Elizabeth:
>
> Mark and I were so saddened to hear of Mike's death. I wish there was something we could say or do to ease the pain. Please know how much I value our friendship, your talents, and your support. I would like to be there for you, too. I will keep in touch to see what we can do to make the next few days, weeks, and months easier for you and your family. You, Jared, and Michelle will be in my thoughts and prayers.
>
> Love,
> Nancy

To the mother of your friend on your friend's death.

> September X, 2XXX
> Dear Mrs. Harper:
>
> I was deeply saddened by my dear friend Alexandra's death. Your daughter was a very special friend, and I feel richer for having had the pleasure of knowing her. I will miss her terribly, and I know you will too.
>
> Alexandra and I shared so much. Our lives were so entwined, and I have the most wonderful memories of her.
>
> In the next few months, I plan to look through my albums and gather together photographs of Alexandra's and my adventures. I will give you a call

when I have finished, and I would like to get together with you to share the photographs.

In the meantime, you have my heartfelt condolences.

Sincerely,
Mary Beth

To a cousin on the death of her father.

August X, 2XXX
Dear Sharon:

We are all so sad your dad died, and know that our grief is only a small portion of what you must be feeling.

I just wanted to take a moment and share some thoughts about your dad and what he meant to me. When I think of your dad, the first word that comes to mind is *fun*. From my earliest recollections, your family always seemed to be such an active and involved bunch, and that is always how I think of your dad. I can only imagine what a great teacher he must have been because he had such a keen interest in so many things. It was always interesting to talk to him.

I am so glad our families were able to share their last years together in such close proximity. They had such a rich and shared history, which we are all connected through and to each other. For this, I am most grateful.

I am thankful that I got to spend a whole afternoon with your dad when I was in Florida in April. Your dad was looking pretty well for all the health problems he was having, and we had a good visit.

He was so proud of you, and he had every right to be. What an achievement your dad's life was. He raised all of you after your mom died at a time when it was unusual to have a single-parent household. Whatever difficulties he experienced in life, he overcame and found such joy in his relationships with his children and grandchildren.

We will all miss him—while we didn't see him regularly, we communicated with him often and knew that he was a part of our life and our family. We will remember him with love, humor, and pride.

You are in my thoughts.

Love,
Ellen

To the daughter of a friend on the death of her mother.

October X, 2XXX
Dear Teresa:

It is with great sorrow that I learned of your dear mother's death. Words cannot tell you how much I will miss her and how much she affected my life. I am sure the pain you must now feel is tempered by all the wonderful memories you have of this extraordinary woman. As the years go by, missing her will bring to mind those meaningful times you spent together. You must know how very proud she was of you. Her conversations were always replete with things about her family, her love, and her pride.

Mothers are very special people in our lives, and it is always difficult to lose them, no matter their age or ours.

May you be a living tribute to your mom's memory. Know that I, too, will remember your dear mother with much love and gratitude.

Caroline

To a nephew's wife whose mom died four months ago.

May X, 2XXX
Dear Cindy:

You are often in my thoughts. How are you, Steve, and the children doing? I remember feeling very much alone several months after my mom's death. Everyone I knew was back to their normal routine, and I had a sense that nothing in my life would be normal again. It was a very sad period, and I missed my mother terribly.

It's a difficult time as you adjust to life without your mom. I know you two had a special relationship, and that will always remain. It takes time for the pain and sense of loss to subside, but when it does, it is wonderful to bring those special feelings and warmth back into your life.

I don't have many words of wisdom. I just wanted you to know that you are thought of and cared for. Be kind to yourself, and give Steve and the children a kiss for me.

With love,
Aunt Jenny

A very belated sympathy letter to an acquaintance on the death of her husband.

June X, 2XXX
Dear Teresa:

Please accept my apology for taking so long to write this note. I was so sorry to hear of John's death last August. We frequently mentioned him in our prayers at services and hoped the treatments he was receiving would work.

We really enjoyed getting to know John through the religious school programs, and his warmth and friendliness made many of the meetings a much more pleasant experience.

What always struck me about John was his smile and his interest in the people around him. His sincerity and easygoing nature made the day brighter. He is sorely missed.

Please accept my deepest sympathy on your loss. You are in my heart and prayers.

Sincerely,
Harriet Brown

For further information:

Bartocci, Barbara. *Nobody's Child Anymore: Grieving, Caring and Comforting When Parents Die.* Notre Dame, IN: Sorin Books, 2000.

Commins, Patricia. *Remembering Mother, Finding Myself.* Deerfield Beach, FL: Health Communications, Inc., 1999.

Deits, Bob. *Life After Loss: A Personal Guide to Dealing with Death, Divorce, Job Change and Relocation.* Tucson, AZ: Perseus Publishing, 1999.

Doka, Kenneth J., Ph.D., ed. *Living with Grief After Sudden Loss: Suicide, Homicide, Accident, Heart Attack, Stroke.* Bristol, PA: Taylor and Francis, 1996.

Kübler-Ross, Elisabeth. *On Death and Dying.* New York, NY: Scribner, 1997.

Mathis, Stuart M., and Arthur J. Magida, eds. *How to Be a Perfect Stranger: A Guide to Etiquette in Other People's Religious Ceremonies.* Woodstock, VT: Jewish Lights Publishing, 1996.

Noel, Brook, and Pamela D. Blair, Ph.D. *I Wasn't Ready to Say Good-bye: Surviving, Coping and Healing After the Sudden Death of a Loved One.* Milwaukee, WI: Champion Press Ltd., 2000.

Rando, Therese A., Ph.D. *How to Go on Living When Someone You Love Dies.* New York, NY: Bantam Books, 1991.

American Association of Retired Persons (AARP), Grief and Loss, a collection of resources, a community of care
www.aarp.org/griefandloss

GriefNet.org is an Internet community of persons dealing with grief, death, and major loss with forty-seven e-mail support groups and two websites.
GriefNet.org

Especially for teens:
Fitzgerald, Helen. *The Grieving Teen: A Guide for Teenagers and Their Friends.* New York, NY: Fireside, 2000.

Grollman, Earl A. *Bereaved Children and Teens: A Support Guide for Parents and Professionals.* Boston, MA: Beacon Press, 1996.

———. *Straight Talk About Death for Teenagers: How to Cope with Losing Someone You Love.* Boston, MA: Beacon Press, 1993.

Wolfelt, Alan D., Ph.D. *Healing Your Grieving Heart for Teens.* Fort Collins, CO: Companion Press, 2001.

Especially for children:
Buscaglia, Leo, Ph.D. *The Fall of Freddie the Leaf.* New York, NY: Henry Holt & Company, Inc., 2002.

Coleman, Dr. Paul. *How to Say It to Your Child When Bad Things Happen: Good Answers to Tough Questions.* Paramus, NJ: Prentice Hall Press, 2002.

———. *How to Say It to Your Kids.* Paramus, NJ: Prentice Hall Press, 2000.

Krementz, Jill. *How It Feels When a Parent Dies.* New York, NY: Knopf, 1988.

Mundy, Michaelene. *Sad Isn't Bad: A Good-Grief Guidebook for Kids Dealing with Loss*. St. Meinrad, IA: Abbey Press, 1998.

See also: WHAT IS GRIEF? UNDERSTANDING THE PROCESS OF MOURNING AND HOW YOU CAN HELP, WHAT CAN I SAY? COMMUNICATIONS THAT COMFORT, and WHAT CAN I DO? HOW TO LISTEN.

SIX

Death of a Child

∞

"The true way to mourn the dead is to take care
of the living who belong to them."

—Edmund Burke

PARENTS expect to die before their children; when a child dies it is not in the natural order of things, and nothing prepares us for burying and mourning our children. Hopes and dreams for the future die along with the child. Because a child is so intimately linked to its parents, it is easy for the parents to feel as if they have lost a piece of themselves.

Parents report an aching sense of guilt and personal responsibility when children die from accidents, homicide, and suicide, the leading causes of death among young people. They might exert enormous effort replaying and reliving the moments of the day the death occurred, desperately trying to figure out what they could have done differently to prevent the outcome.

The death of a child is deeply unsettling, and because of its infrequency, it is easy for parents to feel very isolated. Parents can feel an enormous emptiness in their homes and in their hearts. It is a loss that is keenly felt by both parents, grandparents, and any surviving children.

Parents describe the grief as so overwhelming that it can bring unique tensions to a marriage. Unlike other losses and disappointments, parents who had previously been able to provide each other with comfort and support might find it difficult to do so when grieving for their child. Each parent might adopt their own coping or grieving approach. These approaches might be neither complementary nor compatible but quite necessary if the parent is to survive the devastating loss.

A parent who experiences the death of a child is forever changed. They don't want to be treated like a victim, and while they yearn to be just like everyone else, this experience has made them different from everyone else. Your job in supporting them in this difficult time is a tough one, but it's absolutely vital.

THINGS TO CONSIDER

- The parent believes that it is his or her role to protect their child, and through no fault of their own, they were unable to do so. They might feel an overwhelming sense of guilt and responsibility.

- Accept that this experience will irrevocably change the parent(s).

- Parents don't "get over it"; they learn to live with the pain.

- Time does not heal all wounds. It makes coping with the loss easier, but the heart never fully recovers.

- Grief might not just be lengthy, it might be everlasting.

- Birthdays of the child and anniversaries of his or her death are particularly painful.

- Recognize that siblings experience a unique loss when a child dies. Take extra care to ensure that you don't ignore the sibling(s), and in your grief, don't imply only the deceased child mattered. If you have a relationship with the sibling(s), continue to nurture it.

EMOTIONS AND FEELINGS TO ANTICIPATE

- Anger
- Blame
- Confusion
- Denial
- Disbelief
- Envy
- Failure
- Guilt

- Helplessness
- Inadequacy
- Incompetency
- Isolation
- Jealousy
- Powerlessness
- Resentment
- Shock

WHAT TO SAY AND DO

- The death of a child is so shocking that the parents might find it difficult to make the simplest decisions or choices. If you are close to the parents, don't ask what you can do, just step in and help them take care of the basic necessities such as caring for other children and pets, meals, snow removal, lawn care, and other daily needs.

- Offer to make calls to places of employment, colleagues, school, family members, or neighbors.

- Do make sure the family's religious leader and congregation are aware of the death; the congregation often has resources in place to provide bereavement support.

- Convey your compassion by acknowledging the loss.

- When you speak about the child, use the child's name.

- Keep in touch on a regular basis.

- Share your memories of the child.

- Do expect the parent(s) to be changed by their experience.

- Do use a "sixth sense" in monitoring your conversations and interactions. Be sensitive when relating news or an experience of your child because it might touch a sensitive or painful nerve.

- If you are a close family member or friend and are willing to help the parent clean the child's room, offer ahead of time. The parent might not know when they will be ready to do so but may appreciate your availability to lend support and comfort.

- Do invite them for holiday celebrations. They probably don't have the energy to prepare a celebration, and they might not be up to it.

- Offer to accompany them to the cemetery.

- Do send a "thinking of you" card to remember them and their child around the child's birthday and the anniversary of the death.

↝ When the parent(s) are ready to socialize, find opportunities to create new memories together because the old ones might be too painful. Suggest a new interest such as taking a cooking class or dance lessons together or attending programs at the museum or through adult education. Try a new sport such as bowling or ice skating—something they never did with you or your family.

■ Do understand that it might be difficult for the parents to attend graduations, showers, engagement parties, weddings, and visits from your family; these may all be reminders of experiences they will never have with their child.

■ Do realize that you might have to accept whatever the parents can give; if you want to continue your relationship, you will have to do so on their terms. They might be emotionally incapable of participating in many of the social rituals you shared in the past, as the memories might be too painful.

■ Continue to share your memories of the child throughout the years after their death. It will make the parents feel good to know that their child's special smile, warm greeting, giving nature, or artistic talent is not forgotten.

HOW TO SAY IT

I am so sorry this has happened.

I really don't know how you are feeling, but I would like to be there for you.

I will always miss her (him).

I will never forget him (her).

I'm sad for you.

Take your time; you will do things when you are ready.

There will always be a special place in my heart for him (her) and you.

We loved her (him), too.

We share your sorrow.

WHAT NOT TO SAY AND DO

- Don't visit without an invitation.

- Don't isolate the parents by not sharing any information about your own family; just be sensitive to their loss when you discuss your news.

- Don't treat them as if they are a martyr by making comments such as "I am so proud of you"; they didn't choose to go through this tragedy.

- Don't try to make life appear normal; it's not. Life will never be the same as they knew it, no matter how much you would like it to be. As the parents redefine their lives, life will take on a new "normal."

- Don't be offended if the parent(s) decline your offer for holidays or dinner at your home. Those events might be reminders of past shared experiences.

- Don't automatically assume or expect the parent(s) to continue lifelong patterns and rituals; they might be too painful.

HOW NOT TO SAY IT

At least you have another child.

Be thankful he (she) wasn't an only child.

Don't you wish it was you instead?

God never gives us more than we can handle.

God only takes the best.

He's (She's) in heaven.

I don't know how you are bearing all this; I could never do it.

It happened for the best.

It was God's will.

It would be worse if it was your husband (wife).

Now you have your very own angel.

You'll have other children.

NONVERBAL STRATEGIES

- Make copies of photos you may have of the child and give them to the parents.

- If you are a family member or close friend, you might want to make a small scrapbook of photos from your collection.

- When holiday invitations are declined, bring the holiday to them. Cook and bake holiday foods and deliver them.

- Is there a special holiday ritual you know brought them pleasure? Do it for them, and bring it to their home to enjoy.

- If you are a teacher or classmate, share a project or schoolwork by the child with the parents.

- All the parents have left are memories; share your special memories by writing them down and presenting them to the parents.

Special Situations

I have a sixteen-year-old daughter, and my close friend's sixteen-year-old son was killed in a car accident. How can I deal with this on an ongoing basis?
Be compassionate and caring to your friend, and reach out to her or him, but don't be surprised if it is just too painful for your friend to resume your friendship. Your daughter is and will continue to be a constant reminder of everything your friend has lost. As your child grows and experiences graduation, prom, and college, your friend's child will forever remain sixteen. If the friendship is important to you, you should make an effort to see him or her in nonfamily situations and focus on sharing the adult facets of your life.

My lifelong friend's teenage daughter just died unexpectedly. We have always shared holidays and special occasions together, even vacations. Now she refuses all my invitations. I am heartbroken, too, and wonder if I must lose my friend as well as her daughter?
This person who has suffered the death of her daughter is now a different person, and the person she is today is not the person she might be in a few years. The loss of a child shakes the very core of a parent's existence, and your holidays

and special occasions are a constant reminder of what was and what your friend will never have again. Accept that it is just too painful for your friend to continue this shared tradition. But it is possible for the two of you to continue your friendship. Don't take your friend's refusal personally; she or he is just protecting themselves. Let them know you are ready to resume a relationship when they are. Suggest that you begin a new routine such as coffee on Saturday mornings or an early morning or afternoon walk. Find new ways to be together that provide you both a fresh start and a new foundation for your relationship. When you build new memories together you will retain your friendship, but it will be a different friendship than your past relationship.

A couple my spouse and I are close with lost their young daughter to cancer. Despite our best efforts, we have seen them very infrequently since the funeral and are not sure if they just need to be alone or if they are sending a message that they want us to back off.

Your friends have a rough road ahead of them, but if you are willing, ride it out with them. Keep in touch, briefly if you must, but let them know that you are thinking of them. Give as much as you can, but don't take it personally if you get nothing back. Grief is exhausting, and it might be impossible for your friends to do anything but grieve. Let your friends know that you are available if they want to talk; be their "safe harbor" through nonjudgmental listening. Remember them in small ways on their birthdays and their daughter's birthday or special holidays. Be a continued presence, and wait for them to be ready to resume a relationship. Be patient.

SAMPLE LETTERS/E-MAILS

To a colleague whose teenage daughter was killed in an accident.

> January X, 2XXX
> Dear Bill:
>
> You have been in my thoughts since I heard the shocking news about Linda. The loss of a child is such a difficult grief to bear, and I am so terribly sorry.
>
> There is really nothing I can say to you except that I share your pain. I didn't know Linda personally, but I remember the family portrait you kept in your office, and I enjoyed your stories of her and all that she accomplished in

her short life. I hope that you and your family will find peace again someday. My thoughts and prayers are with you.

Sincerely,
Jim Smith

To the parents of a young child who died after battling cancer for two years.

November X, 2XXX
Dearest Beth and John:

Kelly's death leaves me speechless and in tears. Our thoughts have been with you and your family during this sad week. Losing a wonderful daughter like Kelly is too painful to imagine.

We have the most wonderful memories of the times we spent together on family outings. Kelly was always the adventurous soul, willing to experience new things with such confidence and pleasure. She was sheer joy to be with, and I will never forget her warmth and charm that went beyond her young years. She had a strength and force that let her live life to the fullest during her terrible struggle. She left a legacy of courage that I will try to use as my model as I face the sad days ahead.

We are thinking of you constantly during this difficult time. May you be blessed with the strength and courage to move ahead.

With much love,
Harriet and Sam Little

To the aunt of a teenager killed in a car accident.

June X, 2XXX
Dear Tina:

There are no words to express the shock and sadness I feel over the tragic death of your dear nephew Marshall.

Children are one of life's greatest gifts. Please let your sister and brother-in-law know that my thoughts and prayers have been and will continue to be with all of you during this difficult time.

Marshall was so outgoing and fun-loving that no one who knew him will ever forget him. Though Marshall's time with us was short, his presence touched many lives. May Marshall's memory forever be a blessing.

So much love is sent your way. I will be in touch.
Marianne White

To a teenage friend's family after the friend's death due to complications after surgery.

September X, 2XXX
Dear Mr. and Mrs. Turner and Will:

I was stunned and saddened to learn of Sara's death. Meg had kept me informed, and we were so happy that the surgery had gone well.

Sara will forever remain a bright and shining star that touched my life. She had the sweetest nature, and her smile is etched in my mind. I truly enjoyed being around Sara and looked forward to spending time with her during her convalescence.

Everyone at school is shocked. It is amazing to see what an impact Sara had on everyone's lives. She was so bright and positive-spirited, she seems to have made an impression even on students who didn't know her or were just acquaintances.

Please know that you are not alone in your sadness and grief. I will always feel blessed to have known her.

I found the enclosed photograph yesterday and thought you might like to have it. The picture was taken in our English class last semester when we dressed up like our favorite character. As you can see, Sara was her beloved Scarlett O'Hara.

Much love,
Erica

From a member of the community to the parents of a local teenager who was killed in a car accident.

March X, 2XXX

Dear Mr. and Mrs. Wilson:

Our family was saddened to learn of your recent tragedy and want you to know that it touched our hearts. We are among the many whom you might not know who mourn your loss with you.

May your memories of this special child be sweet and everlasting. You will continue to be in our thoughts and prayers.

Please accept my deepest sympathy.

Sincerely,

Ms. Sharon Landry

For additional information:

Bernstein, Judith R. *When the Bough Breaks—Forever After the Death of a Son or Daughter*. Kansas City, MO: Andrews McMeel Publishing, 1998.

Doka, Kenneth J., Ph.D., ed. *Living with Grief After Sudden Loss: Suicide, Homicide, Accident, Heart Attack, Stroke*. Bristol, PA: Taylor and Francis, 1996.

Finkbeiner, Ann K. *After the Death of a Child: Living with Loss Through the Years*. Baltimore, MD: The Johns Hopkins University Press, 1998.

McCracken, Anne, and Mary Semel. *A Broken Heart Still Beats—After Your Child Dies*. Center City, MN: Hazelden, 2000.

Mehren, Elizabeth. *After the Darkest Hour the Sun Will Shine Again*. New York, NY: Simon & Schuster, 1997.

Rosof, Barbara D. *The Worst Loss: How Families Heal from the Death of a Child*. New York, NY: Henry Holt and Company, Inc., 1994.

Sanders, Catherine M., Ph.D. *How to Survive the Loss of a Child*. Roseville, CA: Prima Publishing, 1998.

Schiff, Harriett Sarnoff. *The Bereaved Parent*. New York, NY: Penguin Books, 1977.

The Compassionate Friends, Inc.

National Headquarters

P.O. Box 3696

Oak Brook, IL 60522-3696
(630) 990-0010 or (877) 969-0010
www.compassionatefriends.org

GriefNet.org is an Internet community of persons dealing with grief, death, and major loss with forty-seven e-mail support groups and two websites. GriefNet.org

Especially for teens:
Fitzgerald, Helen. *The Grieving Teen: A Guide for Teenagers and Their Friends*. New York, NY: Fireside, 2000.

Grollman, Earl A. *Bereaved Children and Teens: A Support Guide for Parents and Professionals*. Boston, MA: Beacon Press, 1996.

———. *Straight Talk About Death for Teenagers: How to Cope with Losing Someone You Love*. Boston, MA: Beacon Press, 1993.

Wolfelt, Alan D., Ph.D. *Healing Your Grieving Heart for Teens*. Fort Collins, CO: Companion Press, 2001.

Especially for children:
Buscaglia, Leo, Ph.D. *The Fall of Freddie the Leaf*. New York, NY: Henry Holt & Company, Inc., 2002.

Coleman, Dr. Paul. *How to Say It to Your Child When Bad Things Happen: Good Answers to Tough Questions*. Paramus, NJ: Prentice Hall Press, 2002.

———. *How to Say It to Your Kids*. Paramus, NJ: Prentice Hall Press, 2000.

Mundy, Michaelene. *Sad Isn't Bad: A Good-Grief Guidebook for Kids Dealing with Loss*. St. Meinrad, IA: Abbey Press, 1998.

See also: WHAT IS GRIEF? UNDERSTANDING THE PROCESS OF MOURNING AND HOW YOU CAN HELP, WHAT CAN I SAY? COMMUNICATIONS THAT COMFORT, WHAT CAN I DO? HOW TO LISTEN, and DEATH OF AN ADULT.

SEVEN

Birth of a Stillborn or Death of a Newborn Baby

∞

"For some life lasts a short while,
but the memories it holds last forever."

—Laura Swenson

THERE is something particularly tragic when a baby dies before birth or shortly after birth. Moms and dads and extended family members have dreamed, planned, and hoped for the day they would meet the new arrival; they wondered who the baby would look like and what characteristics he or she would inherit. This special time winds up filled with sorrow rather than the much-anticipated joy. The mom and dad come home with empty arms and a heavy heart.

The National Center for Health Statistics, Centers for Disease Control Prevention, reports that out of almost 4 million births in the United States in 2000, about 18,737 babies or infants died in the first month of life and 9,250 additional babies died by twelve months. The death of babies up to twenty-eight days is referred to as neonatal death.

Forty-five percent of all infant deaths in 1999 were linked to three leading causes:

- Congenital malformations
- Disorders related to short gestation and low birth weight
- Sudden Infant Death Syndrome (SIDS)

No one knows what to say or do to comfort moms and dads who have lost a baby. Rituals and procedures that provide spiritual and emotional comfort and strength to the bereaved might not exist for stillborns or newborns who live fewer than a full thirty days.

Many adults still turn to their own parents when they need comfort, but it is difficult for the moms and dads to reach out to their own parents for solace when their baby dies because their parents are hurting, too; they have just lost a much-anticipated grandchild and are also bereaved.

Although it might be difficult to comfort someone experiencing such an intensely painful loss, the bereaved will need your prolonged support and help to voice their feelings and fully grieve.

THINGS TO CONSIDER

- Birth defects account for approximately 25 percent of neonatal deaths.

- Premature birth and resulting complications account for approximately 20 percent of neonatal deaths.

- Heart defects account for almost a third of birth-defect-related neonatal deaths.

- Grief and loss are profoundly painful, no matter how old the baby.

- Recognize that siblings experience a unique loss when a fetus or baby dies. Take extra care to ensure that you don't ignore the sibling(s) in your grief. Children are very sensitive to their parents' emotions, so if parents, grandparents, and other adults grieve in a healthy way, the children will learn how to grieve, too.

EMOTIONS AND FEELINGS TO ANTICIPATE

■ Anger	■ Emptiness
■ Confusion	■ Failure
■ Disappointment	■ Fear
■ Disbelief	■ Guilt

- Helplessness
- Incompetence
- Jealousy
- Pain

- Resentment
- Sadness
- Shock
- Sorrow

WHAT TO SAY AND DO

- It's okay if you cry when you hear the news or when you are with the parent(s).

- Do make sure the family's religious leader and congregation are aware of the death; the congregation often has resources in place to provide bereavement support.

> ✎ If you do visit the family, offer to fix a food they love or bring along a favorite treat. Comfort foods can be nurturing, so consider indulging one or both of the parents' fondness for a special candy, ice cream, bagels, donuts, or a deli sandwich. Even if they have no appetite for it right now, it will warm their heart that you remembered them in such a personal way.

- Plan to attend the funeral or memorial service.

- Offer transportation to and from the airport if family members or friends are coming in from out of town.

- Ask the parent(s) if they picked out a name for their baby. If so, refer to the baby by name.

- Offer to help with household tasks like grocery shopping, laundry, or running errands.

- Bring prepared meals and other groceries the family will need.

- Offer to make phone calls to notify people.

> ✎ If you do accompany the mother to the doctor, suggest you go out for coffee or a diversion afterward.

- Offer to write notes to acknowledge kindnesses if the mom and dad are not up to it.

- Send them a gift certificate for a restaurant or take-out food service.

- The parent(s) might need some household help; an offer to personally help or a gift certificate for a cleaning service will be appreciated. You can always propose this idea as a group or neighborhood endeavor.

> ↪ If you have a baby yourself, do wait until they ask or offer to hold or help with your baby. They are the only ones who know whether it would be painful or not.

- Offer to accompany the mom to her post-delivery checkup with the obstetrician.

- Give the mom a gift certificate for a haircut or spa treatment; it won't take away the pain, but she will look and subsequently feel better.

HOW TO SAY IT

Help me know what I can do to help you.

I can't imagine how sad you must feel.

I love you, and I am so sorry this has happened.

I want to help. What can I do for you?

Is there anything I can do for you?

This must be terribly difficult.

What can I do to help you?

What is your baby's name?

WHAT NOT TO SAY AND DO

- Don't visit without an invitation.

- Don't insist on visiting if the mom and dad tell you they are not up to visitors.

- Don't expect the parent(s) to entertain you. If you are served something, take the initiative to clean up the kitchen before you leave.

- Don't bring your children without checking first.

- If your children accompany you, bring something to keep them occupied and feed them first so they won't be hungry.

- If you have a baby, don't hide the baby from the parents. But don't hand your baby to them to hold; it might be too painful.

- Don't suggest that giving of themselves would make them feel better, for example, donating some of their maternity clothing to someone you know who is pregnant and needy or giving some of the baby clothing and accessories to a needy family.

HOW NOT TO SAY IT

At least you have other children.

At least your baby didn't suffer long.

Don't be so sad.

God doesn't give you more than you can handle.

I hope you didn't hold him (her).

It was better the baby died before you got to know her (him).

It wasn't meant to be.

It's a blessing in disguise.

It's God's will.

There's a reason for everything.

You can have more children.

You're still young.

NONVERBAL STRATEGIES

- If the mom is taking some time off, offer to bring her lunch and share a meal with her.

- If the baby died as an infant, give a baby book as a gift so they can include photos and memories of the baby.

- If they are not up to filling in a baby book, ask them if they would like you to do it for them.

- Save a copy of the local newspaper for them to commemorate and remember the day the baby was born.

Special Situations

A cousin was pregnant with twins. Just before delivery, one baby died; she gave birth to a stillborn and a healthy baby. How do I commemorate this happy-yet-sad occasion?

Although the birth of a child is a joyous event, the parents of these twins have entered a time of great sorrow mixed with great joy. It would be a mistake to assume that the healthy child makes up for the loss of the other twin. The parents lovingly awaited the birth of the two babies, and they will have to mourn the baby who died. It is important to address both the death and the birth separately; if you were to address them together, you would not be recognizing the great sadness and loss for the baby who did not live. You can send a sympathy note for the baby who died, and it would be appropriate to make a donation in memory of the child. You can check with a family member or their religious organization to learn if there is an organization or charity designated for this purpose. You should also send a congratulations, separately, for the healthy baby in whatever way you planned—either by card, flowers, and/or a gift.

A friend had an uneventful pregnancy, but at thirty-two weeks, the baby died and she was induced to deliver a stillborn baby.

It is very important that you acknowledge the baby's death—you will compound her loss if you stay away or never mention that it happened. If your friend chose a name for the baby, it is appropriate to refer to the baby by name. You can send a card, note, or flowers expressing your sympathy. Take your cues from your friend as far as a visit goes; if you do visit with her, give her and her partner a hug, keep them company if they cry, and make yourself available to listen.

SAMPLE LETTERS/E-MAILS

To a friend's daughter and son-in-law whose baby was stillborn.

July X, 2XXX
Dear Hillary and Tom:

We were so saddened to hear that your sweet baby daughter died. Words can't possibly express the sorrow we feel for your loss. I know how much you loved your daughter and anticipated her birth.

I hope that you will find some comfort in knowing that your loss is shared by so many who love you. Please accept our deepest sympathy.

Fondly,
Steve and Melissa Smith

To friends whose baby died from a congenital problem at three weeks old.

September X, 2XXX
Dear Nan and Max:

I was so terribly sorry to hear that Megan died. It was such a joy to share the excitement of her anticipated birth, and I know just how much you treasured her.

You have been in my thoughts constantly in the last few days. I pray that you will find solace and comfort in your memories of this special child. May these memories be sweet and everlasting.

With love,
Shannon

To a distant cousin who has had a stillborn baby.

April X, 2XXX
Dear Natalie:

Jackie called this morning with the news of your son's birth, and I was terribly saddened to hear that he had died. I have felt so close to you during this pregnancy and share your sorrow.

While I haven't had your experience, I suspect that I know very much how you are feeling. You see, I also lost a baby in infancy.

I've only known you a short time, Natalie, and learned of your pregnancy early in our relationship. I didn't share this with you earlier because I didn't want to frighten you with my story.

You are such a gifted and special person, Natalie. I want nothing more for you and your family than all the goodness you deserve. Let this experience bind you and Aaron closer together. Lean on each other, because no one else knows quite what you are experiencing.

I send much love to you. If you want to share any thoughts with me, please do. I will always be there for you.

Love,
Linda

To a friend on the death of her two-month-old daughter from SIDS.

July X, 2XXX
Dearest Ann:

How does one express such sorrow? You waited so long for Jamie to come into your life. I feel so terribly sad, and I am sorry that you must be asked to endure such grief.

I send my love and support on the loss of your sweet Jamie. The beauty of this child will be locked in your hearts forever.

I will keep you, Jamie, and your dear husband in my prayers.

With love,
Madeline

For further information:

Davis, Deborah L., Ph.D. *Empty Cradle, Broken Heart: Surviving the Death of Your Baby*. Golden, CO: Fulcrum Publishing, 1996.

Douglas, Ann, and John R. Sussman, M.D. *Trying Again: A Guide to Pregnancy After Miscarriage, Stillbirth, and Infant Loss*. Dallas, TX: Taylor Publishing Company, 2000.

Horchler, Joani Nelson, and Robin Rice Morris. *The SIDS Survival Guide: Information and Comfort for Grieving Family and Friends and Professionals Who Seek to Help Them*. Hyattsville, MD: SIDS Educational Services, 1994.

Kohn, Ingrid, MSW, and Perry-Lynn Moffitt, with Isabelle A. Wilkins, M.D. *A Silent Sorrow—Pregnancy Loss: Guidance and Support for You and Your Family*. New York, NY: Routledge, 2000.

Lothrop, Hannah. *Help, Comfort and Hope After Losing Your Baby in Pregnancy or the First Year*. Boulder, CO: Perseus Publishing, 1997.

National Sudden Infant Death Syndrome Resource Center (NSRC)
2070 Chain Bridge Road, Suite 450
Vienna, VA 22182
Toll Free: (866) 866-7437
(703) 821-8955
Fax: (703) 821-2098
www.sidscenter.org

SHARE is a not-for-profit nondenominational organization providing support to those whose lives are touched by the tragic death of a baby through early pregnancy loss, still-birth, or newborn death.

National SHARE Office
St. Joseph Health Center
300 First Capitol Drive
St. Charles, MS 63301-2893
(636) 947-6164 or (800) 821-6819
Fax: (636) 947-7486
share@nationalshareoffice.com
www.nationalshareoffice.com

The Compassionate Friends, Inc.
National Headquarters
P.O. Box 3696
Oak Brook, IL 60522-3696
(630) 990-0010 or (877) 969-0010
www.compassionatefriends.org

Especially for children:

Buscaglia, Leo, Ph.D. *The Fall of Freddie the Leaf*. New York, NY: Henry Holt & Company, Inc., 2002.

Coleman, Dr. Paul. *How to Say It to Your Child When Bad Things Happen: Good Answers to Tough Questions*. Paramus, NJ: Prentice Hall Press, 2002.

———. *How to Say It to Your Kids*. Paramus, NJ: Prentice Hall Press, 2000.

See also: WHAT IS GRIEF? UNDERSTANDING THE PROCESS OF MOURNING AND HOW YOU CAN HELP, WHAT CAN I SAY? COMMUNICATIONS THAT COMFORT, WHAT CAN I DO? HOW TO LISTEN, DEATH OF AN ADULT, and DEATH OF A CHILD.

EIGHT

Suicide

∞

*"Do not dwell in the past, do not dream of the future,
concentrate the mind on the present moment."*

—Buddha

SUICIDE is sudden, unexpected, and traumatic. Even if there is a prior history of attempts, suicide is shocking, and nothing prepares the bereaved for the loss.

The National Center for Health Statistics ranks suicide as the eleventh leading cause of death in the United States. Approximately 30,000 individuals die by suicide each year. Suicide ranks as the third leading cause of death for teens and young adults; more teens and young adults die from suicide than from cancer, heart disease, congenital birth defects, AIDS, chronic lung disease, influenza and pneumonia, and stroke combined.

Although suicide is not that uncommon, it bears a social stigma that makes it different from any other death. The bereaved, sometimes referred to as "suicide grievers," might feel shunned by society. They might also feel ashamed; they might be embarrassed to tell people about the death and how it happened, and it is not uncommon for them to keep the cause of death a secret. If a child commits suicide, the parents might feel that sharing the information will reflect negatively on their parenting skills.

The bereaved might feel a sense of responsibility for their loss—shouldn't they have seen it coming, or couldn't they have done something differently that could have prevented the suicide? It isn't just the people closest to the deceased that feel the burden of responsibility; many acquaintances and friends might think they, too, could have done something differently that would have made a difference.

The bereaved might replay past experiences and conversations, searching for clues or some explanation for the suicide. Guilt is unavoidable; their brain is trying to reconcile how this could have happened.

Spiritual and societal rituals and routines that bring comfort to the bereaved might not be available to those dealing with the aftermath of suicide. Some religions might even consider suicide a sin, and burial might be discreet.

The bereaved who witness the suicide or who find the body might compound their grief and experience post-traumatic stress.

It is quite common for the bereaved to experience social withdrawal, and this can easily make them feel isolated at a time when they desperately need support. You can ease this sense of isolation by reaching out to them through oral, written, and nonverbal communications.

THINGS TO CONSIDER

- Police will initially conduct an investigation to rule out homicide before declaring death a suicide. A crime scene must be maintained to identify and analyze the evidence. You will need to check in at the perimeter of the crime scene and request to be with a loved one before entering the area.

- Suicide carries a negative stigma, and it is very common for the bereaved to experience significant shame.

- You might have some experience dealing with death but little or none with suicide.

- Lack of experience makes some folks uncomfortable and fearful; be careful not to treat suicide grievers differently than you would others who grieve the death of a loved one.

- The bereaved might be distressed over unresolved issues.

- The bereaved might be reluctant to talk about their feelings because of the stigma of suicide.

EMOTIONS AND FEELINGS TO ANTICIPATE

- Anger
- Bewilderment
- Confusion
- Despair

- Disbelief
- Embarrassment
- Fear
- Guilt
- Helplessness
- Rage

- Rejection
- Remorse
- Resentment
- Shame
- Shock

WHAT TO SAY AND DO

- Do make sure the family's religious leader and congregation are aware of the death. The congregation often has resources in place to provide bereavement support.

- Do participate in all mourning rituals—attend the wake, funeral, memorial service, or reception.

- Give unconditional support. It is very appropriate to let the bereaved know that no matter what they are feeling, it is okay.

> ✄ The bereaved experience a great deal of guilt, and it can easily be misplaced. If you don't attend the funeral or memorial service, they might think you are avoiding them. Assuage these feelings by sending a card or note to express your condolences if you are unable to attend.

- Do bring meals and help out in all the ways you would for anyone who is mourning the death of a loved one. See Chapter Five for ideas, customs, and suggestions.

- Be patient and understanding, and roll with the myriad emotions that can be very intense and long-lasting.

- Do bring comfort to the bereaved by mentioning the name of the person who has died.

- Do share your special memories of the person who has died.

- Be sensitive in discussing the deceased; they might have ended their own life, but that doesn't take away from their good character and the life they led.

- Encourage the bereaved to release their feelings. Troubles that are locked inside will fester.

- Allow the bereaved to tell their story over and over again. This is an experience that they might not get over, but in time, their feelings will stabilize.

- Listen and say nothing. No one expects you to have the answers.

- Do keep in touch, as suicide grievers can feel especially isolated.

- Include the bereaved in invitations to a dinner out, a concert, or a movie, and include a few close family members or friends.

- Help the bereaved reestablish routines. If the bereaved is a member of a book club, bridge club, bowling league, etc., offer to pick them up and encourage them to attend.

- Suggest sharing a walk once or twice a week; exercise goes a long way to reestablishing routines and physical health. They might need some coaxing to get out; you might need to let them know you will stop by on Monday and Wednesday at ten in the morning to pick them up.

- Do remember the bereaved at the anniversary of the suicide and other special holidays and events; your thoughtfulness will lighten the sadness.

HOW TO SAY IT

I am here to listen, not to judge.

I am not going to pretend to know how you feel.

I am not going to suggest how you should respond.

I don't have answers, but I will help in any way you'd like.

I know this is a rough time for you.

I might not have any experience with this, but I want to help you.

If you would like some company, I am here for you anytime.

It's good to see you.

Let's take a walk so you can talk and I can listen.

This must be very painful for you.

Would you like to go to a movie with me?

Would you like to talk?

WHAT NOT TO SAY AND DO

- Don't tell the mourner how they should respond; grieving for someone who has committed suicide is different than any other death.

- Don't express your anger at the deceased for taking their life. That is something you will have to deal with, and it is unfair to burden the bereaved with your angry feelings.

- Don't ask if there was a suicide note.

- Don't ask details of the suicide such as "How did Paula take her life?" The bereaved will need to talk about the experience and tell their story many times, but they need to do that with caring people they are comfortable with. Rather than ask questions about the circumstances, offer to be available to listen whenever the bereaved needs to talk.

- Avoid statements that oversimplify the magnitude of loss, such as "Time heals all wounds."

- Avoid judgmental statements relating to the deceased and the cause of death.

- Don't speculate on the reasons for the suicide.

- Don't pass judgment on the bereaved; the experience of suicide might irrevocably change the bereaved, and you'll need to accept the person they have become.

- Don't criticize.

- Don't refer to the deceased as crazy or insane or their actions as irrational.

- Don't compare the experience of the bereaved to that of another suicide griever; everyone adjusts differently, and no two mourners grieve alike.

- Don't avoid the bereaved; if you cross the street or pretend you don't see them, you will heighten their isolation.

- Don't repeat mean-spirited remarks made about the deceased; you'll hurt the bereaved, and you'll look as bad as the person who made the remarks.

HOW NOT TO SAY IT

How are you feeling?

How did they do it?

It was a terrible accident.

It was such a selfish act.

It's God's will.

Snap out of it, already.

The pain will pass.

There must have been signs that she (he) was depressed.

They were crazy.

They were out of their mind.

Think of what you have to be thankful for.

Time is a great healer.

What happened? You'll feel better if you talk about it.

You are holding up so well.

You must be strong for your other children.

You'll get over it in time.

NONVERBAL STRATEGIES

■ Offer to help the bereaved create a scrapbook of photos and memorabilia to honor the deceased.

■ If the deceased was a part of your group, for example, co-workers or members of a fraternal, professional, or community organization, you might create a memory book for the bereaved. Ask each member to write a personal note about their experience working with the deceased and their thoughts and feelings about them on a more personal level. Include them in a photo album or scrapbook, and present to the bereaved.

■ Make a donation to a charitable organization in the deceased's memory.

■ Offer to help plant a shrub or garden in memory of the deceased.

■ Provide information on local support groups for suicide grievers.

■ If the bereaved is uncomfortable going to a support group meeting alone, arrange for a family member to accompany them or offer to accompany them yourself.

■ Locate online support groups for suicide grievers. Go to any search engine (www.google.com or www.alltheweb.com) and enter "suicide grief" for the search. You will find a great deal of information that should provide comfort along with interactive list serves where the bereaved can vent their feelings to individuals with common experiences.

Special Situations

A friend's mother was terminally ill with cancer, and she just died. But I don't think her death was from the illness; I think she took an overdose of pain medication.

The end stages of cancer can be brutally painful, and your friend's family has just gone through a terrible ordeal. It would be inappropriate to question your friend on the circumstances of his mom's death; if he chooses to share that with you, it would be a blessing if you could listen and offer compassion. If he does not choose to share this information with you, accept his silence. It is difficult to cope with a parent's illness and subsequent death, and your friend needs understanding. Extend him the same caring support you would provide for any death. Chapter Five will provide you with details on how to help the bereaved deal with the death of an adult. If you have personal or religious reasons that make you uncomfortable or prevent you from lending support, send a sympathy note that expresses your sadness for your friend's loss.

I bumped into an old friend I haven't seen in years, and she shared that her husband died. Surprised, I inquired, "What from?" She told me he committed suicide. I was so shocked, I mumbled something quickly and left. How do I handle the unexpected news of a suicide?
It is shocking to learn that someone you know has taken their life. The survivor is shocked, too, as well as traumatized by the experience. If you leave suddenly, you are expressing your discomfort, which compounds their sorrow. It's okay to be shocked; you could touch your friend lightly on the arm and tell them how sorry you are to learn about their spouse's death. Ask "How are you doing today?" If you have time and are willing, ask them to join you for a cup of coffee. Let them know you have fond memories of them or the spouse. Mention that you will keep them in your prayers.

SAMPLE LETTERS/E-MAILS

To a former co-worker whose husband has taken his life.

> January X, 2XXX
> Dear Mollie:
>
> My deepest sympathy to you and your children on Anthony's sudden death. What a terrible loss to you and everyone who knew Anthony. I have the most wonderful memories of our annual office picnics at Craggy Lake. Anthony was a charismatic storyteller, and I always looked forward to hearing his tales. Anthony will be greatly missed. I will keep you in my prayers.
>
> With fondness,
> Elizabeth Green

To neighbors whose son took his life.

> May X, 2XXX
> Dear Bob and Sheila:
>
> Thinking of you both at this sad time. Robert was a lovely young man with a generous nature and a quick smile. He will be missed by everyone who had the good fortune to cross his path.
>
> We hope that knowing that our love and thoughts are with you will help you through this difficult time.
>
> Love,
> Beth and Michael

To a friend whose wife took her life.

> June X, 2XXX
> Dear Bill:
>
> I am terribly saddened at Susie's death. Susie had many wonderful qualities, and she will be missed. I just don't know what else to say or do because I have never experienced what you are going through. You and the children are in my thoughts and prayers.
>
> Fondly,
> Philip

To an old friend whose teenage son has taken his life.

> February X, 2XXX
> Dearest Sandy:
>
> Words cannot express the deep sorrow I have felt since learning of Alex's death. Memories of our friendship and all the joy we have shared with the children have filled my heart over the last few days.
>
> I remember Alex as a sensitive and loving child. I regret that distance has kept us from spending more time together in the last few years. He will forever be frozen in my memories as the child I dearly loved.

I am so sorry that you are faced with such sadness. I pray that you and your family find the strength to deal with what has to be one of the most difficult losses to bear.

May love and the beautiful memories sustain you. You are in my thoughts and prayers.

Love,
Stacey

For further information:

Doka, Kenneth J., Ph.D., ed. *Living with Grief After Sudden Loss: Suicide, Homicide, Accident, Heart Attack, Stroke.* Bristol, PA: Taylor and Francis, 1996.

Levy, Naomi. *To Begin Again—The Journey Toward Comfort, Strength, and Faith in Difficult Times.* New York, NY: Ballantine Books, 1998.

Robinson, Rita. *Survivors of Suicide.* Franklin Lakes, NJ: Career Press, 2001.

Ross, E. Betsy. *Life After Suicide: A Ray of Hope for Those Left Behind.* New York, NY: Perseus Publishing, 1997.

Viscott, David. *Finding Your Strength in Difficult Times—A Book of Meditations.* Chicago, IL: Contemporary Books, 1993.

American Foundation for Suicide Prevention
120 Wall Street, 22nd Floor
New York, NY 10005
(212) 363-3500 or (888) 333-AFSP
www.afsp.org/

Survivors of Suicide

An independently owned and operated website, in no way associated with any specific group, organization, or religious affiliation, to help those who have lost a loved one to suicide resolve their grief and pain in their own personal way.
www.survivorsofsuicide.com

Beyond Indigo

A privately held company called Kelasan, Inc., based out of Minnesota, Minnesota. The company provides grief support, products, and services to individuals and companies that assist people who are grieving.

www.death-dying.com

See also: WHAT IS GRIEF? UNDERSTANDING THE PROCESS OF MOURNING AND HOW YOU CAN HELP, WHAT CAN I SAY? COMMUNICATIONS THAT COMFORT, WHAT CAN I DO? HOW TO LISTEN, DEATH OF AN ADULT, and DEATH OF A CHILD.

NINE

Miscarriage

∞

"Friendship improves happiness, and abates misery,
by doubling our joy, and dividing our grief."

—Joseph Addison

MEDICAL professionals define a miscarriage as any pregnancy loss that occurs before twenty weeks gestational age, approximately up to the fifth month, with most miscarriages occurring during the first twelve weeks.

Clinically, miscarriage is defined as the premature expulsion of a nonviable fetus from the uterus. Medical professionals might view the miscarriage experience in clinical terms and suggest it really isn't a baby but a "product of conception." But to the parents who hoped and dreamed for this pregnancy, the miscarriage is a death in the family and should be treated as such.

There is often no explanation for a miscarriage; almost 50 percent of miscarriages happen because the fetus has failed to develop normally, and the remaining 50 percent occur for no known reason. And sometimes the baby begins life not inside the womb but forms outside the fallopian tube; this is called an ectopic pregnancy. Ectopic pregnancy must be terminated, as the mother's life is at risk if the fallopian tube ruptures; a surgical procedure takes place in which the embryo and part of the fallopian tube is removed. The mother can get pregnant again if the other fallopian tube is healthy.

Couples can feel very vulnerable—they have experienced a loss that was beyond their control. Because many miscarriages happen so early in the pregnancy, sometimes before anyone is told, family, friends, co-workers, and neighbors might not know the couple is grieving until long after the miscarriage.

Mothers and fathers grieve for the child they never knew and will never know. They might have already selected a name, decorated a room, and filled their hearts with love. They grieve for the loss of their baby and yet, in many religions, there is no custom for burying the fetus and no mourning rituals to bring spiritual comfort.

Women might feel extreme guilt after a miscarriage, thinking they are to blame; they might wonder if they should have done something different or contacted their physician earlier. They might exert great effort searching for clues—if only they can figure out what it was they did or experienced during their pregnancy that caused them to miscarry.

Some women feel as if their own body has betrayed them. It is not uncommon for the mom to feel like a failure because it was her body that was to have nurtured and carried the baby to term. Some grieving moms might think irrational thoughts in their grief; they might see babies everywhere they look and wonder why everyone else was able to complete their pregnancy and she couldn't seem to do it.

Miscarriage is not just an emotional loss; it has physical implications as well. The woman's body has undergone hormonal and physical adjustments; she might experience bleeding, cramping, sleeplessness, fatigue, and lack of appetite. She'll need rest and time to regain her strength and emotional well-being. You can play a pivotal role in restoring her emotional well-being through thoughtful and caring verbal, written, and nonverbal communications.

THINGS TO CONSIDER

- No one is at fault. Many miscarriages happen not because of something the mother did or didn't do.

- The family has experienced a death, and they need time to grieve for their loss.

- The mom and dad might grieve differently, but both will need support to talk through their feelings.

- There might be no mourning or burial rites for fetuses.

EMOTIONS AND FEELINGS TO ANTICIPATE

- Anger
- Emptiness
- Failure
- Fear
- Guilt

- Helplessness
- Hopelessness
- Jealousy
- Sadness
- Self-blame

WHAT TO SAY AND DO

- Acknowledge the loss.

- Do show that you genuinely care.

- Do make yourself available to listen.

- It's appropriate to send a card or note.

- Send a bouquet of flowers with a simple note that says "Thinking of you" or "Sending love your way."

> ᨞ The mom has experienced physical and hormonal changes and would appreciate some pampering. Offer to help with meals or child care if there is a child at home, or just request that she tell you what would make her feel better.

- Offer a truly funny movie or a comedy tape to provide them with a distraction and release.

- Make yourself available to drive them or accompany them to a medical procedure or doctor appointment.

- Reassure the parents that the miscarriage was not their fault and they should not blame themselves.

- Encourage them to be patient with themselves and the world around them as they adjust to the loss.

- If the couple has other children, offer to babysit so the couple can have some time to themselves.

- Ask the mom and dad if there is something you can do to help them memorialize the baby.

- If they would like to do something in the baby's memory, suggest you plant a tree together.

- If the mom and dad are having difficulty expressing their grief, you can research and provide them with information on local support groups where they can share their experience with others who know what they are feeling.

HOW TO SAY IT

How is your husband/wife?

I am here for you no matter how you need me.

I am not going to pretend to know how you feel.

I am so sorry you lost your baby.

I am thinking of you during this sad time.

I can't imagine how you must be feeling.

I love you, and I am here for you.

I've had a miscarriage, too; if you ever want to talk, let me know.

This must be so hard for you.

This wasn't your fault.

Why don't we sit down and talk about how you are feeling.

WHAT NOT TO SAY AND DO

- Don't ignore the mom or dad and say nothing at all because you don't know what to say.

- Don't ask questions about the experience; if they choose, they will tell you about it in their own time.

- Don't tell them you know someone who had multiple miscarriages. They might think you are minimizing their loss or they should get used to the experience and pain because there might be more.

- Don't tell them they can try again. Another child will not take away the grief of losing this baby who was already loved and cherished.

- Don't allow your discomfort to keep you away. The absence of friends and loved ones could compound an already painful experience.

- Don't change the subject when they try to talk about their loss or their feelings.

- Don't avoid sharing your good news of a pregnancy or birth.

- Don't visit without an invitation.

- Don't ask anything of them. They need time to heal physically and emotionally.

HOW NOT TO SAY IT

At least you can get pregnant.

At least you have another child.

Don't worry; you'll get pregnant again.

It wasn't meant to be.

It wasn't really a person yet.

It's for the best.

It's nature's way of dealing with a problem.

Nature takes care of its mistakes.

So what does this mean for you?

There was probably something wrong with the baby.

You should be feeling better by now.

You're young; you'll have other children.

Special Situations

My friend has had multiple miscarriages.
Your friend must be feeling terribly sad and frustrated. She probably feels that her body has betrayed her, and she will need your support and willingness to hear her out. Women with multiple miscarriages can still successfully carry a baby through term. Be aware that if she becomes pregnant again and is frightened and panicked, these emotions are normal. She'll need love and understanding, and that's what you, as her friend, can give her.

My friend just miscarried, and I am expecting a baby in a few weeks.
Don't assume your friend who has lost a baby will resent you for having a baby. Take your cues from the person who has had the loss. If you exclude her from baby showers and baby announcements, she might feel even more isolated. You could ask her how involved she would like to be. She might indicate it would be too painful to be close to you right now, but it might give her a lift to be involved and share your happiness.

My friend had a second ectopic pregnancy.
Because ectopics often are removed surgically to preserve the mother's life, there is a risk of infertility on the affected side. Your friend is dealing with issues of loss while going through the process of recovering her health. She is probably frightened that she might never get pregnant again and that if she does, she will not carry a healthy baby through delivery. It will be harder for your friend to have a successful pregnancy but not impossible. Be supportive and let her know you are sad for her. Offer support in helping her through her convalescence. Let her know that you intend to support whatever decision she makes in pursuing her desire to be a mom. She needs a willing listener to vent her frustrations and injustice at the difficulty in carrying a baby to term.

SAMPLE LETTERS/E-MAILS

To a friend who has just miscarried early in her first pregnancy.

March X, 2XXX
Dear Jane:

I am so sorry to hear about your loss. This must be such a difficult time for you and John. I will call you in the next week to see what I can do to help. In the meantime, know that you are often in my thoughts.

Love,
Sandy

To a co-worker who has miscarried.

June X, 2XXX
Dear Teresa:

I just learned about your miscarriage, and I wanted to tell you how sorry I am. I can't possibly know how you are feeling, but I know how thrilled you were with your pregnancy and this must be a terrible disappointment. I am looking forward to your return to work. We'll have lunch as soon as you feel like it. Until then, I will keep you in my thoughts and prayers.

Fondly,
Marie

To a sister-in-law who has a child and has miscarried a second time.

April X, 2XXX
Dear Madeline:

Will called last night to tell us you miscarried. I am so sorry this has happened. I know how much the three of you have been looking forward to this baby, and it's a terrible loss. I wish there was something I could do or say to make this easier. John and I love you all and are thinking of you constantly. If you'd like some help and company, we are available this weekend and could drive down on Saturday. I will call you in a day or so to see what you need. I'm sending hugs to all of you.

Much love,
Lilly

To a colleague who has had an ectopic pregnancy and lost a fallopian tube, which will make it harder for her to get pregnant again.

June X, 2XXX
Dear Liz:

I know how excited you were about your pregnancy, and I am so sorry this has happened. It's a terrible blow and so unexpected. You and Steve are such special people, and I know you will make wonderful parents. Don't lose faith. I will call you soon to see what I can do for you. I am more than willing to help in any way.

I am thinking of you both with love and a hopeful heart.
Marianne

For further information:

Allen, Marie, Ph.D., and Shelly Marks, M.S. *Miscarriage—Women Sharing from the Heart.* New York, NY: John Wiley & Sons, 1993.

Douglas, Ann, and John R. Sussman, M.D. *Trying Again: A Guide to Pregnancy After Miscarriage, Stillbirth, and Infant Loss.* Dallas, TX: Taylor Publishing Company, 2000.

Kohn, Ingrid, M.S.W., and Perry-Lynn Moffitt, with Isabelle A. Wilkins, M.D. *A Silent Sorrow—Pregnancy Loss: Guidance and Support for You and Your Family.* New York, NY: Routledge, 2000.

Lothrop, Hannah. *Help, Comfort and Hope after Losing Your Baby in Pregnancy or the First Year.* Boulder, CO: Perseus Publishing, 1997.

Luebbermann, Mimi. *Coping with Miscarriage: A Simple, Reassuring Guide to Emotional and Physical Healing.* Rocklin, CA: Prima Publishing, 1996.

SHARE is a not-for-profit nondenominational organization providing support to those whose lives are touched by the tragic death of a baby through early pregnancy loss, stillbirth, or newborn death.

National SHARE Office
St. Joseph Health Center
300 First Capitol Drive
St. Charles, MS 63301-2893
(636) 947-6164 or (800) 821-6819
Fax: (636) 947-7486
share@nationalshareoffice.com
www.nationalshareoffice.com

See also: WHAT IS GRIEF? UNDERSTANDING THE PROCESS OF MOURNING AND HOW YOU CAN HELP, WHAT CAN I SAY? COMMUNICATIONS THAT COMFORT, WHAT CAN I DO? HOW TO LISTEN, and DEATH OF A STILLBORN OR NEWBORN BABY.

TEN

Pet Loss

∞

"Animals are such agreeable friends—they ask no questions,
they pass no criticisms."

—George Eliot

Pets fulfill a wide range of physical and emotional needs, and they share a place in our lives as companions, substitute relatives, protectors, and a means to express our affection. Pets are good for us; they are a source of pleasure, unconditional love, acceptance, and comfort. It's been proven that pets play a positive role in wellness and recovery.

So it should be no surprise that the loss of a pet is a painful experience. And although pet loss is not the same as human loss, the grieving and mourning processes are very similar.

Friends, family members, co-workers, neighbors, and acquaintances who have lost their pet will most likely experience a period of mourning. They might feel guilty for feeling so terribly sad, but if they are to heal they must express their grief and mourn for their pet.

A lack of support compounds the grief of someone who is mourning a loss. Traditionally, society has generated little sympathy when a pet dies. There have been no religious or social rituals to comfort the bereaved. Some view pet cemeteries and pet funerals as bizarre. Comments such as "She was a sweet dog; will you get the same kind next time?" would be considered heartless if you were commenting on human loss.

It's important to understand that the bereaved will grieve, and you can significantly help them by acknowledging their loss rather than minimizing it. Grief must be expressed if one is to heal; grief that is suppressed hampers physical and emotional well-being and extends the grieving period.

The actual experience of pet loss can trigger an individual's feelings of grief over previous losses—animal *and* human. Even if you do not have a pet or don't feel the depth of attachment to your pet as the bereaved feels to theirs, it is important to acknowledge the loss and support the mourner during this difficult period. Your support in encouraging the bereaved to express their grief will positively impact their healing.

THINGS TO CONSIDER

- Not all pet owners view their pets in the same light; many owners consider their pets as companions and members of their family. They cultivate a special bond with their beloved pet, and there is a depth of emotion and attachment. Others might view their pet as a special part of their life without the deep, emotional attachment. Gauge your response by what you know of the personal involvement, and take your cues from the pet owners when responding to their loss.

- Is the loss a result of a prolonged illness or natural death?

- Is the death sudden?

- Was the pet euthanized?

- Did the loss occur through someone's negligence or by an accident?

- Was the pet placed in a new home?

EMOTIONS AND FEELINGS TO ANTICIPATE

- Anger
- Depression
- Emptiness
- Guilt

- Helplessness
- Loneliness
- Regret
- Sadness

WHAT TO SAY AND DO

- Allow the pet owner to talk openly about their pet and their feelings of loss.

- Demonstrate interest by asking the owner the circumstances surrounding the pet's death or loss.

- If the pet is lost, offer to help circulate flyers in the area or recommend placement of a notice in the local newspaper.

> ༄ If the pet is to be taken to the veterinarian for euthanasia, offer to accompany the owner to the veterinarian.

- Encourage the mourner to share stories and memories about their pet.

- Share your own memories of the pet or your recollections of what the person has told you about their pet.

- Send a condolence card. There are cards specifically created for pet loss, and if you can't locate one, convey your own message in a note.

- Plan on following up in a few weeks or months with a note, e-mail message, or phone call to let them know you are thinking of them.

- Send a donation in memory of their deceased or lost pet to any animal-related organization.

- If you have a photograph of the pet, have a copy made for the bereaved or have it framed.

- Offer to help the bereaved create a photo album or scrapbook in memory of the pet.

HOW TO SAY IT

I am so sorry.

I'll always remember your stories about Buddy.

Lucy was a special dog.

Please accept my deepest sympathies.

What a comfort Sally was to you; she will truly be missed.

What sad news; I am so sorry for your loss.

WHAT NOT TO SAY AND DO

- Don't make fun of the pet owner for feeling so sad.

- Don't minimize the loss.

- Don't change the subject when the bereaved begins to share their feelings of loss.

- Don't tell the bereaved to stop dwelling on their pain and remember their happy memories of their pet. Grief must be expressed if the bereaved is to heal.

- Don't minimize the depth of their loss and pain by telling them it was only a pet.

- Don't tell the owner to get on with their life.

- Don't suggest they replace the pet. They need time to grieve before making a decision to get another pet.

HOW NOT TO SAY IT

Be grateful it wasn't a family member.

Don't be so upset; it was only a pet.

It was only a dog (cat, bird, horse, etc.).

Now, now . . . don't cry.

Time heals all wounds.

You can always get another dog (cat).

Special Situations

My seventeen-year-old friend had to sell her horse to pay for college expenses.
You can tell your friend how sorry you are and give her a hug. Or you could

send her a note and acknowledge what a difficult choice she had to make. Let her know that her horse was so lucky to have a caring human companion. Remind her that the memories she has will bring her comfort and will stay with her always. If you have memories of her horse, she would appreciate having you share them with her. Close your note by letting her know that you are thinking of her.

My neighbor's dog was aggressively difficult. She tried several dog obedience programs, but they just didn't work. She finally had to have him put to sleep.
It is always difficult to make the decision to put an animal to sleep. Let your neighbor know that she did everything she could to help her dog. Make sure she understands that her dog was lucky that his life ended in such caring hands.

My niece's cat was lost. She posted notices but got no response, and she doesn't know what happened to her cat.
Let your niece know how sorry you are that she has lost her cat. Acknowledge that it must be so difficult not knowing what has happened. Remind her that she has done everything she could possibly do, and if you volunteer to help, she won't feel so alone. Let her know that you hope the cat comes back to her.

Someone left my neighbor's gate open; his dog ran out of his yard and was killed by a passing car.
Make sure your neighbor knows that this could have happened to anyone. Let him know that he was a caring owner and did his best to keep his dog safe. He might appreciate it if you share any stories you have of his dog.

My cousin's dog became sick quite suddenly and died.
Express your shock at the sudden and untimely death of your cousin's dog. Be honest and say that you can only imagine how difficult this is for her to deal with. Share with her any special memories you have of her dog, and let her know that her dog was lucky to have her in his life.

SAMPLE LETTERS/E-MAILS

To a colleague who is a freelance writer specializing in dogs, on the death of her Collie.

> March X, 2XXX
> Dear Megan:
>
> I'm so very sorry to hear that you lost Maggie. What a blow. You've been very much in my thoughts this afternoon, and you have my warmest wishes for strength in your grieving and eventual acceptance and peace.
>
> I think of Maggie quite often—the scene you painted in your June article about her rounding up everyone for dinner always comes back to me when I see a certain Collie every morning on my commute in to work—it trots along so beautifully with its owner and always lifts my spirits.
>
> Take good care of yourself and your family, and again, my wishes for strength and peace.
>
> Sincerely,
> Stephanie

To a young niece on the death of her cat.

> June X, 2XXX
> Dearest Lynne:
>
> Your mom called me last night to tell me the sad news about Patches. I am so sorry, Lynne. Patches was a real sweetie and leaves behind wonderful memories. When I think of Patches, I'll always remember her curled at your feet no matter where you sat. Patches was special, and I know you will miss her.
>
> I'm sending love to you, Lynne. Know that you and Patches are in my thoughts. Please extend my sympathies to your mom and dad, too.
>
> Love,
> Aunt Mollie

To a sister whose dog had a terminal illness and had to be put to sleep.

> October X, 2XXX
> Dear Beth:
>
> I'm so sorry—I had no idea. I can only imagine how difficult this is for you and how much courage it took to do the right thing in not prolonging Bailey's suffering.
>
> I really don't know what I can do to help, but if there is something I can do, I hope you will let me know. You're in my thoughts.
>
> With love,
> Kathy

For further information:

Anderson, Moira K. *Coping with Sorrow on the Loss of Your Pet.* Loveland, CO: Alpine Publications, 1996.

Lee, Laura, and Martyn Lee. *Absent Friend, Coping with the Loss of a Treasured Pet.* Bucks, England: Henston Ltd., 1992.

Montgomery, Herb, and Mary Montgomery. *Goodbye My Friend.* Minneapolis, MN: Montgomery Press, 1991.

Sife, Wallace. *The Loss of a Pet.* New York, NY: Howell Book House, John Wiley & Sons, 1998.

The American Veterinary Medical Association
Pet Loss Support Hotlines
www.avma.org/careforanimals/animatedjourneys/goodbyefriend

The Association for Pet Loss and Bereavement (APLB)
P.O. Box 106
Brooklyn, NY 11230
(718) 382-0690
aplb@aplb.org
www.aplb.org

Especially for children:

Rogers, Fred. *When a Pet Dies.* New York, NY: Penguin Putnam, 1998.

White, E. B. *Charlotte's Web.* New York, NY: HarperCollins Juvenile Books, 1999.

Viorst, Judith. *The Tenth Good Thing About Barney.* New York, NY: Aladdin Library, Simon & Shuster, 1976.

See also: WHAT IS GRIEF? UNDERSTANDING THE PROCESS OF MOURNING AND HOW YOU CAN HELP, WHAT CAN I SAY? COMMUNICATIONS THAT COMFORT, and WHAT CAN I DO? HOW TO LISTEN.

ELEVEN

Mental Illness

∞

"He gives little who gives with a frown; he gives much
who gives little with a smile."

—Talmud

MENTAL illness shows no partiality to age, ethnicity, race, or financial standing. Mental illness, according to the National Mental Health Association, causes mild to severe disturbances in thought and/or behavior, resulting in an inability to cope with life's ordinary demands and routines. An estimated 54 million Americans suffer from some form of mental disorder in a given year.

Major depression, bipolar disorder, schizophrenia, and obsessive-compulsive disorder account for four of the ten leading causes of disability in the United States. Depression is the leading cause of disability; the National Institute of Mental Health reports that approximately 18.8 million American adults or about 9.5 percent of the population age eighteen and older have a depressive disorder in a given year. Nearly twice as many women (12.0 percent) as men (6.6 percent) in the United States are affected; these figures translate to 12.4 million women and 6.4 million men.

Mental illness is a contributing factor in suicide, a leading cause of death in the United States.

Individuals experiencing mental illness and their loved ones need your caring support. You can help them best by demonstrating your love and acceptance through verbal and nonverbal communications.

THINGS TO CONSIDER

- Mental illness can be difficult to diagnose and treat. It is essential to find a psychiatrist who will work well with both the individual and family members.

- Mental illness carries a stigma, but with proper care and treatment, many individuals can cope and recover.

- Medication, support systems, mental health programs, and vocational rehabilitation help many people lead productive lives.

- It is important to support parents, spouses, children, caregivers, and other family members of people with a mental disorder. These folks are often forgotten but bear burdens as well.

EMOTIONS AND FEELINGS TO ANTICIPATE

- Anger
- Denial
- Despair
- Exhaustion
- Fear
- Guilt
- Helplessness

- Inferiority
- Loneliness
- Misery
- Pain
- Panic
- Sadness
- Shame

WHAT TO SAY AND DO

- If a loved one is diagnosed with a mental illness, learn all you can about the particular mental illness, forms of treatment, and side effects.

- Access information and resources through your local mental health association. You can find these listed in the Yellow Pages of your local phone directory. Additional resources are also listed at the end of this chapter.

- Conduct research using the Internet. Access the websites listed at the end of this chapter.

- Speak with mental health professionals about the illness prognosis, coping techniques, and how you can help your loved one.

- Encourage your loved one to see a therapist or counselor.

- If they don't like the therapist or counselor, help them find one who is more compatible.

- Find support through your clergy, family physician, or family service agencies. Your clergy can help you identify resources in your area.

- Find supportive family members and friends to vent and share your feelings and frustrations.

- Research and locate support groups to find others who have coped with the same experiences and problems.

- Listen to your loved one.

- Set limits on how much time you will listen and what you can do to help them.

> ✎ If they accept an invitation and call at the last moment to cancel, communicate your disappointment. Let them know that if they need to cancel an invitation in the future, you would like more notice.

- Recognize your own limitations in what you can do.

- Hold them accountable for basic human courtesies.

- Retain your own interests, hobbies, relationships, and work experiences to keep your balance and perspective.

- Seek ways to minimize your stress through exercise, creative outlets, and supportive relationships.

- Know when and how to get help for yourself when you are overwhelmed with what your loved one is experiencing.

HOW TO SAY IT

I care about you.

I know I can never completely understand what you are going through, but I would like to try.

I love you.

I will be available Sunday afternoon.

I will be here for you.

It's never too late.

This must be painful for you.

You can count on me.

WHAT NOT TO SAY AND DO

- Do not offer to solve their problems.
- Do not tell them what to do.
- Don't criticize.
- Don't shut them out.
- Don't deprive them of your love and support.
- Don't ignore them.
- Don't take on more than you can handle.

HOW NOT TO SAY IT

Count your blessings.

If you think you have problems . . .

Don't worry.

What will we tell people?

Just forget about it.

You're being silly.

For further information:
Adamec, Christine. *How to Live with a Mentally Ill Person.* New York, NY: John Wiley & Sons, 1996.

Bockian, Neil R., Nora Elizabeth Villagran, and Valerie Porr. *New Hope for People with Borderline Personality Disorder: Your Friendly, Authoritative Guide to the Latest in Traditional and Complementary Solutions*. Roseville, CA: Prima Publishing, 2002.

Carter, Rosalynn, with Susan K. Golant. *Helping Someone with Mental Illness*. New York, NY: Times Books, 1999.

Golant, Mitch, and Susan K. Golant. *What to Do When Someone You Love Is Depressed*. New York, NY: Henry Holt & Company, Inc., 1998.

Karp, David Allen. *The Burden of Sympathy: How Families Cope with Mental Illness*. Oxford, England: Oxford University Press, 2001.

Mason, Paul T., M.S., and Randi Kreger. *Stop Walking on Eggshells—Taking Your Life Back When Someone You Care About Has Borderline Personality Disorder*. Oakland, CA: New Harbinger Publications, 1998.

Miklowitz, David J. *The Bipolar Disorder Survival Guide: What You and Your Family Need to Know*. New York, NY: Guildford Press, 2002.

Nasar, Sylvia. *A Beautiful Mind: The Life of Mathematical Genius and Nobel Laureate John Nash*. New York, NY: Simon & Schuster, 2001.

O'Connor, Richard. *Undoing Depression: What Therapy Doesn't Teach You and Medication Can't Give You*. New York, NY: Berkley Publishing Group, 1999.

Olen, Dale R., Ph.D. *Defeating Depression—Lifting Yourself from Sadness to Joy*. Holmes Beach, FL: Learning Publications, 2003.

National Alliance for the Mentally Ill (NAMI)
Colonial Place Three
2107 Wilson Boulevard, Suite 300
Arlington, VA 22201
(703) 524-7600
NAMI HelpLine: 1 (800) 950-NAMI
www.nami.org

National Institute of Mental Health (NIMH)
6001 Executive Boulevard, Room 8184, MSC 9663
Bethesda, MD 20892-9663

(301) 443-4513 or toll-free (866) 615-NIMH
www.nimh.nih.gov

National Mental Health Association
2001 N. Beauregard Street, 12th Floor
Alexandria, VA 22311
(703) 684-7722
www.nmha.org

See also: WHAT CAN I SAY? COMMUNICATIONS THAT COMFORT and WHAT CAN I DO? HOW TO LISTEN.

COMMUNICATING IN THE FACE OF CRIME AND VIOLENCE

Nothing in life prepares us for the shocking experience of crime and violence—the feelings of sorrow, helplessness, and loss are devastating, and the aftermath of crime and violence may last for years. Support is crucial to the healing process, but grief can be intense and prolonged, taxing even the most loyal supporters.

You can help your loved one, friend, co-worker, or community member cope with crime and violence by remaining patient and understanding. Your consistent presence, for however long it takes, can help them through this traumatic experience.

Part Four provides specific insight into nonviolent crime, violent crime, sexual assault or rape, domestic violence, natural disasters, terrorism, and legal or criminal problems, with guidelines on verbal, written, and nonverbal communications that are sure to comfort.

TWELVE

Nonviolent Crime

∞

"It is one of the most beautiful compensations
of life, that no man can sincerely try to help another
without helping himself."

—Ralph Waldo Emerson

A CROSS the United States, nonviolent crimes have declined since 1973. Although these statistics are heartening, if you happen to be a victim of property or nonviolent crime, the experience can be devastating. Other property and nonviolent crime statistics by the Bureau of Justice Statistics indicate:

- Property crime, consisting of burglary, theft, and motor vehicle theft, makes up about three-quarters of all crime in the United States.

- In 2001, 78 percent of males and 51 percent of females reported the individual who robbed them was a stranger.

- About 85 percent of burglaries were successful.

- About 72 percent of all motor vehicle thefts were successful.

- Of the 13.7 million completed thefts of property in 2001, there were 4.7 million property thefts of less than $50, 4.8 million thefts between $50 and $249, and 3.2 million thefts of $250 or more.

Victims of nonviolent crime are fortunate they were not physically hurt, but their psyche is badly shaken. They will need your help and support to regain a sense of control and security.

VICTIM OR SURVIVOR?

You will find differing opinions on the appropriate way to identify the person upon whom a crime was perpetrated. Some people feel they should be called a "survivor," which is more empowering. Others prefer to be identified as "victims of crime." For the purpose of unity, this chapter and Chapter Thirteen (Violent Crime) will refer to crime victims as "victims of crime."

THINGS TO CONSIDER

- The type of crime.

- The victim's personal and financial needs as a result of the crime.

- Victims of any type of crime feel personally violated.

- The damage to the victim's psyche even though no one was physically injured.

- Reactions to traumatic events can last a long time.

- There is no single standard of coping; each person is unique and copes in their own way and in their own time.

EMOTIONS AND FEELINGS TO ANTICIPATE

- Anxiety
- Deep anger
- Disorientation
- Fear
- Guilt
- Insecurity
- Pain
- Powerlessness
- Shock
- Terror
- Violation
- Vulnerability

WHAT TO SAY AND DO

- Communicate that you really do want to listen, and try to really hear what the victim of crime is saying.

- Do try and get a sense from the conversation as to what the victim of crime needs from you; it might just be someone to listen.

- Ask if they would like to stay with you or have you stay with them until they are feeling safer.

- Do let them know that whatever they are feeling is a normal response to their experience.

- Do understand their fear and how shaken they are.

- Validate that it is okay to get help if they are unable to cope with their feelings and fears.

> ⏳ Offer to research resources for victims of crime or, if you have knowledge of resources for victims of crime, provide them to the victim.

HOW TO SAY IT

How are you feeling?

How can I help you?

I am really sorry this has happened.

I am sorry you have been through something so frightening.

I'd like to help in any way I can.

This must be very hard for you.

Whatever you did was the right thing.

You are not at fault.

You couldn't have known.

WHAT NOT TO SAY AND DO

- Don't assume that there was something they could have done differently to prevent the crime.

- Don't ask questions that cause the victim to blame themselves for what happened.

- Don't second-guess the decision the victim made that might have made them or their property vulnerable.

- Don't try to find something good in the crime experience, such as "You are lucky you weren't in the car when it happened."

- Don't try to minimize the crime experience, such as "It could have been so much worse."

- Don't make them feel that they were at fault for the crime by telling them what they could have done differently and what they should do in the future to avoid this type of situation.

HOW NOT TO SAY IT

At least you weren't hurt.

Didn't you bolt the door?

How could it have happened?

I told you that wasn't a good neighborhood.

I've told you before not to talk to strangers.

Look on the bright side . . .

Why didn't you lock your car?

You could have been really hurt.

SAMPLE LETTERS/E-MAILS

To a friend whose home was burglarized.

> January X, 2XXX
> Dear Toni:
>
> I was saddened to hear your home was burglarized. What a frightening experience to go through. I am thankful that you were all out of the house at the time and none of you were harmed.
>
> It is awful to go through this type of experience and have your safety and personal space violated. Allow yourself to experience and work through your feelings and emotions. Give yourself time to heal, and do whatever you need to do to feel safe again.

I will be in your area during spring break. I would love to see you then, but in the meantime, know that you are in my thoughts. Take good care of yourself.

Love,
Sheila

To a daughter whose car was stolen.

October X, 2XXX
Dear Stella:

I hope things have settled down since we last spoke. Dad told me you rented a car and took care of all the required notifications.

This was an awful experience for you, Stella, and I am so sorry you had to go through it. Losing your beloved Volvo along with your personal papers is a terrible loss. As sad as it is, I am so very grateful that you were not injured. You can replace the material things, Stella, but you yourself are irreplaceable.

Know that Dad and I are thinking of you. Please plan on having dinner with us on Thursday. I will fix the spaghetti dinner you love so much. Until then I send my love.

Mom

For further information:

Levy, Naomi. *To Begin Again—The Journey Toward Comfort, Strength, and Faith in Difficult Times.* New York, NY: Ballantine Books, 1998.

Matsakis, Aphrodite, Ph.D. *I Can't Get Over It: A Handbook for Trauma Survivors, Second Edition.* Oakland, CA: New Harbinger Publications Inc., 1996.

National Center for Victims of Crime
2000 M Street, NW, Suite 480
Washington, DC 20036
(202) 467-8700
www.ncvc.org

National Organization for Victim Assistance (NOVA)
1730 Park Road NW
Washington, DC 20010

(202) 232-6682

Information and referrals for victims of crime and disaster (800) TRY-NOVA

www.try-nova.org

Victim Services Helpline

(800) FYI-CALL

gethelp@ncvc.org

See also: WHAT IS GRIEF? UNDERSTANDING THE PROCESS OF MOURNING AND HOW YOU CAN HELP, WHAT CAN I SAY? COMMUNICATIONS THAT COMFORT, and WHAT CAN I DO? HOW TO LISTEN.

THIRTEEN

Violent Crime

∞

"A real friend is one who walks in when the
rest of the world walks out."

—Walter Winchell

N OTHING in life prepares us for the traumatic experience of violent crime such as homicide, rape, sexual assault, or domestic violence. Although violent crime rates have declined in recent years, the Federal Bureau of Investigation reports that in the United States in 2000, one violent crime occurred every 22.1 seconds, one aggravated assault occurred every 34.6 seconds, and someone was murdered every 33.9 minutes.

Victims of violence and their families and friends experience crisis reactions; the levels of extremes will differ from person to person based on their personal situation at the time of the crime, the impact of the crime, and resulting injuries. As each person is unique, so are victim reactions, responses, and recovery. It is impossible to compare one experience, response, or recovery to another.

How the victim of crime and their loved ones are treated immediately following the crime impacts their ability to cope and recover. They will need to know what comes next by way of the crime investigation and the resulting criminal justice process.

In times of crisis, friends, acquaintances, and loved ones willingly provide support. But support wanes along with the months, and it is easy to lose patience as time passes. You can play a pivotal role in the recovery process by remaining a presence in their life—no matter how long it takes.

The topics of sexual assault and rape are covered in Chapter Fourteen.

The topic of domestic violence is covered in Chapter Fifteen.

VICTIM OR SURVIVOR?

You will find differing opinions on the appropriate way to identify the person upon whom a crime was perpetrated. Some people feel they should be called a "survivor," which is more empowering. Others prefer to be identified as "victims of crime." For the purpose of unity, this chapter and Chapter Twelve (Nonviolent Crime) will refer to crime victims as "victims of crime."

THINGS TO CONSIDER

- Victims of crime will experience both physical and psychological trauma.

- It is imperative that victims of crime regain a sense of safety and develop outlets to express their emotions.

- Victims of crime might have financial difficulties resulting from the crime—there might be uncovered medical expenses, counseling services, property loss, funeral expenses, transportation costs, and unpaid employment leave to participate in the criminal justice system and attend court. There might also be a significant income loss.

- Victims of crime must be treated with dignity, compassion, and respect to facilitate recovery.

- There is no single standard of coping; each person is unique and copes in their own way and in their own time.

EMOTIONS AND FEELINGS TO ANTICIPATE

- Anger
- Anxiety
- Denial
- Devastation
- Distrust
- Fear
- Guilt
- Helplessness
- Hopelessness
- Humiliation
- Hurt
- Injustice
- Insecurity
- Irritability
- Isolation
- Loss
- Numbness
- Rage

- Sadness
- Self-blame
- Shame

- Shock
- Terror
- Vulnerability

WHAT TO SAY AND DO

- Express sympathy and sorrow for what has happened.

- Anyone who has lost a loved one to a violent crime will need your caring patience. It takes a long time to heal, and they will need your support during the process.

- Anger is a natural response to a violent crime. Listen with patience; the victim of crime is not looking for answers but an opportunity to vent their anger.

- Recognize that they will grieve in their own way.

> ✒ Offer to help with the basic necessities—grocery shopping, cleaning, laundry, food preparation, child care, and carpooling—as they might find it impossible to resume their normal housekeeping and caregiver tasks.

- Do communicate your willingness to support the victim of crime in whatever ways you can. Individuals who have someone to lean on increase their chances of healing from the trauma.

- Locate victim assistance services through your local police department.

- Offer to help research other community and counseling support services.

- Encourage them to participate in the judicial process to restore a sense of control.

- Offer to listen. The individual will need to tell their story over and over again to process what has happened.

- Allow them to grieve in their own way.

- Encourage them to express their grief and sorrow for as long as they need.

- Those who experience violent crime are changed; many victims of crime find that they reconstruct and change their lives in the aftermath and recovery process. Support them and accept the changes.

- Do continue to keep in touch with them and remember them during significant dates and difficult periods, such as the anniversary of the crime, a birthday, or holidays.

HOW TO SAY IT

I am here for you when you need me.

I care about you and will support you however you might need me.

I have never experienced this before; please let me know how I can help you.

I will always be your friend; nothing can change that.

I will miss him (her), too.

I'd like to help any way I can.

I'm glad you survived.

It's not your fault.

This was a terrible crime, and I am sorry it happened to you.

What you are feeling is normal.

You are safe now.

You can talk to me at any time.

You did the best you could.

You were in no way to blame for what happened.

WHAT NOT TO SAY AND DO

- Don't disbelieve their account of the crime.

- Don't be alarmed with their anger or rage. It is a natural expression, and they must voice their anger and life's unfairness if they are to heal.

- Stay clear of questions that begin with the word *why*—these questions tend to put the blame on the victim rather than the assailant.

- Don't judge the victim of crime in what has happened, their response, or how they are handling their grief.

- Don't try to hurry their grief along. They need the time to heal in their own way and at their own speed.

- Avoid telling the victim of crime how you would have reacted in the same situation.

- Don't ask for details. The event might be too painful for them to share.

- Don't suggest they could have avoided the crime by doing something different.

HOW NOT TO SAY IT

How could you have let them into your house?

How could you have trusted him (her)?

It's time to move on.

What was he doing there?

Why did you go there?

Why didn't you fight back?

Why were you there in the first place?

You need to get over it.

SAMPLE LETTER/E-MAIL

To a friend who was badly injured in an assault.

September X, 2XXX
Dear Will:

You have constantly been in my thoughts and prayers these last few days, and I have been struggling to find some words to comfort you. I am at a loss at how this could have happened and how I can best help you.

There have been so many times when you sat and listened to me and lent me your shoulder to cry on. You didn't offer advice or comment on my woes; you just let me talk endlessly until I either exhausted myself or somehow figured out a solution. Your very presence was the solace I needed, and that is what I would like to give to you.

Mary told me you weren't up to having visitors, and it might be a while before you will see anyone. I have patience, and when you are ready to see me, I will be available. I will help you in any way you wish, and I'm in this with you for the long haul.

In the meantime, I will continue to pray for your recovery and keep in touch by mail. I send love and comfort to you, Will. Get well soon.

Love,
Meredith

For further information:

Doka, Kenneth J., Ph.D., ed. *Living with Grief After Sudden Loss: Suicide, Homicide, Accident, Heart Attack, Stroke*. Bristol, PA: Taylor & Francis, 1996.

Levy, Naomi. *To Begin Again—The Journey Toward Comfort, Strength, and Faith in Difficult Times*. New York, NY: Ballantine Books, 1998.

Matsakis, Aphrodite, Ph.D. *I Can't Get Over It: A Handbook for Trauma Survivors, Second Edition*. Oakland, CA: New Harbinger Publications, Inc., 1996.

Wolfelt, Alan D., Ph.D. *Healing Your Traumatized Heart: 100 Practical Ideas After Someone You Love Dies a Sudden, Violent Death*. Fort Collins, CO: Companion Press, 2002.

Department of Justice, Office for Victims of Crime (OVC)
www.ojp.usdoj.gov/ovc

Families and Friends of Violent Crime Victims
P.O. Box 1949
Everett, WA 98206
(425) 355-6822
(800) 346-7555
www.fnfvcv.org

Mothers Against Drunk Driving (MADD)
669 Airport Freeway, Suite 310

Hurst, TX 76053
(817) 268-MADD

National Center for Victims of Crime
2000 M Street, NW, Suite 480
Washington, DC 20036
(202) 467-8700
www.ncvc.org

The National Coalition of Homicide Survivors, Inc.
www.mivictims.org/nchs

National Organization for Victim Assistance (NOVA)
1730 Park Road NW
Washington, DC 20010
(202) 232-6682
Information and referrals for victims of crime and disaster (800) TRY-NOVA
www.try-nova.org

National Organization of Parents of Murdered Children (POMC)
100 East Eighth Street, Suite B-41
Cincinnati, OH 45202
(513) 721-LOVE or (513) 242-8025

The Compassionate Friends, Inc.
National Headquarters
P.O. Box 3696
Oak Brook, IL 60522-3696
(630) 990-0010 or (877) 969-0010
www.compassionatefriends.org

Victim Services Helpline
(800) FYI-CALL
gethelp@ncvc.org

See also: WHAT IS GRIEF? UNDERSTANDING THE PROCESS OF MOURNING AND HOW YOU CAN HELP, WHAT CAN I SAY? COMMUNICATIONS THAT COMFORT, WHAT CAN I DO? HOW TO LISTEN, NONVIOLENT CRIME, SEXUAL ASSAULT OR RAPE, and DOMESTIC VIOLENCE.

FOURTEEN

Sexual Assault or Rape

∞

*"You can't live a perfect day without doing something for
someone who will never be able to repay you."*

—John Wooden

ACCORDING to the American Medical Association, sexual assault or rape is one of the most rapidly growing and most serious violent crimes in the United States. The Federal Bureau of Investigation reports that in the United States in 2000, a forcible rape occurred every 5.8 minutes. Often unreported, rape is referred to as a silent crime.

Sexual assault or rape can be committed by an unknown offender, an acquaintance or someone known to the victim, or by a marital partner. According to a 2001 report issued by the U.S. Department of Justice, Bureau of Justice Statistics, six in ten sexual assault or rape survivors stated they knew the offender as an intimate, other relative, friend, or acquaintance.

When a sexual assault or rape is committed by someone known to the survivor, it is referred to as acquaintance rape. When sexual assault or rape occurs on a date or between two individuals who expect to or who already have an intimate relationship, it is referred to as date rape.

Females aged sixteen to twenty-four appear most vulnerable according to a U.S. Department of Justice, Bureau of Justice Statistics report. They experienced the highest per capita rates of intimate violence—19.6 victimizations per 1,000 females.

The sexual assault and rape numbers are staggering. A study conducted in 1992 by the National Center for Victims of Crime and Crime Victims Research and Treatment Center states that 12.1 million American women have been victims of forcible rape.

Women are not the only victims of sexual assault and rape; these same crimes are committed against males. The American Academy of Pediatrics estimates that 5 percent of committed sexual assaults are against men.

Although they might be fortunate to have survived rape or sexual assault, those who survive violent crimes aren't feeling lucky. They'll need your continuous support, so check in with them frequently to see how they are doing and let them know you are there for them.

VICTIM OR SURVIVOR?

There is a real dispute among professionals whether victims of crime are victims per se or survivors. I took all the comments and decided victims of crime was appropriate for Chapters Twelve and Thirteen, but for rape, survivor was more empowering. I felt "survivor" was certainly not an appropriate term for domestic violence—the "abused" or "victim of domestic violence" seemed most appropriate. The four chapters are very different and I wanted to show their distinction rather than treating them all under one umbrella.

THINGS TO CONSIDER

- Studies estimate that as many as one in eight women may be sexually assaulted in their lifetime.

- Sexual assault or rape survivors might feel so embarrassed or shamed by the experience that they tell no one and withdraw socially.

- Many rapes go unreported or survivors are unwilling to press charges because they know the assailant and are afraid they will be harassed by them and/or mutual friends.

- Sexual crimes against men are frequently underreported; men are less willing to press charges and have a greater fear of the criminal justice system and how their case will be handled.

EMOTIONS AND FEELINGS TO ANTICIPATE

- Anger
- Confusion
- Denial
- Depression

- Disbelief
- Embarrassment
- Fear
- Frustration
- Guilt
- Helplessness
- Hopelessness
- Humiliation
- Insecurity

- Irritability
- Numbness
- Panic
- Self-blame
- Shame
- Shock
- Terror
- Violation
- Worry

WHAT TO SAY AND DO

- Recommend that they contact a sexual assault crisis center. The Rape, Abuse, and Incest National Network (RAINN) 24-hour hotline at (800) 656-HOPE will help you find a center near you.

- Suggest that they report the assault, but don't push it. If the survivor resists, let it go.

- Encourage them to seek medical care.

- Offer to accompany them to the police station or the hospital.

- Help them find any information they might need by way of phone numbers or support and counseling services.

- If the survivor has children, offer to watch the children while they report the assault.

- Let them make their own choices; this will help them regain control of their life.

- Let them know that they do not have to face this alone.

- Consistently be there for them.

- Let them know that whenever they would like to talk, you will be ready to listen.

- Be willing to listen without judging.

- Communicate that you believe them.

- Allow them to speak at their own pace; don't try to hurry them along.

- Reinforce that it is not their fault the assault occurred; no one asks to be sexually assaulted or raped.

- Ask them what you can do to make them feel comfortable.

- Ask if there is anyone you can call for them.

- Offer to stay with them or take them to your home.

- Validate their feelings; let them know that whatever they are feeling is okay.

- Encourage them to seek professional help if they are unable to talk about the assault.

> ☞ If you have difficulty dealing with the sexual assault or the emotional response, you can also call the local sexual assault center to learn how you can handle your own feelings and the survivor's emotions while providing the needed support.

HOW TO SAY IT

I love you and care about you.

I will help you in any way you need me to.

I'd like to help if I can.

If you ever want to talk about it, I am here for you.

It wasn't your fault.

Please let me know how I can help you.

This doesn't change the wonderful person you are.

We'll get through this together.

Whatever you are feeling is okay.

Whatever you did was the right thing for you at the time.

When you are ready to talk, I am here.

You are not to blame.

You can talk to me any time.

You couldn't have known.

You didn't ask for it.

WHAT NOT TO SAY AND DO

- Don't suggest they were to blame for the assault. Under no circumstances were they at fault.

- Don't imply that they could have done something different, such as kicking the assailant or running, that would have prevented the attack.

- If you are uncomfortable with what has happened, don't demonstrate your discomfort by way of your body language and your approach to the survivor.

- Don't imply that it wasn't rape because they knew the assailant.

- Don't avoid the survivor once they have told you what has happened. If you choose to stay away, they might interpret your actions incorrectly. Your absence might signal that you don't believe them or that you are shocked or repelled by their experience.

- Don't finish their sentences. They might speak slowly, and it is important to allow them time to control their emotions and form their own thoughts.

- Don't criticize the survivor for the clothing they wore, their circle of friends or acquaintances, what they said, or where they were when the assault occurred.

- Don't imply that the survivor used poor judgment in their behavior, despite the circumstances they might have put themselves in prior to the assault. Even if they drank or had too much to drink, they did not provoke the assault or deserve to be assaulted. No one deserves to be raped.

- Avoid any statements beginning with "If you had only." This implies that the survivor rather than the assailant is to blame.

- Don't pressure them to talk. They do need to talk about the experience, but they will talk about it when they are ready.

- Don't push for details of the assault. It might be too painful to share or too embarrassing. If they want to share this information with you, they will do so when they are ready.

- Don't tell anyone what has happened without first obtaining permission. It is important to respect their right to privacy.

- Don't criticize how they handled themselves.

- Don't tell them how you would have handled it.

- Don't tell them it would have never happened to you.

- Don't judge them.

- Don't try to relate it to yourself. Your story is not their story. This is about them, not you.

- Don't look at the survivor any differently than you did before.

- Don't suggest that the survivor is damaged goods because of the assault.

- Don't ask them how it could have happened without their consent. Sexual assault or rape is a violent crime of power and control; it has nothing to do with sexual desire.

- Don't touch them without asking, even a hug. The survivor's personal space was violated, and because you don't know exactly what happened during the assault, you might inadvertently touch them in a way that triggers reminders of what happened.

- Don't behave differently when you are with them.

- Don't act as if you pity them. They need your loving care and concern, not your pity.

HOW NOT TO SAY IT

How could it have happened?

I feel sorry for you.

I told you he wasn't good for you.

I told you not to drink so much.

I wish you hadn't gone to that party.

If only you didn't dress so suggestively.

She was asking for it.

This was my greatest fear, and now it's happened.

What exactly happened?

Why didn't you yell?

SAMPLE LETTERS/E-MAILS

To a college friend who has experienced date rape.

> June X, 2XXX
> Dear Diane:
>
> You have been in my thoughts all morning. I am so sorry that such a terrible thing happened to someone as special as you. I know this is a difficult time, and although I do not fully understand what you are going through, please know that I want to be there for you in any way I can. If you want company, I will be there; if you want to talk, I want to listen.
>
> How about if we plan to be together this weekend? I could fix that chicken dish you like so much, and you can spend the night if you like.
>
> Know that I will be thinking of you today. I will call you later so you can let me know what I can do to help. Take care, stay strong, and I will see you soon.
>
> I love you,
> Jo Ann

To a friend who has been sexually assaulted.

February X, 2XXX

Dear Anna:

I left you a message today, but I wanted to write as well to let you know that I have been thinking about you. I know this is an extremely difficult time for you, but I also know that you are strong and will get through this. Please remember, though, that you don't have to get through it alone. You are surrounded by family and friends who love you and want to support you in any way we can.

No one knows better than you how much it hurts, so I won't pretend to know how you feel. But I do know that the pain you are feeling is part of the grieving process. Allow yourself to work through your feelings at your own pace. It might not seem like it now, but you will feel better with time.

I understand that the Sexual Assault Center's support group has helped many rape survivors cope with feelings of loss and distrust. If you'd like, I can go with you to a meeting. If you aren't ready now, we can talk about it later.

Anna, you are a beautiful, intelligent, and loving woman. No one can take that away from you. I am here for you. Call me anytime, day or night, if you want company or just want to talk.

I love you,

Lynne

For further information:

Aranow, Vicki, C.S.W., and Monique Lang, C.S.W. *Journey to Wholeness—Healing from the Trauma of Rape.* Holmes Beach, FL: Learning Publications, 2000.

Ledray, Linda E. *Recovering from Rape.* New York, NY: Henry Holt & Company, 1986.

Levy, Naomi. *To Begin Again—The Journey Toward Comfort, Strength, and Faith in Difficult Times.* New York, NY: Ballantine Books, 1998.

Sebold, Alice. *Lucky: A Memoir.* New York, NY: Scribner, 1999.

Warshaw, Robin. *I Never Called It Rape: The Ms. Report on Recognizing, Fighting, and Surviving Date and Acquaintance Rape.* New York, NY: HarperCollins Publishers, 1994.

Department of Justice, Office for Victims of Crime (OVC)
www.ojp.usdoj.gov/ovc

National Center for Victims of Crime
2000 M Street, NW, Suite 480
Washington, DC 20036
(202) 467-8700
www.ncvc.org

National Organization for Victim Assistance (NOVA)
1730 Park Road NW
Washington, DC 20010
(202) 232-6682
Information and referrals for victims of crime and disaster (800) TRY-NOVA
www.try-nova.org

The Rape, Abuse, and Incest National Network (RAINN) 24-hour hotline
(800) 656-HOPE
www.rainn.org

Victim Services Helpline
(800) FYI-CALL
gethelp@ncvc.org

See also: WHAT IS GRIEF? UNDERSTANDING THE PROCESS OF MOURNING AND HOW YOU CAN HELP, WHAT CAN I SAY? COMMUNICATIONS THAT COMFORT, WHAT CAN I DO? HOW TO LISTEN, and VIOLENT CRIME.

FIFTEEN

Domestic Violence

∞

"Good friends are good for your health.".

—Irwin Sarason

I N a report issued by the U.S. Department of Justice, Bureau of Justice Statistics, domestic violence is defined as violent crimes by current or former spouses, boyfriends, or girlfriends. Violent crimes include lethal (homicide) and nonlethal (rape, sexual assault, robbery, aggravated assault, and simple assault) offenses.

Studies by the Surgeon General's office and reported in the *Journal of the American Medical Association* reveal that domestic violence is the leading cause of injury to women between the ages of fifteen and forty-four; domestic violence is a more common cause of death to this age group than automobile accidents, muggings, and cancer combined.

In a survey conducted by the Commonwealth Fund in 1998, almost one third of American women reported being sexually or physically abused by a spouse or boyfriend at some point in their lives.

Another report issued by the U.S. Department of Justice, Bureau of Justice Statistics provides startling facts about domestic violence:

- Women were much more likely to be victims of domestic violence, experiencing more than ten times as many incidents of violence by an intimate than males.

- Six times as many women victimized by intimates (18 percent) as those victimized by strangers (3 percent) did not report their violent victimization to police because they feared offender reprisal.

- Nearly two in three female victims of violence were related to or knew their attacker.

If you suspect that someone you care about might be a victim of domestic violence, she (or he) might not be ready to take control of their situation. The abused have every reason to fear retribution if they report the crime, and they are likely to be financially dependent on the abuser.

Although it might be frustrating to see someone you care about struggling in this type of situation, remain actively understanding and empathetic. They desperately need your steadfast support if they are to break this violent cycle.

VICTIM OR SURVIVOR?

You will find differing opinions on the appropriate way to identify the person upon whom a crime was perpetrated. Some people feel they should be called a "survivor," which is more empowering. Others prefer to be identified as "victims of crime." This chapter will refer to crime victims as "victims of domestic violence" or as "the abused."

THINGS TO CONSIDER

- Domestic abuse is a silent crime; a great many cases go unreported.

- Domestic abuse isn't just committed against women; about 5 percent of reported cases are committed by women against men.

- Physical abuse, such as a punch, slap, or shove, isn't the only form of abuse. Domestic violence can take the form of verbal or emotional abuse by way of threats, intimidation, domination, or isolation. It can also take the form of financial abuse by way of controlling or concealing money or joint assets.

- Domination or control in the areas of religion, spirituality, sex, or social relationships also constitutes domestic abuse.

- Stalking is a form of abusive behavior, and the majority of cases involve women being stalked by ex-husbands or former boyfriends.

EMOTIONS AND FEELINGS TO ANTICIPATE

- Denial
- Dependency
- Embarrassment
- Fear for safety
- Fear of retribution
- Guilt
- Helplessness

- Humiliation
- Incompetency
- Insecurity
- Isolation
- Self-blame
- Shame
- Terror

WHAT TO SAY AND DO

- Demonstrate your concern if someone you care about is in an abusive situation, but be careful—domestic violence is a deadly crime.

- Encourage them to deal with a professional who can help them assess their personal situation.

- If the abused is having difficulty accessing information, call the National Domestic Violence Hotline yourself to secure the latest information to pass on.

> ๛ Recommend they locate and contact professionals at domestic violence hotlines. The National Domestic Violence Hotline is 1(800) 799-SAFE and is available twenty-four hours a day.

- Communicate your willingness and availability to listen.

- Offer support, and be empathetic and understanding.

- If you are told about abuse, reinforce that you believe the abused.

- Research and identify available community services through your local phone book.

- Call the Department of Social Services to learn about domestic violence services such as crisis counseling, medical care, legal assistance or advocacy, shelters, housing, or employment.

- Contact these organizations and find out what they provide for someone experiencing domestic abuse. Record key information in a notebook.

- Locate support groups.

- Suggest the abused change their routines.

- Recommend that they prepare a safety plan before they experience a crisis; an effective plan establishes ways to reduce risk.

HOW TO SAY IT

How can I help you?

I am concerned about you.

I am concerned about your safety.

I care about you.

I have no experience with this, so you will have to let me know what I can do to help you.

I would like to help you.

If you would like to talk, I'm available to listen.

Is there something I can do to help?

No one deserves to be hurt by someone else.

You are a wonderful person.

You are not to blame.

You did not cause this.

WHAT NOT TO SAY AND DO

- Don't blame the abused.

- Don't say anything that makes the abused think you don't believe them.

- Don't question their ability to make it on their own.

- Don't act judgmental if someone shares a domestic violence experience with you that happened long ago.

■ Don't make someone feel guilty for not taking action against prior abuse.

■ Don't give conditional support, for example "I will only help you if you leave him."

HOW NOT TO SAY IT

Get out while you can.

Have you no shame?

How can you stand this?

I can't believe he (she) would do this.

What are you doing to anger them?

Where is your pride?

Special Situations

My co-worker comes to work every Monday with bruises.
Approach your supervisor and tell them that your co-worker shows up with bruises every Monday morning. The organization you work for should have procedures in place to handle this type of problem. Let your supervisor be the one to take charge of the situation.

For further information:

Brown, Louis, Francois Dubau, and Merritt McKeon, J.D. *Stop Domestic Violence: An Action Plan for Saving Lives.* New York, NY: St. Martin's Press, 1997.

Cook, Philip W. *Abused Men: The Hidden Side of Domestic Violence.* Portsmouth, NH: Praeger Trade, 1997.

Dugan, Meg Kennedy, A.M., and Roger R. Hock, Ph.D. *It's My Life Now—Starting Over After an Abusive Relationship or Domestic Violence.* New York, NY: Routledge, 2000.

Lissette, Andrea, M.A. C.D.V.C., and Richard Kraus, Ph.D. *Free Yourself from an Abusive Relationship.* Alameda, CA: Hunter House Publishers, 1999.

Nicarthy, Ginny, M.S.W. *Getting Free: You Can End Abuse and Take Back Your Life.* Seattle, WA: Seal Press, 1997.

Rosenberg, Marshall B., Ph.D. *Nonviolent Communication: A Language of Life, Second Edition.* Encinitas, CA: PuddleDancer Press, 2003.

Statman, Jan Berliner. *The Battered Woman's Survival Guide.* Dallas, TX: Taylor Publishing Company, 1995.

Center for Nonviolent Communication
www.cnvc.org/main.htm

Department of Justice, Office for Victims of Crime (OVC)
www.ojp.usdoj.gov/ovc

National Organization for Victim Assistance (NOVA)
1730 Park Road NW
Washington, DC 20010
(202) 232-6682
Information and referrals for victims of crime and disaster (800) TRY-NOVA
www.try-nova.org

The National Coalition Against Domestic Violence
www.ncadv.org

The National Domestic Violence Hotline
(800) 799-SAFE, available twenty-four hours a day

See also: WHAT IS GRIEF? UNDERSTANDING THE PROCESS OF MOURNING AND HOW YOU CAN HELP, WHAT CAN I SAY? COMMUNICATIONS THAT COMFORT, WHAT CAN I DO? HOW TO LISTEN, and VIOLENT CRIME.

SIXTEEN

Natural Disasters

∞

"Kindness is gladdening the hearts of those who are
traveling in the dark with us."

—Henri-Frederic Amiel

EACH year, millions of people find themselves in the wrong place at the wrong time, encountering a wide range of natural disasters such as floods, hurricanes, tornadoes, earthquakes, mud slides, wildfires, volcanic eruptions, and blizzards.

Those who make it through these disasters might have experienced the death of loved ones, personal injuries, and/or potential loss of their home, employment, earthly possessions, and communities. They might have witnessed extremes in physical harm, injuries, or death. The more extensive the loss and trauma, the greater the risk for severe stress symptoms and lasting readjustment problems.

Although they might be fortunate to have survived, they will need a great deal of help and support in restoring their lives.

THINGS TO CONSIDER

- Despite warnings, natural disasters are always unexpected.

- No matter how prepared one is for the natural disaster, the actual event puts survivors at risk for psychological and readjustment problems.

- The National Center for Post Traumatic Stress Disorder (PTSD) reports that as many as one in three disaster survivors experience some or all of the following severe stress symptoms, which may lead to lasting PTSD, anxiety disorders, or depression: blank periods of time with no memory, nightmares, flashbacks, extreme attempts to avoid disturbing memories, extreme emotional numbing, panic attacks, rage, severe anxiety, and/or severe depression.

EMOTIONS AND FEELINGS TO ANTICIPATE

- Anxiety
- Confusion
- Desperation
- Disorientation
- Dislocation
- Grief
- Helplessness
- Fear
- Numbness
- Resentment
- Self-blame
- Shock
- Sorrow

WHAT TO SAY AND DO

- Offer safe shelter.

- Ensure that the survivor has privacy to reflect quietly and get some sleep.

- Locate and contact the local and state health departments to identify services for survivors.

> ✄ Help the survivor contact disaster-relief agencies to secure help in restoring their lives. The resources listed at the end of this chapter provide support in cleanup, health, housing, and basic emergency assistance.

- Provide whatever help is needed as soon as it is safe, such as retrieving belongings after a tornado or flood; don't wait to be asked.

- Assess the survivor's condition, and provide support if they are injured. For suggestions on what you can do to help, see Chapter Four.

- Help connect them with other survivors to share their experiences and learn coping mechanisms.

- Be patient with the survivor, encouraging them to share their feelings and experience when they are ready.

- Be a willing listener. Allow the survivor to tell their story as often as they would like. Repeating their story over and over will help the survivor in the healing process.

- Let the survivor set the pace and speak as slowly as they need to in gathering their thoughts.

- Help them transition back into healthy living habits.

- Encourage good nutrition and restoration of wholesome eating patterns.

- Assist them in securing comfortable clothing that they will enjoy wearing, as they might have left their home quickly or experienced damage to personal belongings.

- Help them find quiet and undisturbed places to sleep so they can resume normal sleeping patterns.

- Encourage the survivor to get as much exercise as possible. Exercise is a great tool in coping with stress. Offer to accompany them on a walk, a swim, or at formal exercise classes.

- Give them a gift certificate for a relaxing massage.

- Allow them to cry.

- If they enjoy reading, encourage them to read the types of books that relax them or suggest rereading an old favorite.

- Suggest the survivor see a physician.

- Survivors might need more help coping with the trauma. Help them find a counselor or therapist, and accompany them to appointments if they need extra support.

HOW TO SAY IT

Come and stay with me.

I am here to listen whenever you need to talk.

I am so grateful you are okay.

I will help you any way I can.

Of course you are shaken; I would be, too.

This must have been a terrible shock.

What can I do to help you?

You can count on us for whatever you need.

You couldn't have known.

You did the best you could in the circumstances.

WHAT NOT TO SAY AND DO

- Don't tell them they are "lucky" because they survived. If they have lost their home, prized possessions, or a sense of community, they are not feeling lucky.

- Don't try to hurry them along. They need time to reflect on the experience and take the time to recover.

- Unless you have had the identical experience, don't tell them you understand.

- Don't compare their loss to someone else's loss.

- Don't tell them other people's losses were worse than their loss.

- Don't tell them to be grateful for what they have.

- Don't tell them what they should have done differently.

HOW NOT TO SAY IT

At least you weren't hurt.

Be grateful it was just material things.

Be thankful you survived.

It could have been worse.

It wasn't that big a deal.

Many people were hurt worse.

Thankfully it only hit a small area.

SAMPLE LETTER/E-MAIL

To a friend whose home was destroyed in a tornado.

June X, 2XXX
Dear Karina:

I was stunned and scared to hear that a tornado had ripped through your town last night. When Diane finally heard from you, I was so relieved to know you, Ken, and the kids were okay, but I understand that, unbelievably, your entire house was demolished.

I am sending this to your mother's house because I know that's where you will be living for a while, but I want to extend an open invitation for you to stay with us for any length of time. In the meantime, I will plan on coming down as soon as the road is reopened to help with the cleanup effort and anything else you need.

I love you, and I am always here for you,
Annie

For further information:

Levy, Naomi. *To Begin Again—The Journey Toward Comfort, Strength, and Faith in Difficult Times.* New York, NY: Ballantine Books, 1998.

Matsakis, Aphrodite, Ph.D. *I Can't Get Over It: A Handbook for Trauma Survivors, Second Edition.* Oakland, CA: New Harbinger Publications, Inc., 1996.

American Red Cross National Headquarters
431 18th Street, NW
Washington, DC 20006
(202) 303-4498
www.redcross.org

Anxiety Disorders Association of America
8730 Georgia Avenue, Suite 600

Silver Spring, MD 20910

(240) 485-1001

www.adaa.org

Federal Emergency Management Agency (FEMA)

500 C Street, SW

Washington, DC 20472

(202) 566-1600

www.fema.gov

National Institute of Mental Health (NIMH)

6001 Executive Boulevard, Room 8184, MSC 9663

Bethesda, MD 20892-9663

(301) 443-4513 or toll-free (866) 615-NIMH

www.nimh.nih.gov

Salvation Army National Headquarters

615 Slaters Lane

P.O. Box 269

Alexandria, VA 22313

See also: WHAT IS GRIEF? UNDERSTANDING THE PROCESS OF MOURNING AND HOW CAN YOU HELP, WHAT CAN I SAY? COMMUNICATIONS THAT COMFORT, and WHAT CAN I DO? HOW TO LISTEN.

SEVENTEEN

Terrorism

∞

*"In times like these, it helps to recall that there have
always been times like these."*

—Paul Harvey

THE unspeakable happened on September 11, 2001. It forever changed our perception of safety and initiated feelings of vulnerability in the fragility and unpredictability of life.

The events of September 11 were particularly personal and close to home, but outrageous and shocking events occur in the world every day, leaving us feeling powerless and with a sense of unreality. We are unprepared for the unexpected trauma resulting from terrorist violence. Those who experience the disasters firsthand are not the only ones affected; anyone who witnesses these events, views the sites, or experiences loss, such as family members, emergency and rescue workers, medical and mental health professionals, and the entire nation, can be impacted by the experience.

We are all vulnerable to trauma, even healthy and well-adjusted individuals. It's important to understand that any experience with trauma can lead to long-lasting problems.

If you suspect that someone you love is having difficulty recovering from trauma or the symptoms seem especially severe and prolonged and you think they might be experiencing post traumatic stress disorder (PTSD), you might want to seek help from a professional—only a trained professional can make a diagnosis of PTSD. If you are interested in exploring and learning more about PTSD, see the resources at the end of this chapter.

The road to recovery from terrorist violence is a slow one. Your patient support and presence, both immediately following the event and in the years to come, will go a long way in helping the survivor heal.

THINGS TO CONSIDER

- Terrorism can be a single act in which one person is hurt or killed or in which thousands are hurt and/or killed. What differentiates the magnitude of this trauma is the sheer numbers of dead and wounded; the impact of the death, destruction, and damage can be very overwhelming.

- Traumatic events can happen to anyone.

- No one can prepare for or protect themselves from a traumatic event.

- Survivors feel an overwhelming loss of control.

- Survivors will be forever influenced by their experience.

- Survivors report their reaction to trauma as feeling as if they are going crazy. They are not. They are experiencing symptoms and problems that are in response to the traumatic experience.

- Survivors can feel a tremendous sense of guilt and wonder why they survived and not others.

EMOTIONS AND FEELINGS TO ANTICIPATE

- Aggressiveness
- Anger
- Anxiety
- Blame
- Denial
- Despair
- Disbelief
- Disorientation
- Distress
- Fear
- Grief
- Guilt
- Helplessness
- Hopelessness
- Horror
- Humiliation
- Hurt
- Irritability
- Resentment
- Sadness
- Self-blame
- Shame
- Shock
- Terror
- Upset

WHAT TO SAY AND DO

- Extend your sympathy and let the survivor know that you care about them and their well-being.

- Be understanding.

- Let them know you are available to listen.

- Be patient; trauma survivors often speak slowly and haltingly while sharing their feelings and experiences.

- Reinforce that you believe them.

- Reassure them that it is normal to feel stressful reactions following a traumatic event.

- Encourage them to experience their feelings and fully grieve for their tragic loss.

- Affirm and believe all their personal responses and reactions to their experience and loss.

- Accept who they have become; trauma can change the survivors, and they need unconditional love to work through the healing process.

> ↣ Volunteer to provide transportation to support group meetings or offer to attend the meetings with them.

- Do learn as much as you can about trauma recovery and PTSD.

- Encourage the survivor to find support groups. It is important for them to relate to others who have been through the same or similar experiences.

- If they are unable to take the initiative, locate support groups for them.

- Invite the survivor to participate in physical exercise such as walking or swimming.

> ↣ Survivors might benefit from relaxation activities. Give them a gift certificate for a massage, a yoga or relaxation videotape, or suggest taking a class together that promotes relaxation.

- Recommend that they keep a journal of their thoughts and feelings.

- Let them know that it is okay to cry, and realize that it is okay for you to cry along with them.

- Suggest the survivor explore education and counseling to recover from the trauma.

- If the survivor is unable to do so, offer to research available support services for them.

HOW TO SAY IT

I am so grateful you survived.

I am so sorry this happened.

I love you, and I will be here for you.

I will be here for you no matter what, no matter when, because I love you and care about you.

I'm here for you.

You couldn't have known.

You did the best you could to protect yourself.

You handled yourself the best way you could under the circumstances.

WHAT NOT TO SAY AND DO

- Don't communicate lowered expectations to the survivor; if you do, they might think you feel they aren't capable or strong enough to overcome the traumatic event.

- Don't judge.

- Don't pressure or force someone to get help.

- Don't exhibit frustration if you feel they are not healing as quickly as you think they should.

- Don't tell them not to think about it.

- Don't tell them it is time to move on with their life.

HOW NOT TO SAY IT

Don't think about it.

It doesn't help to dwell on it.

It's time to move on with your life.

Just put it behind you.

Pretend it didn't happen.

Why can't you get over it, already?

SAMPLE LETTER/E-MAIL

To a friend who experienced a traumatic event.

October X, 2XXX
Dear Shawn:

I was so saddened to hear that you were injured and shocked to learn how it happened. Your sister shared that you will spend some time in rehabilitation while your injuries heal.

No one could possibly have predicted that this would happen, and I am grateful you survived. I have never experienced anything like this, and I find myself at a loss for what I can say that would bring you comfort.

You demonstrated tremendous courage, Shawn, in a very difficult situation. I respect your strength and tenacity and know that you did everything humanly possible to survive.

When you are up for some company, I would like to visit. In the meantime, I am sending positive thoughts your way. May you feel the warmth of the sun shine on you again soon.

Fondly,
Danielle

For further information:

To locate specialists or support groups for PTSD:

- The Sidran Foundation, (410) 825-8888.

- Anxiety Disorders Association of America, (212) 543-5355.

- American Psychological Association, (800) 964-2000.

- National Alliance for the Mentally Ill (NAMI), (800) 950-6264.

- Check in the Yellow Pages of your local telephone book pages for Mental Health Services.

Cart, Michael, ed., with Marc Aronson and Marianne Carus. *911—The Book of Help.* Chicago, IL: Cricket Books, 2002.

Doka, Kenneth J., ed., Ph.D. *Living with Grief After Sudden Loss: Suicide, Homicide, Accident, Heart Attack, Stroke.* Bristol, PA: Taylor & Francis, 1996.

Lattanzi-Licht, Marcia E., and Kenneth J. Doka, eds. *Living with Grief: Coping with Public Tragedy.* Washington, DC: Hospice Foundation of America, 2003.

Matsakis, Aphrodite, Ph.D. *I Can't Get Over It: A Handbook for Trauma Survivors, Second Edition.* Oakland, CA: New Harbinger Publications, Inc., 1996.

Wolfelt, Alan D., Ph.D. *Healing Your Traumatized Heart: 100 Practical Ideas After Someone You Love Dies a Sudden, Violent Death.* Fort Collins, CO: Companion Press, 2002.

American Red Cross National Headquarters
431 18th Street, NW
Washington, DC 20006
(202) 303-4498
www.redcross.org

Anxiety Disorders Association of America
8730 Georgia Avenue, Suite 600
Silver Spring, MD 20910
(240) 485-1001
www.adaa.org

Coping with Disaster
www.nmha.org/reassurance/anniversary/index.cfm

Coping with War and Terrorism: Tips for the Workplace
www.nmha.org/reassurance/workplaceWarCoping.cfm

Federal Emergency Management Agency (FEMA)
500 C Street, SW
Washington, DC 20472
(202) 566-1600
www.fema.gov

National Center for Victims of Crime
2000 M Street, NW, Suite 480
Washington, DC 20036
(202) 467-8700
www.ncvc.org

National Institute of Mental Health (NIMH)
6001 Executive Boulevard, Room 8184, MSC 9663
Bethesda, MD 20892-9663
(301) 443-4513 or toll-free (866) 615-NIMH
www.nimh.nih.gov

National Organization for Victim Assistance (NOVA)
1730 Park Road NW
Washington, DC 20010
(202) 232-6682
Information and referrals for victims of crime and disaster (800) TRY-NOVA
www.try-nova.org

The Salvation Army National Headquarters
615 Slaters Lane
P.O. Box 269
Alexandria, VA 22313
www.salvationarmyusa.org/www_usn.nsf

Especially for children:
Reactions and Guidelines for Children Following Trauma/Disaster
www.apa.org/practice/ptguidelines.html

Tragic Times Healing Words
www.sesameworkshop.org/parents/advice/article.php?contentId=49560#1

See also: WHAT IS GRIEF? UNDERSTANDING THE PROCESS OF MOURNING AND HOW YOU CAN HELP, WHAT CAN I SAY? COMMUNICATIONS THAT COMFORT, and WHAT CAN I DO? HOW TO LISTEN.

EIGHTEEN

Legal or Criminal Problems

∞

"You never know when a moment and a few sincere words
can have an impact on a life."

—Zig Ziglar

I<small>T</small> is shocking to open the daily newspaper and read that your neighbor's son has been arrested for drunk driving or a childhood friend's brother has been indicted for tax fraud. We know everyone is "innocent until proven guilty," but investigations, indictments, and arrests all raise the suspicion of guilt. Despite pleas of innocence, any conviction, fine, forfeiture of license, or incarceration carries a guilty stigma.

Anyone who experiences legal and/or criminal problems feels extreme shame, confusion, and fear; their problems shadow their loved ones, who experience the same emotions. Whether guilty or innocent, the experience is traumatizing— even more so if the news is broadcast locally or nationally in newspapers or on the radio or television.

Everyone reacts differently to these experiences, and it is impossible to predict how someone you care about will respond. They might desire seclusion or want your companionship or support.

Dealing with criminal or legal issues is both stressful and isolating. But if you are to continue the relationship, you can't ignore what has happened. Communications require great sensitivity, and the right words at the right time will demonstrate your support and keep the lines of communication open.

THINGS TO CONSIDER

- No one is prepared to deal with their own criminal or legal problems, even if they have a legal or criminal background.

- Individuals and their families who find themselves dealing with investigation, arrest, incarceration, or indictment need a great deal of information, resources, and support.

- Loved ones might experience severe financial hardship by hiring legal and investigative experts.

EMOTIONS AND FEELINGS TO ANTICIPATE

- Anger
- Denial
- Desire to flee
- Desperation
- Embarrassment
- Fear
- Guilt
- Loss
- Sadness
- Shame

WHAT TO SAY AND DO

- Let your family members, friends, or neighbors know that you are thinking of them and are sorry they are experiencing such a difficult situation.

- If they are uncomfortable speaking with you by telephone, communicate with them by notes and e-mail.

- If you don't get much of a response from them, continue to keep in touch, reinforcing again and again that you care about them.

- Offer to help in ways that are compatible with the type of relationship you have. For some, a note or phone call is sufficient; those with closer relationships can volunteer to research legal experts, provide meals, offer transportation, or volunteer to attend legal meetings, hearings, or court proceedings to extend support and take notes.

- Be patient. Your loved ones might be overwhelmed with emotions they have never experienced, or they might be at a loss for how to deal with their feelings and the world at large.

> ☞ Your loved ones might be embarrassed and prefer their privacy. With patience, they may be willing to resume their relationship with you.

HOW TO SAY IT

I am available for whatever you need me to do.

I am so sorry this is happening.

I have no idea what you might need, but I will help you in any way I can.

I know John is a fine person, and he will get through this.

I love you, and I will be there for you.

Know that you are often in my thoughts.

You are a wonderful person, and nothing can change that.

WHAT NOT TO SAY AND DO

- Don't ask for details of what happened. If someone wants to share detailed information with you, they will initiate the conversation themselves.

- Don't pressure them to talk to you.

- Don't pester them. If they won't take your calls or respond to your e-mail messages, they probably need privacy.

- Don't try to force them to see you by showing up uninvited or appearing in court or at a public venue.

- Don't break down when you see them, appearing as if you are the one who needs comfort.

HOW NOT TO SAY IT

How could he (she) do this?

How did this happen?

Is he (she) guilty?

Is it true?

It's in the newspaper; everyone is going to know.

How much is this all going to cost?

What is everyone going to think?

Special Situations

My cousin's son has been arrested for assault.
Send your cousin a note and let them know you are sorry this has happened. Remind them that you care about them and are ready to support them in any way. Refrain from making judgments or coming to any conclusions on the arrest charges. If your cousin would like to share any experiences with you, be there to listen. Do not give advice unless specifically asked to do so. The greatest gift you can give your cousin is to be there for them. Let them know what you are available to do, such as attend hearings with them, fix a meal, or just keep them company in the evening. If you receive no response from your outreach, continue to send notes or cards and keep in touch. This might be so difficult for your cousin that they are unable to respond to your efforts.

SAMPLE LETTERS/E-MAILS

To a friend whose son is under investigation for embezzlement.

> January X, 2XXX
> Dear Tom:
>
> You have frequently been in my thoughts. Having no experience in what you are going through, I am uncertain what to say or do to help you. Our friendship spans decades, and our children further cemented our relationship. It's been a pleasure to be part of Peter's life, and I am so terribly sorry this has happened. Please know that Beth and I think the world of you and your family. Nothing will change that.
>
> I will give you a call in a week or so to see how you are doing. I will be available to listen or support you in any way you'd like.
>
> Take good care of yourself.
> John

To a friend whose son is experiencing legal problems.

> October X, 2XXX
> Dear Carolyn:
>
> Just sending a note to say hello. I really enjoyed getting together for lunch last month—let's do it again and see if Tara's available.
>
> Carolyn, I can't say I know how you feel, but you are not alone. I know several people whose kids have been arrested—but you'll never know about it! Part of suburban (maybe "modern" would be a better description) life is maintaining the front that your own family is just fine, thank you. I think we'd all be better off dropping the charade and sharing more of what really goes on.
>
> I just wanted you to know that I'm thinking of you and will help in any way. If you're looking for a good juvenile attorney, I can provide some names. I can write a reference for David, or if you just want to talk, give me a call or e-mail.
>
> I've known David since our kids were in kindergarten together, and he is one fine young man, thanks to you and Ted. This experience might be unpleasant for everyone, but I'm confident he'll get through it and go on to college and a successful life.
>
> So take care of yourself, and keep in touch.
>
> Best,
> JoAnn

For further information:

Bergman, Paul, and Sara J. Berman-Barrett. *The Criminal Law Handbook: Know Your Rights, Survive the System (Criminal Law Handbook, 5th Ed.).* Berkeley, CA: Nolo Press, 2003.

Feinman, Jay. *Law 101: Everything You Need to Know About the American Legal System.* Oxford, England: Oxford University Press, 2000.

Herskowitz, Suzan. *Legal Research Made Easy (Self-Help Law Kit).* Naperville, IL: Sourcebooks Trade, 1998.

Hill, Douglas J. *Federal Criminal Defendant's Handbook.* New York, NY: Kensington Publishers, 1999.

AllLaw.com
Find legal information or a lawyer in your geographic area.
www.AllLaw.com

American Bar Association
Extensive online source of legal information.
www.abanet.org

American Law Sources On-Line
Comprehensive, uniform, and useful compilation of links to freely accessible online sources of law for the United States and Canada.
www.lawsource.com

FindLaw.com
Research your legal questions online or search directly for a lawyer in your area.
www.findlaw.com

Nolo—Law for All
Nolo is the nation's leading provider of self-help legal books, software, and web-based information and tools.
www.nolo.com

See also: WHAT IS GRIEF? UNDERSTANDING THE PROCESS OF MOURNING AND HOW YOU CAN HELP, WHAT CAN I SAY? COMMUNICATIONS THAT COMFORT, and WHAT CAN I DO? HOW TO LISTEN.

PART FIVE

COMMUNICATING ABOUT PERSONAL AND FAMILY ISSUES

❧

Although change is inevitable, some of life's personal and family challenges are unanticipated, unwanted, or terribly disappointing. How individuals cope with personal and family losses and whether they move forward in their lives often depends on their network of support.

You can play a crucial role in helping your loved one, friend, co-worker, or community member recover from loss and disappointment.

Part Five provides specific insight into infertility, adoption, a baby or child with special needs, physical disability, separation, divorce, job loss, financial troubles, caregiver responsibilities, and personal disappointment, with guidelines on verbal, written, and nonverbal communications that you can use to comfort.

NINETEEN

Infertility

∞

"One kind word can warm three winter nights."

—Asian saying

Infertility, the inability to conceive a child, is a highly personal medical condition that can be emotionally devastating to the couple trying to start a family. The National Center for Health Statistics reports infertility affects 6.1 million Americans—approximately one in six couples.

To women who were lectured in their early teens to avoid the risk of pregnancy, it is a cruel irony that when they are ready to take on the responsibility and role of parenthood, they can't. It is incredibly frustrating to reach the status of an adult and find you have no control over your fertility.

Many women feel an overwhelming sense of failure and wonder "Why me?" Why are they being singled out when it seems like everyone else can get pregnant whether they want to or not? Women are not alone in their feelings of failure and frustration; infertility is a real blow to the male ego. Many men are demoralized when undergoing infertility testing, and they might feel their masculinity threatened if the results indicate problems with their sperm.

Medical professionals can provide details of the physical and physiological barriers that prevent pregnancy, but there are no known psychological barriers. Well-meaning family members and friends often suggest behavioral adjustments, but there is no proof that an optimistic outlook, how hard the couple try or don't try, or their degree of relaxation has any impact on the likelihood of achieving gestation.

Modern medicine has made significant breakthroughs in helping infertile couples achieve pregnancy. Technology continues to provide new opportunities, which lead to innovative options for individuals and partners to have children.

It is important to understand that although many of these options have helped individuals and partners have children, they can be expensive, painful, complicated, not in line with someone's religious beliefs, or just not feasible for the individuals or couples. Some of them are just too high a price to pay to become pregnant, and none of them are guaranteed.

Parents, siblings, grandparents, and other relatives, in their love and desire to expand the family, have the capacity to exacerbate an already stressful situation. In-laws should be particularly sensitive in broaching the subject of fertility.

Infertility is a sensitive topic, and if not handled well, you can easily cause a serious strain or rift in the relationship between you and the individual or partner. Communications require diplomacy and tact, and your caring support will help them work through this difficult and frustrating experience.

THINGS TO CONSIDER

- Infertility does not discriminate—it strikes all income levels and all races.
- The inability to conceive is a deeply personal experience.
- The relationship you have with the individual or partner.
- Did you have difficulty getting pregnant?
- Do you have children? If so, are they biological or adopted?
- Moods and emotions may be erratic as a result of infertility medications.

EMOTIONS AND FEELINGS TO ANTICIPATE

- Anger
- Anxiousness
- Confusion
- Depression
- Desperation
- Embarrassment
- Failure
- Frustration
- Guilt
- Isolation
- Jealousy
- Longing
- Misery
- Obsessiveness
- Sadness
- Vulnerability

WHAT TO SAY AND DO

- Do be understanding and supportive.

- Do make yourself available to listen. If the individual shares his or her feelings, be empathetic.

- Do be thoughtful if continued infertility is causing stress and depression. Lift their spirits with movie tickets for two, a gift certificate to a spa, or a CD from their favorite artist.

> ↪ You can demonstrate support if they are going through medical procedures by offering to take them to physician appointments or bringing dinner the night of a procedure.

- Do understand if the couple is sensitive or uncomfortable in attending baby showers or family events that focus on pregnancy and babies.

- Do offer the couple the opportunity to attend an event late or leave early so they can make a quick "cameo" appearance.

- Do understand if they choose not to attend.

HOW TO SAY IT

Go ahead and cry; I'll stay with you.

How would you like me to be there for you?

I would like to support you; please let me know how I can be there for you.

If you need me, I am here for you.

It must be hard to go through this.

There is always hope.

What can I do that will help you?

You can talk to me; I care.

WHAT NOT TO SAY AND DO

- Don't ask a childless couple "When do you plan to have children?"

- Don't initiate conversations on infertility; always take your cues from the couple.

- Don't downplay the problem by telling them "At least you have each other and your health" or "Thank goodness you already have a child."

- Don't give any unsolicited advice on how to get pregnant or recommendations of unproven techniques such as herbal remedies or sexual timing.

- Don't tell them to relax or suggest their intense focus on pregnancy is causing them unnecessary stress.

- Don't tell personal stories about your own fertility, such as "I got pregnant both times I tried."

- Don't second-guess their physician by telling them medical techniques to pursue; assume they have conducted research and are using a competent medical professional.

- Don't blame them for their infertility.

- Don't tell them anything that might make them feel guilty, such as "You should have tried sooner."

- Don't pressure a woman to attend any event that makes her feel uncomfortable and is a reminder that she is not pregnant.

- Don't share stories about other couples who either failed to become pregnant or who successfully became pregnant; these stories won't make them feel better.

- Don't express negative opinions on fertility treatments and adoption; these might be their best alternatives to have a child.

HOW NOT TO SAY IT

All I have to do is look at my husband and I get pregnant.

Don't be so blue.

Go away for a romantic weekend.

My friend adopted a baby, and she got pregnant right away.

Take a cruise.

When are you going to have your next one?

Whose fault is it you can't get pregnant?

You are trying too hard.

You need to relax.

Special Situations

It took my cousin years before she was able to conceive, and her daughter is now five years old. I think she might be experiencing infertility again and I would like to be supportive.

She might have made the choice to have an only child. Or she might be experiencing secondary infertility. She has not mentioned anything to you about the subject, so I would keep quiet. She will initiate a conversation if and when she wants to discuss this with you.

My co-worker has completed her third attempt at in vitro fertilization, and this last attempt failed like the others.

Your co-worker is terribly disappointed and needs your support. This is not the time to give advice or opinions concerning fertility methods or even adoption. She and her partner need to make their own decision on what path to choose. Let her know that you care about her and will support whatever decision she makes. The decision to pursue further fertility treatments is a decision only your friend and her partner can make.

SAMPLE LETTER/E-MAIL

To a friend who has just confided that she has been unable to conceive.

> January X, 2XXX
> Dear Elizabeth:
>
> My thoughts have been with you all morning. Thank you so much for sharing your feelings and experiences with me yesterday.
> Now I understand better how difficult this has been for you and Bill. I will be here for you in any way I can. Know that I am praying that things will work out and your dreams will come true. You are always in my heart.
>
> Love,
> Kate

For further information:

Domar, Alice D., Ph.D., and Alice Lesch Kelly. *Conquering Infertility: Dr. Alice Domar's Mind/Body Guide to Enhancing Fertility and Coping with Infertility.* New York, NY: Viking Press, 2002.

Indichova, Julia. *Inconceivable: A Woman's Triumph over Despair and Statistics.* New York, NY: Broadway Books, 2001.

Marrs, Richard, M.D., Lisa Friedman Bloch, and Kathy Kirtland Silverman, *Dr. Richard Marrs' Fertility Book: America's Leading Infertility Expert Tells You Everything You Need to Know About Getting Pregnant.* New York, NY: Dell Books, 1998.

The Staff of *Resolve* and Diane Aronson. *Resolving Infertility.* New York, NY: HarperCollins Publishers, 2001.

Zouves, Christo, and Julie Sullivan, cont. *Expecting Miracles: On the Path of Hope from Infertility to Parenthood.* New York, NY: Henry Holt & Company, 1999.

American Society for Reproductive Medicine

(Formerly The American Fertility Society)
1209 Montgomery Highway
Birmingham, AL 35216-2809
(205) 978-5000
www.asrm.org

CDC's Reproductive Health Information Source
Division of Reproductive Health
National Center for Chronic Disease Prevention and Health Promotion
Centers for Disease Control and Prevention
4770 Buford Highway, NE, Mail Stop K-20
Atlanta, GA 30341-3717
(770) 488-5200

MEDLINE plus Health Information—Infertility
A Service of the U.S. National Library of Medicine and the National Institutes of Health
www.nlm.nih.gov/medlineplus/infertility.html

RESOLVE, Inc.
National Headquarters
1310 Broadway
Somerville, MA 02144
(888) 623-0744
www.resolve.org

See also: WHAT IS GRIEF? UNDERSTANDING THE PROCESS OF MOURNING AND HOW YOU CAN HELP, WHAT CAN I SAY? COMMUNICATIONS THAT COMFORT, and WHAT CAN I DO? HOW TO LISTEN.

TWENTY

Adoption

∞

"An 'adoptive parent' is a special kind of person.
Not just any grown-up can be one."

—Carole Livingston, *Why Was I Adopted?*

As parents of adopted children will tell you, adoption is just another way to form a family. Individuals and couples choose adoption for a variety of reasons, but primarily because they want to love and share their life with a child and raise that child as their own.

Married couples might choose to adopt because they can't have a child together, or because they already have a child and want to give another child a home and a family. Single adults might choose to adopt because they want to be a parent and feel they can raise a child on their own. In stepfamilies, a stepparent can adopt the child or children of their spouse. And in some instances, a family member adopts a child who was parented by another family member.

The joys and challenges of parenting are the same for adoptive families as they are for biological families. Approximately 120,000 children are adopted annually, and the number has remained consistent through the last decade. Slightly less than half of all adoptions are *related adoptions,* meaning children were adopted by stepparents or other family members.

Chances are that you know someone who is adopted. About 1.5 million children in the United States reside with adoptive parents—approximately 2 percent of all children age eighteen and under. More than 7 million adopted individuals of all ages live in the United States.

A survey conducted by the Adoption Institute found that 60 percent of Americans have had a personal experience with adoption; either they or a family member or close friend was adopted, they themselves had adopted, or they had placed a child for adoption. Approximately one third of the country—close to 100 million Americans—has adoption within their immediate family.

Parents have begun looking to other countries to adopt healthy babies and children. Between the years 1971 and 2001, 265,677 children from other countries were adopted by U.S. citizens. International adoptions have more than doubled in the last eleven years, from 9,000 in 1991 to 20,099 in 2002.

The U.S. State Department reported that more children were adopted from abroad in 2002 than in any year since records were kept. China led all countries for the third consecutive year in U.S. adoptions; the top eight countries include China, 5,053; Russia, 4,939; Guatemala, 2,219; South Korea, 1,779; Ukraine, 1,106; Kazakhstan, 819; Vietnam, 766; and India, 466.

A new family addition is a time for joy, but a period of adjustment follows the excitement. They will need your help and support during this transitional period.

THINGS TO CONSIDER

- Adoption is another way to be a family; adopting or being adopted is just different, not second-best.

- Insensitive attention or questions, no matter how well intentioned, can hurt adopted children, their siblings, and their parents.

- Families who adopt a child from a foreign country do so to build a family; the adopted children become their "own" children.

EMOTIONS AND FEELINGS TO ANTICIPATE

- Anxiety
- Apprehensiveness
- Excitement
- Fear
- Gratefulness
- Happiness
- Joy
- Nervousness
- Relief
- Uncertainty
- Vulnerability

WHAT TO SAY AND DO

■ Congratulate the parent(s).

■ Just as you might inquire about the due date of an expectant mother, it's okay to ask prospective adoptive parents if they have information about the arrival, such as "Do you have any idea when this will happen?"

■ If you know someone who has adopted children from the same type of agency or the same country, you can ask "Would you like to meet another international family?" or "Would you like to know another family who adopted privately?" But don't be offended if the parent(s) don't accept your offer; it is a period of vulnerability that leaves the parent(s) exhilarated but emotionally drained while waiting for a child to be offered and waiting for the child to arrive. The parent(s) might wish to keep this time private.

> ↶ If the adoption requirements necessitate the family traveling to and possibly staying in a foreign country to await the adoption, ask what you can do for them while they are away. You can take care of the mail, the newspaper, watering the plants, or any other household chores.

■ Familiarize yourself with the adoption process so you will understand how the adoption is proceeding, how you can help, and what it's all about.

■ Send flowers if that's what you would do for the birth of a baby.

■ Write cards and notes of congratulations.

■ Choose a gift appropriate for the child's age.

■ Offer to bring lunch or a dinner.

> ↶ Be specific in asking how you can help. Letters of recommendation may be part of the adoption process, and you can offer to write a letter on their behalf. If photographs are required, you can offer to take and print the photographs.

■ Do refer to the child as their daughter or their son; avoid describing them as their "adopted daughter" or "adopted son."

■ If the parent(s) adopt a child from another race, be sensitive in your comments.

- Do approach the family with kindness and accept them as a family. Avoid asking any questions that make the parents and children feel uncomfortable. Parents and children want to be accepted for what they are—a family—and they do not enjoy being questioned about personal matters.

HOW TO SAY IT

How are you feeling?

How can I help?

How exciting!

I am so happy for you!

I can't wait to meet him (her).

That's terrific!

This is great!

What can I do to help?

What lucky parents to have such a wonderful child.

What wonderful news!

> ᔕ Before you say anything to a parent of an adopted child, ask yourself if this is appropriate commentary for a parent of a biological child. If you would say the same thing to a parent of a biological child, then it is probably appropriate to say to a parent of an adopted child.

WHAT NOT TO SAY AND DO

- Don't imply that an adopted child is not quite as good or is second-best to a biological child.

- Don't relate horror stories that you might have heard about adoption in general or adoption from a particular country or source; rest assured that the parent(s) have investigated and weighed all sources of information.

- Don't ask intimate questions about the child's history, such as "So what is the story with the birthparents?" or "Was he (she) abandoned?"

- Don't ask questions on any facet of the adoption or their child's heritage in front of the child.

- Avoid comments that imply the parents "saved" the child they adopted. In that same vein, don't describe the parents as selfless or saints; they adopted this child because they wanted to be a family.

- Don't express negative opinions or your personal concerns about adoption.

- There are certain ways of referring to adoptive family members that you should avoid; don't refer to the child's birth parents as the "real parents," and don't refer to the child that is adopted as an "orphan" or as an "unwanted" child.

> ๛ Outdated language needs to be replaced with a more modern vocabulary that will protect an adopted child's privacy and preserve their self-esteem. The "parents" are the parents who are raising the child and the "birth parents" are the child's biological parents.

- Don't suggest friends or family members who are interested in adoption call someone you know who is in the process of adopting. Individuals going through the adoption process are dealing with many emotions and fears, and it is important to respect their privacy during the adoption process.

- Many children experience problems during different phases of their development. If someone's adopted child is having difficulty, don't inquire "Do you think that behavior is related to their adoption?"

- Do not ask parents of young international children if their child has characteristics of the parent country, such as "Does your child speak Korean?" or "Is he a Communist?"

HOW NOT TO SAY IT

Are they real sisters?

Are those kids really yours?

Aren't you nice for doing that.

Can you love this child as much as you would your own?

Can't you have a child of your own?

Do you have children of your own?

Do your kids know they are adopted?

How could the real mother give him (her) away?

How much did it cost?

How much did you pay for the child?

Is she yours?

What happens if you have natural children?

Why did you do that?

You are doing these kids such a favor.

NONVERBAL STRATEGIES

Sometimes, the parents have little notice that a child is available. In some cases, the parents might not be ready for the child, and there are a number of things you can do to help out.

- Offer to purchase the basic necessities such as diapers, wipes, bottles, formula, baby food, and other sundry items.

- Volunteer to arrange or pick up furniture for the nursery or to help set up the nursery.

- Offer to loan the prospective parents equipment such as a stroller, car seat, high chair, or age-appropriate clothing.

Special Situations

My friend's adoption fell through.
This is a painfully disappointing experience. Call your friend and tell them how sorry you are. If they are not accepting phone calls, write a note. Let them know that you care and will be there for them however they might need you. Offer to visit and be willing to sit with them and listen. Avoid telling them there will be

another chance and another child; they need to grieve for the child they have already taken into their hearts.

My friend and her husband entered into a private adoption. They had the baby for three weeks and then the birth mother changed her mind and took custody of the baby.
Your friend and her husband are devastated. They loved this baby, and they will need to grieve for their loss. Treat this situation like you would a death, with the same thoughtfulness, compassion, and kindness. Your friends will need time and patience to heal from this experience.

My friend adopted a child from Russia, and the child has health problems that require several surgeries.
Your friend is feeling blessed to have this child, and you should focus your efforts on welcoming and celebrating this new addition to the family. Offer your congratulations and emphasize the joy this child brings, responding in the same way you do for any new baby. You can send a card or a gift, bring a meal, or do something special for your friend. Your friend is not looking for sympathy, but he or she could probably use some help when the child is hospitalized. Be specific in offering help—volunteer to do some grocery shopping, bring a meal, provide child care or carpooling (if there is a sibling), and run errands.

SAMPLE LETTERS/E-MAILS

From an acquaintance, a gift of an Asian baby doll in a traditional red dress, in celebration of the adoption of a baby daughter born in Korea.

> October X, 2XXX
> Dear Margaret and John:
>
> Red is the color of joy and happiness according to Eastern culture. The birth of a baby is celebrated by passing out red-dyed eggs, and the newborn is dressed in red. I know Suzanne has brought you much joy and will continue to do so. Congratulations! I hope she will enjoy this doll.
>
> Fondly,
> Debbie, Bill, Lisa, and Hillary

From a family friend on the adoption of a son.

> May X, 2XXX
> Dear Maggie and Griffin:
>
> Just got a call from Charlie Jones with the good news of your baby son, Jason. So very delighted for you both—and, of course, our wishes for a wonderful life together always.
>
> I am sure you are both thrilled and Jason is blessed to have such terrific parents. Please give him a big kiss for us.
>
> Much love,
> Dorothy and Jack

For additional information:

Adamec, Chris. *The Complete Idiot's Guide to Adoption.* Indianapolis, IN: Alpha Books, 1998.

Johnston, Patricia Irwin. *Adopting After Infertility.* Indianapolis, IN: Perspectives Press, 1996.

Register, Cherie. *Are Those Kids Yours?* New York, NY: Free Press, 1990.

Van Gulden, Holly, and Lisa M. Bartels-Rabb. *Real Parents, Real Children: Parenting the Adopted Child.* New York, NY: Crossroad, 1995.

The National Adoption Center
1500 Walnut Street, Suite 701
Philadelphia, PA 19102
(800) TO-ADOPT
www.adopting.org

National Adoption Center's Learning Center offers a variety of online adoption education, information, and support services.
www.adoptnet.org

For comprehensive resources on all aspects of adoption:
The National Adoption Information Clearinghouse
330 C Street SW
Washington, DC 20447

(703) 352-3488 or (888) 251-0075
www.naic.acf.hhs.gov/index.cfm

RESOLVE, Inc.
National Headquarters
1310 Broadway
Somerville, MA 02144
(888) 623-0744
www.resolve.org

Especially for children:

Krementz, Jill. *How It Feels to Be Adopted.* New York, NY: Alfred A. Knopf, 1988.

Livingston, Carole. *Why Was I Adopted?* New York, NY: Carol Publishing Group, 1997.

Watkins, Mary, and Susan Fisher. *Talking with Young Children About Adoption.* New Haven, CT: Yale University Press, 1995.

TWENTY-ONE

Baby or Child with Special Needs

∞

*"Friends in your life are like pillars on your porch. Sometimes
they hold you up, and sometimes they lean on you. Sometimes it's just
enough to know they're standing by."*

—Anonymous

Most of us go into parenthood with great expectations; we long to share our love with our offspring and nurture them through a healthy and happy childhood. But this dream is not always a reality. It can be devastating for parents to learn that their dearly anticipated baby or child may be disabled and require a lifetime of special care.

The Maternal and Child Health Bureau estimates that 18 million children in the United States have "special health needs." And although these babies and children are special and beloved, the challenges to parenting can be exhausting and overwhelming.

Children with special health needs are defined as all children who have, or are at increased risk for, chronic physical, developmental, behavioral, or emotional challenges. These children will require health and related services of a type or amount beyond the normal requirements of children.

Approximately 18 percent of children have significant chronic conditions, and they consume 60 to 70 percent of the health-care resources spent on children. Examples of chronic conditions include asthma, cancer, autism, cerebral palsy, depression, and complications of prematurity. Care for these children requires coordination between primary and specialty health-care systems, schools, child care, early intervention programs, and community services.

Parenting the special needs child offers many rewards, but parents must first acknowledge that their dreams might be altered, postponed, or no longer possible. They might grieve for what they will not have the opportunity to experience—the typical childhood that might never be and the life that might be very different than the one they envisioned. They must work through this grief while dealing with difficult issues as they strive to ensure appropriate medical and developmental services for their child.

While raising a child with special needs is not the life the parent(s) dreamed, this different life will provide ample opportunities for childhood achievements. You can help support them by remaining a consistent presence in their lives. They will continue to need assistance and companionship throughout their child's life.

THINGS TO CONSIDER

- Parent(s) will spend a tremendous amount of time and energy mapping out diagnostic plans and new life, educational, and medical goals.

- Parent(s) will be sleep deprived, but especially so in the first year.

- Parent(s) might be severely impaired in maintaining almost any segment of their lives.

- The parents' relationship will meet unremitting stress and test every aspect of their relationships.

- Friends will need to understand that the difficult constraints will shift the balance of the relationship. The parent(s) will want and need to continue the friendship, but friends will need to expend 75 percent of the initiative with the parent(s) expending the other 25 percent.

- The parents' financial resources might be stretched to a point that previous expected and/or typical expenditures may end up being delayed, postponed, or eliminated.

- Parents will experience tremendous fear for what the future holds, the unknown parameters of the parents' altered life, and what will happen to the child when the parents die.

- Despite the inherent stresses, there will be pride and joy at different milestones, and even the simplest accomplishments are a cause for rejoicing.

EMOTIONS AND FEELINGS TO ANTICIPATE

- Anger
- Anxiety
- Fear
- Grief
- Happiness
- Hurt
- Jealousy

- Joy
- Love
- Pride
- Regret
- Resentment
- Sadness

WHAT TO SAY AND DO

- Do call rather than write a note; parents feel isolated, and they might falsely assume you are uncomfortable and avoiding them if you chose to write rather than call.

- Express your love for the child now and in the future.

- Do encourage the parent(s) to get a second opinion.

- Do let the parent(s) know it is okay to challenge the diagnosis and the doctor.

- Do let the parent(s) know it is okay to change doctors if the relationship is not working, and it is okay to get professional health-care assistance.

- Do ease any guilt by making them aware that what works for one family doesn't work for every family.

- Do bring a meal.

- Ask questions about the child's progress on a regular basis.

> ☞ Solicit a sign-up sheet to deliver meals from members of the neighborhood, congregants, parents and faculty at the school, and any other club, institution, business, or organization that has a relationship with the family.

- Do take your cues and talk if they would like or be quiet together if they do not choose to talk.

- Encourage your relationship and a dialogue.

- Be persistent; the parent(s) might be insecure or uncomfortable participating in social activities and events, but keep asking.

- Engage any related faith-based organization for all types of support.

> ✒ Include siblings in activities and special events so they won't get lost in the shuffle.

- Ease the stress by offering to partner in any form of exercise; it is always easier to stay on an exercise regimen if someone is there to keep you on track.

- Offer to come to the house, answer the phone, and maintain some order while they take a nap.

- Understand and respect the necessary and existing boundaries.

- Share and take pride in the child's accomplishments.

- Encourage hobbies and special interests by ordering them a gift subscription to a hobby magazine or gift certificate to a hobby or craft store for a hobby or special interest they either enjoy or would like to pursue.

- If siblings are not in a support group, find information for them on local groups available for their special needs.

- Recommend that parents communicate with their police department and fire department that there is a child with special needs in the home.

- Suggest the child wear an identification bracelet should he (she) become separated from the caregiver.

- Do understand that holidays are especially stressful; they alter routines, and routines are necessary for a child with special needs.

- Do ask what you can do to make holidays less stressful.

- Do offer to do the traveling during holidays and try to accommodate the family in any way you can.

HOW TO SAY IT

Give yourself some time.

I don't know what you are going through, but you are in my heart and prayers.

I have a few free hours; can I come over and do (laundry, grocery shopping, etc.)?

It's okay to hope for more.

This is really hard.

This must be really rough for you.

We love you all; nothing will change that.

WHAT NOT TO SAY AND DO

- Don't ignore the family.

- Don't pretend it hasn't happened or act as if nothing is wrong; avoid comments such as "He'll grow out of it" or "I think she is just fine."

- Don't put a label on the child.

- Don't assume that you know the child's status and medical condition.

- Don't take it personally if your invitations are refused.

- Don't let them think they have to reinvent the wheel; encourage them or help them find out what has worked for other parents.

- Don't force conversation; it is okay for the parent(s) not to talk about it.

- Don't second-guess their parenting skills with comments such as "You are not strict enough" or "Don't you think you are being too overprotective?"

HOW NOT TO SAY IT

God will only give you what you can handle.

He (she) can't talk because he has nothing to say.

What do I tell the family?

What kind of life will he (she) have?

When will he (she) be normal?

Will he (she) ever go to school?

Will she (he) need to be institutionalized?

NONVERBAL STRATEGIES

- Offer to go grocery shopping or locate information on grocery delivery services.

- Volunteer to do the laundry.

- Ask for a list of errands to do while running your own.

- Offer to stay in the home while the child is sleeping so the parent can get some relief or run some errands.

- Provide help in researching physicians, medical facilities, articles, and other resources.

- Make a list of who they should be contacting, and locate the contacts for them.

- Help them find appropriate support groups; attend in their place to collect information or, if they are available to attend, go with them for support.

- Locate qualified respite care so they will have backup help and a breather from caregiver responsibilities.

- Do offer to care for another child or children in the family.

- Offer a gift certificate for a cleaning service.

- Provide transportation to medical appointments.

- Accompany the parent(s) to medical appointments; either watch the child while they are getting information or volunteer to take notes; they might not be able to process all the information.

- Encourage them to keep specific milestone, goal, medical, and prescription records.

- Offer to help organize their records or establish a system.

- Suggest maintaining a journal on all the physicians they have seen.

Special Situations

A friend and I had our babies around the same time, and the children played frequently. Her son has recently been diagnosed with autism.
Be persistent in retaining the relationship with your friend, but be aware that your child's milestones might cause her pain. Continue to invite her to outings, but don't be upset if she declines. You might have to work hard to find one special thing that is a successful experience for everyone such as an outing or activity whose physical requirements meet the child's special needs. It will be well worth the effort to preserve your relationship while your child learns appropriate ways to treat another person whose needs and life experience differ from his (her) own.

My cousin has a typically developing child and a child with special needs. Must both children be invited to birthday parties?
Invite both children and let your cousin know that she is welcome to come late or leave early to meet her special child's needs. It would be appropriate for another family member to volunteer to pick up or take home her other child so they can enjoy the full party. If the child with special needs is disruptive and your cousin allows the child to spoil the event, you can extend just one invitation to the nondisruptive child.

My friend has a child with special needs who enjoys going out to dinner. We join them for dinner out once a month, but occasionally an incident occurs involving the child and the adult friend is reprimanded by another adult in public.
Don't let the incident destroy your evening out. I bet your friend has lots of experience dealing with and diffusing these situations. Let her (him) know that the incident was awful; you are sorry it happened, but they handled it well. Be empathetic and let them know that you think they are doing a great job. You need to

be supportive of your friend, and if you are uncomfortable in these situations, find another way to spend time together.

For further information:

Klein, Stanley D., Ph.D., and Kim Schive, eds. *You Will Dream New Dreams: Inspiring Personal Stories by Parents of Children with Disabilities*. New York, NY: Kensington Publishing Corporation, 2001.

Lavin, Judith Loseff. *Special Kids Need Special Parents: A Resource for Parents of Children with Special Needs*. New York, NY: Berkley Publishing Group, 2001.

Morel, Janet. *Playing the Hand That's Dealt to You: A Guide for Parents of Children with Special Needs*. Melbourne Beach, FL: Canmore Press, 2000.

Naseef, Robert A. *Special Children, Challenged Parents: The Struggles and Rewards of Raising a Child with a Disability*. Baltimore, MD: Paul H. Brookes Publishing Company, 2001.

National Network for Childcare
www.nncc.org

Parenting Special Needs
specialchildren.about.com

Woodbine House
Publishers of the special-needs collection
www.woodbinehouse.com

See also: WHAT IS GRIEF? UNDERSTANDING THE PROCESS OF MOURNING AND HOW YOU CAN HELP, WHAT CAN I SAY? COMMUNICATIONS THAT COMFORT, and WHAT CAN I DO? HOW TO LISTEN.

TWENTY-TWO

Physical Disability

∞

"People seldom refuse help, if one offers it in the right way."

—A. C. Benson

M ANY people feel apprehensive when it comes to interacting with individu-als with physical disabilities. Apprehension is rooted in fear, and it could be that we experience fear in not knowing what to say or do when we encounter someone with a physical disability. Or it might be that persons with disabilities are poignant reminders of life's fragilities. We might fear that we could easily be disabled, too.

Current statistics indicate that approximately 54 million Americans—about one in five—have a disability that interferes with their life activities. Disabilities are expected to impact 50 percent of the population by 2010.

Physical disability is defined by the Americans with Disabilities Act (ADA) as a person who has a physical or mental impairment that substantially limits one or more major life activities. The U.S. Census breaks disability into two categories—sensory disability, which includes blindness, deafness, or severe vision or hearing impairment; and physical disability, which includes a condition that substantially limits one or more basic physical activities such as walking, climb-ing stairs, reaching, lifting, or carrying.

Modern science has improved the quality and longevity of life for those with disabilities, and assistive technology and services have facilitated and enhanced independent living.

A disability can alter or change a person's life, but it doesn't necessarily change the person. You can help support individuals with disabilities by treating them with the same respect and reverence you use for anyone.

THINGS TO CONSIDER

- Some individuals might have genetic disabilities, while others might have become disabled later in life.

- Individuals with disabilities are each unique; they will have diverse skills, abilities, interests, and personalities.

- Individuals with disabilities are like everyone else; they possess the same feelings and emotions as other individuals.

- Individuals might not view their disability as a liability.

EMOTIONS AND FEELINGS TO ANTICIPATE

- Adaptable
- Anger
- Denial
- Despair
- Depression
- Determination
- Fear
- Focused

- Isolation
- Loneliness
- Loss
- Motivated
- Persuasive
- Sadness
- Sensitivity

WHAT TO SAY AND DO

- Relax and behave as you would in any social situation.

- Do communicate in ways that demonstrate respect for the individual's dignity.

- Do give them the freedom to interact and participate in any activity they choose.

- Do use positive rather than negative terms when referring to the individual's abilities; use "She walks with a walker" rather than "She cannot navigate without a walker."

- Do treat the individual the same way you would like to be treated.

- Do take your cues from the individual; if you offer help and they refuse, accept the refusal. If you offer help and they accept, allow them to instruct you how you can best help them.

- If they use an assistive device such as a wheelchair, crutches, a cane, or a walker, ask how you could help them. Do ensure that pathways are clear and accessible for easier access.

- Be specific when asking how you can accommodate them.

- Do let them know the dimensions of doorways and if doorways and entrances to restrooms are accessible. Do give them advance warning if there will be a problem with logistics.

> ⌖ Always consider an alternative, inclusive location.

- Do treat them in the same way you would have treated them before; even if it is awkward to hug them, do so if you hugged them before.

- Speak to them at eye level if you will be speaking for any duration; either sit down on a seat or squat.

- Do take your cues from the individual in inquiring about their disability. Some individuals are comfortable in discussing it; others are not.

> ⌖ If you are going to have an ongoing relationship with this individual, you will need to learn personal information about each other. It's okay to express genuine personal interest; it's not okay to inquire just because you are curious.

CHOOSE WORDS WITH DIGNITY

Basic Guidelines:

Make reference to the person first, then the disability, for example "A person with a disability" rather than "a disabled person."

The following words are affirmative and reflect a positive attitude.	*The following words have strong negative connotations.*
Words with Dignity	**Do Not Use**
Disability	Handicap
Person who has multiple sclerosis	Stricken with multiple sclerosis
Paraplegic (person with limited or no use of lower limbs)	Para
Quadriplegic (person with limited or no use of all four limbs)	Quad
Person who has cerebral palsy	Spastic
Person who has a speech impairment	Speech defect
Person with a head injury	The head injured
Person with AIDS	AIDS victim
Person who has polio, arthritis, etc.	Crippled with polio, arthritis, etc.
Person with mental retardation	Retard
Person with learning disability	Dim witted, slow

Words with Dignity	Do Not Use
Person with a mental disorder	Mentally ill
Person with an emotional disorder	Crazy
Person who is blind, partially blind	Blind guys, visually impaired*
Person who is deaf	Deaf and dumb, deaf mute
Person who is hard of hearing	Hearing impaired*
Sign language interpreter	Deaf interpreter
Born with "_____"	Birth defect
Caused by "_____"	Afflicted by
Nondisabled (referring to nondisabled persons as normal insinuates that disabled persons are not normal)	Normal
Person in a wheelchair	Confined/restricted to a wheelchair**
Person who walks with crutches, a walker, a cane, a limp, etc.	Crippled

*Many blind persons and deaf persons consider the words *visually impaired* and *hearing impaired* offensive. *Blind* simply means without the sense or use of sight. *Deaf* simply means partially or totally unable to hear. They believe these two words describe their situation best. They do not wish to be identified as diminished in strength or value, as the word *impaired* denotes.
**Crutches, walkers, and wheelchairs are mobility aids. Without the use of these mobility aids, the person might be restricted from participation in their community.

Used with permission from Iowa Department of Human Rights, Division of Persons with Disabilities, Des Moines, Iowa.

HOW TO SAY IT

How can I be most helpful?

Please let me know what would make you most comfortable.

What do I need to know about to accommodate your wheelchair?

WHAT NOT TO SAY AND DO

- Don't say a visit or a location will be okay if there are obstacles; let them know up front.

- Don't express pity when speaking to the individual.

- Don't avoid making eye contact or speaking without looking at them.

- Don't touch him or her without permission.

- Don't automatically push their wheelchair or take their arm.

- Avoid asking intimate questions that you would not ask an able-bodied person, such as "How do you eat?" or "How do you use the restroom?"

> ‿ Before you say anything to a person with a disability, ask yourself if this is appropriate commentary for an able-bodied person. If you would say the same thing to an able-bodied person, then it is probably appropriate to say to a person with a disability.

HOW NOT TO SAY IT

Do you mind telling me what happened?

How long have you been handicapped?

I am really amazed at how well you do.

It must be tough to have to use a walker.

It's unfortunate that you are confined to a wheelchair.

You should really be proud of yourself.

Special Situations

I would like to meet a new friend for lunch at a restaurant. He is in a wheelchair, and I want to make it comfortable for him.
Ask your friend whether he prefers sitting in his wheelchair or a regular chair. When you call to make a reservation, let them know that your friend is in a wheelchair and his preferences so they can accommodate you. If they don't take reservations, find out what time you should arrive to limit your wait. Ensure the logistics match your friend's needs, and inquire whether their restroom facilities can accommodate a wheelchair. Ask your friend for any other logistical information to ensure the experience is a good one.

My friend is hard of hearing, and I am unsure how to best communicate.
It's important to speak directly to your friend, as people who are hard of hearing may read lips. Ensure that you continue to look directly at him during your conversation, and avoid walking away while speaking. Understand that you might need to repeat your information; do so in a respectful manner without raising your voice.

SAMPLE LETTERS/E-MAILS

To an uncle who recently had a stroke.

> January X, 2XXX
> Dear Uncle Phil:
>
> Mary has been calling to keep me updated on your progress. I can only imagine how difficult this is for you. Everyone in the family has always said you were the one to tap for the toughest jobs. Little did we know how tough the jobs would become. I know in my heart that if anyone can surmount this challenge, it is you.
>
> I was so very happy to hear that you had regained some movement on your right side. That's the encouragement you need to keep motivated. Mary said both the physical therapist and speech therapist are encouraged.

You are in my prayers constantly, Uncle Phil. I look forward to hearing continued progress. I miss you terribly.

Love,
Jeanette

To a friend whose mother has a disability from a cerebral hemorrhage.

March X, 2XXX
Dear Fran:

You've frequently been in my thoughts and prayers. Although I don't know what you are feeling, I have some idea of what you are experiencing, as I also found it extremely difficult to watch my independent mother go through such massive changes as a result of a cerebral hemorrhage.

The role reversal when a parent is ill is hard. My siblings and I learned to lean on each other, and we rallied for one purpose—my mom's recovery. The reality is that your journey through life has been changed. But you have been given a precious gift: more time together.

Know that I keep you in my prayers. I will check in often and be there for you. Give your mom a big kiss for me. I'll speak to you soon.

Love,
Liz

For further information:

Albrecht, Donna. *Raising a Child Who Has a Physical Disability*. New York, NY: John Wiley & Sons, 1995.

Formulated by the Committee on Handicaps, Group for the Advancement of Psychiatry. *Caring for People with Physical Impairment*. Washington, DC: American Psychiatric Press, 1993.

Meyer, Donald J, ed. *Uncommon Fathers—Reflections on Raising a Child with a Disability*. Bethesda, MD: Woodbine House, 1995.

Mouth Magazine
Voice of the Disability Nation
P.O. Box 558

Topeka, KS 66601
www.mouthmag.com

The Ragged Edge
Ragged Edge magazine and Ragged Edge online are publications of The Advocado Press, Inc., a nonprofit 501(c)3 organization founded in 1981 to publish materials on disability rights.
www.ragged-edge-mag.com

Disability and Business Technical Assistance Centers (DBTACs)
A comprehensive resource for information on the Americans with Disabilities Act.
www.adata.org/dbtac.html

ILUSA
Directory of Independent Living Centers in the United States, typically nonresidential, private, nonprofit, consumer-controlled, community-based organizations providing services and advocacy by and for persons with all types of disabilities. Their goal is to assist individuals with disabilities to achieve their maximum potential within their families and communities.
www.ilusa.com/links/ilcenters.htm

Let's Face It
A nonprofit network that links people with facial disfigurement and all who care for them to resources that can enrich their lives.
www.faceit.org

National Council on Disability
1331 F Street, NW, Suite 1050
Washington, DC 20004
(202) 272-2004 or TTY number (202) 272-2074
www.ncd.gov

National Information Center for Children and Youth with Disabilities
P.O. Box 1492
Washington, DC 20013
(800) 695-0285, voice and TTY or (202) 884-8200, voice and TTY
www.nichcy.org

Woodbine House
Publishers of the special-needs collection.
www.woodbinehouse.com

Especially for children:
Krementz, Jill. *How It Feels to Live with a Physical Disability*. New York, NY: Simon & Schuster, 1992.

See also: WHAT IS GRIEF? UNDERSTANDING THE PROCESS OF MOURNING AND HOW YOU CAN HELP, WHAT CAN I SAY? COMMUNICATIONS THAT COMFORT, and WHAT CAN I DO? HOW TO LISTEN.

TWENTY-THREE

Separation

∞

"Friends are made by many acts—and lost by only one."

—Anonymous

MARITAL separation ranks as one of the top three most stressful life events, after death and divorce. When couples separate, whether they plan to divorce or not, they begin a period of enormous change that necessitates a life-altering and restructuring process. Separation might come as a couple prepares to divorce, or the couple might not yet have reached that decision but are taking a break to see if they can repair the marital relationship.

Separation is an emotional time for both spouses, and although the emotions might not be as extreme as those experienced during divorce, they are very similar.

The couple enters a period of uncertainty while they must deal with the process of loss, day-to-day challenges, and problems such as changes in housing, finances, relationships, potential return to the workforce, or child care.

During this period of uncertainty and upheaval, your companionship and support will help restore stability in their lives.

THINGS TO CONSIDER

- Couples must address and deal with multiple losses such as loss of roles, security, and sense of self.

- The length of the marriage has no correlation to the depth of pain and loss separating couples experience.

- Separations might occur as a result of infidelity. The word *infidelity* conjures images of extramarital affairs, but an emotional attraction and

bond with another individual can be just as damaging to the marital relationship as a sexual relationship.

- Separation and infidelity do not necessarily mean the end of a relationship. Couples can repair and heal their relationships.

EMOTIONS AND FEELINGS TO ANTICIPATE

- Agitation
- Anger
- Betrayal
- Bewilderment
- Blame
- Confusion
- Denial
- Depression
- Disappointment
- Disbelief
- Embarrassment
- Emotional turmoil
- Fear

- Guilt
- Hurt
- Loneliness
- Numbness
- Pain
- Panic
- Rage
- Resentment
- Self-blame
- Shame
- Shock
- Vulnerability

WHAT TO SAY AND DO

- Remain objective, even if they try to draw you in.

- Listen and allow the speaker to vent.

- Your job is to provide support, not to comment on their angry and sometimes hostile observations or feelings about their spouse.

> ↜ Accept what they share and what they don't. They might not choose to share with you, and this is okay.

- Encourage them to share their emotions when it feels safe and comfortable; individuals must experience the
full range of grieving emotions to
heal.

- Suggest that they take some time to think through their feelings and
avoid making quick decisions on what they will do.

- Bring a meal or take them out to eat. Loss of appetite is very common, and they will need optimal health to work through this difficult and stressful experience.

- Include him or her in your holiday plans.

- Offer to help with child care.

- If you live nearby, help the children maintain neighborhood contacts by offering your home as the designated household for the children to play. Do this only if you will not be in the middle of custody issues.

- Respect their privacy and right for confidentiality; they might not want to make the separation public knowledge.

- Offer to help them pack, relocate, and get settled.

- Include the separated spouse in social activities such as dinners out and the movies.

HOW TO SAY IT

Can I call you next week?

How are you doing?

I am available to support you; don't hesitate to call me.

I am here if you want to talk.

I care about you.

I miss you.

I really don't know how you feel.

I will not repeat anything you say.

It's okay to feel sad. I feel sad, too.

Let me know what I can help you with.

Let's get together for coffee on Friday.

Please keep in touch.

Take all the time you need.

What can I do to help?

You can count on me.

WHAT NOT TO SAY AND DO

- Don't initiate the subject of divorce. If they want to speak about it, they will initiate the conversation.

- Don't take sides.

- Don't try to place the blame on anyone.

- Avoid saying negative things about the spouse. The couple might reconcile, and this will cause hard feelings.

- Don't play favorites.

- Avoid passing judgment.

- Don't ask for details.

- Don't suggest that they move on; they will make adjustments and move at their own pace.

- Don't fix them up with a date.

- Don't recommend a divorce attorney unless you are asked to help find one.

- Don't tell them what to do.

- Don't try and rush them through the grieving and recovery process.

- Don't measure how they are doing with someone else; everyone has their own unique way of resolving their problems, coping, and healing.

HOW NOT TO SAY IT

Didn't you see it coming?

Drop him (her).

Have you been to counseling?

He (she) was a philanderer all along.

How could you leave Sally and the children?

I never really trusted him (her).

I predicted this all along.

I told you it was never going to work.

If that's what you think will make you happy . . .

It's about time.

This is a good thing to do.

You don't deserve this.

You should have left him (her) long ago.

You should have listened to me.

Special Situations

My neighbors are separating, and I would like to retain both friendships. My children are close friends with their children.
Keep in touch with both individuals to let them know you value their friendship. Ask them how they are doing, and include them separately in family events. Inquire if they would like to be included when the other spouse is included in neighborhood social occasions. Use the children as an opening and an opportunity to continue the relationships. See the adults separately.

My spouse and I went to dinner with friends. During dinner, the husband forced his wife to confess that she is having an affair. How should my spouse and I handle the relationship with the husband, the wife, and as couples?
Sometimes the best response is no response; treat it as if it never happened. If you feel the need to help, ask the wife and husband (separately) what you can do. They might need a friend to listen or a recommendation for a good therapist.

SAMPLE LETTERS/E-MAILS

To a neighborhood friend who has separated and moved out of her home.

January X, 2XXX
Dear Liz:

I wanted to let you know that John and I are both sorry to hear about your separation from Josh. I know things are up in the air for you, but when I said I was here to help you in any way, I meant it.

It must have been very difficult for you to make the decision to move out. We are available to help you with the physical move next week; you can use our van and our muscle (or lack thereof!).

I know you are worried about the kids. Bill has already told Matt that his mom and dad are separating and his mom will be moving to a townhouse where he will live part-time. I have told Matt that Bill might seem to be doing okay but he needs his friends now and he must be supportive and extra nice to him.

While you and Josh work out the logistics of the separation, please keep in mind that I am willing to help watch the kids. All you have to do is call, and I will be happy to help.

You mentioned your concern about feeling lonely when you won't have the kids. That could be a time when we do some fun things together. Let me think of some ideas for the next time we speak.

Take care of yourself, Liz. I will call you soon.

Love,
Cate

To a friend who has been separated for several months.

June X, 2XXX
Dear Michelle:

I was cutting flowers from the garden yesterday and came upon the pink rosebush you gave me for my birthday several years ago. It was full of blooms, and as I cut them, I thought of you and the wonderful friendship we have shared.

Even though we haven't seen each other in a while, I think of you often. I understand your desire for space and the time to sort through all the changes in your life. I would love to see you and will continue to keep in touch. No matter how you might need me, I will be here for you.

For now, the scent of these beautiful roses will keep you close to me.

With love,
Allison

For further information:

Brown, Emily M. *Affairs: A Guide to Working Through the Repercussions of Infidelity*. San Francisco, CA: Jossey-Bass, 1999.

Davis, Laura. *I Thought We'd Never Speak Again: The Road from Estrangement to Reconciliation*. New York, NY: HarperCollins Publishers, 2002.

Harley, Dr. Willard F., Jr., and Dr. Jennifer Harley Chalmers. *Surviving an Affair*. Grand Rapids, MI: Fleming H. Revell Co., 1998.

Lusterman, Don-David, Ph.D. *Infidelity: A Survival Guide*. Oakland, CA: New Harbinger Publications, 1998.

Perry, Susan K. *Loving in Flow: How the Happiest Couples Get and Stay That Way*. Naperville, IL: Sourcebooks, Inc., 2003.

Spring, Janis Abrahms, Ph.D. *After the Affair: Healing the Pain and Rebuilding Trust When a Partner Has Been Unfaithful*. New York, NY: HarperCollins Publishers, 1996.

Viorst, Judith. *Grown-Up Marriage: What We Know, Wish We Had Known, and Still Need to Know About Being Married*. New York, NY: Simon & Schuster, 2003.

Weiner-Davis, Michelle. *Divorce Busting*. New York, NY: Summit Books, 1992.

See also: WHAT IS GRIEF? UNDERSTANDING THE PROCESS OF MOURNING AND HOW YOU CAN HELP, WHAT CAN I SAY? COMMUNICATIONS THAT COMFORT, WHAT CAN I DO? HOW TO LISTEN, and DIVORCE.

TWENTY-FOUR

Divorce

∞

"Divorce is the psychological equivalent of a
triple coronary bypass."

—Mary Kay Blakely, *American Mom*

T HE dissolution of a marriage ranks as one of the most disruptive and difficult experiences, second only to the death of a spouse. Although death is a devastating experience for the surviving spouse, the bereaved usually find a wellspring of support in the community. Not so for divorcing spouses, who must go through a similar grieving process and life-changing adjustments, often with little community support.

The National Center for Health Statistics reports that 43 percent of first marriages end in separation or divorce within fifteen years. Despite the frequency of divorce, many individuals feel tremendous pain and shame and might delay telling family and friends. This tumultuous period leaves many feeling shaken, unsettled, and disoriented. The Centers for Disease Control and Prevention report higher mortality rates, more health problems, and increased frequency of risky behaviors such as drug and alcohol use after divorce.

Divorce is a major transition as individuals sever ties from their past, restructure their lives, and refashion their relationships. It might be a surprise to learn that both partners, whether they initiated the divorce or not, go through a grieving and adjustment process. For the partner who initiates the divorce and leaves, it is still a massive undertaking. Years later, some still recount painful feelings of guilt for the grief they caused their partner. For the partner who did not initiate the divorce, it can be crippling.

Many people feel a sense of failure, reliving experiences and trying to discern what went wrong. They might exert great energy analyzing past situations and actions, trying to figure out if they had said or done something different or made other choices they might have saved the marriage. They might endure sleeplessness, anger, and agitation as they try to determine who or what is to blame.

Divorce is not just the loss of the marriage; it often means the end of a lifestyle, shared relationships, financial security, future plans, and the family home. Partners lose not only a spouse, but often relationships with the spouse's family. This sad experience turns sadder when family members feel the need to take sides and once-loving family relationships turn sour.

The process of coupling leads to a merged identity, and once that couple ceases to exist, so does that identity. In an unsettled and disoriented state, individuals must find fresh identities that reflect their new status.

An adjustment to the magnitude of these changes is extremely difficult, and mental health professionals predict it takes a minimum of two years to heal from a divorce. However, each person reacts differently; for some this recovery period could take longer, and for others, shorter.

Individuals must allow themselves the time to grieve for the end of their relationship and work through the anger, sadness, fear, and sorrow. Under this cloud of stress, they might experience emotions that frighten them and their loved ones; some withdraw from family and friends and deliberately isolate themselves.

Individuals will need support from their family, friends, co-workers, and neighbors during this time period but especially during the first several months.

THINGS TO CONSIDER

- Two and a half million individuals divorce each year.

- Life will never be the same for these individuals.

- Dreams and relationships are lost.

- Forty-five percent of females have a drop in their standard of living after a divorce.

EMOTIONS AND FEELINGS TO ANTICIPATE

- Anger
- Anxiety
- Bitterness
- Blame

- Confusion
- Denial
- Depression
- Fear
- Guilt
- Hurt
- Inadequacy
- Insecurity
- Jealousy
- Loneliness
- Loss
- Pain
- Panic
- Rage
- Resentment

WHAT TO SAY AND DO

- Reassure them that they are not a failure.

- Make overtures to include them in social activities to reduce their isolation and boost their morale.

- Offer to help with meals and child care to provide stability; the transitional period before and after a divorce is particularly disorienting.

- Reassure them that anger is a very normal response, but suggest they channel their anger in positive ways such as talking it out with a friend or in a support group setting.

> ↬ An excellent way to redirect the anger is through physical activity such as aerobic exercise, jogging, walking, gardening, or painting.

- Allow them the time to become an independent, single person.

- Inquire if there is a difficult activity or chore you can help them with or get them started on.

- Suggest joining an exercise class and offer to attend with them or provide child care so they can attend.

- Recommend they keep a journal to vent emotions and establish goals. It will be helpful to maintain a steady course in their healing process and to gauge how they progress.

- Invite them to your home for a home-cooked meal and your good company.

- Introduce them to some of your friends and acquaintances to foster new relationships.

- Encourage them to share their feelings and vent their emotions.

- If there are children, volunteer to take them for a special activity to give the parent a break.

- Offer to help with carpooling. If the custodial parent is working, let them know you are available for extra turns in carpooling until they feel more comfortable in their new situation.

> ↝ Do remember them with a card on Valentine's Day or any other special holiday such as Easter, Passover, Halloween, or Thanksgiving.

- Initiate a steady date for coffee, a manicure, or a game of racquetball or tennis to offer friendship and reestablish routines.

- If you are available, volunteer to help with child care on a regular basis to ease the transition and provide some stress relief.

- Recommend they pursue participation in support groups where they can vent their feelings with individuals who share common experiences. Check your local

> ↝ An offer of child care in case of emergency is reassuring.

newspaper calendars or contact social service agencies for referrals.

- Encourage them to find a support group specifically for children if there are children involved. It will be a big relief for the child(ren) to know that this has happened to other children and they are not alone.

HOW TO SAY IT

Consider me your support person; just let me know what I can do to help.

How can I help you?

I am here for you in any way you need me.

I am here to listen anytime you would like to talk.

I am so sorry this has happened.

I love you and will support you through this.

It's okay to be angry.

Please come and share dinner with me (us).

This must be very painful for you.

You're doing great.

WHAT NOT TO SAY AND DO

- Don't make negative comments about the spouse; be aware that negative comments about the spouse reflect also on children.

- Don't give your opinions.

- Don't judge them.

- Don't tell them what to do.

- Don't comment on anyone's behavior.

- Don't take the other spouse's side.

- Don't tell the partner to stop complaining and get on with their life.

- Don't throw away the photos with the divorcing spouse; ask the partner how they feel or put them away until emotions die down.

- Be very careful in front of the children; don't malign the divorcing partner or make nasty comments.

- Don't look for someone to blame.

- Don't pressure them to begin dating.

- Avoid rushing them to become a couple again.

HOW NOT TO SAY IT

But no one in our family has ever been divorced before.

But you always seemed so happy.

But you were such a great couple.

Didn't you see it coming?

Have you tried praying?

I never liked Jane anyway.

If you'd only worked less (cooked more often, had waited to have a family, etc.).

Snap out of it.

You could have made it work.

You have such a tough situation with a special needs child that no one will ever want to date you.

You should have tried harder.

You'll be sorry.

Who will be interested in you?

NONVERBAL STRATEGIES

- The spouse who does not traditionally take care of household repairs, car maintenance, physician appointments, or laundry will appreciate help when assuming these responsibilities.

- Offer to provide training in some task they have not had to handle before such as yard work or cooking.

- Distract them with a movie, a sports event, a game of bowling, or an afternoon of antiquing.

- Purchase a book or tape on meditation so they can integrate relaxation exercises into their routine to reduce stress.

Special Situations

Our neighbors have divorced, but our daughter has remained friends with their son. Our daughter is getting married soon; who should we invite to the wedding?

Invite all three of them to the wedding. Each one will have to take responsibility and decide whether they will accept or decline your invitation. Do seat all three of them at different tables, and carefully select the guests they will sit with so they can enjoy their companions and your special event.

Close friends of mine are getting divorced. How do I continue my friendship with both of them?

It is very difficult to continue relationships with both friends, but not impossible if you are passionate and committed to retaining both friendships. You'll need to be diplomatic, tactful, and nonjudgmental, not laying blame on either party nor taking sides on any issue. Although it might seem sexist, it might be more comfortable if you continue the relationship in the early stage with just same-sex activities; males participating in sports activities together and females shopping or taking in a movie. You'll need to move along with the friendship, not dwelling on what was and what will no longer be, and see what is comfortable with all involved parties. It will be essential that you support dating relationships, new ventures, and new lifestyles.

My sister-in-law had an affair and has initiated a divorce. I love my brother-in-law, and he is a terrific father to my niece and nephew. I really want to retain a relationship with him.

It is not only possible to retain your relationship, but important to do so because he will still be a big part of your niece's and nephew's lives. Keep in touch with him by phone and e-mail. If you have photos of his children, he will enjoy receiving copies along with a message from you. He is your children's uncle, so keep him updated on your children, too, because he will want to know how they are doing. If your sister-in-law is resistant, let her know that you feel it important that you foster positive family relationships for the sake of her children.

SAMPLE LETTERS/E-MAILS

To a friend who is in the process of getting a divorce.

> January X, 2XXX
> Dear Bill:
>
> It's hard to know what to say. You've both been my closest friends since college, and we have had so many great times together. I feel foolish that I was unaware that you two were having such difficulties and am so sorry to hear that you plan to divorce.
>
> There have been so many times when you have been there for me. I'll keep in touch to see how I can help you.
>
> My thoughts are with you during this difficult time.
>
> Fondly,
> Jim

To a childhood friend whose spouse has asked for a divorce.

> May X, 2XXX
> Dear Meredith:
>
> You've been in my thoughts constantly the last few days. I have truly been at a loss for what I could possibly say to comfort you.
>
> I have no experience in this area, Meredith, and yet I want to help you so much. I don't want to add to your burden, but I need your guidance so you can tell me how best I can support you and the children. Whatever you need, just let me know. I can bring a dinner, take the kids to the movies, or just sit with you and keep you company. If you want to come to my house for a change of scenery, you have an open invitation.
>
> I am so sorry this has happened, Meredith. You are a terrific person and a wonderful friend. You deserve only the best life has to offer.
>
> I will give you a call so we can make a plan to get together. Speak to you soon.
>
> Love,
> Laura

To the spouse of a girlfriend who initiated a divorce after she had an affair.

May X, 2XXX
Dear Phil,

At your wedding six years ago, I could never have imagined that I would be writing this note to you. I am so sad that your journey with Sharon as your life partner has ended. With so little choice in the matter and such painful circumstances, this must be a very hard time for you.

I trust you know how much I value our friendship and hope that we will continue to be friends. I wish Sharon had made better choices and given your marriage, which started out so strong, the time and attention it deserved.

You are a terrific person, Phil, and I wish you all the best in the future. Please take care and keep in touch.

With warm regards,
Janice

To a friend whose parents are divorcing.

October X, 2XXX
Dear John,

I was surprised to hear the news about your parents' divorce. They seemed so right together. I never thought of them individually but only as a wonderful couple.

Hearing the news brought back all the feelings I had several years ago when my parents divorced. I remember thinking, "How could it be my parents?" I also recall questioning my own ability to have a lasting relationship in the future. If my own parents were divorcing, was I destined to the same fate? These might be some of the same questions you are asking yourself.

John, this is going to be a long and challenging road. Although I still find my parents' divorce painful, I have gone on to have a happy marriage and learned from my parents' mistakes. You will, too. I want you to know that I am here for you, and I will make myself available anytime you would like to talk. I'll give you a call soon to see how you are doing.

Best regards,
Marco

For further information:

Ahrons, Constance, Ph.D. *The Good Divorce*. New York, NY: HarperCollins Publishers, 1994.

Blakeslee, Sandra, and Judith Wallerstein. *Second Chances: Men, Women and Children a Decade After Divorce*. Boston, MA: Houghton Mifflin Company, 1996.

Clapp, Genevieve, Ph.D. *Divorce and New Beginnings: A Complete Guide to Recovery, Solo Parenting, Co-Parenting, and Stepfamilies, Second Edition*. New York, NY: John Wiley & Sons, Inc., 2000.

Deits, Bob. *Life After Loss: A Personal Guide to Dealing with Death, Divorce, Job Change and Relocation*. Tucson, AZ: Perseus Publishing, 1999.

Hetherington, E. Mavis, and John Kelly. *For Better or For Worse—Divorce Reconsidered*. New York, NY: W.W. Norton & Company, 2003.

Divorce Resource Network—a guide for families in transition
www.divorceresourcenetwork.org

Especially for children:

Krementz, Jill. *How It Feels When Parents Divorce*. New York, NY: Knopf, 1988.

Lansky, Vicki. *It's Not Your Fault, Koko Bear: A Read-Together Book for Parents and Young Children During Divorce*. Minnetonka, MN: Book Peddlers, 2003.

Neuman, M. Gary, LMHC, with Patricia Romanowski. *Helping Your Kids Cope with Divorce the Sandcastles Way*. New York, NY: Random House, 1999.

Schneider, Meg. *Difficult Questions Kids Ask and Are Afraid to Ask About Divorce*. New York, NY: Fireside, 1996.

See also: WHAT IS GRIEF? UNDERSTANDING THE PROCESS OF MOURNING AND HOW YOU CAN HELP, WHAT CAN I SAY? COMMUNICATIONS THAT COMFORT, and WHAT CAN I DO? HOW TO LISTEN.

TWENTY-FIVE

Job Loss

∞

"Employment is nature's physician,
and it is essential to human happiness."

—Galen

WE spend more of our waking hours at work than we do at home or with our families. Many of us devote years to planning and building our careers, studying to obtain degrees, sitting for certification and licensing exams, completing and updating our training, and taking continuing education courses. So it should be no surprise to find that many of us define ourselves by our work; our identity is what we do for our livelihood and who we do it for.

Whether someone loves or hates their job, co-workers, or commute, job loss is a disorienting experience. Daily routines are disrupted, relationships are changed, personal roles might become reversed, and financial circumstances are altered.

Employees leave jobs for many reasons, and they might receive advance, little, or no warning. Organizations might downsize and lay off staff when they are acquired, merged, sold, closed, relocated, or reorganized due to bankruptcy or a quest for greater profitability. Or they might lose funding or a contract. Employees might be dismissed for poor performance, or they might terminate voluntarily to relocate for personal reasons or due to a significant other's relocation.

But no matter why individuals lose their jobs, it is often a painful experience. Employees dedicate themselves to working toward organizational goals. They feel they make a difference and assume organizations are as loyal to them as they are to their organizations. If they find they are replaceable or the organization can easily operate without them, they mourn the loss of their value to the organization, their relationships with their co-workers, and their security.

Individuals who worked for organizations that were closed or suffered severe hardships from fraudulent business practices or dishonest senior executives will experience not only a sense of loss but betrayal as well. They might lose not only their jobs but stock value, investment funds, pension, and other benefits.

Job loss can be a frightening experience, and it is common to feel anxious. Individuals have financial responsibilities that must be maintained despite a loss or decrease in income. Families must be supported, mortgages paid, and financial commitments met.

Many individuals may be consciously aware that changes are impending after a merger, acquisition, or poor financial performance; yet many report that they still feel startled and shocked when they learn their organization will lay off staff.

Individuals experiencing job loss grieve and mourn the loss of their job, security, routines, friendships, and future. They might be in denial, unable to believe that so many people they know and care about will be out of a job. There might be anger and resentment for the lost years spent devoted to the organization and the effort exerted to climb the ladder to their current level. They might have contributed to the organization's profitability and salability, and they are justified in feeling anger, especially if the organization meets its goals and terminates staff to pursue even higher levels of profitability.

Job seekers must display confidence when interviewing for jobs. This may prove daunting to someone who has just been laid off or dismissed and is feeling like a failure. You can help to support them and boost their confidence with the right words at the right time.

THINGS TO CONSIDER

- Whether job loss is due to a major lay off or downsizing.

- Whether the organization has merged, been acquired, or closed, which might impact vested retirement payouts, severance packages, and benefit settlements.

- The number of years since the individual's last job search.

- Whether skills and experience are current.

- Whether their occupation is declining or in demand.

- Length of time they worked for their most recent employer.

- Whether they received outplacement benefits.

EMOTIONS AND FEELINGS TO ANTICIPATE

- Anger
- Anxiety
- Betrayal
- Bitterness
- Denial
- Depression
- Disbelief
- Fear

- Frustration
- Helplessness
- Insecurity
- Instability
- Isolation
- Loneliness
- Sadness
- Vulnerability

WHAT TO SAY AND DO

- Recognize the loss, and express your sympathy.

> ✍ If the job loss is due to a downsizing or layoff, assure them they lost their job through no fault of their own. Organizations go through changes, and this had to do with the organization rather than the individual, their performance, and their skills.

- Tell the person you care about them and you'll provide emotional support through the job search process.

- Allow them to feel their way through the experience and make choices in their own time and in their own way.

- Provide them with positive reinforcement on how good you think they are.

- Bolster their ego by reinforcing their talents, skills, and achievements. Job loss shakes even the most confident, and it is not unusual for someone who has lost their job to question and trivialize their accomplishments.

- Do offer to help, but don't be offended if they don't take you up on it.

- Provide advice only if you are asked directly.

- Offer to critique or proofread their résumé.

- Provide contacts through your network.

- Distribute copies of their résumé.

- Offer to role play the interview process to strengthen their interview skills.

- Purchase a job search book as a gift.

> ↪ Act as a support system, scheduling meetings for coffee or lunch to review search progress and recommend suggestions.

- Give a gift certificate to a professional résumé writer or their favorite clothing store.

- Offer to be a reference.

- Brainstorm potential employers or job search opportunities.

- Offer to provide another opinion on any aspect of the search.

- Volunteer to help with Internet research.

- Encourage them to get additional training if it will make them more marketable.

- Do return their phone calls.

HOW TO SAY IT

Fully explore your options.

Have you applied for unemployment benefits yet?

How are you doing?

I know how hard you've worked, and this must be really difficult for you.

I love you, and I'll help you in any way I can.

I'm sorry this has happened.

It's not your fault.

Take your time and find the right job.

The economy's bad; it's not you.

What can I do to help?

You are very talented, and another company will be lucky to have you.

WHAT NOT TO SAY AND DO

- Don't pity them.

- Don't ignore or avoid them.

- Don't criticize their résumé.

- Don't harass them into finding a job too quickly.

- Don't insist that they allow you to help.

- Don't pressure them into taking just anything so they will have a job; allow them to make their own decisions.

- Don't shake their confidence.

- Don't tell them they should have anticipated the layoff and been better prepared. Hindsight is always better.

- Don't blame them for quitting.

- Don't tell them this is a particularly bad time to be unemployed. It is never a good time to be out of a job.

HOW NOT TO SAY IT

Did you find a job yet?

Don't be so lazy; what are you waiting for?

Haven't you found a job yet?

I'm sure you'll find something quick.

Look on the bright side—your spouse has a job.

You better take what you can get.

You can't be too choosy.

You have nothing to worry about.

You poor thing; what a difficult thing to go through.

You'll never find the same salary.

You're still unemployed?

Special Situations

My friend keeps getting laid off.
Some industries and occupations have been particularly hard hit in the last few years. Be supportive and keep in touch. Be available to brainstorm ideas, and encourage your friend to be persistent. Invite them for dinner. Remind them that successful people succeed because they persist until they find success.

My cousin is chronically unemployed and just can't seem to stay in a job more than eighteen months.
It might be the positions or organizations your cousin pursues are not a good fit. You might encourage him to explore different types of organizations, such as federal, state, and local government; educational institutions; nonprofit organizations; corporations; or different industries. Continue to support him, and avoid making judgmental comments that might undermine his confidence in his job search efforts.

My co-worker's husband accepted a promotion, and they are relocating. Although the co-worker is happy for her husband, she is depressed because she is leaving her job and will be unemployed.
Order a subscription to the largest local newspaper in her new area so she can begin to learn the business and job opportunities in the new community. You

can also suggest you have lunch and brainstorm job search strategies. If she needs a jump start, purchase a spiral notebook and take notes for her. She will be more confident making the move and initiating a search with a notebook of ideas and an understanding of the local economy.

My friend has sixteen years of tenure with a state government and is being laid off because of budget cuts. He has only four years left to full retirement and needs to stay with his health insurer because of a previous condition. He is worried and depressed.

Encourage your friend to explore other job openings in the state, even though he might be forced to relocate or take a position with less responsibility and salary. He might not get relocation reimbursement, but it would be in his best interest to remain in the system until he is eligible for retirement. Suggest that he view the job change as an opportunity and that he maintain a positive outlook. If he finds the new job is not satisfying, he can balance his life with outside activities and community interests that will bolster his self-esteem.

My friend works for a large grocery chain that has been bought out by a larger company. He has not been laid off, but he was offered an incentive package to voluntarily leave. He has worked for this company since high school graduation and has no further education. My extensive network is in a different industry, and I think he would do well there.

Introduce your friend to key people in your network and make some calls to hiring personnel in your organization. Your friend should make the initial contacts to schedule interviews, but you can provide background information on the organization and culture prior to his meetings. It would be helpful to coach him so he knows what questions to anticipate and the personalities of the interviewers. You'll lay the groundwork so your friend will be comfortable and relaxed, anticipating a positive interview experience.

The company my spouse works for has been sold three times in the last eight years and they have downsized four times. My spouse keeps getting lucky, but I am afraid his luck is about to run out.

When you are working for an unstable organization or industry, it is imperative that you remain ready to enter the job market. Encourage your spouse to update his résumé, activate his network, and hone his job search skills. He should apprise his network members of his organization or industry instability and communicate what opportunities interest him. Suggest he continually explore and pursue job opportunities, and be prepared to move when an offer presents itself.

SAMPLE LETTERS/E-MAILS

To a former co-worker who has been laid off.

> January X, 2XXX
> Dear John:
>
> I was sorry to hear about the layoff at XYZ Company. I know you worked hard on the expansion project, and it is disappointing that things didn't work out the way you anticipated.
>
> Whatever you need, John, I'll be here for you. I can link you up with some of my contacts or set up a meeting for you with the sales manager. Feel free to use me as a reference.
>
> I will call you next week to see how you are doing and schedule a lunch. You are a great worker, John, and any organization will be lucky to have you.
>
> All the best,
> Tom

To a friend whose organization filed for bankruptcy and who was laid off with no notice.

> March X, 2XXX
> Dear Debra:
>
> What a shock this must be. I was so sorry to learn that Hall and Brighton is closing this week.
>
> You do a terrific job, Debra, and I would like to help you in any way I can. I will call you later this week and find out how I can assist you best.
>
> In the meantime, know that I am thinking of you and sending good thoughts your way.
>
> Fondly,
> Betty

To a cousin whose organization closed and the organization both laid off staff and merged several business groups with a rival firm; your cousin was offered and accepted a lesser position with the rival firm.

March X, 2XXX
Dear Malcolm:

I was surprised and sorry to hear the news about XYZ. I know how much you enjoyed working there, and you have every right to be distressed over the firm's dissolution.

The new position with Big Blue is good news. I hope you will soon feel as comfortable there as you were at XYZ.

Although I know this position is not at your previous level, I feel confident that you will do well. Keep yourself open to new opportunities; they will soon see what an asset you are, and this move might take your career in a whole new direction.

Know that I'm always here for you. I'll keep in touch, but in the meantime, if I can help in any way, please don't hesitate to call.

Take care,
Linda

To a friend who was laid off.

January X, 2XXX
Dear Collin:

There are two sayings I frequently use when faced with difficult situations: The sun will come up tomorrow, and it's not how often you get knocked down but how many times you get back up again.

My experience with two employment layoffs gives me a unique perspective on your current position. First of all, the sun will come up tomorrow. This might be hard to grasp in your current frame of mind, but you will face and overcome many feeling and emotions—self-doubt, worthlessness, and fear are among them. I remember the first time I was informed that my services were no longer needed. However the news was couched or soft-sold, it was a staggering blow. You hear none of the conversation after the "revelation." Instead, your mind races in many directions, none of which are particularly inviting. Sound familiar so far?

This blow to your ego seems crushing, but it is not! You might have self-doubts about your abilities or lack of them and question your career path to date—don't! You might feel as if you are swimming in a sea of perceived worthlessness. The key word is *perceived*. You deem yourself a failure, and fear begins to set in. Fear is healthy. You fear the inability to provide for yourself and your family, being ostracized by loved ones and friends, substantial financial setbacks, and drastic lifestyle changes. This fear is natural and simply put—okay.

Collin, you're much stronger and resilient than you think you are. You can and will handle this situation. Draw upon your family and friends for support. They all want you to succeed and enjoy life. They are in your corner. Use them openly and often. Never consider the act of turning to them to be a sign of weakness. Aren't you pleased when someone approaches you for help or advice? You will learn, improve, and flourish from this experience. I know I have twice!

In closing, my friend, you've been knocked down hard perhaps. But get up, brush yourself off, and figure out a plan of action with your head held high. There's no time for self-doubt, no place for self-worthlessness, and your fears are slowing abating. It's time to start a new chapter in your life. It will take courage, pride, and action. You have the first two already. Just add the third and don't look back.

I'm here for you! All the best,
Ted

For further information:

Bolles, Richard Nelson. *What Color Is Your Parachute?* Berkeley, CA: Ten Speed Press, 2003.

Cohen, William A., Ph.D. *Break the Rules—The Secret Code to Finding a Great Job Fast.* Paramus, NJ: Prentice Hall Press, 2001.

Critchley, Robert K. *Rewired, Rehired, or Retired?* San Francisco, CA: Jossey-Bass/Pfeiffer, 2002.

Deits, Bob. *Life After Loss: A Personal Guide to Dealing with Death, Divorce, Job Change and Relocation.* Tucson, AZ: Perseus Publishing, 1999.

Kaplan, Robbie Miller. *How to Say It in Your Job Search.* New York, NY: Prentice Hall Press, 2002.

————. *Résumé Shortcuts.* Manassas, VA: Impact Publications, 1997.

Lussier, Don, with Tom Noteman and Donna M. Henderson, ed. *Job Search Secrets.* Lincolnwood, IL: VGM Career Horizons, 1998.

Nielsen, Niels H. *Princeton Management Consultants Guide to Your New Job.* New York, NY: John Wiley & Sons, Inc., 2003.

Podesta, Sandra, and Andrea Paxton. *201 Killer Cover Letters.* New York, NY: McGraw Hill, 2003.

Simon, Mary. *Negotiate Your Job Offer.* New York, NY: John Wiley & Sons, Inc., 1998.

Wendleton, Kate. *Getting Interviews.* Franklin Lakes, NJ: Career Press, 2000.

————. *Interviewing and Salary Negotiations.* Franklin Lakes, NJ: Career Press, 1999.

Job Resources
www.job-resources.com

Job-Hunt.Org
Website providing comprehensive listing of useful Internet-accessible job search resources and services on the web, including lists of links by category or location for job websites where you can search for a job and/or leave a copy of your résumé and websites that provide information and/or support useful in the job search process.
http://www.job-hunt.org

See also: WHAT IS GRIEF? UNDERSTANDING THE PROCESS OF MOURNING AND HOW YOU CAN HELP, WHAT CAN I SAY? COMMUNICATIONS THAT COMFORT, and WHAT CAN I DO? HOW TO LISTEN.

TWENTY-SIX

Financial Troubles

∞

*"There is no such thing as failure for people
who have done their best."*

—Anonymous

PERSONAL bankruptcies increased 5.7 percent in 2002 and set a record at more than 1.5 million according to the Administrative Office of the U.S. Courts. While studies show that people are often pushed to bankruptcy through job loss, illness, divorce, or a call to active military duty, financial difficulty can also arise from compulsive shopping or spending, credit card abuse, or debt abuse.

Who's at greatest risk? Individuals who earn far less than their potential are vulnerable to financial problems, but individuals who earn far more than they are used to are vulnerable, too. They might have difficulty balancing their needs and newfound desires.

How you respond to someone experiencing financial difficulty will depend on your personal relationship and the underlying circumstances. You might be reluctant to offer financial assistance to a habitual spender but quite willing to help out if the financial difficulties were beyond their control. Whatever you choose to do, the right words and nonverbal communication strategies will help them through a difficult and uncertain time.

THINGS TO CONSIDER

- Fiscal responsibility and stability requires basic money management skills, including balancing a checkbook, establishing a budget, tracking income and expenses, saving, and investing.

- Individuals must have a good grasp of their income and an understanding of how to live within their means.

- There are financial counseling services available to resolve financial and credit problems such as budget counseling, money management services, debt management, debt consolidation repayment, mortgage counseling, bankruptcy counseling and/or assistance with bankruptcy, and public-service educational programs.

EMOTIONS AND FEELINGS TO ANTICIPATE

- Denial
- Embarrassment
- Fear
- Helplessness
- Hopelessness
- Incompetency
- Insecurity
- Instability
- Panic
- Self-blame
- Shame
- Uncertainty
- Worry

WHAT TO SAY AND DO

- If they haven't already, suggest they meet with a credit counselor if they have a lot of credit card debt or are in serious financial trouble. They can locate a reputable counselor through the Association of Independent Consumer Credit Counseling Agencies (AICCCA) or the National Foundation for Credit Counseling (NFCC). Find details for both at the end of this chapter.

- If they are unable to pay off their debts and have to file for bankruptcy, suggest they locate an attorney. They can ask around for a referral or use one of the Internet sources at the end of this chapter to locate bankruptcy attorneys in their geographic area.

- If they are experiencing other non-credit-related financial difficulties— for example, a spouse loses a partner to death or divorce and has never managed the household finances—suggest they locate a certified financial planner through the Financial Planning Association (FPA). Find details at the end of this chapter.

- Continue to socialize, but switch to low-cost activities.

- Invite them over for a home-cooked meal.

- Prepare extra food when they are sharing a meal with you, and ask if they would like you to pack some extras to take home.

- If you have traditionally shopped together in the past, suggest inexpensive activities such as going for a walk.

> ✄ Instead of going out to lunch, invite them over or offer to prepare a lunch and have a picnic.

- Research free or low-cost social activities in your local newspaper such as concerts, gallery openings, or art exhibits.

- If you usually attend movies together, rent a movie, go to an afternoon matinee, or locate an inexpensive movie theater.

- Give them a gift card to their hair salon or a mall they really enjoy.

HOW TO SAY IT

I am so sorry this is happening.

Let me know what I can do to help.

Let's meet for coffee and talk.

Please let me help you; you would do the same for me.

This must be very difficult for you.

This really isn't your fault.

WHAT NOT TO SAY AND DO

- Be cautious in offering them money.

- Do not tell them it is their own doing.

- Do not find fault in how they handled their money.

- Don't point fingers on who is to blame; it is more productive to support them through this financial crisis.

HOW NOT TO SAY IT

How could this have happened to you?

I hope you enjoyed it while it lasted.

I told you this was going to happen.

You have to live within your means.

You should have seen it coming.

Special Situations

My sister is declaring bankruptcy, and I don't know what type of help is appropriate.
Your sister needs support while going through this difficult process. What you choose to do to help her will depend on your relationship and the circumstances that led to this very personal decision. Be frank and ask her what she needs, whether it is a loan to pay the attorney and filing fee, transportation if her car is repossessed, help in organizing her bills and paperwork, or a place to stay.

My son and his wife have an opportunity to buy a home but do not qualify for a mortgage due to credit card debt.
It is hard to see your children struggling. How you respond will depend on your personal financial situation, your relationship, the behaviors that led to their financial predicament, and their willingness to resolve the problem. You can choose from a wide range of options such as verbal support, invitations to dinner, help in organizing their financial papers, or an early disbursement of their inheritance.

SAMPLE LETTER/E-MAIL

To a friend who had a car accident and some medical bills that the insurance would not cover, and subsequently wound up with a large credit card debt.

November X, 2XXX
Dear Wendy:

I appreciate your trust in sharing such a personal experience with me. I had no idea your health insurance did not cover all your expenses from the accident. This has been a terrible burden for you to carry all by yourself. Please let Mark and me help you sort things out.

Mark is such a whiz in accounting he has offered to help you prepare a budget. He would also like to help negotiate a payment arrangement with your credit card company.

In the meantime, you have a standing invitation for dinner any night. Just let me know when you will join us, and I'll set a place. We'll do everything we can to help you stay on a course to reduce your debt. I am confident we can help you get back on track.

With love,
Angie

For further information:

Bierman, Todd, and Nathaniel Wice. *The Guerrilla Guide to Credit Repair.* New York, NY: St. Martin's Griffin, 1994.

Casanova, Karen. *Letting Go of Debt.* Center City, MN: Hazelden, 2000.

Eichhorn, Brian. *Credit Repair Made Simple.* Richmond Hill, GA: Beak Press, 2000.

Sember, Brette McWhorter. *Repair Your Own Credit and Deal with Debt, Second Edition.* Naperville, IL: Sourcebooks, 2003.

AllLaw.com
Find legal information or a lawyer in your geographic area
www.AllLaw.com

American Law Sources On-Line
Comprehensive, uniform, and useful compilation of links to freely accessible online sources of law for the United States and Canada.
www.lawsource.com

The Association of Independent Consumer Credit Counseling Agencies (AICCCA)
PMB 626
11350 Randoms Hill Road, Suite 800
Fairfax, VA 22030
(703) 934-6118
Locate a Member Agency by calling (800) 450-1794.

Financial Planning Association (FPA)
5775 Glenridge Drive, NE
Suite B-300
Atlanta, GA 30328
(404) 845-0011 or (800) 322-4237
www.fpanet.org

FindLaw.com
Locate attorneys in your geographic area.
www.FindLaw.com

National Foundation for Credit Counseling (NFCC)
(800) 388-2227 for twenty-four-hour automated office listings for an NFCC member location near you.
www.nfcc.org

See also: WHAT IS GRIEF? UNDERSTANDING THE PROCESS OF MOURNING AND HOW YOU CAN HELP, WHAT CAN I SAY? COMMUNICATIONS THAT COMFORT, and WHAT CAN I DO? HOW TO LISTEN.

TWENTY-SEVEN

Caregiver Responsibilities

∞

"When I give, I give myself."

—Walt Whitman

MEDICAL and technological advances have increased our life span, but medical innovations do not necessarily translate into healthier lives. We are living longer, and more and more of us will need assistance in meeting the challenges of our daily lives.

In a survey conducted by the National Family Caregivers Association, more than one quarter (26.6 percent) of the adult population provided care for a chronically ill, disabled, or aged family member or friend in the year 2000. Based on the 2000 census data, that translated into more than 50 million people.

Most care recipients are elderly, but care is also provided to family members and friends who are ill, disabled, or injured from accidents as well as children unable to live on their own.

In a survey of 1,000 adults conducted by the National Family Caregivers Association, 59 percent responded that they either were or expected to be a family caregiver.

The National Women's Health Information Center reports that recent surveys indicate more than 7 million persons are informal caregivers to older adults. Other surveys found that almost 26 million family caregivers provide care to adults, age eighteen and over, with a disability or chronic illness, and 5 million informal caregivers provide care for older adults age fifty and over with dementia.

One of the most important things a caregiver can do is to take care of themselves. They will need a great deal of help, and you can play a vital role in supporting them.

THINGS TO CONSIDER

- Hospital stays continue to shorten as hospitals discharge patients more quickly.

- Both short-term and long-term situations require caregiver support. Some people become caregivers for a few weeks and others for a few years.

- Caregivers need a wide range of support.

- Caregivers need to relate to others who have been caregivers and understand the challenges and difficulties they face.

EMOTIONS AND FEELINGS TO ANTICIPATE

- Anger
- Anxiety
- Compassion
- Confusion
- Denial
- Desperation
- Fear
- Frustration
- Fulfillment
- Guilt
- Isolation
- Loneliness
- Regret
- Resentment
- Sadness
- Satisfaction
- Understanding

WHAT TO SAY AND DO

- Offer to conduct research on the illness, home health care, respite care, or alternative living arrangements.

- Volunteer to research available services for physical therapy, occupational therapy, nutritional counseling, meals, or medical equipment rentals.

- Volunteer to relieve the caregiver of responsibility for a few hours a week.

- Offer to stay at the home for an hour at a time so the caregiver can run errands.

- Suggest the caregiver make time for pleasant activities or interests and offer to accompany them to the movies, an exhibit, or a concert.

> ∿ Suggest or offer to help prepare a comprehensive list of all medications, including name, dosage, prescription number, and prescribing physician. Offer to make copies for all health-care professionals.

- If the caregiver can't get away to a favorite restaurant or coffee spot, bring it to them. Provide take-out treats and share with them.

- Encourage exercise as an outlet for stress. Offer to be an exercise buddy to make exercise a regular activity.

- If they aren't comfortable going out and leaving you as the caregiver, suggest you stay in the house while they take a bubble bath, a hot shower, and/or some private time for themselves.

- Help with outings. It is easier and more pleasant to have some company.

- If they are having difficulty getting adequate rest, take over their responsibilities for a few hours and encourage them to nap.

- Bring a nutritional food or meal. A container of homemade soup or a basket of muffins will be appreciated.

- When shopping, pick up an extra item at the bakery and drop it off for a treat.

- Bring a large container of sliced fresh fruit instead of sending flowers or a plant.

> ∿ If you play an instrument, bring it along. Live music will brighten any day. Or offer music to relax. Share your CDs or tapes of different types of music. If the patient is able to get about, research music programs that might be appropriate at the local high school or park.

- Think of simple ways to lighten the caregiver's schedule while providing living necessities.

- Remember the patient, too. If they like reading mysteries, working crossword puzzles, watching

> ⚥ Offer to install a bird feeder or bird bath at a window accessible to the patient and caregiver. Watching wildlife is soothing and renewing, especially for those confined indoors.

videos/DVDs, or reading the local paper, keep them supplied.

- Pets can relieve anxiety and reduce loneliness. If the patient and caregiver are agreeable, bring your pet over for a visit.

- Pick up books on tape or CDs while visiting the local library. Choose interesting topics or best-sellers as a pleasurable way to pass the time.

- Visit as often as you can. Companionship for the caregiver and the patient speeds the passage of time and brightens the day.

- Please the senses of the caregiver and patient. Give a gift of a scented candle, bag of potpourri, wind chimes, or flavorful herbal teas.

- Call on a regular basis just to chat.

HOW TO SAY IT

Do you need anything from the grocery store today?

How are you and your dad doing?

How can I help you this week?

I am on my way to the pharmacy; can I pick up anything for you?

I think you are doing a great job.

I would love to see you both.

What can I do to help?

Would you like some company?

WHAT NOT TO SAY AND DO

- Don't stay away because you think you will be in the way.

- Don't avoid a visit because you are uncomfortable with the illness or injury. Instead, research it on the Internet or at the library or ask questions. You will feel more comfortable when you know what to expect.

- Don't refer to the individual who is requiring help as a burden. The responsibilities might be difficult, but they might be perceived as an act of love.

- Don't express your opinions on what they should do with their patient.

- Don't give unsolicited advice.

HOW NOT TO SAY IT

He doesn't even know you are there.

I wouldn't want to end up like that.

What a burden you have taken on.

You should think about putting your mom in a nursing home.

Special Situations

My sister lives near my mother and is her primary caregiver. I live 1,000 miles away.

Despite your physical distance, there are many ways you can support your sister and your mom. Frequent notes, telephone calls, or e-mails will let them know they are in your thoughts. You can inquire if there is a specific chore you can take over, such as reconciling the medical bills. Your sister would appreciate an occasional note or a bouquet of flowers to thank her and acknowledge her efforts. You can volunteer to stay with your mom for specific weekends or a week or pay for respite care so your sister can have a break or take a vacation. You can also arrange to have a meal delivered from a favorite restaurant on a weekly or bimonthly basis.

My neighbor's husband had a stroke. He is totally incapacitated, and she is the primary caregiver.

There are some simple things you can do to help your neighbor. Call her before running your errands to see if you can run an errand for her at the same time. Prepare a double recipe once a week and take your neighbor a dinner. Offer to stay at her house for an hour so she can run an errand or have some private time. Recruit other neighbors to help mow the lawn or shovel snow. When you have free time, suggest a visit with your neighbor. She would probably enjoy some companionship.

SAMPLE LETTERS/E-MAILS

To a cousin taking care of your aunt and to the aunt who is terminally ill.

> July X, 2XXX
> Dear Aunt Gayle and Mary:
>
> Just a short note to let you know that you are in my thoughts. I hope you are both managing well.
> Summer has finally arrived here, and I suspect in your neck of the woods, too. I am happy for the warm weather and the chance to do some work in the garden. I enjoy watching the birds take a bath, and it's a pleasure to watch them pecking away at the bird feeder.
> My girls have been busy with summer camp and music activities. There are several concerts coming up, and they are hard at work. They asked me to send along their greetings and good wishes.
> I spoke with Sarah last week, and she said she had a good visit with you. I wish I was closer so I could see you, too. I know how much you enjoy a cup of tea in the afternoon, and when I take mine, I always think of you.
> I will call in the next few days, and if my timing is off, please let me know when you will be up for a chat, Aunt Gayle. The sound of your voice always lifts my spirits.
> You are both constantly in my thoughts. Know that I send much love your way.
>
> Love,
> Rosie

A grown daughter writes to her mother's cousin.

October X, 2XXX
Dear Ellie and Matthew:

I have been meaning to write to you for a while now—ever since I got your new address. The days pass so quickly that I never seem to get to all the things I'd like to do. Today is my catch-up day, and you are at the top of my list.

I understand that the move to your new home went well. I am glad for that. It must have been hard to decide to make such a big change. I know that when my mom finally made the move to a retirement community, she loved it.

Congratulations on your eighty-first birthday, Ellie. I was surprised to hear that you had passed such a milestone. My mom always spoke of you as the much younger cousin. I guess when you are children, four or five years seems like a huge difference.

I hope both of you are meeting the challenges this new decade brings. Recent experiences have shown me that sometimes we learn to appreciate the small steps and victories when the larger ones are no longer within our grasp. My mother really seemed to appreciate all the small kindnesses and comforts she received. Some of the things that used to annoy or bother her were no longer an issue. It really taught me a lesson about enjoying the moment and appreciating the things that were really important, like my kids, my husband, and even fresh air and sunshine.

I hope that each day you find some small treasure to make you smile or feel contentment.

Love,
Andie

To a former neighbor who is the primary caretaker for her terminally ill husband.

April X, 2XXX
Dear Joan:

I have been thinking of you often over the past several weeks. How are you both doing? I am finding that now that spring has arrived I am able to face the day with new energy. My garden is beginning to come to life, and today I noticed that at least one of the lupines I planted last year has decided to return. Maybe I will actually get some blooms this year—anything is possible.

Joan, I hope you are finding the time you need to take care of yourself while you are meeting Jim's needs. Caretaking is a full-time job, and you need to make sure to get help and respite so you can provide Jim the kind of care I know you want to give him. There is nothing wrong with asking for help and taking a break. And please remember, if you need for me to come and visit, all you have to do is ask.

You are a wonderful person, Joan. So many marriages fail even at the best of times, and the two of you have been there for each other through thick and thin. I know you probably have days that are difficult to get through. But I also hope you are getting a great deal of satisfaction knowing that the care you are giving Jim is irreplaceable and that he appreciates it more than you know—even if he can't tell you so.

I will give you a call soon. In the meantime, I am sending good thoughts and my love.

Hannah

For further information:

Carr, Sasha, M.S., and Sandra Choron. *The Caregiver's Essential Handbook: More Than 1,200 Tips to Help You Care for and Comfort the Seniors in Your Life.* New York, NY: Contemporary Books, 2003.

Carter, Roslynn. *Helping Yourself Help Others.* New York, NY: Times Books, 1996.

Collier, Andrea King. *Still with Me.* New York, NY: Simon & Schuster, 2003.

Cooper, Joan Hunter, et al. *Fourteen Friends' Guide to Eldercaring.* Herndon, VA: Capital Books, Inc., 1999.

Gray-Davidson, Frena. *The Caregiver's Sourcebook.* New York, NY: Contemporary Books, 2001.

Gruetzner, Howard. *Alzheimer's—A Caregiver's Guide and Sourcebook.* New York, NY: John Wiley & Sons, Inc., 2001.

McLeod, Beth Witrogen. *Caregiving—The Spiritual Journey of Love, Loss, and Renewal.* New York, NY: John Wiley & Sons, 1999.

Visiting Nurse Association of America. *Caregiver's Handbook: A Complete Guide to Home Health Care.* New York, NY: DK Publishing Merchandise, 1998.

Administration on Aging
Center for Communication and Consumer Services
330 Independence Avenue, SW
Room 4656
Washington, DC 20201
(202) 619 7501
www.aoa.gov/eldfam/FOR_Caregivers/FOR_Caregivers.ASP

Alzheimer's Association
(800) 272-3900
www.alz.org

American Association of Retired Persons (AARP) Webplace Caregiving:
Finding Help
www.aarp.org/life

Caregiver.com
A print and web magazine dedicated to those caring for loved ones
www.caregiver.com

Eldercare Locator service is a nationwide toll-free service to help older adults and their caregivers find local services for seniors. It operates Monday through Friday, 9 A.M. to 8 P.M., Eastern time and can be reached at (800) 677-1116. The U.S. Administration on Aging makes part of this service available online so consumers can easily link to the information and referral (I&R) services of their state and area agencies on aging. These I&R programs help identify appropriate services in the area where the caregiver or family member resides.
www.eldercare.gov

Family Caregiver Alliance
690 Market Street, Suite 600
San Francisco, CA 94104
(415) 434–3388
www.caregiver.org/index.html

Hospice Foundation of America
www.hospicefoundation.org

National Association for Home Care and Hospice's
Virtual Headquarters
www.nahc.org/home.html

National Family Caregivers Association
10400 Connecticut Avenue, #500
Kensington, MD 20895-3944
(800) 896-3650
www.nfcacares.org

See also: WHAT IS GRIEF? UNDERSTANDING THE PROCESS OF MOURNING AND HOW YOU CAN HELP, WHAT CAN I SAY? COMMUNICATIONS THAT COMFORT, and WHAT CAN I DO? HOW TO LISTEN.

TWENTY-EIGHT

Personal Disappointment

∞

"Only those who dare to fail greatly can ever achieve greatly."

—Robert F. Kennedy

PERSONAL disappointments can be terribly painful. Individuals may covet leadership opportunities, attempt to win a competition, run for public office, or desire membership with a team. In the scheme of things, these disappointments might seem on the lower end of the "difficult times" scale, but to someone who has trained, planned, and prepared extensively and over a long time period to achieve their goal, this loss can be devastating.

Individuals study, practice, put in relentless hours, or spend exorbitant amounts of money for training, lessons, professional services, and equipment to achieve goals. They might sacrifice friendships and relationships, place themselves in debt, or miss out on other opportunities to experience and pursue their dreams. When an opportunity no longer exists or is earned or given to someone else, the private disappointment can become public knowledge.

You can help them through this difficult time by letting them know that you value them, their efforts, and their integrity.

THINGS TO CONSIDER

- This might have been the only opportunity to achieve this goal.

- Restrictions might exist that preclude the individual from making another attempt.

- They might never again have the opportunity to pursue their dream.

EMOTIONS AND FEELINGS TO ANTICIPATE

- Anger
- Bitterness
- Depression
- Disappointment
- Disbelief
- Embarrassment
- Hopelessness

- Inadequacy
- Incompetency
- Regret
- Sadness
- Self-blame
- Shame

WHAT TO SAY AND DO

- Take your cues from your personal relationship. A hug when you are together might be enough, followed with a note.

- Acknowledge how hard they have worked.

- Validate their skills and abilities.

- Express pride in all they have accomplished.

- Let them know their efforts and focus were not in vain.

- Reinforce that you value the skills and expertise gained by the experience.

- Tell them you love them.

- Let them know how special they are.

HOW TO SAY IT

Congratulations for a great job.

I am so proud that you set your sights on this goal.

I am sorry this didn't work out for you.

I am very proud of how hard you worked.

It is so important to reach for your goals, and you did just that.

You are my inspiration.

You did a great job.

You have accomplished so much.

You were wonderful, and I am so proud of you.

WHAT NOT TO SAY AND DO

- Do not trivialize their pain. Disappointments are terribly painful, especially when you have worked so hard to achieve a specific goal.

- Do not tell them to put their disappointment in perspective. Individuals have the right to grieve for their loss.

- Don't minimize their loss by telling them that what they hoped to achieve wasn't that important.

- Do not compare the loss to someone else's loss. If you do this, you are sending a message that their loss is not as significant or as painful.

HOW NOT TO SAY IT

And you hurt your leg for what?

It could be so much worse.

It's probably for the best.

Look on the bright side; you are in great physical shape now.

Look on the bright side. You have your health.

Put things in perspective; it's really not a big deal.

This is nothing in the scheme of things.

You'll get over it.

Special Situations

My best friend's fiancé broke their engagement three months before the wedding. How can I help my friend?

Console your friend and let her know how very sorry you are that her relationship has ended. You can lift her spirits with a bouquet of flowers and/or a note to let her know how very special she is and that she is loved. Offer concrete support to contact vendors and cancel the arrangements. Volunteer to review contracts to evaluate cancellation clauses, negotiate cancellation penalties, write letters, make phone calls, pick up purchased items that cannot be cancelled, or return gifts.

A friend in my writer's network had her book contract cancelled after she completed the manuscript.

Either call or write your friend a note to say how sorry you are that the contract was cancelled. Reassure her that someone liked her book idea before, and someone will like it again. If she does not have an agent, suggest she look for one or volunteer to help her locate recommendations. Offer to brainstorm ideas on how she can rewrite or repackage the material for another publisher.

SAMPLE LETTER/E-MAIL

To a niece who competed in a pageant and lost.

> June X, 2XXX
> Dearest Ellie:
>
> It has been such a joy to watch you grow into the lovely young woman you have become. You worked so very hard to develop your musical talent and train for the competition. Your dedication and achievements demonstrated your talents to everyone who worked with you and got to know you.
>
> The competition results disappointed you, and I am so very sorry. But I can't help but feel the real prize was the preparation and participation. You have shown wisdom and dedication far beyond your years. I am in awe of the innate ability to single-handedly focus that drives you to excellence. You are a real winner, Ellie, and I am so very proud to be your aunt.
>
> Lots of love,
> Aunt Leah

For further information:

Sell, Colleen, ed. *A Cup of Comfort.* Avon, MA: Adams Media Corporation, 2001.

———. *A Cup of Comfort for Inspiration.* Avon, MA: Adams Media Corporation, 2003.

Thomas, Marlo, and friends. *The Right Words at the Right Time.* New York, NY: Atria Books, 2002.

Zadra, Dan, comp. *I Believe in You: To Your Heart, Your Dream, and the Difference You Make.* Edmonds, WA: Compendium, Inc., 1999.

See also: WHAT IS GRIEF? UNDERSTANDING THE PROCESS OF MOURNING AND HOW YOU CAN HELP, WHAT CAN I SAY? COMMUNICATIONS THAT COMFORT, and WHAT CAN I DO? HOW TO LISTEN.

About the Author

Robbie Miller Kaplan is a trainer and writer with an expertise in communications. She is a frequent speaker and lecturer for business, academic, community, association, and governmental organizations. She is the author of *How to Say It in Your Job Search, Sure-Hire Résumés, Sure-Hire Cover Letters, 101 Resumes for Sure-Hire Results, The Whole Career Sourcebook, Résumé Shortcuts,* and *Résumés: The Write Stuff* and is a contributing author to the *Strong Interest Inventory Applications and Technical Guide*. She holds a Bachelor of Arts in English from George Mason University and has a management background with Xerox Corporation.

Index

A

Accidents, car
   co-worker in, 391
   teenager killed in, 424, 425–428
Administration on Aging, 603
Adoption, 528, 530, 531, 534–542
   emotions/feelings on, 535
   international, 535, 536, 537, 538, 540
   letters/e-mails on, 540–541
   nonverbal strategies on, 539
   organizations, 542–543
   publications, 541, 542
   special situations of, 539–540
   things to consider with, 535
   what not to say/do with, 537–539
   what to say/do with, 536–537
Adoption Institute, 534–535
Adult, death of. *See* Death of adult
Affairs, marital. *See* Infidelity
AIDS, 554
AllLaw.com, 524, 593
Alzheimer's Association, 603
American Academy of Pediatrics, 491
American Association of Retired
      Persons (AARP), 359, 417, 603
American Bar Association, 524
American Cancer Society, 394
American Foundations for Suicide
      Prevention, 449

American Heart Association, 394–395
American Law Sources On-Line, 524, 594
American Lung Association, 395
American Medical Association, 490
American Parkinson Disease
      Association, Inc., 395
American Psychological Association, 516
American Red Cross National
      Headquarters, 509, 516
American Self-Help Group
      Clearinghouse, 373
American Society for Reproductive
      Medicine, 532
American Veterinary Medical Associa-
      tion, 466
Americans with Disabilities Act
      (ADA), 551, 559
Anger
   crime and, 478, 484, 485, 491
   grief and, 358, 387
   suicide and, 441
Anxiety Disorders Association of
      America, 509–510, 516
Association for Pet Loss and
      Bereavement (APLB), 466
Association of Independent
      Consumer Credit Counseling
      Agencies (AICCCA), 594

B

Babies. *See* Death of baby; Illness;
  Miscarriage; Special needs,
  baby/child with
Bankruptcy, 589, 590, 592
Beyond Indigo (organization), 449
Blindness, 555
Books. *See* publications
Buddhism, 404
Bureau of Justice Statistics, 477
Burglary victims, 477, 480–481
Burial. *See* Funerals

C

Cancer
  chemotherapy during, 391
  child lost to, 425, 426
  organizations, 394, 396
  suicide and, 446–447
Cards/notes, 365. *See also*
    Writing
  on death of child, 421
  on illness, 390, 391
  on miscarriage, 453
  on pet loss, 462
  sympathy, 371
Caregiver responsibilities, 595–604.
    See also Illness
  emotions/feelings on, 596
  letters/e-mails on, 600–602
  organizations, 595, 603–604
  publications,, 602–603
  special situations of, 599–600
  things to consider with, 596
  what not to say/do with,
    598–599
  what to say/do with, 596–598
Caregiver.com, 603

Cars
  accidents in, 391, 424, 425–428
  stolen, 477, 481
Catholic Church. *See* Roman
    Catholic funerals
Center for Nonviolent Communi-
    cation, 504
Centers for Disease Control and
    Prevention, 568
Cerebral Palsy, 554
Charities. *See* Donations, charitable
Children. *See also* Adoption; Death
    of baby; Death of child;
    Miscarriage; Special needs,
    baby/child with; Teenagers
  cancer death in, 425, 426
  communicating with, 373
  death of adult and, 399, 417–418,
    429, 439
  death of baby and, 431, 439
  death of sibling and, 420, 431
  disabilities and, 559, 560
  divorce and, 571, 572, 573, 574,
    576, 577
  grief and, 360
  marital separation and, 561, 563,
    565
  pet loss and, 465, 467
  suicide of, 440, 448
  traumatic events and, 518
Chinese funerals, 405
Commonwealth Fund survey, 499
Communication. *See also* Listening
  basic, 361–380
  with children, 373
  to comfort, 363–373
  phrases, 366–367
  what not to say in, 369–370
  what to say in, 367–368
  words to use in, 366
  in writing, 370–372

The Compassionate Friends, Inc.,
    428–429, 438, 489
Congenital malformations, 347–348,
    430, 431, 436
Courts, U.S., Administrative Office of,
    589
Co-worker
    arrest of son of, 522
    in car accident, 391
    death of, 400
    death of daughter of, 425–426
    death of parent of, 412
    domestic violence abuse of, 503
    illness of, 391
    infertility of, 531
    layoff of, 585
    miscarriage of, 457, 458
    pet loss of, 465
    suicide of, 446
    suicide of husband of, 447
Credit debt, 589, 590, 592, 593–594
Crime, 475. *See also* Domestic
    violence; Legal/criminal
    problems; Sexual assault/rape
    anger and, 478, 484, 485, 491
    date rape as, 496
    emotions/feelings on, 478,
        484–485
    letters/e-mails on, 480–481,
        487–488
    nonviolent, 477–482
    publications, 481, 488
    things to consider with, 478, 484
    victim v. survivor, 478, 484, 491, 500
    victims organizations, 481–482,
        488–489, 490
    violent, 483–489
    what not to say/do after, 479–480,
        486–487
    what to say/do after, 478–479,
        485–486

Crime Victims Research and
    Treatment Center, 490
Crutches, use of, 553–555
Crying
    after death of adult, 400, 401
    after death of baby, 432, 435
    after natural disaster, 507
    grief and, 365, 369
    infertility and, 529

D

Date rape, 496
Deafness, 555, 557
Death, 381. *See also* Funerals; Grief;
    Pet loss
    communication and, 363–373
    coping with, 351–360
    fear of, 398
    talking and, 363–373
Death of adult, 397–419
    belated sympathy for, 412, 416
    bringing food after, 403, 404, 405,
        406, 407, 409, 411
    charitable donations and, 404,
        407–408, 409, 410, 411, 412
    children and, 399, 417–418, 429,
        439
    co-worker, 400
    crying and, 400, 401
    cultural differences and, 403–411
    emotions/feelings on, 399
    friend's mother, 414
    friend's wife, 413
    high school friend, 412
    incapacitated spouse, 413
    letters/e-mails after, 413–416
    parents, 412, 414, 415, 446–447
    publications, 417–418
    religion and, 398, 399, 403–411

Death of adult (*cont.*)
  special situations of, 412–413
  teenagers and, 417
  what not to say/do after, 401–403
  what to say/do after, 399–402
Death of baby, 430–439
  bringing food after, 432, 434
  children and, 431, 439
  from congenital malformations,
    347–348, 430, 431, 436
  crying after, 432, 435
  emotions/feelings on, 431–432
  funeral for, 432
  letters/e-mails after, 436–437
  nonverbal strategies after,
    434–435
  organizations for, 438
  publications on, 437–438, 439
  religion and, 432
  from short gestation/low birth
    weight, 430, 431
  from SIDS, 430, 437, 438
  special situations of, 435
  as stillborn, 435–438
  things to consider with, 431
  twin, 435
  what not to say/do after,
    433–434
  what to say/do after, 432–433
Death of child, 419–429
  as adult, 413–414
  from cancer, 425, 426
  in car accident, 424, 425–428
  emotions/feelings on, 420
  holidays after, 421, 423, 424–425
  letters/e-mails after, 425–428
  nonverbal strategies after, 424
  organizations for, 428–429
  publications on, 428–429, 489
  religion and, 421
  special situations of, 424–425

  things to consider with, 420
  what not to say/do after, 423
  what to say/do after, 420–421, 422
Department of Justice, U.S.
  Bureau of Justice Statistics, 490,
    499–500
  Office for Victims of Crime
    (OVC), 488, 498, 504
Depression, 468
Disabilities. *See* Physical disabilities
Disability and Business Technical
    Assistance Centers (DBTACs),
    559
Disappointment, personal, 605–609
  emotions/feelings on, 606
  letters/e-mails after, 608
  publications on, 609
  special situations of, 607–608
  things to consider with, 605–606
  what not to say/do after, 607
  what to say/do after, 606–607
Disasters. *See* Natural disaster; Terror-
    ism; Traumatic events
Divorce, 568–577
  children and, 571, 572, 573, 574,
    576, 577
  emotions/feelings on, 569–570
  holidays after, 571
  letters/e-mails after, 575, 576
  nonverbal strategies on, 573
  publications/organizations, 577
  Special needs, baby/child and, 573
  special situations of, 574
  things to consider with, 569
  what not to say/do with, 572–573
  what to say/do after, 570–572
Divorce Resource Network, 577
Domestic violence, 483, 499, 504
  emotions/feelings on, 501
  organizations, 501, 504
  publications, 503, 504

special situations of, 503
support groups, 501
things to consider with, 500
what not to say/do with, 502-503
what to say/do with, 501-502
Donations, charitable
after suicide, 446
death of adult and, 404, 407-408,
    409, 410, 411, 412
in memory of pet, 462

E

Ectopic pregnancy, 451, 456, 458
Eldercare Locator (service), 603
E-mails, sample
on adoption, 540-541
on caregiver responsibility,
    600-602
on crime, 480-481, 487-488
on death of adult, 413-416
on death of baby, 436-437
on death of child, 425-428
on divorce, 575-576
on financial trouble, 593
on illness, 392-394
on infertility, 532
on job loss, 585-587
on legal/criminal problem,
    522-523
on natural disaster, 509
on personal disappointment, 608
on pet loss, 465-466
on physical disability, 557-558
on sexual assault/rape, 496-497
on suicide, 447-449
on traumatic event, 515
E-mails, sending, 370, 371-372
Employment. See Co-worker; Job loss
Engagements, broken, 607-608

F

Faith. See Religion
Families and Friends of Violent Crime
    Victims, 488
Family Caregiver Alliance, 603
Fear
of death, 398
helping with, 387
Federal Bureau of Investigation, 490
Federal Emergency Management
    Agency (FEMA), 510, 517
Financial Planning Association (FPA),
    590, 594
Financial trouble, 589-594
bankruptcy as, 589, 590, 592
credit debt as, 589, 590, 592,
    593-594
emotions/feelings on, 590
letters/e-mails on, 593
publications/organizations,
    593-594
special situations of, 592
things to consider with, 589-590
what not to say/do with, 591-592
what to say/do with, 590-591
FindLaw.com, 524, 594
Flowers
funeral, 403, 404, 405, 407, 408,
    409, 410, 411
in hospital, 385
when to send, 403
Food, bringing, 365
after death of adult, 403, 404, 405,
    406, 407, 409, 411
after death of baby, 432, 434
after suicide, 442
Funeral(s), 400
after miscarriage, 452
attending, 365
baby, 432

Funeral(s), (*cont.*)
  Buddhist, 404
  Chinese, 405
  cultural differences in, 403–411
  flowers, 403, 404, 405, 407, 408,
    409, 410, 411
  Hindu, 405–406
  Islamic, 406–407
  Japanese, 407–408
  Jewish, 408–409
  Protestant, 410
  Roman Catholic, 411
  for suicide victims, 442
  what not to do/say at, 404, 405,
    406, 407, 408, 409, 410, 411
  what to bring to, 404, 405, 406,
    407, 408, 409, 410, 411
  what to do at, 404, 405, 406
    407–408, 409, 410, 411
  what to expect at, 404, 405, 406,
    407, 408–409, 410, 411
  what to wear to, 404,1 405, 406,
    407, 409, 410, 411

G

Greeting cards. See Cards/notes
Grief, 397–398, 399. *See also* Death;
    Death of adult; Death of baby;
    Death of child; Funerals
  anger and, 358, 387
  in children, 360
  crying and, 365, 369
  helping with, 356–358
  Kübler-Ross, Elisabeth, on,
    354–355
  over divorce, 568–569
  for pet, 460–461, 463
  publications/organizations,
    358–360, 429
  stages of, 354–356, 363, 398
  understanding, 353–360
  GriefNet.org, 359, 429

H

Head injuries, 554
Hearing loss, 555, 557
High school friend, death of, 412
Hindu funerals, 405–406
Holidays
  after death of child, 421, 423,
    424–425
  divorce and, 571
  illness during, 386
  marital separation and, 563
Hospice Foundation of America, 395,
    604
Hospital(s)
  flowers in, 385
  visits, 365, 383, 384–385, 392

I

Illness, 381, 383–387. *See also* Care-
    giver responsibilities; Mental
    illness
  cancer as, 391
  cards/notes, 390, 391
  chronic, 390, 392
  co-worker, 391
  emotions/feelings on, 384
  during holidays, 386
  letters/e-mails on, 392–394
  in newborn babies, 391–392
  nonverbal strategies on, 389–390
  publications/organizations,
    394–396
  religion and, 369

special situations of, 390–392
stroke as, 557–558, 599–600
support groups, 386, 390
terminal, 600, 601–602
things to consider with, 384
visits and, 384–385
what not to say/do with, 387–389
what to say/do with, 385–387
ILUSA (directory of Independent
    Living Centers in United States),
    559
Infertility, 527–533
    emotions/feelings on, 528
    letters/e-mails on, 532
    organizations, 532–533
    publications, 532
    special situations of, 531
    things to consider with, 528
    what not to say/do with, 530–531
    what to say/do with, 529
Infidelity, 561–562, 565, 574, 576
International Communication
    Association, 380
International Listening Association,
    380
Internet, locating information on,
    389, 469
Islamic funerals, 406–407

J

Japanese funerals, 407–408
Jewish funerals, 408–409
Job loss, 578–588
    emotions/feelings on, 580
    letters/e-mails on, 585–587
    publications, 587–588
    resources, 588
    special situations of, 583–585
    things to consider with, 579–580

what not to say/do after, 582–583
what to say/do after, 580–581
Job-Hunt.org, 588
*Journal of American Medical
    Association (JAMA),* 499

K

Kübler-Ross, Elisabeth, 354–355

L

Layoffs. *See* job loss
Learning disabilities, 554
Legal/criminal problems, 519–524
    emotions/feelings on, 520
    letters/e-mails on, 522–523
    organizations for, 524
    publications on, 523–524
    special situations of, 522
    things to consider with, 519–520
    what not to say/do with, 521–522
    what to say/do with, 520
Let's Face It (network), 559
Letters, sample
    on adoption, 540–541
    on caregiver responsibilities,
        600–602
    on crime, 480–481, 487–488
    on death of adult, 413–416
    on death of baby, 436–437
    on death of child, 425–428
    on divorce, 575–576
    on financial trouble, 593
    on illness, 392–394
    on infertility, 532
    on job loss, 585–587
    on legal/criminal problems,
        522–523

Letters, sample (*cont.*)
  on natural disaster, 509
  on personal disappointment, 608
  on pet loss, 465–466
  on physical disability, 557–558
  on sexual assault/rape, 496–497
  on suicide, 447–449
  on traumatic events, 515
Leukemia and Lymphoma Society,
    395
Listening
  communication and, 364, 365,
    374–380
  hearing v., 375
  loss and, 364, 365, 374–380, 507
  publications/organizations,
    379–380
Loss. *See* Death

M

Marriage. See Divorce; Separation,
    marital
Maternal and Child Health Bureau, 543
Meals. *See* Food, bringing
MEDLINE plus (information service),
    533
Memorial service. *See* funerals
Mental illness. *See also* Suicide
  depression as, 468
  emotions/feelings on, 469
  organizations, 468, 469, 472–473
  publications, 471–472
  religion and, 470
  stigma of, 469
  suicide as, 468
  support groups, 470
  things to consider with, 469
  what not to say/do with, 471
  what to say/do with, 469–471

Mental retardation, 554
Miscarriage, 451–459
  ectopic pregnancy and, 451, 456,
    458
  emotions/feelings on, 453
  funeral after, 452
  letters/e-mails on, 457–458
  multiple, 454, 456, 457–458
  organizations, 460
  publications, 459
  special situations, 456
  support groups, 454
  things to consider with, 452
  what not to say/do with,
    454–455
  what to say/do with, 453–454
Mothers Against Drunk Driving
    (MADD), 488–489
Mourning. *See* Grief
Mouth Magazine, 558–559
Multiple sclerosis, 395, 554

N

National Adoption Center, 541
National Adoption Information
    Clearinghouse, 541–542
National Alliance for Mentally Ill
    (NAMI), 472, 516
National Association for Home Care,
    604
National Association of People with
    AIDS, 395
National Cancer Institute, 396
National Center for Chronic Disease
    Prevention and Health
    Promotion, 533
National Center for Health Statistics,
    430, 440, 527, 568
National Center for PTSD, 505–506

National Center for Victims of Crime, 481, 489, 490, 498, 517
National Coalition Against Domestic Violence, 504
National Coalition of Homicide Survivors, Inc., 489
National Council on Disability, 559
National Domestic Violence Hotline, 501, 504
National Family Caregivers Association, 595, 604
National Foundation for Credit Counseling (NFCC), 594
National Information Center for Children and Youth with Disabilities, 559
National Institute of Mental Health (NIMH), 468, 472, 510, 517
National Mental Health Association, 468, 472-473
National Network for Childcare, 550
National Organization for Parents of Murdered Children, 489
National Organization for Victim Assistance (NOVA), 481-482, 489, 498, 504, 517
National SIDS Resource Center (NSRC), 438
National Women's Health Information Center, 595
Natural disaster, 505-510
    emotions/feelings on, 506
    letters/e-mails on, 509
    organizations, 509-510
    publications, 509
    things to consider with, 505-506
    what not to say/do after, 508-509
    what to say/do after, 506-508
Nolo-Law for All, 524

Notes. See Cards/notes
Nursing home, returning from, 393-394

O

Organizations. See also specific organizations
    adoption, 542-543
    cancer, 394, 396
    caregiver responsibility, 595, 603-604
    crime victims, 481-482, 488-489, 490
    death of baby, 438
    death of child, 428-429
    divorce, 577
    domestic violence, 501, 504
    financial trouble, 593-594
    grief, 358-360, 429
    illness, 394-396
    infertility, 532-533
    legal/criminal problems, 524
    listening, 379-380
    mental illness, 468, 469, 472-473
    miscarriage, 460
    natural disaster, 509-510
    pet loss, 466, 467
    physical disability, 559
    sexual assault/rape, 490, 492, 498
    special needs, 550
    suicide, 449-450

P

Paraplegics, 554
Personal disappointment. See disappointment, personal

Pet loss, 402, 460–467
    charitable donation after, 462
    children and, 465, 467
    co-workers, 465
    emotions/feelings on, 461
    grief, 460–461, 463
    letters/e-mails on, 465–466
    publications/organizations, 466,
        467
    special situations of, 463–464
    things to consider with, 461
    what not to say/do after, 463
    what to say/do after, 461–462
Pets, visits from, 598
Phrases, communication, 366–367
Physical disabilities, 551–560
    emotions/feelings on, 552
    letters/e-mails on, 557–558
    organizations, 559
    publications, 558–559, 560
    special situations of, 557
    things to consider with, 552
    what not to say/do with, 556
    what to say/do with, 552–553, 556
    wheelchairs and, 553, 555,
        556–557
    words with dignity and, 554–555
Post Traumatic Stress Disorder. See
        PTSD
Pregnancy. See Death of baby; Ec-
        topic pregnancy; Infertility;
        Miscarriage
Protestant funerals, 410
PTSD (Post Traumatic Stress Disor-
        der), 505–506, 511, 513
Publications
    adoption, 541, 542
    baby/child with special needs, 550
    caregiver responsibility, 602–603
    crime, 481, 488
    death of adult, 417–418
    death of baby, 437–438, 439
    death of child, 428–429, 489
    divorce, 577
    domestic violence, 503–504
    financial trouble, 593–594
    grief, 358–360, 429
    illness, 394–396
    infertility, 532
    job loss, 587–588
    legal/criminal problems, 523–524
    listening, 379–380
    mental illness, 471–472
    miscarriage, 459
    natural disaster, 509
    personal disappointment, 609
    pet loss, 466, 467
    physical disability, 558–559, 560
    separation, marital, 565–567
    sexual assault/rape, 497
    suicide, 449
    terrorism, 516–518
    writing, 372–373

Q

Quadriplegics, 554

R

Ragged Edge (magazine), 559
Rape. See Sexual assault/rape
The Rape, Abuse, and Incest National
        Network (RAINN), 492, 498
Religion
    death and, 369, 398, 399, 403–411
    death of baby and, 432
    death of child and, 421
    illness and, 369
    mental illness and, 470

special needs baby/child and, 546
suicide and, 442
RESOLVE, Inc., 533, 542
Roman Catholic funerals, 411

S

Salvation Army National Headquarters, 510, 517
Separation, marital 561–577
  children and, 561, 563, 565
  emotions/feelings on, 562
  holidays and, 563
  publications, 565–567
  special situations of, 565–567
  things to consider with, 561–562
  what not to say/do with, 564–565
  what to say/do with, 562–564
September 11, events of, 511
Sexual assault/rape, 483, 490–498
  Date rape as, 496
  emotions/feelings on, 491–492
  letters/e-mails after, 496–497
  organizations, 490, 492, 498
  publications, 497
  things to consider with, 491
  what not to say/do after, 494–496
  what to say/do after, 492–494
SHARE (organization), 438, 459
The Sidran Foundation, 516
SIDS (Sudden Infant Death Syndrome), 430, 437, 438
Special needs, baby/child with, 543–550
  divorce and, 573
  emotions/feelings on, 545
  how to say it, 547
  learning disabilities and, 554
  nonverbal strategies for, 548–549
  publications/organizations, 550

  special situations of, 549–550
  support groups, 548
  things to consider with, 544
  what not to say/do with, 547–548
  what to say/do with, 545–546
State Department, U.S., 534–535
Stillborn birth. See Death of baby
Strokes, 557–558, 599–600
Sudden Infant Death Syndrome. See SIDS
Suicide, 440–450. See also Mental illness
  anger and, 441
  bringing food after, 442
  cancer and, 446–447
  charitable donations after, 446
  of child, 440, 448
  of co-worker, 446
  of co-worker's husband, 447
  emotions/feelings on, 441–442
  of friend's spouse, 448
  funerals for, 442
  handling news of, 447
  letters/e-mails after, 447–449
  as mental illness, 468
  nonverbal strategies after, 446
  organizations, 449–450
  publications, 449
  religion and, 442
  social stigma of, 440
  special situations of, 446–447
  support groups, 446
  teenage, 448–449
  things to consider with, 441
  what not to say/do after, 444–445
  what to say/do after, 442–444
Support groups
  domestic violence, 501
  illness, 386, 390

Support groups (*cont.*)
  mental illness, 470
  miscarriage, 454
  special needs, 548
  suicide grief, 446
  traumatic event/terrorism, 513,
    516–517
Support systems, 364
Surgeon General, U.S., 499
Surgery, 393, 427
Survivors of Suicide (organization),
    449
Sympathy, belated, 412, 416. *See also*
    Cards/notes

T

Talking, loss and, 363–373
Teenager(s)
  death of adult and, 417
  killed in accidents, 424, 425–428
  post-surgery death of, 427
  publications on grief for, 429
  suicide of, 448–449
Terrorism, 511–518
  emotions/feelings on, 512
  publications on, 516, 518
  support groups, 513, 516–517
  things to consider with, 512
  what not to say/do with,
    514–515
  what to say/do with, 513–514
Tornadoes, 509

Touch, therapeutic, 365
Traumatic events, 511–518
  children and, 518
  recovering from, 511
  responding to, 363–364
  support groups, 513, 516–517
Twins, death of one, 435

U

USLAW.com, 524, 594

V

Victim Services Helpline, 482, 489,
    498
Victim v. survivor, 478, 484, 491, 500
Violence, *See* Crime

W

Walkers, use of, 552, 553, 555
Wheelchairs, use of, 553, 555, 556,
    557
Woodbine House (publishers), 550,
    560
Words, use of, 366, 554–555
Writing. *See also* Cards/notes;
    E-mails, sample; Letters, sample
  communicating in, 370–372
  publications on, 372–373